HISTORY OF OLD AGE

In memory of Geoffrey Gordon Cole

'He was a man, take him for all in all, I shall not look
upon his like again.'

William Shakespeare, *Hamlet*, 1,2

History of Old Age

From Antiquity to the Renaissance

Georges Minois

Translated by
Sarah Hanbury Tenison

The University of Chicago Press

Originally published as *Histoire de la vieillesse: De l'Antiquité à la Renaissance*, © 1987, Librairie Arthème Fayard.

The University of Chicago Press, Chicago 60637

Polity Press, Cambridge

© 1989 by Polity Press

All rights reserved. Published 1989

Printed in Great Britain

98 97 96 95 94 93 92 91 90 89   54321

Library of Congress Cataloging-in-Publication Data

Minois, Georges, 1946–
    [Histoire de la vieillesse en Occident. English]
    History of old age : from antiquity to the Rennaissance /
Georges Minois ; translated by Sarah Hanbury Tenison.
        p.   cm.
    Translation of: Histoire de la vieillesse en Occident.
    Includes bibliographical references.
    ISBN 0-226-53031-0
    1. Old age—Europe—History.   2. Aged—Europe—Social
    conditions.
    3. Social structure—Europe—History.   I. Title.
    HQ1064.E8M5613   1990
    305.26'094—dc20   89–5221
                                                                 CIP

Contents

Foreword

by Jean Delumeau

Simone de Beauvoir thought it 'impossible to write a history of old age'. The present work – which will be continued in a second volume – proves brilliantly that she was wrong. Georges Minois's book is an astonishing success and I can't help wondering how this young historian, the author of a truly monumental thesis on the diocese of Tréguier from the fifteenth to the eighteenth centuries, was able to find the time to cull the immense documentation which he has used for this history of old age, which follows closely behind the research and writing of his thesis.

Was he led to the subject by the present-day granny boom which France is experiencing – by the year 2000 there will be 865,000 persons aged over 85 in our country? To some extent undoubtedly. The position of the old in our society invites us to dwell on their distant past. But historiography nowadays, especially in France, makes it a point of honour to follow untrodden paths and to open up new fields of work. If these masterful activities are impelled by current events, all the better! Especially if they do so on the basis of very serious investigations, conducted by professionals who both work hard and write well. At this point I would like to say briefly that Georges Minois's work is very well written; it belongs to a long French tradition, going from Voltaire to Braudel and which is being continued among us. Consequently this book is written in an easy style, with plenty of well-chosen quotations and remarkably apposite formulas. In saying this, I feel real pleasure at acknowledging a rising talent.

The danger for this sort of subject, and for the ancient or relatively ancient periods it covers, is of being imprisoned by the literature and the iconography. Their testimony is certainly necessary and Georges Minois has not failed to evoke the Book of Job, Plautus' Comedies, Shakespeare's plays or Quentin Metsys's *Ugly Duchess*. But other documents appear in his book: medical writings, funerary inscriptions from antiquity, medieval cartularies, witnesses' statements at canonization proceedings, demographic calculations, statistics bearing on the age of popes and kings, or of the great English administrators during the Tudor period. He has mastered this varied and by its very nature heterogeneous documentation with ease, and has exploited it with consummate skill.

The vast fresco he has painted for us includes some unusual aspects; that is, new interpretations which will surprise or will give rise to debate. Georges Minois takes issue in particular with the theory that the old were in a very small minority in the Middle Ages and did not play an important role in medieval society. However, quite apart from the rather incredible case of Eleanor of Aquitaine, whose personal career began at the age of 69, many popes in the eleventh to thirteenth centuries and several doges of Venice were old men. By collating all recent research on the Plague, our historian has been able to set an important fact in strong relief: the Black Death and the epidemics following it spared (relatively speaking) the old. The logical consequence was that they pulled more weight in society, as well as in the economy and in politics. This resulted in a tendency towards gerontocracy which had as its corollary, at least in cultivated circles, a revival of criticism against the old. It became the fashion once again to satirize marriages between old men and very young girls, as it had been in Plautus' age, when Roman youth was trying to topple the over-weighty power of the *pater familias*. These are connections which would not have occurred to one before.

The re-establishment of the role of old people in medieval society was followed by another revival, one related to the Renaissance and its revival of Greco-Roman ideals and paganism, which is known to have pitched into the ugliness of old age and especially into the decrepitude of women. However, until now, the discrepancy between actual events and this theoretical condemnation has not been sufficiently stressed. In reality, in the domains of politics and art, there were numerous very active old men in the sixteenth century, when the septuagenarian Andrea Doria could be seen fighting the octagenarian Barbarossa, when Michelangelo would reach the age of 89 and Titian that of 99. Of the 47 Italian artists in the fourteenth to sixteenth centuries mentioned by Vasari, 72 per cent lived longer than 60 years.

These figures invite the author, and us with him, to be prudent about drawing conclusions. During the long period under consideration, starting with the first old man to talk about himself – an Egyptian scribe 4,500 years ago – and ending with the deaths of Elizabeth I and Henri IV, neither old age nor its status experienced a linear evolution. The place granted it and the way it was viewed were the result of many factors which could combine in a more or less complex way: the structuring of society, the respective places of oral and written traditions, the dimension of the family, patriarchal or nuclear, the accumulation of movable wealth, the ideal of beauty, which itself was governed (or not) by religious concepts.

In spite of all this, one point common to ancient civilizations does emerge: they provided an abstract model of old age and judged old people – kindly, or more often unkindly – in relation to this theoretical picture. They had not yet discovered the concrete specificity of the age of retirement.

Acknowledgements

The author, translator and the publishers are grateful to the following for permission to quote at length from their publications: Basil Blackwell Ltd for material from *Chaucer's Romaunt of the Rose and Le Roman de la Rose*, ed. Ronald Sutherland, Oxford, Basil Blackwell, 1967, pp. 8–9; J.M. Dent & Sons Ltd (Publishers) for material from Baldassare Castiglione, *The Book of the Courtier*, trans. Sir Thomas Hoby, London, Dent, 1974, book II, pp. 86–8; Oxford University Press for material from *On the Properties of Things. John Trevisa's translation of Bartholomaeus Anglicus' De Proprietatibus Rerum*, ed. M.C. Seymour, 2 vols, Oxford, Oxford University Press, 1975; Penguin Books Ltd for material from Erasmus of Rotterdam, *Praise of Folly*, trans. Betty Radice, London, Penguin, 1971, translation copyright © Betty Radice, 1971; and from Plato, *The Republic* trans. Desmond Lee, London, Penguin, 1974, pp. 62–3, copyright © H.D.P. Lee, 1955, 1974; and from Christine de Pisan, trans. Sarah Lawson, London, Penguin, 1985, pp. 162–7, 160, copyright © Sarah Lawson, 1985; and from Geoffrey Chaucer, *The Canterbury Tales*, trans. Nevill Coghill, London, Penguin, 1977, pp. 106, 281–2, 283, 390–1, 123–4, 379, 305, 306, 309, 266, 270, 308–9, copyright © Nevill Coghill, 1958, 1960, 1975, 1977; University of Wales Press for material from *Early Welsh Gnomic Poems*, ed. K.H. Jackson, Cardiff, University of Wales Press, 1961, pp. 54–5.

Introduction

Old age: a term which generally arouses a shudder, two words loaded with anxiety, frailty and sometimes anguish. Yet an imprecise term, whose meaning is still vague, its reality difficult to perceive. When does one become old? At 55, 60, 65 or at 70 years? Nothing fluctuates more than the contours of old age, that physiological, psychological and social complex. Is one as old as one's arteries, as one's heart, as one's brain, as one's morale or as one's civil status? Or is it the way other people come to regard us – one day – which classifies us as old? The only rite of passage is a contemporary and artificial one; the passage into retirement, a moment determined more by socio-economic constraints than by actual age. Biologically speaking, people start to age from their birth onwards, but at very different speeds. Their social situation, manner of life and cultural environment accelerate or slow down bio-physiological evolution and cause us to enter old age at very different ages.

In spite of everything, growing old is still an essentially biological phenomenon to which modern medicine is paying ever greater attention, without having yet managed to understand its mechanics. While gerontologists all affirm that human longevity has not varied since the emergence of our species and is situated at around 110 years, the ageing process is still much debated. How is it that cells, which are potentially immortal, end by weakening and dying through non-regeneration? Leslie Orgel and his partisans attribute this phenomenon to the accumulation of errors in the translation of the genetic message, leading to a final catastrophe (the error catastrophe theory). Strehler proposes a related theory: with the passage of time, the cell's mechanism for decoding genetic messages weakens, and ends by modifying its bio-synthetic activity. Others, such as Burnet, promote the idea of old age being genetically programmed. For the moment, however, none of these explanations has achieved unanimous support.[1] As Edgar Morin remarked, we are still at the stage of probabilities:

> At the level of polycellular creatures, it seems that, for many
> vegetal and animal species, death is, if not programmed, at least
> genetically foreseen. Senescence would then be the product of a
> 'programmed deprogramization' . . . Where human ageing is
> concerned, the average length of our lives would not be merely a
> statistical phenomenon but due to the fact of a roughly average
> and certainly unequal ageing process, which would be, if not
> genetically controlled, at least genetically decontrolled.[2]

Whatever its causes, old age is a reality feared by those who have not
yet reached it, and is often unappreciated by the old. Devalued, despised
and relegated by some to the ranks of an incurable disease which serves
as the harbinger of death, old age is denied by others who refuse to
accept their physical transformation. They want to show that they are
'still young' and there are many examples in the performing arts, and
in the worlds of sport and politics, some even bordering on the
ridiculous, of elderly individuals of either sex behaving like young
people, spurred on by the partisans of the theoretical equality of all
mankind. But whether they exaggerate their ills or deny them against
all the evidence, these old people witness to the generalized depreciation
of old age in the modern world.

Our age, however, has witnessed a renewal of interest in the old.
Never before have they been talked about so much or have they had
so much attention paid them. Every discipline is studying this
phenomenon which apparently concerns people all over the place. This
is partly due to the natural growth of the range of modern scientific
research, but especially to the pressure of socio-demographic conditions.
Never have our western societies included such a high proportion of
old people: those 'over 65s' who formed 11.4 per cent of the French
population in 1950, and 13.4 per cent in 1975, will represent 14.5 per
cent of the total population in the year 2000, and apparently 18.5 per
cent in 2025 and 20.4 per cent in 2050. The proportion of very old
people will increase even further: we have seen the number of 'over 85s'
grow from 200,000 in 1950 to 500,000 in 1975 and it will reach 865,000
in the year 2000, 75 per cent of which will be women.[3] It is worth
noting that the old are about to become the commonest sort of citizen.

This new market force has already aroused considerable interest. Old
men and women, experienced, wise, the possessors of worldly knowledge,
have penetrated advertising, recommending such and such a brand of
washing machine or dog food. 'The marketers of leisure activities have
taken these models of how to age well and have subtly re-injected the
old into an economic circuit from which they had been definitively
removed'.[4] Clubs and universities aiming at 'a new sales target', the world

of the third age (our senior citizens), have also multiplied; sociologists, psychologists and doctors are attentively studying its specific problems,[5] while economists worry about the growing volume of retirement money to be paid to this mass of non-productive persons, and demographers bemoan the grotesque upside-down age pyramid which our 'wrinkled France' has in store for the beginning of the twenty-first century.

Confronted with this invasion of hoary locks, some people have even wondered whether old age is not a creation of our age:

> Human old age as we know it today is in other terms a historical creation. This remark justifies both the hypothesis of a change in the status of the old during the history of human societies, and the difficulty of verifying it, in so far as one can envisage that it is not only their status, but the old themselves who have changed.[6]

According to Michel Philibert, old age is a typically human phenomenon, of recent date, thanks to life-prolonging advances in medicine. From here it is only a step to denying the existence of old people before the nineteenth century, a step we must be careful not to take. One of our aims is precisely to resuscitate these old people of the past, dead twice over and forgotten twice over: dead and forgotten in the minds and writings of their contemporaries before experiencing the natural death and oblivion born of time.

Present-day interest in old age is consequently new and it touches all spheres of life. Every discipline gradually modifies its point of view by refining it, as if surprised to find in this hitherto neglected subject an essential component of individual and social life. The case of medicine is most characteristic. For thousands of years, medicine has tried to understand the causes of ageing and to delay its effects, but, given their impotence before this natural fatality, doctors had ended by limiting themselves to enumerating the pathologies typical of old people, classifying them among the incurably sick. The old were uninteresting patients because incurable, and so were relegated to hospices.

The first signs of an evolution can be distinguished in the 1950s, with the emergence of retirement schemes, and the growing intervention of the state in this domain. The traditional form of assistance was denounced as degrading; a new terminology was adopted, the 'third age', with its strong suggestion of dynamism and autonomy, replacing 'old age', which had long ago become synonymous with avarice and incapacity. Doctors who specialized in the treatment of old people began to contest the devaluation of their work and services and denounced the harmful effects of the semi-totalitarian system then reigning in the hospices. Encouraged by the state and by the new retirement funds, they gradually succeeded in promoting a new approach to the problems of old age under the name of 'geriatrics'. Based on a fundamental distinction between normal ageing and pathological ageing, the new discipline advocates a global approach to old age, taking account of the physiological, psychological, social and cultural aspects of old people. Parallel with this, psychoanalysis has undertaken a specific approach to old people, remedying Freud's silence on the subject.[7]

As we have already said, the state was growing more aware of the extent of the problem. Old age, which had previously been an essentially private and family concern, became a social phenomenon so widespread that it could not but attract the attention of an administration anxious to endow this hitherto ignored category with status and regulations. While the inadequacies and excesses of this intervention (when will we get a ministry of the third age?) and even the hypocrisies it conceals may certainly be deplored (Edgar Morin pointed out that 'We are in a phase of gentle relegation, the category called third age conceals the process of putting old people aside, to be comforted with a few gadgets and the assurance that they will not starve to death'[8]) one fact is, however, certain: old age has since then been a major preoccupation of the state and of the experimental sciences.

How are we to explain the historians' silence on the subject? Have they been discouraged by Simone de Beauvoir's statement at the start of her famous essay written in 1970: 'It is impossible to write a history of old age'?[9] That is not very likely. The latest generations of Clio's children have not shied away from any subject: death, childhood, married life, sexuality, contraception, madness, medicine, medication, poverty, charity, fear . . . nothing inhibits them. In any case, Philippe Ariès launched a few ideas in 1983 and announced the forthcoming emergence of this theme: 'There will now be studies about old people; they have already started. And I think that if someone tackles the undergrowth, the university bulldozers will soon follow and that there will soon be a whole library on old age.'[10] A prediction which is beginning to be realized, first of all by Anglo-Saxon researchers, among them H.C. Lehmann, a pioneer of the 1950s, followed by David Troyanski, Peter Stearns, Peter Laslett and many others who have already produced significant work. In France we could pick out many names on the university bulldozer as it sets off, but we will mention only Jean-Pierre Bois, whose recent doctoral thesis on the old soldiers of the eighteenth century constitutes a monument of exceptional quality, and who is preparing a very ambitious synthesis on old age under the ancien régime.[11]

The fact remains that for once historians are behindhand. Various explanations for their lack of enthusiasm for a history of old age have been given. Philippe Ariès, when drawing a parallel with his history of childhood, thought that the humanities' lack of interest in the old was due to their degraded image in the twentieth century, whereas children, who nowadays are precious commodities, are a much more popular theme. More important, perhaps, is the fact that in the past old people never constituted a homogeneous category, capable of being isolated from the rest of society.

There have certainly always been old people, and more of them than one might think, in Egypt, Palestine, Mesopotamia, Greece and Rome; in the Middle Ages too. How difficult it is, though, to spot them in the documents of those remote ages! 'It is not easy to study the condition of old people throughout the ages. The written evidence that we have rarely mentions them: they are included in the general category of adults'.[12] Simone de Beauvoir's remark underlines the real problem: ancient societies did not divide life up into slices as we do. Life began with a person's entry into the labour market and ended at death. Even the theories of the 'ages of life' which flourished in the Middle Ages were only abstract dissertations, intellectuals' games, which did not correspond with any practical distinctions. As long as there was no legal age for retirement, old age was not recognized as such in the texts. Given this, how is the category of the old to be distinguished? Old people were only elderly adults. The old never emerged as a social category; they dissolved into a multitude of elusive individual cases.

Let us recall further the aversion to numbers felt by traditional societies, which frequently deprives us of an individual's precise age, both through ignorance of a date of birth and through a tendency towards exaggeration. To all these imprecise quantities must be added the silence and disparity of the sources. The chronicles tell us about great acts, exploits, outstanding warriors; the archives of an economic nature count and enumerate useful and profitable things. Old people are generally absent from all these records.

This leaves us with the literary texts. They are our only source for the most distant periods, but one which provides only a partial vision of reality, the vision of the higher social categories, and one distorted by art. For the whole period between antiquity and the Renaissance, we have to depend on disparate and rare data and to use the slightest allusion picked up while perusing a text. This is why this present study stops at the sixteenth century. With the start of the seventeenth century we enter a different world, in which the statistics, medicine, literature and general level of inquiry make a more detailed study possible, one which Jean-Pierre Bois is undertaking.

The ancient civilizations discussed in this book have been the object of only very little research into old age. They offer however a very interesting field of research: that of the social role of old people in traditional societies before the massive invasion of printing and state bureaucracy. A role which appears to have existed from the most distant ages onwards. Konrad Lorenz thinks it can even be distinguished among the higher primates and social animals; it is the old stag who leads the herd of deer, and no other male, however strong, dares rebel; it is the oldest crow who watches over the group; in a troupe of baboons studied by researchers, two old males were in command.[13]

Anthropologists remark just as frequently on the importance of the privileges enjoyed by old people in present-day traditional societies. Georges Condominas noted concerning South-East Asia:

> This privilege of old age can be found at every level. The old man, surrounded by affection, is entitled to a huge number of privileges. It is regarded as normal for him to make use of what strength is left to him to obtain all sorts of satisfactions . . . If the old man is thus surrounded by considerations, it is not on account of the duty to protect a weaker creature but because happiness imbues and favours the entourage of a man thus privileged. Attaining a great age is considered a happiness and a cause of rejoicing, especially if the old man has many descendants; he has then reached the height of felicity. He cannot be put aside, as happens with us, and be sent off to an old people's home, he stays among his own people, because he is the living proof of the group's success.[14]

For his part, Louis-Vincent Thomas observed in black Africa how the old enjoyed considerable prestige among the 22 ethnic peoples he was able to study.

> Experience, availability, eloquence, wisdom, knowledge, these all justify the idyllic picture black Africans have of old people, in spite of the reality of old people who can be senile, egoistical, tyrannical or cantankerous, just as they are everywhere in the world. This is because a purely oral society needs its old people, the symbols of its continuity, both in their role as the group's memory and as the prerequisite of its reproduction. So, in order to make their power more bearable and also to enhance one's own value by esteeming them, the group does not hesitate to idealize them. Since nothing can be done without old people, they might as well be attributed every quality – and their somnolence taken for meditative contemplation.[15]

This social role, initially so important, was to be unceasingly challenged in the historical societies of the west. The experience and wisdom of the old were contested in more complex types of society. And again, a parallel evolution can be observed among the African peoples we have just mentioned. Louis-Vincent Thomas has noted how the recent penetration of books, of writing, within these oral civilizations has sapped the prestige of old people: 'Nowadays however, the spoken word does not measure up to books. The power of the gerontocracy is henceforth demystified, and even attacked. The young inveigh against the old society. The old, cruelly trivialized, fall back into line'.[16] In the same way, the emergence of a type of democratic government and the progressive elimination of religion in politics are factors contributing to the demise of gerontocracy.

Western history from antiquity to the Renaissance is marked by fluctuations in the social and political role of the old. What we are seeing is not so much a continuous decline as a switchback evolution; the general tendency however is towards degradation. The concept of a curved scale of ages was imposed on our society very early on, with its peak situated at around 40 or 50 years, preceding the irremediable and definitive decline towards a devalued old age. This scheme includes many variants and exceptions, as will be seen, but the psychology of old people is profoundly and enduringly affected by it, making them internalize the degradation of their social status.

Every society has the old people it deserves, as is amply demonstrated by ancient and medieval history. Every type of socio-economic and cultural organization is responsible for the role and image of its old people. Every society treasures a model of the ideal man, and the image of old age depends on this model, whether it is depreciated or esteemed. Thus classical Greece, which was orientated towards beauty, strength and youth, relegated old people to a subaltern position, whereas the Hellenistic period, which was freed from a good many conventions, allowed some old men to break with norms and taboos and return to the forefront. This fact encapsulates one of the essential opportunities of old age; it often allows one to rise above all sorts of conventions which must be submitted to in order to make one's career in adult life; freed from these constraints, an old man could give free rein to his creativity, allowing some people to reveal their genius at the age of 70 or 80.

1

The Middle East of Antiquity:

The Experience of Old Age between Myth and History

'And all the days that Adam lived were nine hundred and thirty years: and he died' (Genesis 5.5); and so it was that the problem of old age and the trauma of death appeared with the first man. A problem which had not often arisen during the three or four million years of our long prehistory; hunting, war, famine, malnutrition and illness left palaeolithic man with few opportunities to watch his hair turn white. The oldest fragments of skeleton yet found all belonged to individuals under 30 years old. Lucy, the palaeontologists' Eve, whose remains were discovered in Ethiopia in 1974, had died aged between 20 and 30. While the neolithic age, with its progressive sedentariness and improved nutrition and security, doubtless allowed a greater number of people to achieve maturity, the proportion of old men must, nonetheless, have remained very small: according to Henri Valois, an examination of 187 prehistoric skulls showed that only three of them had belonged to people aged over 50.[1]

PRIMITIVE SOCIETIES IN THE PREHISTORIC AGE

The very rarity of these prehistoric old men gave them importance. Their contemporaries felt that the ability to survive for so long was such an extraordinary phenomenon that it couldn't be completely natural. Used as they were to interpreting all exceptional events as divine interventions, they very probably attributed longevity to supernatural protection or to a degree of participation by the old person in the spiritual world. But as far as this is concerned we are confined for ever to the realm of hypothesis and risky reconstructions and we shall not venture further over such shaky ground.

The game of comparing and contrasting prehistoric societies with the primitive societies of the twentieth century studied by anthropologists is just as risky and beguiling. The arguments and difficulties implicit in this approach should make us cautious – the more so since the position of the old in primitive societies varied considerably from one people to the next, depending on circumstance and on the way of life and general organization of a particular culture. The position granted to the old depended on the general cultural context. This observation can be verified throughout the ages, and it is illustrated by cultures with no writing.

In favourable times, when the tribe's food supply and survival were secure and it was not threatened by any major danger, an old man would enjoy a enviable position. He possessed an aura of supernatural prestige conferred on him by his longevity and was honoured and respected, playing an important social role. In the religious domain 'he whose age brought him closer to the beyond was the best mediator between this world and the next', as Louis Vincent Thomas observed.[2] This explains the advanced ages of most witch-doctors, witches and priests. But the beyond is also the domain of the forces of evil, which explains the old person's fundamental ambiguity, expressed in two contradictory attitudes towards him: The Turco-Mongols of the sixth to the tenth centuries held some old women to be 'divine' and venerated some old men, calling their god 'the rich old man', while putting other old people to death because they were suspected of evil associations. In black Africa, while two or three of a tribe's old people would be regarded as sacred and placed within the third rank of the supernatural hierarchy, after genies and souls, the rest would be rejected.

The role of the old man among all peoples with oral traditions was clearer and wider, since he was a fund of knowledge, and his 'wisdom' and experience entitled him to be the clan's memory and consequently its educator and judge. An African motto states: 'When an old man dies, a library burns down.' Among the Ashanti, the old man transmits knowledge, educates the children with his stories and advice, while serving as a real live toy, whose beard and hair can be tugged. The ruler and all those with responsibilities, whatever their age, were called 'old men', a feature found among many other peoples. In this respect a remark reported by Leo Simmons is characteristic. It was made by the elders of the tribe of the Akamba to a young man who was telling them what he had seen on his distant travels: 'Young man, if you speak the truth, you are old, you have seen much, we are but children . . . You are older than us, because you have seen with your eyes what we have only heard with our ears.'[3] The idea that age has nothing to do with years is to be found in the Bible and in the writings of some Church Fathers for whom true old age is wisdom.

Alleged wisdom and experience also explain the political role of old people among primitive peoples: 'the beards' or 'the white hairs' are village chiefs in Afghanistan, where the patriarch has great authority over his tribe. In oral civilizations, the elders' advice constitutes one of their most venerable institutions. Old women too often enjoy a privileged status, and accede to power on account of their age. This is one of the most striking contrasts with modern developed societies. In the Lemba tribe

> after the menopause the woman is often admitted into the masculine circle, and may then, being freed from numerous female taboos, play a role alongside the men in the affairs of the tribe and she takes her place in the space on the right, although the right side is forbidden to young women of childbearing age and reserved to men.[4]

In Afghanistan, when a woman becomes a mother-in-law, she acquires authority over her daughter-in-law and exerts strong influence over her son.

We must, however, take care not to idealize. Where old age is concerned, primitive societies contain the same contradictions as our own, and they express these in a far cruder manner. They are not blind to decrepitude and physical ugliness. The Nambikwara Indians have one word for both young and beautiful, and one word for old and ugly. It was not unusual for the old to be despised. The Turco-Mongols respected only healthy old people, neglecting the others and sometimes abandoning them or killing them by suffocation. Old people who had become useless on account of their physical or mental infirmities were often killed, because they represented a burden which these societies with their precarious food supplies could not support. The Ojibwa Indians of Lake Winnipeg abandoned their oldest members or killed them in ritual sacrifice as did the Siriono of the Bolivian rain forest. Among the people of the great Siberian North, when times are hard, an old man who can no longer hunt will decide, with the consent of his band, to commit suicide: he lets himself freeze to death or walks until he collapses. The same practice has been recorded in the most distant regions of the island of Hokkaido.

The fate of the old depended finally on the level of resources within the community:

> In poor societies, defenceless, at the brink of destitution, old people seem to have to be abandoned: not only are they refused food, but they are even left behind when the group undertakes a long journey . . . An old man, without strength, without wealth or children, is the object of constant scorn; worse still, he is treated like a burden.[5]

Many African peoples got rid of their senile old men; if they were chiefs, they committed suicide. Herodotus, our first ethnologist, reported in the fifth century AD that the Massagetae, a people from the northern Caucasus,

> have one way only of determining the appropriate time to die, namely this: when a man is very old, all his relatives give a party and include him in a general sacrifice of cattle: then they boil the flesh and eat it. This they consider to be the best sort of death. Those who die of disease are not eaten but buried, and it is held a misfortune not to have lived long enough to be sacrificed.[6]

Similarly, among the Indian tribe of the Padaei,

> If anyone is lucky enough to live to an advanced age, he is offered in sacrifice and devoured – this, however, rarely happens because most of them will have had some disease or other before they get old and will consequently have been killed by their friends.[7]

The problem of the ambiguity of old age has thus been with us since the stage of primitive society; it was the source both of wisdom and of infirmity, of experience and of decrepitude, of prestige and of suffering. Old people were respected or despised, honoured or put to death according to circumstance.

> Impotent, useless, he is also intercessor, magician, priest; beneath or beyond the human condition, and often both at once . . . a sub-human and a superman . . . The practical solutions adopted by primitive peoples towards the problems presented by their old are very diverse: they are killed, left to die, granted the bare necessities of life, assured a comfortable end or even honoured and showered with gifts.[8]

Simone de Beauvoir concluded that 'the condition of the old depends on their social context', which is only partially true because, as D.B. Bromley's study demonstrates, the way old people are treated does not necessarily reflect the prevailing attitude towards old age.[9] The cultural context also intrudes and interferes with the economic situation; among certain peoples the old may be detested but well treated out of fear that their spirits may take revenge, and among others they may be honoured but put to death because their incapacity and dependence threaten the group's survival.

OLD PEOPLE IN A TOTALITARIAN STATE: THE INCAS

When a people or a group of peoples achieves a superior level of organization, often expressed by establishing a state of the totalitarian type, it tries to solve these contradictions by giving the old a precise role. The best known case is that of the Inca empire, strictly defined as a 'prehistoric empire', because it had no writing. Its remarkable organization has frequently been studied, starting with the Spanish descriptions which followed the Conquistà; the reaction against the conquerors' abuse of the Inca empire has aroused sympathy and admiration for it. It had in fact been, within the limited means of the age, a truly totalitarian regime imposed for the benefit of the Inca and his family, with all that that meant in terms of indoctrination and regimentation, the distribution of labour, the mobilization of energy to benefit the state, the limitation of individual freedom and the elimination of idleness.

In such a society, each person had his place and his role to play, as in a termites' or ants' nest, and the old formed an integral part of the mechanism. Inca society has often been admired for not rejecting its old, for integrating them, keeping them busy and supporting them. But this was at the price of merciless indoctrination, described in detail by Garcilaso de La Vega. Proud of his Indian ancestry, he told how the Andes were civilized by the Incas when they occupied the region. Before then, he assures us, the Indians had killed and eaten their old people, but since their conquest by Manco Capac in the twelfth century, a new organization has been introduced which ensured security for the old. Counted every five years, along with the rest of the population, they were split up into different classes according to their age: those aged between 50 and 78 were the 'old who still walk well'; above them came the categories of the 'toothless', the 'hard of hearing', the 'old who only eat and sleep' and others older still, implying a fairly extraordinary longevity, which contemporary ethnologists have confirmed. The study of baptismal registers, which have been kept in some villages since 1840, reveals a sturdy proportion of centenarians, still going strong, smoking, drinking alcohol and maintaining a respectable level of sexual activity.

In this pre-Columbian and illiterate society the old retained their traditional role as living archives, and Garcilaso himself obtained his information from a very old Indian. As the rulers' counsellors, 'the old men, being the most well-advised' formed an informal council within every tribe and surrounded the heir to the throne in order to guide him. The Inca 'twice sent Maita Capac, the heir to the throne, to visit the kingdom in the company of elderly and experienced men, in order that he might get to know his subjects and rule them well.'[10] Old women had a medical role and were midwives; those who had entered the Temple of the Sun at Cuszo as virgins became *mamacuna*, or matrons; held in great honour, they were responsible for instructing novices. 'These *mamacunas* had grown old in the house and they were honoured with this name and this responsibility because of their age, as though to say that they were mothers and capable of ruling the convent.'[11] As for elderly virgins of royal blood, they were venerated by everyone:

> I remember knowing one of these women when she was extremely old, called 'ocllo', who had never married. According to what I was told, she would sometimes pay my mother a visit, whose (great)aunt she was, her grandparents' sister. They all held her in such veneration that they gave her precedence, wherever they might be. I can attest that my mother treated her like this as much on account of their relationship as of her age and her dignity.[12]

The old members of the populace were cared for by the community. The peasants had to work their land immediately after that of the domains of the Sun, and for nothing; each one brought his own lunch when doing this task. 'They said in fact that the old, the sick, the widows and orphans had enough troubles without having to bother about anyone else.'[13] The grain was supplied from public stores. A special levy was raised in the form of labour dues for making clothes and shoes for the old, and Indians aged more than 50 years were exempt from paying tax.

Garcilaso may certainly be suspected of having idealized his picture out of nostalgia for this lost world. He admits in any case that 'many Spaniards insist on saying the contrary', and his numerous allusions to the poverty of the old are sufficient evidence that the Inca empire was not quite the paradise of the old imagined by some historians, with their guilt feelings about the brutality of the Spanish Conquistà. It is probable that the material condition of the old had improved compared to that of more primitive societies, since it was no longer a matter of abandoning the old. But the Inca system of social security had its dark side in its strict prohibition of idleness and mendicancy: 'All those who were healthy enough put their hand to the task, and they considered it a great disgrace for someone to be punished in public for shirking.'[14]

Judges, called *ilactamayu*, would walk into the houses and check that every one was engaged in useful work; the blind, the lame, the deaf and dumb, all had their tasks to accomplish, according to their capacity. 'The judges and visitors took diligent care . . . that the old men and women and those unsuited to work were employed in some useful exercise, at least at collecting twigs or straw, at ridding themselves of vermin and at bringing their lice to their decurions or corporals.'[15] They were ordered to scare birds off the fields or to make ropes, and begging was forbidden, in theory at least, because Garcilaso tells us about Isabel, an old beggar woman of Cuzco, who was despised by all for 'her life of shirking and begging'.

This was an ultra-organized society, which irresistibly evokes the utopian worlds germinating in the same period within European imaginations. Everyone in his place, with a role to play benefiting the community. The Inca empire was the Utopia of civilizations without writing, which, when confronted with the problem of old age, already present all the types of responses which we will meet in historical societies: respect, rejection, indifference, taking into care; these attitudes are brutal expressions of fear, incomprehension and impotence before the phenomenon of growing old. Simone de Beauvoir observed this accurately, 'every society wants to live, to survive; it exalts vigour, fecundity, which are linked to youth; it fears the attrition and sterility of old age.'

Old age is feared everywhere, whatever attitude is adopted. Efforts are made to drive it off with rites of regeneration; the Indians would have preferred finding the flower of perpetual youth, which was said to grow along the present confines of Peru and the Equator, to living in the Incas' 'welfare state'. Whether the old are killed or honoured, abandoned or maintained, nobody would want to take their place. Old age is a personal and a social drama, and primitive societies fear it just as much as we do. Agonizing and, mysterious as it is, it acknowledges only one remedy, perpetual youth, all the others are but palliatives. Humanity has searched for this remedy since its origins. Since the beginning, old age has been the only really incurable illness: distraught mankind could only try to alleviate its suffering. Prehistoric solutions were simply more excessive than our own, and just as desperately ineffectual.

The old enter history: in the Fertile Crescent, the ambiguity of old age was felt from the start

The old people of prehistory have left no confessions. We can only glimpse them through the attitude of their group towards them. But the oldest written text on the subject to come down to us is unequivocal. The first old man to have talked about himself was an Egyptian scribe who lived 4,500 years ago, and his words are a cry of distress, moving both because of their antiquity and because of their immediacy. His cry shows that nothing has changed in the drama of decrepitude between the age of the Pharaohs and the atomic age. It bridges the generations and expresses all the anguish of old people in the past and the present:

O sovereign my Lord! Oldness has come; old age has descended. Feebleness has arrived; dotage is here anew. The heart sleeps wearily every day. The eyes are weak, the ears are deaf, the strength is disappearing because of weariness of heart, and the mouth is silent and cannot speak. The heart is forgetful and cannot recall yesterday. The bone suffers old age. God is become evil. All taste is gone. What old age does to men is evil in every respect.[16]

Thus spoke Ptah Hotep, Vizir to Pharaoh Izezi, in the fifth dynasty, around 2,450 years BC.

His complaint has been echoed millions of times throughout history. 'I am an old man, there is serious illness in my body', declares one of the tablet-letters at el-Amarna around 1,270 BC.[17] In the first century of our era, another Egyptian papyrus grumbles: 'He who has lived sixty years has lived all that lay before him. If his heart desires wine, he cannot drink until he is intoxicated. If he desires food, he cannot eat as he is used to. If his heart desires his wife, for her, the time of desire never comes.'[18] Hieroglyphs use a bent silhouette leaning on a stick to represent the term 'old' and 'growing old' and this ideogram first appears in an inscription of 2,700 BC to the east of the Fertile Crescent, in Babylonia. Another old man lamented, 700 years before our era: 'I am forgotten . . . my strength has vanished . . . the date wine, vivifier of men, in my case fails', the Akkadian cuneiform texts tell us.[19] And Atossa, wife to Darius, King of the Persians, advised him that 'As the years pass and the body weakens, the mind loses its edge.'[20]

The Semitic and Aryan old of the near East thus felt bitter about the physical and intellectual decay connected with old age. Old age was an evil for anyone who achieved it and all the resources of magic, sorcery, religion and medicine were enlisted to heal it. A first attempt to understand the causes of decrepitude was made; as in many other fields, the Egyptians appear to have been the first to ponder this problem which is still unsolved today. Medical theory of the Middle Empire considered the heart, the source of life, to be also the origin of ageing. In the sixteenth century BC, the papyrus Ebers declared that: 'As to debility through senile decay, it is due to the fact that purulency is on his heart.'[21] However, the wise men of the Near East preferred mythological or magical explanations and they did not research very far into the natural causes. No further movement was made in this direction until the appearance of classical Greece and its rationalism.

In the same period Far Eastern thinking adhered to solutions which were more philosophical than medical. *The Yellow Emperor's Classic of Internal Medicine*, a huge Chinese compilation undertaken during the Han dynasty (200 BC to 200 AD) but including much older traditions, was based on Taoist concepts: ageing is a form of illness due to an imblance in the body between the two universal and opposite principles, the yin and yang. According to this work, man's natural longevity could be much greater than it actually is, but, by drawing away from the Way, which alters the correct functioning of its natural faculties and accelerates decrepitude: 'the limit of man's life can be perceived when man can no longer overcome (his diseases); then his time of death has arrived.'[22]

In India the *Sushruta Samhita* affirms that health resides in the harmony of the body's elementary substances. When this harmony is ruptured, this gives rise to illnesses, which are of four kinds: traumatic (due to exterior and physical causes), corporal (due to foodstuffs, blood and humours), mental (due to excessive emotion), and natural (due to the loss of physical capacities and to the process of ageing). The work contains implicitly the very modern idea according to which the germs of death are present in man, which 'program' him ineluctably towards his decline and death.[23] Thus ageing is a natural process, which weakens resistance to illness. A remarkable intuition, which was never to be made explicit.

Although the causes of illness remained a mystery, there was no shortage of suggestions about remedies. It was characteristic of the pre-scientific age for prophylactics to be studied while neglecting the pathology. In fact, people were trying above all to remedy the superficial effects of old age. Some Assyrian tablets dating from 700 BC, but copying texts from the fifteenth century BC, present a treatment against white hairs and against the loss of acute vision. In the Egyptian tradition, the deified Vizir Imhotep, architect and doctor under the third dynasty (*c.*2,900 BC), is credited with various remedies against the ills of old age. The 'Smith papyrus', dating from the Old Empire, is the oldest text of medical prescriptions against the effects of old age. It contains a 'recipe for transforming an old man into a youth', which was really a cosmetic for concealing the marks of age. It consisted of a paste, kept in a coffer of semi-precious stone, which was to be applied as follows:

> Anoint a man therewith. It is a remover of wrinkles from the head. When the flesh is smeared therewith it becomes a beautifier of the skin, a remover of blemishes, of all disfigurements, of all signs of age, of all weaknesses which are in the flesh. Found effective myriads of times.[24]

This is an extraordinary text, the ancestor of all advertising for ointments and beauty creams with quasi-magical properties. Given that Egyptian medicine was almost exclusively in the hands of priests, it probably did enjoy a supernatural efficacy. This is confirmed a thousand years later by other papyri, dated round 1600 and 1550 BC, which propose treatments based on incantations and magical and religious rites, as well as drugs, for recovering lost youth.[25]

The Indians and Chinese also sought for the secret of rejuvenation. But whereas the latter only hoped for the opportunity to enjoy a longer

Table 1.1 Longevity of Sumerian kings

The first king was	A-lulim,	who reigned	28,800 yrs
then came	Alalgar	who reigned	36,000 yrs
	En Men Lu Anna	who reigned	43,200 yrs
	En Men Gal Anna	who reigned	28,800 yrs
	Dumu-Zi	who reigned	36,000 yrs
	En Sipa Zi Anna	who reigned	28,800 yrs
	En Men Dur Anna	who reigned	21,000 yrs
	Ubar Tutu	who reigned	18,600 yrs

life, the Yogi's fervent desire for health is the result of his need to extend life as much as possible so as to have a longer period of spiritual preparation for the final goal of Nirvana, when his soul may be freed from transmigration and can rejoin the world soul.[26] Consequently, the *Sushruta Samhita* provides a very elaborate system of rejuvenation.

The complete failure of the diverse methods proposed explains why this unfulfilled dream was transposed into the realm of mythology. The lists of the Sumerian kings attribute their antediluvian rulers with extraordinary longevity, beating all the biblical records hollow (table 1.1).

This golden age of old men lasted 241,000 years and ended with the Flood, whose effects reduced the rulers' longevity to 1,200 years for the first, and to less than 1,000 years for his successors.[27] The mythical Sumerian poem of Enki and Ninhursag describes a marvellous country where old age does not exist, where
Its old woman says not: I am an old woman:

> Its old woman says not: I am an old woman:
> Its old man says not: I am an old man.[28]

In the *Epic of Gilgamesh*, composed at the beginning of the second millenium, the hero, in despair about growing old and dying, searches for the secret of immortality. Utanapishtim shows him where he can procure the plant of eternal youth, which grows at the bottom of the sea.[29] In the fourteenth century, the Akkadian myth of Adapa includes a similar search.[30] At the boundary where myth and history meet, Herodotus relates how Cambyses, the Persian conqueror of Egypt, entered into contact with the 'Long Lived Ethiopians' and searched for the secret of the fountain of long life. As is fitting, this people lived at the end of the world, there where geography and nature merge with the unreal and the supernatural, 'towards the eastern sea . . .' Cambyses sent the Ichthyophagi (Fish-Eaters) of the Elephant Isle in an embassy to the Ethiopians, because they knew the Ethiop language. The ensuing dialogue immediately revolved around a comparison between the longevity of the Persians and that of the Ethiopians:

> He [the king of the Ethiopians] then asked what the Persian king ate and what was the greatest age that Persians could attain. Getting in reply an account of the nature and cultivation of wheat, and hearing that the Persian king ate bread, and that the people in Persia did not commonly live beyond eighty, he said he was not surprised that anyone who ate dung would die so soon, adding that the Persians would doubtless die younger still, if they did not keep themselves going with drink – and here he pointed to the wine, the one thing in which he admitted the superiority of the Persians.
>
> The Fish-Eaters in their turn, asked the king how long the Ethiopians lived and what they ate, and were told that most of them lived to be a hundred and twenty, and some even more, and that they ate boiled meat and drank milk. When they expressed surprise that anyone should live to such an advanced age, they were taken to a spring, the water from which smelt like violets and caused a man's skin, when he washed in it, to glisten as if he had washed in oil. They said that the water of this spring lacked density to such a degree that nothing would float in it, neither wood nor any lighter substance – everything sank to the bottom. If this account is true, then their constant use of it must be the cause of the Ethiopians' longevity.[31]

This astonishing passage reveals the preoccupation of the men of antiquity with old age. The question of the superiority of one people over another is here not set on the level of wealth or military power, but on that of human longevity. The Ethiopians were immensely proud of theirs, and the text assumes that this is one of the greatest benefits available to man. The imperceptible progress we have achieved thanks to these documents has allowed us to expose the fundamental ambiguity of people's attitude to old age. We will find it throughout the whole of history; having begun by searching for remedies against the evils of the illness of old age, men then find that their ultimate desire is to prolong this very same old age, the illness that they suffer. The old man complains about his great age, but he also vaunts it and tries to prolong his days.

THE FIRST EVALUATIONS OF HUMAN LONGEVITY

Symptomatic of this are the numerous and precocious attempts at evaluating the maximum span of human life. This is one of the rare fields where the civilizations of the Middle East of antiquity have been fairly scrupulous about the truth of their estimates. If we exclude the mythical duration of the Sumerian kings' reigns, we observe that the maximum records for advanced longevity in the Fertile Crescent 3,000 or 4,000 years ago are very plausible, even more reasonable than all the alleged and unproven records of today about certain Russian and Japanese people. This provides a clue about how important the question was to the men of antiquity: the subject was too serious to be treated lightly. While the estimates certainly vary considerably, they do remain plausible.

The men of antiquity seem to have had a more exact idea of age than did the Europeans of the medieval world, who tended to exaggerate. The Persians knew precisely how old they were. Herodotus mentions how important birthday celebrations were to them: 'Of all days in the year a Persian most distinguishes his birthday and celebrates it with a dinner of special magnificence. A rich Persian on his birthday will have an ox or a horse, or a camel, or a donkey baked whole and served up at table, and the poor some smaller beasts.'[32] So they knew what they were about when they reckoned the extent of human life among their people at around 80 years. Although Herodotus established the age of the Ethiopians at 120 years, this figure is still within the bounds of possibility for these mountain people.

The Egyptian texts are just as reasonable. Ptah Hotep in the middle of the third millenium reckoned he had reached the end of his road at the age of 110 years. This age seems to have been the ideal term of life under the Old Empire: an inscription mentioning the words of salutation by a prince to an old magician stipulate that the latter was 110 years old. '. . . the age of death, the time of placement in a sarcophagus, the time of burial.'[33] Much later on, in the first century of our era, the 'Insiger papyrus' is more pessimistic: it reckons that one should consider oneself happy to achieve 60 years and that not one man among millions goes beyond that. This reduction by half is partly explained by the effects of the invasions, destruction and mortality of the last centuries, and also by the literary genre, since this a book of Wisdom, a bitter reflection on human life, such as is found for the same period in Hellenistic and Hebraic centres. Life is tiring; during the first ten years of childhood one knows nothing, the next ten years are spent learning, then ten years for acquiring experience, and very few make it to the end: 'For the rest of the whole of life, until 60 years of age, prescribed by Thot for the man of God, only one among millions blessed by God exceeds it, when fate is favourable to him.'[34]

We can readily believe that only a few men achieved old age in the Near East of antiquity: in neighbouring Crete, a study of 112 skeletons for the middle Minoan age (*c.*2000 BC) reveals a life expectancy of 48 years for men and of 45 years for women.[35] Precise cases, however, show that maximum longevity in more robust cases must have been over a hundred years: this is the age attributed to Cyrus by Lucian, and the case of Ramses II is universally known. Herodotus stated that 'Next to the Lybians, they (the Ethiopians) are the healthiest people in the world', which he attributed to the virtues of the climate, which did not change, and to the hygienic life of the inhabitants, who purged themselves every month and applied emetics and clysters.[36]

It is obviously impossible to know the exact proportion of old people in these ancient populations. However, all the monarchies, all the organized states which acquired writing were careful to count their populations. The practice of taking censuses with the aim of calculating a state's resources is almost as old as history. Some fragments of family name lists have been found in Egypt, dating from the twentieth dynasty (eleventh century BC). The Far East seems to have been more precise in this field. In Gupta India the minister Kautilya (third century BC) advised the sovereign to have 'the number of women and men, children and old persons . . .' written up; in China the ritual of the Tchu (eleventh century BC) also recommended distinguishing between 'those who are old and those who are young', and some fragments of name lists of 416 AD concerning a village in Kansu give each person's age and profession; we thus find three generations gathered in a household consisting of seven persons, the grandparents being 66 and 63 years old. The Japanese were equally careful to count the number of old people separately, as demanded by Emperor Sujin in 86 BC. From the seventh century onwards, the Japanese registers classify the population according to age, distinguishing between 'old men' (60 to 65 years old) and 'elders' (more than 65 years old).[37]

OLD AGE, A DIVINE BLESSING

In these ancient and profoundly religious societies old age touched on the supernatural world. The simple fact of attaining 70 or 80 years of age was in itself such an extraordinary exploit that it could only be realized with the assistance and protection of the gods. This is certainly what Ptah Hotep meant when, after lamenting his physical decay, he boasted of having benefited from divine favour and hoped his son would achieve the same age as himself: 'May you live as long as me. What I have done on the earth is negligible. The king has granted me a hundred and ten years of life and a preeminent favour among the ancients, because I have served the king well until death.' A long life is a divine reward granted to the just.

This idea was widespread in the Near East. A Canaan inscription near Aleppo attributes to the deceased Agbar, a priest of Sahr, the moon-god, the following:

Because of my righteousness, he gave me a good name and prolonged my days. On the day I died, my mouth was not closed to words and with my eyes, what do I see? Children of the fourth generation who wept for me, being distraught.[38]

So it was normal to pray that the divinity would grant the king life into old age. There are many Elamite, Babylonian and Egyptian invocations along these lines.[39]

Relations between old age and the religious world also extended to a further field, that of magic. There was always a supernatural element to old people, who already stand as it were beyond this world and its passions. They no longer have much in common with other men; their very appearance is no longer really human. So the old are attributed with a certain familiarity with the gods and demons. Among the Hittites, their magic rituals were accomplished by old people: 'the old woman' would pronounce the ritual formulas against domestic arguments.[40] The old man of 110 years referred to in the inscription of Ptahetep's mastaba was also a magician, and among the Persians it was a very old man, Artabanus, who was charged with interpreting the dreams of King Xerxes. He was considered at the same time as 'the memory-man of the dynasty'.

Familiarity with holy things, combined with the experience and wisdom conferred by longevity, explains the importance of the political role played by the old in all the ancient societies of the Near East. In the most basic type of organization, the clan, which we find all over the semitic world, the natural chief was the patriarch, the oldest member of the group: surrounded by great respect, he took all the important decisions involving the life of the clan, which he incarnated. Babylonian inscriptions show that he was frequently held responsible for wrongs committed by members of his family[41] and, inversely, the Bible speaks of Achan, who was put to death for the sins of his patriarch. In the same way, the arab term *shaikh* designates both the chief and the old man.

In states with a more complex political organization, the great monarchies of the Fertile Crescent, the 'council of the elders' was a quasi-universal institution. We find it in Uruk from the fourth millennium: beside the 'lord', the texts of Jemdet Nasr mention the 'elders' who were certainly invested with political power.[42] We find them again in the towns of the Akkadian kingdom, where they ran the administration accompanied by governors answerable to the king.[43] In the ancient Assyrian kingdom, an 'assembly of the elders' possessed legislative and judiciary attributes.[44] The archives of Mari, in the second millennium, speak of 'elders' who defend the interests of the community.[45] The city-states of Phoenicia conformed to this model: the Book of Ezekiel (279) speaks of the elders of Byblos.

The role of old men was just as pre-eminent in the judiciary. In the thirteenth century BC the precious hieroglyphic texts relating to the organization of the Egyptian village of Deir el-Medina show us that the local tribunal was partly made up of the oldest workers and their wives.[46] The Code of Hammurabi frequently mentions the sibu, men with white hair: they intervened as witnesses and, generally speaking, every important form of business seems to have been concluded in the presence of the elders. Among the Persians, the 'royal judges' were old men, who retained their function until their death. 'These royal judges', Herodotus tells us, 'are specially chosen men who hold office either for life or until they are found guilty of some misconduct. Their duties are to determine suits and to interpret the ancient laws of the land, and all points of dispute are referred to them.'[47]

Xenophon, who also lauded the Persian institutions of the age of Cyrus, relates how in every town the population was divided into four categories classed by age. Twelve rulers were appointed over each of these divisions including that of the old men, the boys being governed by 12 men too old for military service and the youths by 12 full-grown men. The last category was achieved at the age of 50, and its members judged public and private affairs, allotted taxes and were able to pronounce the death sentence.[48]

RELATIONS BETWEEN YOUNG AND OLD IN THE FERTILE CRESCENT

Several references seem to indicate that the powers conferred on the old were contested by the young and that the latter submitted impatiently to their elders' tutelage. This theme of conflicting generations appears very frequently in the myths. In most cases, the young prevail, as in the Sumerian *Epic of Gilgamesh*. In this long poem from 3,000 BC, the hero, who proposes starting a war against Agga of Kish, opposes his council of elders, which favours peace. So Gilgamesh appeals to the youth, to the warriors, who approve him, and the advice of the elders is rejected.

Ugaritic mythology suggests a similar evolution. El, the great god of the local pantheon, is represented as an old man, with white beard and hair. He lives in retirement on a mountain and is surnamed 'father of humanity', and most of the other gods are his descendants. A bas-relief carving of Ras Shamra, in the fourteenth century BC, shows him with the features of an old man sitting surrounded by young gods. Principal among these is Baal, a true incarnation of youth and vigour. Several archaeologists and historians tend to think that the mythological texts of Ugarit infer a struggle between El and Baal, which ended with a victory by the young god over the old one. This theme can be found again among the Hurrians, whose old god Kumarbi was replaced by the young god of the storms; among the Babylonians, whose old Enlil gave way to the young Marduk, and even among the Greeks, where Kronos was deposed by Zeus.[49] But a further myth in Ugarit, about Keret, illustrates the same conflict: the demi-god Keret, king of Khubur, having grown very old, falls ill and Yassib, one of his sons, then attempts to seize the throne.[50] Let us also mention the old god Apsu of the Akkadians, who was rejected by his descendants.

To what extent, however, do myths reflect human reality? Reading the former is not sufficient basis for reaching conclusions about the latter. There is no doubt that frictions between young and old did exist, as evidenced by the moralists' recommendations:

> Stretch not forth thy hand against the approach of an old man,
> Nor steal away the speech of the aged.

says Amen-em-opet, an Egyptian scribe of maybe the seventh or sixth centuries BC.[51] 'Thou shouldst not sit when another who is older than thou is standing' a father in *circa* the tenth century BC was already telling his son on a papyrus:[52] in the twenty-second century BC Pharaoh Meri-ka-Re advised imitating one's father and ancestors[53] and in the twenty-fifth century BC Vizir Ptah Hotep recommended filial piety: 'If a son accepts what his father says, no project of his miscarries.'[54]

Do these reminders prove that the old were despised in Egypt? I don't think so. Assassination is not a common practice, in spite of being repeatedly forbidden. On the contrary, respect for the old was probably greater in these ancient societies imbued with a sense of religion than it would be in more rationalist societies. Herodotus witnesses to this evolution, himself a 'modern' Greek of the fifth century BC, who admired the veneration surrounding old people in the archaic Egyptian world as an extraordinary thing. He judged this mental feature as worthy of comment because it contrasted with the current Hellenic practice of his age, when, as we will see, only the Spartans seemed to respect old age: 'There is another point in which the Egyptians resemble one section of the Greek people – the Lacedaemonians, I mean the custom of young men stepping aside to make room for their seniors when they meet them in the street, and of getting up from their seats when older men come in.'[55]

Herodotus also observed that old Egyptians were not abandoned, since their daughters were obliged by custom to look after them: 'Sons are under no compulsion to support their parents if they do not wish to do so, but daughters must, whether they wish it or not.'[56] The same author also observed the absence of conflict between the generations among the Persians: 'They declare that no man has ever yet killed his father or mother; in the cases where this has apparently happened, they are quite certain that inquiry would reveal that the son was either a changeling or born out of wedlock, for they insist that it is most improbable that the actual parent should be killed by his child.'[57]

The fate of the childless old must have been unhappy indeed, and from the second millennium onwards an old man on his own was assimilated among the poor, the ill and the infirm of all kinds. But the existence of some charity hospitals dependent on the temples cannot be excluded for this period, which would have offered a shelter for some of the most destitute, as suggested by a collection of letters from the archives of Nippur in Mesopotamia, dating from the fourteenth century BC.

As a result of all this, it is extremely difficult to acquire an idea of the exact condition of the old in the Near East of antiquity. Any attempt at a synthesis is rendered very chancy by the rarity of texts about the old. Taking a realistic look at the excessively thin information presented in this chapter, one can say that the pre-hellenic world, if it was already fully aware of the fundamental ambiguity of old age, granted the old an honourable place, which they would find only exceptionally in the centuries to come.

The absence of satires directed against the old is significant. Old men and women, whom the art and literature of later ages took pleasure in ridiculing, were treated worthily here. The most ancient portrait of an old man is perhaps the statue of Ebih-il, the intendant of the town of Mari, executed around 2,700 BC. Bald and bearded, it is expressive of great dignity and reminds us that every old person in that society was in contact with the world of divinity. The old enjoyed all the more prestige in that they were few, and in a world where writing was a rarity, they were living archives and represented the law. In an unchanging universe, their experience was never outdated and always useful. Living in an environment which did not idolize physical beauty and often preferred wisdom, old women did not symbolize ugliness, as they would later on.

The golden age never was, neither for the old nor for anyone else. But, compared to the conditions of existence of the age, the conditions of the old in the Middle East of antiquity seem to have been relatively bearable. In spite of the physical sufferings brought by old age, they were not wrong to consider their longevity as a divine blessing. Listened to and held in honour, they exercised real power as patriarchs or counsellors. The last centuries of our era will see their position worsen perceptibly; an evolution which we can trace by looking at the books of the Bible.

2

The Hebraic World:

From Patriarch to Old Man

Thanks to the enormous advances achieved by exegesis, we have a relatively exact idea of the date and order of composition of the different books of the Old Testament. This extremely precious collection, composed of 45 works written down between the ninth and first centuries BC, allows us to trace the evolution of the institutions and the mentality of a people through the vicissitudes of its history over a millennium. These are legal, historical, prophetic, poetic and philosophical writings, giving us a fairly precise picture of the role of the old within a small Semitic group in the Near East.

It is however important fully to grasp the historical breadth of this document, because around a thousand years flow between the first drafts of the Book of Samuel or the Proverbs and the final composition of the Book of Wisdom. This means that the Old Testament should not be used as a whole, as is too often done, in order to extract unspecific references to 'the life of the Hebrew people'. Secondly, it is vital to use the books of the Bible in the chronological order of their composition, as restored to us by exegesis, and not in the order in which they are presented in the canonical Bibles. If these two conditions are respected, it is possible to reconstitute a history of old age among the Hebrews during the first millennium BC. This history is that of a progressive deterioration of the condition of the old under the influence of internal and external events.[1]

THE GOLDEN AGE: PATRIARCH AND ELDER BEFORE THE EXILE

The fundamental break in the history of the Hebrew people was their exile in Babylon, from 587 to 538 BC, a traumatic event which brought about total change. Before the exile was the monarchic period; a sole monarch with Saul, David and Solomon (end eleventh to beginning tenth centuries BC), then came a dual monarchy with the kingdoms of Israel and Judah, the former being defeated by the Assyrians in 721 BC, the latter by the Babylonians in 586 BC. This monarchic period corresponded with the first great wave of Jewish literature. While these writings reflect the conditions of life in a small Near Eastern kingdom, precariously placed between its powerful neighbours, they also echo the oral traditions transmitted from age to age since the nomadic phase, the sojourn in Egypt, the Moses epic and the reconquest of Palestine. It is hard to untangle these two influences, but the most ancient reminiscences, going back to the period of organization in clans, probably provide the most favourable evidence about old age.

According to the oldest writings, during the nomadic period, old men had a fundamental role and were considered to be the natural leaders of the people. Moses made his decisions only after consulting them: God spoke to him from the burning bush and asked him to unite the elders of Israel (Exodus 3, 16); when, in the desert, he made water issue from the rock, he also had the elders with him, whom God had expressly asked him to bring along (Exodus 17.5). Further, the Book of Numbers recounts the creation of the council of the elders as a divine initiative:

the lord said unto Moses: Gather unto me seventy men of the elders of Israel, whom thou knowest to be the elders of the people, and officers over them: and bring them unto the tabernacle of the congregation, that they may stand there with thee. And I will come down and talk with thee there: and I will take of the spirit which is upon thee and will put it upon them: and they shall bear the burden of the people with thee, that thou bear it not thyself alone. (Numbers 11.16–17)

The elders were thus considered to be the bearers of the divine spirit, invested with a holy mission, the people's guides. They possessed enormous religious and judicial powers; at the sacrifices of atonement for a sin committed by the community, they lay their hands upon the sacrificial animal (Leviticus 4.15). When a son rebelled against his parents, it was they who made the decision to lapidate him (Deuteronomy 22.13–21). In every town the council of the elders was all-powerful. When a murderer fled to one of the sanctuary towns designated by the Law, the elders sent someone to have him extradited and handed him over to the avenger of blood (Deuteronomy 19.12). They accompanied the leader in his lamentations before the Ark of the Covenant (Joshua 7.6). They even had a military role because they followed Joshua at the head of the army in the campaign against Ai (Joshua 8.10).

The elders' role appears to have been strengthened during the period of the Judges. As written in the book of that name, composed around the seventh century BC, but using traditions going back to the twelfth century BC, they decided to appeal to the temporary leaders, the Judges, and to dismiss them; when Israel was attacked by the Ammonites, the elders of the tribe of Galaad went to find Jephta to ask him to assume leadership of the people, although they had previously exiled him (Judges 11.15). When wives had to be found to populate the tribe of Benjamin, it was again the elders of Israel who discussed the matter and who decided to abduct the daughters of Shiloh (Judges 21.16). The neighbouring peoples had the same institution: when Gideon defeated the men of Succoth, east of the Jordan, he had their leaders and elders killed (Judges 8.13–16).

The distinction between them was important and can already be found in Joshua (23.2 and 24.1): the elders formed a sort of council of wise men alongside the leader. The duality of power which was gradually established in the tribes apparently corresponded to an age difference. In the period of the 'giants', of Moses and Joshua, the leader was the Jews' guarantee of invincibility by reason of divine protection and he retained power and all his faculties until his death: 'Moses was an hundred and twenty years when he died; his eye was not dim, nor his natural force abated' (Deuteronomy 34.7). Aaron lived 123 years; Joshua, although old and stricken in years, completed the conquest and died at 110 years (Joshua 13, 29). But in the period of the Judges, who did not have the prestige of the old leaders, the people demanded that the oldest be retired: the elders themselves asked Samuel for a king because they reckoned he was too old to lead them (I Samuel 8.1–5). Being charged with military duties, the leader had to be in full possession of his faculties, with the elders retaining an essential role as the council of the wise. Samuel also insisted that king Saul honour him before the elders, in order to endow this gesture with a more official allure (I Samuel 15.30).

This advisory role was established during the royal period. The sovereigns deferred to the elders and respected their prerogatives: David sent them part of the spoil taken from the Amalekites (I Samuel 30.26); during the war between David and Saul, they both tried to get the elders on their side, having assessed the value of their support (2 Samuel 3.17). Their agreement with David was apparently perfect: when the king acceded to the throne, he concluded an alliance with the elders (2 Samuel 5.3). When the king did penitence for having taken the wife of Uriah the Hittite, the elders came to console him (2 Samuel 12.17). During Absalom's rebellion, he relied on the elders of Israel (2 Samuel 17.5) and David relied on the elders of Judah (2 Samuel 19.11), providing new evidence of their political importance. This understanding continued under the reign of Solomon, who convoked the elders for all important business, such as transferring the Ark of the Covenant into the Temple (I Kings 8.1). Later on, when Jehu fought the king of Samaria, he addressed the elders of the town, telling them to organize the rebellion

(2 Kings 10.1 and 5); when Josiah undertook his social reform he summoned the elders of Judah and Jerusalem (2 Kings 3.14).

The first challenges to the elders' advisory role appeared after 935, from the reign of Rehoboam onwards. For the first time, the king was in conflict with them and disregarded their advice, following that of the young men. The first sign of a clash between the generations is reported in the Book of Kings, written in the seventh century BC: the people had demanded that their taxes be reduced and Rehoboam 'consulted with the old men, that stood before Solomon his father while he yet lived' (I Kings 12.6). The elders suggested he reduce taxation. Rehoboam did not agree 'and consulted with the young men that were grown up with him'; they advised on the contrary to increase taxation, and the king followed their advice (I Kings 12.8). This conflict was to become a classic feature of monarchic states, in which the young king would be urged by his courtiers to rid himself of the irritating tutelage of the 'beards' of the preceding reign.

THE FIRST SIGNS OF DECLINE

The image enjoyed by the old began to decline alongside this development. The oldest records all insist on the nobility, the wisdom, the venerable characters of the aged, who were all the more respectable in that they were old. Their model was the patriarch, whose astonishing longevity was the sign of divine blessing. As in Mesopotamia, the mythological antediluvian leaders were attributed with an extraordinary old age: 930 years for Adam, 912 for Seth, 905 for Enos, 910 for Cainan, 895 for Mahalaleel, 962 for Jared, 365 for Enoch, 969 for Methuselah (absolute record holder for longevity in Western culture), 777 for Lamech and 950 for Noah (Genesis 5). From then on, longevity would diminish gradually and unevenly, the result of divine anger: Shem, Noah's son, lived 600 years, Arphaxad 438, Salah 433, Eber 464, Peleg 239, Reu 241, Serug 230, Nahor 158, Terah 205 (Genesis 10 and 11), Abraham 175, Ismael 137, Isaac 180, Jacob 147, Joseph 110.

As with the neighbouring peoples, a long life was a mark of divine favour. We find a curious episode in Genesis in which Joseph presents his father to Pharaoh. The only question that the latter asks him concerns his age; this is the best way of judging the power of a people: how many years can it provide for its adepts? The author of Genesis was careful to attribute 130 years to Jacob, that is, 20 years more than the Egyptian wise men, which could not fail to impress Pharaoh and to inspire in him the greatest respect for Yahweh, the more so since Jacob stressed that his antediluvian ancestors had lived much longer still.

And Pharaoh said unto Jacob, How old art thou?
And Jacob said unto Pharaoh, The days of the years of my
pilgrimage are an hundred and thirty years: few and evil have the
days of the years of my life been, and have not attained unto the
days of the years of the life of my fathers in the days of their
pilgrimage. (Genesis 47, 8–10)

'Those who observe the Law shall prolong their life', says the Book of
Deuteronomy (32.47). Inversely, the absence of old men is a sign of a
curse on the family: 'There shall not be an old man in thine house for
ever', the prophet says to Eli, whose children are behaving badly (I
Samuel 2.32). God promised Solomon to grant him a long life if he
kept faith (I Kings 3.14).

The old man was held in honour. He enjoyed his master's confidence.
When Abraham decided to marry his son Isaac, he charged his oldest
servant, who was also the steward of his estate, with choosing a wife
for him (Genesis 24.2). The old man, who witnesses to the past,
represents the living link between the generations, and it is he who is
consulted about ancient custom (Deuteronomy 37.2). As a witness to
the period of greatness, he is the guarantor of his people's faithfulness.
Israel keeps faith with the Lord as long as the elders who knew the
heroic times of the conquest are alive (Joshua 24.31) and the Book of
Joshua ends significantly with the death of the son of Aaron, the priest
Eleazar (Joshua 24.33): the death of an old man marks the true end of
an era.

The Proverbs and Psalms compete with one another in heaping praises
on the old: 'The hoary head is a crown of glory, if it be found in the
way of righteousness' (Proverbs 16.31); 'The beauty of old men is the
grey head' (Proverbs 20.29). The good live a long time, the wicked die
young: 'The fear of the Lord prolongeth days: but the years of the
wicked shall be shortened' (Proverbs 10.27); 'Hear, O my son, and
receive my sayings: and the years of thy life shall be many' (Proverbs
4.10); 'Bloody and deceitful men shall not live out half their days'
(Psalm 55.23); 'With a long life will I satisfy him and shew him my
salvation' the Lord says to the just man (Psalm 91.16).

These writings were mostly established since the beginning of the
monarchy and were shaped and transcribed in royal administrative
circles; they reflect the thoughts of cultivated court circles. It is possible
that old age was shown greater honour in these wealthy and traditionalist
circles than among the populace. But the prophetic writings of the
eighth and seventh centuries BC, which originated in more varied circles
and were often at odds with the wealthy classes, lambasting the abuse
of wealth, agree with them on this point. Thus Isaiah shows us God
enthroned on Mount Sion in the presence of his elders (Isaiah 24.23).
For him, the elder's mission was to guide his people: 'The ancient and

the honourable, he is the head' (Isaiah 9.14), and the clearest sign of anarchy was lack of respect for the old. The seizure of power by the young men comes high on the list of catastrophes announced by Isaiah: 'I will give children to be their princes and babes shall rule over them. . . . The child shall behave himself proudly before the ancients' (Isaiah 3.4–5). For Jeremiah, the depth of desolation was the fact that even the old were affected by deportation (Jeremiah 6.11 and 51.22). When he was himself charged with announcing their future sufferings to the people, he was told by God to surround himself with elders (Jeremiah 19.1); they were wiser than the priests, against whom they battled to defend the prophet (Jeremiah 26.17).

Added to this, Mosaic Law guaranteed respect for old men and aged relations: 'Thou shalt rise up before the hoary head, and honour the face of the old man' (Leviticus 19.32). 'Honour thy father and thy mother, that thy days may be long upon the land which the Lord thy God has given thee' (Exodus 20.12). The blessing given by the old father was holy and irrevocable, and the son thus blessed is the heir: as when Isaac blessed Jacob instead of Esau by mistake (Genesis 27), or when Jacob blessed his sons (Genesis 49). In certain cases, among the Moabites, but especially the Ammonites, an old father could sleep with his daughters, as evidenced in the Lot episode (Genesis 20.30–8). All this demonstrates the prestige and power of the old man in the ancient period. Furthermore, old age was habitually qualified as 'good': Abraham 'died in a good old age, an old man and full of years' (Genesis 25.8); Isaac died 'being old and full of years' (Genesis 35.29); Gideon 'died in a good old age', surrounded by his 70 sons (Judges 8.32).

Thus, growing old in the time of the patriarchs and even of the kings does not appear to have been too disagreeable, relatively speaking. In any case, this long-distant era compares favourably with the periods which followed after. Although we have not heard any old people talking about themselves, and all the texts mention them in the third person, it is already remarkable that the literature of the tenth and twelfth centuries BC dedicates so much space to them without including one dissonant note. Old people seem to have been genuinely respected, cosseted and obeyed in a general way; they benefited from a semi-religious prestige. Their fate would be envied by future generations.

Their sole real burden was a natural one: physical pain and dwindling ability. It is in this domain that we can distinguish the beginnings of a loss of their prestige in the period of the Kings. The evolution of references to the physical handicaps of old age is revealing, for instance. The growing insistence on the limitations and evils of old age indicate that its image was deteriorating.

This could be seen first of all in the evaluation of longevity. Genesis is generous on this point: God fixes the span of human life at 120 years (Genesis 6.3), and the Book of Joshua fills the Mosaic age with vigorous old men like Caleb, who undertook war at the age of 85 with all the enthusiasm of a young man: 'I am this day fourscore and five years old. As yet I am as strong this day as I was in the day that Moses sent me: as my strength was then, even so is my strength now, for war, both to go out and to come in' (Joshua 14.10–11). The Book of Samuel is already less optimistic. At the age of 80, Barzillai the Gileadite thought he had reached the end of his life and complained of his infirmities: 'How long have I to live, that I should go up with the King unto Jerusalem? I am this day fourscore years old: and can I discern between good and evil? Can thy servant taste what I eat or what I drink? Can I hear any more the voice of singing men and singing women?' (2 Samuel 19.32–40). As for the Psalms, they reduce longevity even further: 'the days of our years are threescore years and ten; and if by reason of strength they be fourscore years, yet is their strength labour and sorrow' (Psalm 90.10).

The oldest writings thus observe the weakness and physical limitations of old age, but in a neutral way, without dwelling on them, and without bitterness. The time of sexual activity had passed, as old Sarah humorously observed: 'Now Abram and Sarah were old and well stricken in age; and it ceased to be with Sarah after the manner of women. Therefore Sarah laughed within herself, saying, After I am waxed old shall I have pleasure, my lord being old also?' (Genesis 18.11–12). David, for his part, did not make fun of his impotence: 'Now king David was old and stricken in years; and they covered him with clothes, but he gat no heat. Wherefore his servant said unto him, Let there be sought for my Lord the king a young virgin: and let her stand before the king and let her cherish him, and let her lie in thy bosom, that my lord the king may get heat' (I Kings 1.1–2). He was given Abishag, a Shunammite, a very lovely young girl. But she failed to revive David's vigour, which distressed the king all the more in that impotence was then a sign of a ruler's inability to reign. Later on, his son Solomon, when he too grew old, was to lose the source of his reputation, his judgement, and his wives were to turn him towards other gods (I Kings, 11.4).

Blindness was one of the most frequent ills notified among the old: 'Ahijah could not see; for his eyes were set by reason of his age' (I Kings 14.4); 'Isaac was old, and his eyes were dim, so that he could not see' (Genesis 27.1); 'Eli was ninety and eight years old; and his eyes were dim, that he could not see' (I Kings 4.18). The latter also died from an accident due to weakness: 'he fell off from the seat backward by the side of the gate, and his neck brake, and he died, for he was an old man and heavy' (I Kings 4.18).

The moment came when even the giants of the heroic age, in spite of their superhuman status, felt their faculties diminish and prepared themselves for giving up: 'I am an hundred and twenty years old this day; I can no more go out and come in', Moses is made to say in Deuteronomy (31.2), which contradicts itself a little later on by stating that he had retained all his vitality. In the same way, Samuel, on observing his decline, established his sons as judges (I Samuel 8.1); the Levites retired at the age of 50, and were restricted to minor duties: 'And from the age of fifty years they shall cease waiting upon the service thereof and shall serve no more. But shall minister with the brethren in the tabernacle of the congregation, to keep the charge, and shall do no service' (Numbers 8.25–6), which could be interpreted two opposite ways: that the old Levite was placed in a subordinate position, or, on the contrary, that he supervised the others.

As far as the common people were concerned, there was no age of retirement. The old worked the fields like the others (Judges 19.16), and some Proverbs from before the exile suggest that aged parents were not always held in respect: 'Hearken to thy father that begat thee, and despise not thy mother when she is old' (Proverbs 23.22). Even though the old were seldom left to suffer on their own, this was not unknown in ancient times: 'Cast me not off in the time of my old age: forsake me not when my strength faileth . . . Now also when I am old and greyheaded, O God, forsake me not' (Psalm 71.9 and 8).

SCRIPTURE AFTER THE EXILE: THE WEAKENED ROLE OF THE
ELDERS

While the exile provided the definitive break with the past, in the literature at least, it also consolidated the position of the old man, who had become the image of divine fidelity: And even to your old age I am he; and even to hoar hairs will I carry you' (2 Isaiah 46.4). The writings of the Babylonian captivity often made use of the character of the old man to show the horrors of siege, deportation and massacre. In Lamentations, the extent of their sufferings is attested by the fact that even the old were not spared, which is a sign *a contrario* of their eminence and dignity in Hebrew society: 'The young and old lie on the ground in the streets' (Lamentations 2.21); 'My priest and mine elders gave up the ghost in the city' (Lamentations 1.19); 'They favoured not the elders' (Lamentations 4.16); 'The faces of the elders were not honoured' (Lamentations 5.12). In this book and in the Book of Ezekiel, the depth of calamity was attained when the elders no longer came to the council, no longer gave their advice, and even turned to idols, evidence of the importance attached to their presence and their behaviour (Ezekiel 7.26 and 8.11). In the public places, the old participated in the general mourning: 'the elders of the daughters of Zion sit upon the ground, and keep silence; they have cast up dust upon their heads' (Lamentations 2.14).

Their reassuring presence was thus to be one of the signs of the return of peace and prosperity – 'There shall yet old men and old women dwell in the streets of Jerusalem, and every man with his staff in his hand for very age' (Zachariah 8.4) – which would then be like a general renewal, marked by lengthened human life, a sign of blessing: 'There shall be no more thence an infant of days, nor an old man that hath not fulfilled his days: for the child shall die an hundred years old' (3 Isaiah 65.20).

The historical writings from after the exile did not cast any further doubt on the prestige of old age. Once again, people died very old and happy: 'Jehoida waxed old, and was full of days when he died; an hundred and thirty years old was he when he died' (2 Chronicles 24.15). The unpleasant picture of the great founding fathers' old age provided in the preceeding writings was even corrected: according to Chronicles, written at the end of the fourth century BC, David died 'in a good old age, full of days' (2 Chronicles 29.28). Killing the old was still the greatest and most shocking crime (2 Chronicles 36.17 and 2 Maccabees 5.13), and all Israel's enemies were unfailingly accused of this. On the contrary, the last great Jewish leaders of the national wars kept the old constantly in mind and Judas Maccabees put part of the booty aside for them (2 Maccabees 9.30). People liked to see them arguing in the public squares, since this was a sign of prosperity for the people: thus, during the period of the high priest Simeon, in 141–140 BC, 'the ancient men sat in the streets, they communed all of them together of good things' (I Maccabees 14.9). The elders represented the people, and they were trusted because they were wise.

The behaviour of Eleazar, a 90-year-old doctor of the Law, was characteristic of this. On being invited to eat pork, he refused categorically to commit this sacrilege because an old man ought to set the young an example; for this reason he even refused to adopt the subterfuge offered him, consisting simply of pretending to eat pork. His words bear witness to his elevated concept of the role of model and example which the old ought to play:

> But he, having formed a high resolve, and one that became his years, and the dignity of old age, and the gray hairs which he had reached with honour . . . For it becometh not our years to dissemble, that through this many of the young should suppose that Eleazar, the man of fourscore years and ten, had gone over unto an alien religion . . . and thus I get to myself a pollution and stain of mine old age. (2 Maccabees 6.23–6)

Of course not all old people were systematically wise, as instanced by Hauran, 'A man far gone in years and not less also in madness' (2 Maccabees 4.40). But they retained an important role in the conduct of public affairs. The elders, for instance, were entrusted by Darius with supervising the work on the reconstruction of the Temple (Ezra 6.7); the elders were consulted by Judas Maccabees before undertaking a campaign (2 Maccabees 13.13); it was with their consent that Jonathan decided to build fortresses in Judea (I Maccabees 12.35); it was with them that he went to seek Demetrius II (I Maccabees 11.23); it was they, finally, who offered up the burnt sacrifice for the king (I Maccabees 7.33).

Nevertheless the term 'elder' had certainly evolved since the Mosaic period and that of the judges. It probably no longer designated a gathering of old men but a group of mature men who were still sufficiently vigorous to participate actively in safeguarding and developing the prosperity of the people. The primitive term had been retained, but was used collectively to designate a council whose leaders gave an opinion in all serious matters. It was also resorted to for designating the exercise of judicial functions: the Book of Ruth shows us the elders seated at the town gate as witnesses and guarantors of the legality of a proceeding (Ruth 4).

Two centuries later, the council of elders was still being mentioned in the Book of Judith, in Bethulia (Judith 7.13, 13.12) and in Jerusalem (15.8), but from then on it was criticized: in the Book of Daniel, the tribunal of the elders was taken in by a false witness and God appealed to a very young man to re-establish the truth – the Spirit no longer necessarily dwelt on the old (Daniel 2.45–9). This had already been proclaimed at the beginning of the fourth century by the prophet Joel: the old men were not the only ones to dream dreams, God would distribute his spirit over everyone, even the young, the servants and the handmaids (Joel 2.28–9). In any case, the council of elders was being shown less respect: those assisting had to be forbidden from chatting (Sirach 7.14). Although this institution carried on in spite of everything for a long time yet, it was under the form of an assembly of notables. The Gospel according to Matthew often mentions it, always as consisting of elders, scribes and high priests; it was in fact the great Sanhedrin, the college of 71 members, made up of representatives of the lay aristocracy (the elders), the interpreters of the Law (the scribes) and the representatives of the great sacerdotal families (the high priests). They played an essential role in the trial of Jesus and the Acts of the Apostles mention them frequently (4.5, 6.12, 24.1).

The first Christian communities were to inherit this institution: thus the funds sent to the church of Jerusalem during the famine of 46–8 AD were sent to the elders. A council of elders is mentioned in Lystra, Iconium, Antioch of Pisidia and Ephesus, and Paul addressed his farewell discourses to them, while charging them with continuing his work (Acts 20.17–38). The elders were nominated by the Apostles (Acts 14.23) and presided over the assemblies, exercising the ministry of the word and of teaching (I Timothy 5.17). They laid hands upon those who received a special chrism (I Timothy 4.14) and annointed the sick (James 5.14). Peter charged them with leading the flock, without abusing their power and asked the young to submit to them (I Peter 5.1). Paul charged Titus with nominating a certain number of them in each town in Crete (Titus 1.5) and they appear to have benefited from prejudice in their favour: 'Against an elder receive not an accusation, but before two or three witnesses', Paul recommended Timothy (I Timothy 5.19). John and Peter called themselves elders, since they were among the fellowship of the first Apostles.

The term 'elder', which we find also in Flavius Josephus' *Antiquities of the Jews* (XII, III, 3), thus acquired a very broad meaning which goes beyond any strict consideration of age; the elder was the important individual in the community, the notable person, renowned for his wisdom; he was no longer necessarily an old man.

THE LITERATURE OF WISDOM: OLD AGE IS CALLED INTO QUESTION AGAIN

Parallel with the loss of public and judicial power in a more complex society, the image of the old man deteriorated strongly in Hebrew circles from the fifth century BC onwards. The first great reflection on the human problem of old age to be qualified as philosophical is the admirable Book of Job. Written shortly before 400 BC, this profoundly original book of the Old Testament reflects the various currents of eastern wisdom in this period, to an extent that it has been asked whether the author really was a Hebrew. He evokes old age in all its aspects, social as well as individual, and in all its ambiguity. Job is old, like most of his interlocutors, and they think this suffices to make wise men of them – 'With us are both the gray-headed and very aged men, much elder than thy father' (Job 15.10) – sufficient reason for believing what they say. While this may well have been true formerly, the authority of old men is henceforth opposed: the young deride them (Job 30.1) and instruct them, because wisdom no longer depends on age. Elihu the son of Barachel the Buzite, after having respectfully allowed the elders to speak, grew angry with them because they had been incapable of defending divine justice, addressing them in the following severe fashion:

I am young and ye are very old: wherefore I was afraid, and durst not shew you mine opinion.
I said 'Days should speak, and multitude of years should teach wisdom.

But there is a spirit in man: and the inspiration of the Almighty giveth them understanding.

Great men are not always wise neither do the aged understand judgement.

(Job 32.6–9)

One of the fundamental bases of the prestige of old age was put in question again. Long life was not a divine blessing because the wicked lived just as long as the good: 'Wherefore do the wicked live, become old, yea, are mighty in power?' (Job 21.7). Nevertheless, traditional morality was preserved for a last time, since Job, the just man, would be re-established in his property and his health, would live a further 140 years, would see his descendants down to the fourth generation and would die 'being old and full of days' (Job 42.17).

A century later in the years between 290–280 BC, the Kohelet, influenced by Hellenistic thought, would venture much further into pessimism. Old age is a long individual tragedy, a sequence of misfortunes. These are the years of which is said: 'I have no pleasure in them' (Kohelet/Ecclesiastes 12.1), in which death is all that can be expected:

Also when they shall be afraid of that which is high, and fears shall be in the way, and the almond tree shall flourish, and the grasshopper shall be a burden, and desire shall fail: because man goeth to his long home, and the mourners go about the streets:

Or ever the silver cord be loosed, or the golden bowl be broken, or the pitcher be broken at the fountain, or the wheel broken at the cistern.

Then shall the dust return to the earth as it was: and the spirit shall return unto God who gave it.

(Kohelet/Ecclesiastes 12.5–7)

The old man could not even pride himself on his wisdom and his experience because 'Better is a poor and a wise child than an old and foolish king, who will no more be admonished' (Kohelet/Ecclesiastes 4.16). The degeneration of the organs was described by means of metaphor: the keepers of the house (the arms) shall tremble, the strong men (the legs) shall bow themselves, the grinders (the teeth) cease because they are few, those that look out of the window (the eyes) are darkened, the shutters (the ears) are closed. Thus is this passage from Ecclesiastes 12.3 interpreted by the Talmud and the *Midrach Rebba*.

The other writings of Wisdom in the same period grumbled that old men were senile gossips who monopolized the conversation: 'Speak, thou that are the elder, for it becometh thee, but with sound knowledge: And hinder not music. Pour not out talk where there is a performance of music, And display not thy wisdom out of season' (Siracid/ Ecclesiasticus 32.3–4). They might also be libidinous old men, like those who lusted after the lovely Susanna and then accused her falsely (Apocrypha, History of Susanna). The Siracid claimed that it was right that these old debauchers be corrected, because love was not suitable at their age (Siracid/Ecclesiasticus 42.8). A theme which has won marked success in all forms of European literature.

Thus, old age, far from being a blessing, was to be feared. It was to be delayed as long as possible by avoiding worry (Siracid 30.24). This is another modern idea which will recur many times. Old couples lived in terror of seeing the other die and being left alone (Tobit 8.7). Allusions to old people being despised multiplied: 'Dishonour not a man in his old age; For some of us also are waxing old', advised the Siracid (Ecclesiasticus 8.6); 'Let us not spare the widow, Nor reverence the hairs of the old man gray for length of years, but let our strength be to us a law of righteousness; For that which is weak is found to be of no service', said the ungodly, who were growing ever more numerous (Wisdom of Solomon 2,10–11). Old parents were frequently abandoned and insulted, and the Siracid had to specify yet again:

> My son, help thy father in his old age;
> and grieve him not as long as he liveth.
> And if he fail in understanding, have patience towards him;
> and dishonour him not while thou art in thy full strength.
> (Siracid/Ecclesiasticus 3.12–13)

At the same time, these very writings concur in saying that old age is not a title which merits respect from others. While 'How beautiful a thing is judgement for gray hairs. And for elders to know counsel': for all that 'How beautiful is the wisdom of old men', on the other hand, 'An old man that is an adulterer lacking understanding', deserves scorn (Siracid/Ecclesiasticus 25.2). This idea reappears in the Book of Wisdom, undoubtedly the last book of the Old Testament (mid first century BC), and would be taken up again by the Church Fathers: the real old man is not he who has lived a long time but he who gives evidence of his wisdom. Old age, dissociated from age, becomes an ideal symbolic time:

> But a righteous man, though he die before his time,
> Shall be at rest
> (For honourable old age is not that which standeth in the length
>   of time
> Nor is its measure given by number of years;
> But understanding is gray hairs unto men,
> And an unspotted life ripe old age) . . .
> Being made perfect in a little while, he fulfilled long years . . .

But a righteous man that is dead shall condemn the ungodly that
   are living
And youth that is quickly perfected the many years of an
   unrighteous man's old age.

(Wisdom of Solomon 4.7–16)

He who follows wisdom is wise from his youth onwards and long
experience is no longer indispensible (Wisdom 8.8). 'I shall have . . .
honour in the sight of elders, though I be young' (Wisdom of Solomon
8.10).

In some ways the Gospels and the Epistles preserved this unfavourable
image of old age. In the episode of the woman taken in adultery, when
Jesus asked those who had never sinned to cast the first stones, the old
were the first to leave with hanging heads (John 8.9). In his letter to
Titus, Paul felt obliged to remind the old men of their duties and a
negative perusal of this passage allows much to be supposed: 'That the
aged men be sober, grave, temperate, sound in faith, in charity, in
patience. The aged women likewise, that they be in behaviour as
becometh holiness, not false accusers, not given to much wine, teachers
of good things' (Titus 2.2–3). Elsewhere the Apostle ordered Timothy:
'Rebuke not an elder, but intreat him as a father; and the younger men
as brethren; the elder women as mothers' (I Timothy 5.1–2).

The situation of the old had thus returned to that of the period before
the exile. The passage from a primitive patriarchal society to that of
kingship and then to the more complex, more organized and more
structured sacerdotal state with its customary institutions established
through the working of centuries, had been fatal for the old. They lost
their security and prestige following the progressive disintegration of
the extended tribal family in which the old relations, who represented
the link with their ancestors, were looked after. Old men and old
women were now the exclusive responsibility of their direct children
and grandchildren, and those who had none were reduced to mendicancy
(Ruth 4.15).

Above all, the old man was now de-sacralized and trivialized.
Influenced by their neighbours' wisdom, notably by the ambient
Hellenism of the end of the fourth century BC onwards, Hebrew
thought no longer envisaged him as more than an aged, suffering and
diminished man, waiting for death. His longevity, previously the source
of his prestige, now only served to increase his culpability when he
committed faults. The type of odious, garrulous, senile, disgusting and
lascivious old man which occurs so frequently in Greek comedies, was
in process of penetrating Jewish life. Once the old had been reduced to
their human dimension, they were left with nothing but their weakness;
they had to drop their responsibilities and go into retirement like Simeon
(1 Matthew 5.13); once they had been dethroned by the mature men in

the council of the elders, they had to begin their careers as useless adjuncts. As institutions became established and the role of the written word grew, they lost their place as guides and the purveyors of living tradition. The old entered the painful gloom in which they are hidden by every advanced society.

The word alone retained its prestige; the Apocalypse of St John represents the community of the faithful by means of the 24 old men who were to appear so frequently on the porches of medieval churches. People still spoke traditionally of the wisdom of the old, but this was only an image, a symbol: 'Miss not the discourse of the aged; For they also learned of their fathers: Because from them thou shalt learn understanding, And to give answer in time of need' (Siracid/Ecclesiasticus 8.9). 'Stand thou in the multitude of the elders; And whoso is wise, cleave thou unto him' (Siracid/Ecclesiasticus 6.34). Finally, the supreme consecration: starting with Daniel (mid second century BC) God himself is an old man, and this image was reproduced by Christian art and would remain anchored in collective mentality until our day: 'I beheld till the thrones were cast down, and the Ancient of days did sit, whose garment was white as snow, and the hair of his head like the pure wool' (Daniel 7.9).

Thus, just as the old man lost his prestige in human society, he made a symbolic entry into eternity by personifying divine wisdom and permanence. This was not the least of the avatars of this age of life, which is subject to perpetual ambiguity.

JEWISH SOCIETY: OLD AGE BETWEEN REMEMBRANCE OF THE
PATRIARCHS AND DE-SACRALIZATION

This ambiguity was to be continued in traditional Jewish society. The rabbinical texts and the Talmud contain numerous allusions to the wisdom of the old man and to the respect due him. In the first two centuries of our era, the *Commentary on Leviticus* by Sifra declares that the old man must be honoured, and that one must 'not sit in his place, not talk in his place, not interrupt his words' because 'an old man is none other than a wise man' (no. 199). Megillah scrupulously resumes the prescriptions of the Torah: 'The Torah prescribes rising up before an old man and honouring him by keeping a distance of four cubits from him. His place is not to be taken, he is not to be contradicted, he is to be shown respect and fear; in commerce and in business they take precedence over the others. If one goes to war, he will dig and will crouch, following Deuteronomy 23.14. He will turn towards the sanctuary and will make water with the sanctuary behind him' (no. 1072). In the consignments relating to vows and promises, Nedarim writes: 'If the young tell you to build and the old to destroy, hearken to the elders, but hearken not to the young, for the building of youth is destruction, whilst the destruction of the old is building. And a sign for this matter is Rehoboam the son of Solomon' (Nedarim 40a).[2] 'Who has a place in the future world? He to who are applied the words, and before his elders shall be glory' (Baba Bathra 10b).[3] 'He who learns from the young, unto what is he compared? Unto one who eats unripe grapes, and drinks wine from his vat. And he who learns from the old, unto what is he compared? Unto one who eats ripe grapes, and drinks old wine (Aboth IV.20).[4]

By taking the text of the Law literally, the Talmudic writings adopted the anachronism of re-establishing the old man of the patriarchal period in honour. Did this notion extend beyond mere words? Was the old man, the elder, the actual poor and diminished old man of real life? Was he not rather the notable learned man, the rabbi? 'Do not read "an old man", but a man of schooling; we learn that they were all capable of sitting in the schools', said Siffre (no. 360); 'The elders were those of whom it is said: – He is worthy, pious, and deserves to be wise' (no. 243); 'Your elders, they are the elder rabbis, according to Numbers 11.16' (no. 353). The Talmud tells the story about the wise man Eleazar ben Azariah, who was nominated head of the sanhedrin at the age of 18, and immediately acquired grey hair, as a sign that he was worthy of the function.

The Talmud and the rabbis distinguished in reality between the venerable old and those who were not. The former, derived from the priestly caste, became wise men as they grew older, while the latter, who belonged to the *amme ka'-ares* (the rude and ignorant common people, observing the Law badly), became idiots. The Kinnim declares:

> Among the old *amme ka'-ares*, as they grow older their minds become confused, according to what is said (Job 12.20): – He removes speech from the faithful and he removes intelligence from the old men. But this is not so for the elders of the Torah: on the contrary, as they grow older, their minds grow stronger, according to what is said (Job 12.12): – To gray hairs wisdom, to aged people prudence. (no. 2314)

Once an elder had become a judge he was surrounded with honours: 'He is raised up and seated in the mountain of the Temple and from there he is raised up and seated in the outer court and seated in the hall of cut stones' (Seqalim no. 970).

In practice, people's attitude to the old varied, but it appears to have been more favourable to them than in the Christian world of those days. Certain rabbis claimed that one should rise up even in the presence of an illiterate old man or of a pagan old man, because his very longevity proved that he must possess some merit. This was why they asked the old not to show themselves in public too much, in order to prevent such ceremonies from being multiplied. Other rabbis felt on the contrary that longevity had nothing to do with merit, morality or divine protection. It was due to good dietary habits, to taking exercise and to bathing. Rabbi Hanina, still going strong at 80, attributed his good health to the hot baths and the oil massages which he had been in the habit of taking since childhood. This would also be Maimonides' opinion in the twelfth century AD. He recommended good physical and intellectual habits for a better life, and quoted the dietary prescriptions of the Talmud:

> Whoever accustoms himself in these ways which I have explained, I guarantee that he will not have illness all his days until he dies in old age. He will need no physician and his body will be sound and healthy all his days, unless his body is unhealthy from its beginning or there was a diathesis which was bad from his birth, or if a plague or famine comes to the world.[5]

Spiritual and physical health are linked; all the rabbis agree on this point. In the fourteenth century, Meir Ibn Adlabi was to demonstrate it once more in his *Shebile Emunah*, in which he mingled Hippocrates and Galen with the Bible and the Rabbis.

Old age began at 60: 'Sixty – for mature age, seventy – for a hoary head' (Aboth V.21).[6] Any death before the age of 60 was considered premature. This age represented life's achievement, whereby what was sown was now harvested; wisdom for some, folly for others. But in any case, in extreme old age, one became useless: even the wisest had to be excluded from the *sanhedrin*, because their age distorted their judgement (Maimonides, Sanhedrin I.3). As for the common people, 'an old man in the house is a burden, an old woman a treasure' (Erahin 19a): old men are often gloomy, whereas old women are always ready to enjoy themselves.

In the Middle Ages the Jewish communities provided specialized charitable organizations for the care of the old. These 'consecrated houses' (*heqdesh*) are mentioned in Germany in the eleventh century, but there must have been some before then.

To sum up, the Jewish world appears to have granted a relatively important place to the old. This attitude was greatly influenced by the Jews' devotion to the oldest writings of the Bible, especially the Pentateuch, which testify to an age when the old were privileged. For those familiar with the Torah, the old man must have retained some of his ancient aura, and this would have enhanced his dignity. The Christian world, on the other hand, based itself on the New Testament, where the old play only an insignificant role, and it was easier there to slip into indifference towards or mockery of the old. The more so, in that Christianity was to inherit the Greco-Roman tradition, itself so unkind to the old.

3

The Greek World:

Sad Old Age

As the mother of western civilization, ancient Greece has bequeathed us a fascinating inheritance which has long formed the basis of our world outlook. In art as in philosophy, theatre and politics, the Greeks asked the fundamental questions and outlined possible solutions, without for all that definitively solving anything.

Western culture has found in Greece, at least since the fifth century BC, all the seeds of its success and its problems. The Greeks had a go at everything, from democracy to tyranny, from science to Dionysiac mysticism, from art for art's sake to chequerboard cities, from the purest faith to scepticism and cynicism, from ontology to sophism. They asked all the questions which man must ask when confronted with the mystery of the world, of life and of consciousness, and they refused to accept any easy answers, whether provided by religious or materialistic creeds. By seeking passionately for Truth they showed that she was not to be found. By searching unceasingly for Beauty, they managed to come closer to her than any other civilization has done. Above all, they raised man to the summit of his capacities; they made him master of his destiny.

Did old age have a place in such a civilization? Yes; in the same way as evil, pain and suffering did, that is to say, on the level of the great mysteries, the questions with no answers, in the gallery of insoluble problems. For a people searching for human perfection, beauty and the achievement of full human potential, old age could be classified among the divine curses. Decrepitude, which shrivels heroes, seemed worse than death, which guarantees the grandeur of destiny. Happy Alexander, who never acquired wrinkles! The conqueror owed his glory to his youth, like his model the divine Achilles, and what a pitiable spectacle would the conqueror of the Persians have afforded, once vanquished by rheumatism!

MYTHOLOGY: THE GODS HATE OLD AGE

In those shadowy times when mythology took shape, which is as far back as we can go in Greek history, old age was always considered a curse. 'Sorrowful Old Age', as Hesiod called her, was she not daughter of the Night, goddess of Darkness and grand-daughter of Chaos? Were her brothers and sisters not Destiny, Death, Destitution, Sleep and Concupiscence? Was her dwelling not the anteroom to Hell, where she rubbed shoulders with Terror, Illness, Indigence, Exhaustion and Death? She haunted the old myths peddled or cobbled together by Hesiod, who tells in his *Works and Days* how Zeus, in order to take his revenge on mankind, to whom Prometheus had given fire, sent them Pandora, who sowed among them the cruel illnesses which old age brings to men; indeed, men age quickly after illness. Before this curse, they had known neither work, nor pain, nor cruel old age; they had always retained the strength of their feet and hands and their death was like falling asleep. Eternity itself was of no value if it had to be accompanied by old age. Poor Tithonus experienced this, when he obtained the gift of immortality from the gods thanks to the intervention of Aurora, his wife: he became so decrepit and wizened as a result that he was changed into a cicada. Eternal youth was the supreme happiness; this was Zeus' magnificent gift to Ganymede, the son of a Trojan king, whom he had abducted. As for Aeson, he experienced the joy of being rejuvenated at the threshold of death by his daughter-in-law Medea's enchantments.

The Olympians did not like old people, as is abundantly demonstrated by mythology. The young rebelled against the tyrannical old, chasing them away or killing them. In every generation, the elders were dethroned by their children. The story of Uranus, castrated by his son Kronos, himself the victim of his son Zeus, goes back to the oldest myths. The gigantic struggle of the Olympians against the Titans has the marks of a conflict between the generations, which ended with the inevitable triumph of youth. The old gods are invariably wicked, perverted and always vanquished. The final generation, that of the Olympians, consisted of gods and goddesses who were either young or eternally in the prime of life, with the exception of Charon and a few marine divinities. We must be extremely careful before drawing any conclusions about the Greeks' attitude towards old age, given the obscure origins of these myths.[1] It is however certain that there was a temple to old age in Athens, in which old age was portrayed as an old woman draped in black, leaning on a stick with a goblet in her hand; near her, stood a water clock which had almost run out.

THE COUNCIL OF THE ELDERS IN HOMERIC GREECE

If we climb down from Olympia in order to try and understand the place of old age among the mortals of the Acheans' heroic age, we are obliged to quote Homer. The debate about the value of the Iliad and the Odyssey as historical evidence lies to a great extent outside the framework of this present book. Whether his 28,000 verses tell us more about the Bronze Age civilization in the twelfth century BC than about Ionia in the eighthcentury BC, or whether they constitute a synthesis of the two, is only relatively important to our theme.[2] Whatever the answer, the Homeric world offers us an irreplaceable reflection of the Archaic age in Greece, when the old seem to have occupied an enviable position.

This is but an illusory impression which careful reading of the text will dissipate. Just as one swallow does not make a summer, so too one Nestor does not make a gerontocracy. His is indeed a genial personality with a specific role to play:

> Nestor the fair-spoken rose up, the kind speaker of Pylos from whose lips the streams of words ran sweeter than honey. In his time two generations of mortal men had perished: those who had grown up with him and they who had been born to these in sacred Pylos, and he was king in the third age.[3]

His advice was solicited in times of difficulty, 'he whose counsels had been listened to before'. When the warriors despaired of taking Troy, the best they could think of was going to find Nestor: 'Nestor, shepherd of the people', who was conscious of the wisdom conferred by his age: 'both of you are younger than I am. Yes, and in my time I have dealt with better men than you are and never once did they disregard me.'[4] He told Diomedes: 'But let me speak, since I can call myself older than you are and go through the whole matter, since there is none who can dishonour the thing I say, not even powerful Agamemnon.[5]

But was wise Nestor more than an individual? Is it not mistaken to make him represent all old Achaeans and so conclude that they were all respected and listened to? The Homeric world was not a world of old people; it was a heroic world and its heroes were the young, the warriors, Achilles, Ajax, Patroclos, Odysseus, Agamemnon and Hector. In any case, Nestor continued to fight and lead his troops; like the others he carried his two lances, his helmet and his belt because, Homer observes, 'he gave no ground to sorrowful old age.'[6] He was not the only old man to enter the arena. The oldest were the first to speak in the general assemblies. Thus, among the Ithacans, at the beginning of the Odyssey, 'Aegyptius, an old man bent with years and rich in wisdom, was the first to speak' in the assembly.[7] Other old men contributed to the debates: 'the old lord Halitherses, Mastor's son, spoke out. He knew more of bird-lore and soothsaying than any man in his generation.'[8] The Phaeacians demonstrably enjoyed the same custom: 'The silence was broken by the venerable lord Echeneaus, a Phaeacian elder who was the most eloquent speaker among them and rich in the wisdom of his forefathers.'[9] Before he left, Odysseus entrusted the administration of his property to an old friend, the proverbial Mentor, 'with orders to defer to the aged Laertes and keep everything intact.'[10]

All these venerable old men, who were generally heard with respect, were elderly heroes, and were honoured more on this account than because of their age. Aegyptius, Halitherses and Mentor were old companions of Odysseus' father and their glorious past conferred prestige and authority on them. Nestor recalled that he had fought and befriended men stronger than those of the present time. They were listened to out of respect for the former hero rather than the old man. People might sometimes not shrink from openly snubbing them, calling their words foolish and threatening them

> Greybeard, he said, enough! Run home and read omens to your children, or they may be getting into mischief. And leave me to interpret these signs. I am a better man than you at that . . . As for Odysseus, he has met his fate abroad: and I wish you too had perished with him. We should then have been spared this flood of divination from your mouth . . . But let me tell you this; and what I say holds good. If you, his senior, with the wisdom of the ages at your disposal, misuse your eloquence to incite this young man to violence, in the first place it will be all the worse for him . . . and for you, old man, there will be the extremely unpleasant consequence that we shall impose on you a fine that it will break your heart to pay.[11]

So what about the council of the elders, which was mentioned so often at difficult moments? Its role appears to have never been more than advisory; the government was more monarchic than senatorial, and the council more aristocratic than gerontocratic. It consisted of old chiefs whose advice was solicited from time to time. As for old men of modest origins, they are more often to be met among the highway beggars than among the places of honour in the city. Even old heroes were not always glorious: Laertes, Odysseus' father, lived as a recluse in the country, tending his vines, and looked after by an old woman. His disguised son commented on his decrepitude:

> Old man . . . you don't look after yourself very well: in fact, what with your squalor and your wretched clothes, old age has hit you very hard . . . You look more like a man of royal blood,

the sort of person who enjoys the privilege of age, and sleeps on a soft bed when he has had his bath and dined.[12]

The Homeric epic exalted youth. If the old do not appear to be despised in it, this was due to their aristocratic origins. Left in the background, they were no more than sometimes over-garrulous advisors. When Calypso tried to detain Odysseus, the best promise she could make him was that of never knowing old age, of staying eternally young. 'The gods hate old age', Homer makes Aphrodite say, and it is only too clear that all his heroes dreaded crossing the 'accursed threshold of old age'. In this rural society, where land was acquired and defended by force of arms, the old were necessarily relegated to an honorific role.

POETS AND PLAYWRIGHTS: THE CURSE OF OLD AGE

The whole of Greek literature reflected these sentiments. Already by the end of the seventh century BC Mimnermus of Colophon was anathematizing old age, to which everything is preferable including death. Happy they who die at the age of 60, since 'once painful old age has arrived, which renders man ugly and useless, his heart is no longer free of evil cares, and the sun's rays bring him no comfort. He dislikes children and women despise him. Thus has Zeus given us an old age full of pains.'

The leitmotifs of ugliness, suffering and rejection by society are repeated untiringly: 'Misery me! Misery! Oh youth! Oh old age which spoils everything! The latter is coming closer, while the former is turning away!' lamented Theognis of Megara, while Archilochus predicted his beloved's decay, and Anacreon evoked grey temples, faded hair and exposed teeth. For the latter, old age was only bearable so long as the individual concerned was able to compete with the young men: 'I am old, no doubt, he said, but I can drink more than the young and, when I lead the dances, my sceptre is a wine-skin' (ode 38), and in his ode about old men he proclaims: 'I like to see the happy dances of the young and old men. An old man who dances is old by his hair, but he is young by his spirit' (ode 47). The old are crashingly boring on account of their garrulity and self-importance, like the old woman of Theocritus' *Idyll XV*, who always expresses herself in a sententious tone. Pindar is the only poet who does not poke fun at the old. In the *Nemaean Games*, he eulogizes Sogenes of Aegina, the winner of the boys' pentathlon, and wishes him a long life with his father, who is enjoying a 'flourishing old age'. He says further that extreme old age can be the source of tranquil satisfaction, and he was no doubt speaking from experience as he himself lived 84 years (518–438).

The very academic character of his poems prevents us from drawing any conclusions about the real situation of the old in Greece. Simone de Beauvoir has already drawn attention to the fact that the witness of literary men should often be treated cautiously: 'Law-givers and poets always belong to the privileged classes, which is one of the reasons why their words have no great value. They never say anything but part truths and very often they lie.'[13] This statement is, however, dangerous and excessive and could too easily rebound on its author, as a bourgeois renegade branded by her class origins. Nor for that matter are popular or populist writers any less prejudiced than those who belong to the wealthy classes. Should we then deprive ourselves of their contribution? That they reflect the ideals of a certain social category only makes them more valuable, so long as one never forgets to allow for their environment and origin. Poets do not in fact lie; they see the world through distorting glasses created by their sensitivity, their social milieu and their education. Do we not all wear these kinds of spectacles? By contrasting different points of view we may eventually come close to the truth.

It is not irrelevant that Greek poets held a negative view of old age. Nor were they contradicted by the playwrights, although the latter generally agreed in attributing wisdom to the elders, like their model Homer. We must however agree with Simone de Beauvoir that their plays are about noble deeds and are staged in aristocratic, divine or royal settings. Within these very restricted circles, the old man could not but be worthy and venerable; his political experience made him a precious counsellor who was consulted and listened to. Aeschylus' plays show us young sovereigns seeking the advice of their mentors before taking important decisions; in Sophocles' plays, old men of politics are entrusted with important missions and sent as ambassadors in periods of crisis: 'It's on account of my age that I was chosen', says Creon in the *Trachiniae*. Euripides shared the same point of view about the usefulness of old counsellors: 'The heart of young people is unsteady, but in all his enterprises the old man takes the ins and outs into account that the end result may be the best for all.'

A feature of aristocratic education in Greece was the liaison between an elder and a younger man. A young nobleman would be entrusted to the care of an older man who guided him with his advice. The first example of this is also to be found in Homer, with Chiron, who raised Achilles and 20 other heroes. And again, when Nestor sent Odysseus and Ajax to try to move this very Achilles, he added Phoinix, a good old man who had looked after the great warrior during his early childhood. 'It is I who have made you what you are', he reminded Achilles in a long speech recalling the past, with the latter giving an affectionate welcome to 'Phoinix my father, aged, illustrious'.[14]

The practice of association between old and young no doubt favoured a better understanding between the generations, with the elder keeping in touch with the interests and activities of his protégé, while the

latter participated in his mentor's serious conversations. The classic
recriminations of the old against the folly and extravagance of the young
are not to be found in the tragedies; everyone keeps his place, without
trying to play a part unsuited to his age. The worthy old man behaves
like a wise man who has renounced worldly and amorous pleasures and
entertainments. He is thus protected from the criticism of the younger
generations.

This model probably did exist in aristocratic circles, although the
foregoing examples owe more to the ideal than to reality. Classical
tragedy offers us models rather than portraits and comedy doubtless
comes closer to real life. Nevertheless, the tragedies do show us that
old age had a role to play, that it need not be a negligible quantity and
that it could hold an important place in society, at least in high society.

However this social role does not obliterate the personal drama which
old age constitutes. Close behind the flattering cliché of the wise old
man come the pitiable figures of decrepit and suffering old men, which
overwhelm the former. Sophocles provides us with one of the most
pathetic examples in the whole of literature in the character of *Oedipus
at Colonos*.[15] The author was 88 years old at the time and he patently
identified with his unhappy hero, old Oedipus, as he is led by his
daughter Antigone and comes at the end of his life to the sacred wood
at Colonos, Sophocles' homeland. Old age is the last curse the gods
load on our fate: the chorus of old men at Colonos, like a troupe of
damned souls, employs terrible words to depict the misery of very old
age, words which were to echo through the generations in the hearts
of all the old people.

> None but a fool would scorn life that was brief.
> None but a fool would cleave to life too long:
> For when an old man draws his lingering breath
> Beyond his fitting season, pain and grief,
> The harsh years' harvesting, upon him throng
> And joy is but a phantom of the past.
> Then soon or late the doom of Hades, death,
> Comes with no dance, no lyre, no marriage song,
> All all alike delivers at the last.
>
> Incomparably best is not to be.
> And next to this, once a man sees the day.
> I wish all speed to hasten whence he came;
> After youth's trifling joy, he is not free,
> He must endure his lot as best he may;
> Envy, sedition, murder, hate and strife,
> Until at length old age, unfriended, lame,
> Reviled and lonely claims him for its pay:

The wretched ending of a wretched life.
                    (*Oedipus at Colonus*, ll. 1166–83)

Resignation can then be the only wise attitude, since, as Oedipus learnt during his life, one cannot struggle against one's fate:

Dear son of Aegeus, only the gods themselves
Are free from age or death. All else is ruined
By overmastering time. The strength of earth,
The strength of the body, both alike decay.
Faith dies, and lack of faith comes into being.
                    (*Oedipus at Colonus*, ll. 579–88)

Oedipus is already resigned when the play opens:

I ask for little.
Though I get less than little, it is enough;
For hardship and the years that have been my lot,
The long years, and nobility of mind
Have taught me patience.
                    (*Oedipus at Colonus*, ll. 5–9)

Euripides was Sophocles' contemporary and almost as old as him, dying at the age of 74 in 406 BC. In *Herakles* he launched a hymn to youth accompanied by a curse at old age:

Chorus:
Youth is what I love
Age weighs on my head like a burden
Heavier than the rock of Etna
It draws a curtain of darkness before my eyes.
Not the wealth of an Eastern throne,
Not a palace full of gold
Would I take in exchange for youth.
Youth is most precious in prosperity,
Most precious in poverty;
Age is miserable, tainted with death:
I hate it. Away with it, let the sea swallow it!
Why must the curse of age fall on men's homes and cities?
Away to the winds with it![16]

This accursed old age re-emerges in *Hecuba*, under the lineaments of the old queen of Troy, Priam's widow, and prisoner of the Greeks, 'an aged, childless slavewoman', and again in the character of Oedipus in the *Pheonician Women*:

Why have you brought me forth to the light,
dragging my blindness along on a stick
with my pitiful tears, from my bed in the dark
a gray, invisible ghost of the air, a corse, a flying dream?[17]

(ll. 1540–5)

Aeschylus had employed the same image in the *Agamemnon*, where the old man wanders like a dream appearing in full day:

> And the passing old, while the dead leaf blows
> And the old staff gropeth his three-foot way,
> Weak as a babe and alone he goes,
> A dream in the noon astray.[18]

These diminished beings, very often blind, certainly had a greater impact on the picture of old age presented by the playwrights than did the wise counsellors we recalled earlier.

COMEDY: THE RIDICULOUS ASPECT OF OLD AGE

This portrait was not softened by the comic writers, indeed quite the reverse. To the pathetic and pitiable aspect emphasized by the writers of tragedies they added the ridiculous aspect by accentuating some of the faults occurring among the very old. The old man and woman were to become the special butts of comic art for centuries to come, because they were no more than caricatures of human beings, and their physical and sometimes mental decay made them at once easy to fool and harmless. Every human passion assumes a grotesque aspect among the old because they are no longer able to enjoy the pleasures of life and because the approach of death renders all their schemes vain. The only old man not to be mocked was he who did nothing, who no longer ate, drank or slept with women. As soon as he tried to 'live', he became repugnant and ridiculous. His vices or simple passions were automatically funny; the old lecher, the old drunkard, the old miser, the old infatuated woman and the old procuress were all guaranteed to raise a laugh.

Greek writers were, however, less nasty about old age than were the Romans, who had an added reason for resenting old people: as we will see, comedy provided Latin audiences with a form of revenge against the tyranny of the *pater familias*. Greek theatre seems to be more restrained in this matter. Even the redoubtable Aristophanes was able to show tenderness and pity towards the old. As was the case in the *Acharnians*, where the chorus-leader is angered by the treatment inflicted on old Thucydides, an adversary of Pericles', who was ostracized and then ruined by trial:

What an injustice that a man, bent with age like Theucidides, should be brow-beaten . . . I wept tears of pity when I saw an Archer maltreat this old man . . . Ah, but if you will not leave the aged in peace, decree that the advocates be matched: thus the old man will only be confronted with a toothless greybeard.[19]

'How sad that I have so many years', says the chorus of coal-burners in the *Acharnians*, while other old people lament their inability to run any more.

Menander was also capable of staging agreeable old men. In the *Girl from Samos*, Demeas, who has passed his sixtieth year and lives with a courtesan, is well-to-do, good-humoured and peaceable; he and his adoptive son Moschion get on well and respect each other. Niceratus, the other old man in the play, is poor and rather miserly, but although he is not endowed with the same qualities he does not descend into caricature. The two men are worthy, but the slightest thing suffices to make them ridiculous; as when they start quarrelling and fighting. Menander treats the old man above all as a victim who is to be pitied: 'He who carries on too long dies disgusted; his old age is painful, he is in need. Wherever he turns, he sees enemies; he is plotted against. He has not gone away in time; he has not had a fine death.' Old age, like death, becomes an allegory, a malignant power which attacks individuals and eats away at them: 'Old age, you are the enemy of human kind, you ravage all the beauty of its forms, you transform the splendour of its limbs into heaviness, speed into slowness.' Old age, not old people, is hateful.

Aristophanes is more biting, his old people are more ridiculous and more guilty than Menander's. He accentuates their physical ugliness sweepingly: 'All bent and wrinkled, with a most pitiful appearance, bald and toothless', thus does the old man in *Plutus* appear.[20] He displays their deficiencies and failings. Being quarrelsome and jealous of their authority, they are frequently at odds with their children and they always lose their case and are ridiculous. In the *Clouds*, the old Strepsiades, who has fallen into debt on account of his son's extravagance, learns that Socrates holds a school in which he teaches strong and weak reasoning, thanks to which he would be able to get rid of his creditors. But he feels too old to take in this teaching: 'At my age, memory has gone and the mind is slow to grasp things. How can all their fine distinctions, these subtleties be learned?'[21] So he sends his son instead, who becomes so skilful at sophism that he proves to his father that he has to beat him. The play further conjures up old men who tell improper jokes and then hit their hearers to make them laugh.

In the *Wasps*, Aristophanes pokes fun at Philocleon and his colleagues among the Heliastae for their mania for judging. While his work constitutes above all a political satire against the popular tribunal of

Heliastae, it is not immaterial that Aristophanes chose old men to represent the judges; advancing as a group, leaning on their staffs, guided by children, they present a sorry picture. When Philocleon is late, he is accused of having all kinds of illnesses due to old age, finishing off with his own son holding him up to ridicule. In *Lysistrata*, the old are again made fun of, when they try in vain to dislodge a troupe of women entrenched on the Acropolis. The lewdness and impotence of old men are also butts for comedy.

It is not useful at this point to appeal to risky psychoanalytical explanations based on what is known as the castration complex, according to which the old man is supposed to represent man's unconscious anxiety about his fear of feeling desire without being able to satisfy it. For Aristophanes as for most of his contemporaries, the old man has passed the age of physical love, basically because his ugliness makes any idea of coupling revolting. Old age is the antithesis of eroticism, and the mere thought of an old man still being capable of desire was enough to make him repugnant in the mind of a Greek, for whom beauty, youth and love could not be dissociated.

Thus the old who cheated about their age were among the favourite subjects for comedy, particularly those who made up their faces in order to wed a much younger partner, as in *Plutus*. Old women are handicapped in this game because they fade much sooner than men:

> A man comes home – he may be old and grey – but he can get himself a wife in no time. But a woman's not in bloom for long, and if she doesn't succeed quickly, there's no one will marry her, and before long she's going round to the fortune tellers to ask them is she's any chance.[22]

THE PHILOSOPHERS: THE MISFORTUNE AND AMBIGUITY OF OLD AGE

The accursed and pathetic old age of the tragedies and the ridiculous and disgusting old age of the comedies are complemented by the contradictory and ambiguous old age of the philosophers. The latter had often studied the mystery of ageing. The abundance of their writings on this subject witness both to their interest and their confusion.

Let us note first of all that most Greek philosophers achieved an advanced age and so spoke of old age not objectively but subjectively. Writing when they were themselves old, their opinions were obviously swayed by the manner in which they lived their old age. Their state of health and their personal relations with the world loomed large in their analyses. Their philosophy is in this instance much more existentialist than when holding forth on Goodness, Evil, Virtue or the Soul. Their witness, albeit less 'rational', gains in human value as a reflection of the condition, opinions and prejudices of the old.

The *Lives of Eminent Philosophers* by Diogenes Laertius, while from many points of view so unreliable, does tell us the age at which most of the philosophers died. Although the higher figures need not all be taken absolutely at face value, they are nevertheless on the whole fairly likely. Moderation is only exceeded in one case, that of Epimenides, whose life is the stuff of legends: having slept for 57 years in a cave, his hibernation endowed him with extraordinary longevity: 154 years according to Xenophon of Colophon, 157 years according to Phlegon and 299 years according to the Cretans.[23] With the exception of this fable, the ages of the other philosophers generally agree with those established by modern scholarship[24] and the witness of contemporaries.

The Greek philosophers correspond in general to the idea we have of them: they were old, as amply demonstrated in table 3.1.

Most of these venerable persons remained active until the last: they watched the games, travelled by chariot, pleaded in court, took part in banquets and several died from excess of wine. At over 70 years of age, Menedemus was renowned for his health and vitality: 'In his habit of body, even in old age, he was as firm and sunburnt in appearance as any athlete, being stout and always in the pink of condition.'[25] Theophrastus regretted that human life was so short when there was so much to do, whereas deer and crows live a long time and are useless. When Diogenes was told: 'You are an old man, take a rest', 'What', he replied, 'If I were running in the stadium, ought I to slacken my pace when approaching the goal? Ought I not rather to put on speed?'[26] As for Epicurus, he stated that one is never too old to engage in philosophy:

Let no one be slow to seek wisdom when he is young nor weary of the search thereof when he is grown old. For no age is too early or too late for the health of the soul. And to say that the season for studying philosophy has not yet come, or that it is past and gone, is like saying that the season for happiness is not yet or that it is now no more. Therefore both young and old ought to seek wisdom, the former in order that, as age comes over him, he may be young in good things because of the grace of what has been, and the latter in order that, while he is young, he may at the same time be old, because he has no fear of the things which are to come.[27]

While some preferred suicide to an excessively advanced and decrepit old age, most of them were preoccupied with the problem of great age: they talked about it frequently in their works and even dedicated whole treatises to it, which have unfortunately been lost: *On old age* by

Table 3.1. Longevity of eminent philosophers

Name	Supposed age at death	Remarks and quotations from Diogenes Laertius
Anaxagoras	72 yrs	
Anaximander	66 yrs	
Appolonius Thyaneus	80 yrs	
Arcelisaus	75 yrs	
Aristippus	79 yrs	
Ariston	old	
Aristotle	63 yrs	
Athenodorus	82 yrs	
Bias	extreme old age	
Carneades	85 yrs	
Chilon	very old	His death took place at Pisa just after he had congratulated his son on an Olympic victory in boxing. It was due to excess of joy coupled with the weakness of a man stricken in years (I.72–4).
Chrysippus	73 yrs	Died from drinking wine (VII.184).
Cleanthes	80 yrs	99 according to B.E. Richardson (starved himself to death).
Cleobulus	70 yrs	
Crantor	old	
Crates	old	He sang about himself: You are going, dear hunchback, you are off to the house of Hades – bent crooked by old age (VI.92).
Democritus	100 or 109 yrs	
Denys	80 yrs	
Diogenes	90 yrs	Committed suicide by holding his breath, or died from cholera.
Empedocles	60 or 77 yrs	Died in an accident, falling from a chariot on his way to a party.
Epicharmus	90 yrs	
Epicurus	72 yrs	
Eudoxus	53 yrs	
Gorgias	100, 105 or 109 yrs	
Heraclitus	60 yrs	
Isocrates	98 yrs	
Lacidas	old	Died from excess of drink.
Lycon	74 yrs	
Menedemus	74 yrs	
Metrocles	very old	Committed suicide.

Table 3.1 contd

Myson	97 yrs	
Periander	80 yrs	
Pittacus	70 yrs	
Plato	81 yrs	
Polemon	old	
Protagoras	70 yrs	
Pyrrho	90 yrs	
Pythagoras	80 or 99 yrs	
Socrates	60 yrs (70)	(executed)
Speusippus	advanced age	(committed suicide)
Stilpo	very old	Silpo died at a great age after taking wine to hasten his end (II.121).
Thales the Sage	78 or 90 yrs	Died as he was watching an athletic contest from heat, thirst, and the weakness incident to advanced age (I.39).
Theophrastus	85 or more than 100 yrs	Died: not long after having relinquished his labours (I.39).
Timon	90 yrs	
Xenocrates	82 yrs	
Xenophon	advanced age	
Zeno	98 yrs	He tripped and fell . . . and died on the spot through holding his breath (VII. 28).

Theophrastus, *Antimachus or the Old Men* by Phaedon, *Book of Longevity* by Phlegon, *On Old Age*, by Demetrius Phalerius.

Pythagoras was one of the first to elaborate a theory of the ages of life corresponding to the seasons, which was to become a very popular theme. He divided life into four times 20 years: childhood–spring (from 0 to 20 years), adolescence–summer (from 20 to 40), youth–autumn (40 to 60) and old age–winter (60 to 80). It is strange that he makes old age follow on directly from a pretty mature youth. For his part, Solon reckoned the average length of life at 70 years; Plutarch made old age begin at 50; Aristotle fixed physical maturity at 35 and spiritual maturity at 49 years.

It is revealing that none of these wise men state whether old age is in itself a good thing. All these old men only accept their age for as long as it is accompanied by health. Cleanthes replied to a man who twitted him about his old age (another significant mental aspect) that 'I too am ready to depart; but when again I consider that I am in all points in good health and that I can still write and read, I am content to wait.'[28]

The philosophers, like other people, did not suffer old age gladly. When they looked at it objectively, their opinion was more subtle but never very favourable. They noticed that they all wished to attain great age, despite its evils. Bion compared old age to a harbour where all ills converge and take refuge;[29] nevertheless, they all wanted a long life, like Solon himself, who upraided Mimnermus for having wished to die only at the age of 60, when he should have said 80.[30] Most of them concurred in recognizing that old age is a defect: it resembles everything that decays, and youth everything that grows, as Pythagoras said.[31] Old athletes 'are worn threadbare, cloaks that have lost the nap',[32] and their instrument was the staff. Diogenes thought that 'the word disabled ought to be applied not to the deaf or blind but those who have no wallet.'[33] Of course, old men had to be honoured, as Chilo and Pythagoras demanded. And of course the Stoics taught that one's parents must be honoured immediately after the gods. But on the whole, the philosophers were muddled about old age, which brought them more torments than it did prestige and wisdom.

PLATO'S IDEAL OLD MAN

The two greatest philosophers adopted radically different positions on this subject as on others. Plato was the main advocate in defence of the old man, whereas Aristotle led the prosecution. But were they talking about the same old man?

Plato does not engage in a description of reality and he envisages his old men such as they might or ought to be. His model old man, Cephalus, a rich merchant of Piraeus, lives in ideal conditions; robust and cultured, he enjoys a high standard of living. His physical powers are, however, certainly diminishing and he tells Socrates (in *The Republic*) that he now has trouble walking the eight miles that separate him from Athens. However, this does not bother him because, he goes on to say, 'I myself find that as age blunts one's enjoyment of physical pleasures, one's desire for rational conversation and one's enjoyment of it increase correspondingly.'[34] The following conversation with Socrates turns on the advantages of old age. Although the piece is quite long it merits being quoted in its entirety, because it is one of the very fine and rare texts in antiquity on the subject:

'As a matter of fact, Cephalus,' Socrates said, 'I enjoy talking to old men, for they have gone before us, as it were, on a road that we too may have to tread, and it seems to me that we should find out from them what it is like and whether it is rough and difficult or broad and easy. You are now at an age when you are, as the poets say, about to cross the threshold, and I would like to find out how it strikes you and what you have to tell us. Is it a difficult time of life, or not?'

'I'll certainly tell you how it strikes me, Socrates,' he said, 'for some of us old men often meet together, like the proverbial birds of a feather. And when we do meet, most of them are full of woes; they hanker for the pleasures of their youth, remembering how they used to make love and drink and go to parties and the like, and thinking it a great deprivation that they can't do so any more. Life was good then, they think, whereas now they can hardly be said to live at all. And some of them grumble that their families show no respect for their age, and proceed to harp on the miseries old age brings. But in my opinion, Socrates, they are putting the blame in the wrong place. For if old age were to blame, my experience would be the same as theirs, and so would that of all other old men. But in fact I have met many whose feelings are quite different. For example, I was once present when someone was asking the poet Sophocles about sex, and whether he was still able to make love to a woman; to which he replied, "Don't talk to me about that; I am glad to have left it behind me and escaped from a fierce and frenzied master." A good reply I thought then, and still do. For in old age you become quite free of feelings of this sort and they leave you in peace; and when your desires lose their intensity and relax, you get what Sophocles was talking about, a release from a lot of mad masters. In all this, and in the lack of respect their families show them, there is only one thing to blame; and that is not their old age, Socrates, but their character. For if men are sensible and good-tempered, old age is easy enough to bear: if not, youth as well as age is a burden.'

I was delighted by what he said, and tried to lead him on to say more by replying. 'I'm afraid that most people don't agree with what you say, Cephalus, but think that you carry your years lightly not because of your character but because of your wealth. For they say that the rich have many consolations.'

'Of course they don't agree with me', he said, 'and there's something in what they say, though not as much as they think. The story about Themistocles is very much to the point. A Seriphian was abusing him and saying that his reputation was due not to his personal merits but to his being an Athenian, and Themistocles answered: "I certainly should not have been famous if I had been a Seriphian, but nor would you if you had been an Athenian." The same remark applies to those who are not rich and find old age a burden: a good man may not find old age easy to bear if he's poor, but a bad man won't be at peace with himself even if he is rich.'[35]

This is indeed spoken by an unusually wise man. The basis of his argument, which was to be taken up again by Cicero, consists of linking happiness in old age to virtue. The good man, trained by a virtuous life, will enjoy happiness in his old age; it will be his life's fulfilment. Freed of the passions which troubled his soul, he will be able from then on to concentrate on intellectual pleasures. Cephalus concedes that this is not very often the case: when old men gather together, they spend the time lamenting the loss of youth and its pleasures; they complain of being the subjects of insults, which gives an idea of the scorn meted out to old people in Athens. The Greek proverb to which Cephalus alludes is also typical: 'At every age, enjoy yourself with people of your own age, but when you are old, enjoy yourself with an old man'; elders were not welcome in the gatherings of younger people. In the *Phaedrus*, the ageing Plato alludes discreetly to a 'face which years have robbed of its beauty, together with other consequences which it is unpleasant to hear mentioned.'[36]

However, scarcely has the gloomy reality been glimpsed, when Plato takes refuge in Utopia. In his dream of the ideal republic the old assume the finest role because 'it is for elder men to rule and for younger to submit.'[37] He was to put the finishing touches to the supremacy of the old men in his last dream, the *Laws*, which he finished *c.*348–7 BC, at the age of 80. The type of government whose details he then reveals has all the features of a gerontocracy. Reminding us once again 'that governing is for the elders and being governed for the young',[38] that children owe absolute respect and obedience to their parents and that the old must set an example to the young, he specifies the powers which will be attributed to age; men older than 60 will preside over the banquets; if any one abandons his parents, he will be denounced to the three oldest guardians of the laws and to the three oldest old women in charge of marriages, who will institute sanctions; if anyone mistreats his parents, he will be judged by a tribunal made up of the 101 oldest citizens; the law courts are to be supervised by persons obligatorily aged between 50 and 70; in all difficult cases, the oldest guardians of the laws will be consulted. In this imaginary city, people will only be able to get drunk from their fortieth year on, which will lighten the misery of old age; since Dionysio bestowed the wine cup 'on us for a comfortable medicine against the dryness of old age, that we might renew our youth, and our harsh mood be melted to softness by forgetfulness of our heaviness.'[38] In passing Plato praises the Spartan constitution, which offset the kings' power against that of 85 old men.

Plato recognized that some people could lapse into madness, that their mental and physical capacities sometimes declined '. . . if disease, age, sullen temper, or all together derange a man's mind with more than common violence.'[40] A very old man no longer in possession of all his faculties might be induced to commit a crime. In short, Plato does admit that old age has its weaknesses, and he prescribes places for relaxing and being cared for, with hot baths. Does not the attention and luxury with which he surrounds the old, the respect they are accorded in his ideal city and the powers which devolve on them in his Utopia, all hint at their inferior situation and their rejection in the real city? Do they not indicate the philosopher's reaction to a state of affairs he wanted to put an end to?

ARISTOTLE AGAINST THE OLD

Aristotle's stance is completely different. For him, old age guaranteed neither wisdom nor political ability. Even the experience of old people was not a positive element since it often constituted no more than an accumulation of mistakes in a mind hardened by age. Contrary to Plato, who considered that people's spiritual capacity improved as their senses grew weaker, thus freeing man from the slavery of his passions, Aristotle pointed out that given the union of soul and body, the decrepitude of the one must ineluctably affect the other. Physical health and full possession of bodily faculties are indispensible for the practice of wisdom. This is why man reaches his maximum potential at around 50 and then declines. 'The mind grows old no less than the body', he declares in the *Politics*.[41] The Spartan *gerousia* represents the very type of bad government, because power, far from being entrusted to the old, ought to belong to young and robust men. Old men should be limited to performing priestly functions.

Aristotle's attitude towards old age was pitiless from the moral point of view, accusing it of every evil in the *Ethics*: old people are miserly; they do not acknowledge disinterested friendship; only seeking for what can satisfy their selfish needs, they attach themselves only to those who can be useful to them; among them, love disappears out of lassitude or only survives out of habit; in any case their difficult characters make the birth of real friendship a very hazardous affair.[42] In the *Rhetoric*, Aristotle draws a very remarkable portrait of the old man, the exact opposite of Cephalus' Platonic discourse. The text presents a repulsive portrait, accusing the old of every fault: they are timorous, hesitant, suspicious, parsimonious, fearful, cowardly, selfish, pessimistic, talkative, avaricious and ill-humoured:

> The old have lived long, have been often deceived, have made many mistakes of their own; they see that more often than not the affairs of men turn out badly. And so they are positive about nothing; in all things they err by an extreme moderation. They 'think' – they never 'know'; and in discussing any matter they always subjoin 'perhaps' – 'possibly'. Everything they say is put thus doubtfully – nothing with firmness. They think evil; that is,

they are disposed to put the worse construction on everything. Further, they are suspicious because they are distrustful, and distrustful from sad experience. As a result, they have no strong likings or hates; rather, illustrating the precept of Bias, they love as men ready some day to hate, and hate as ready to love. They are mean-souled, because they have been humbled by life. Thus they aspire to nothing great or exalted, but crave the mere necessities and comforts of existence. And they are not generous. Property, as they know, is one of the necessities, and they have learned by experience how hard it is to acquire, how easy to lose. They are cowards, apprehensive about everything – in temperament just the opposite of youth; for they are grown cold, as youth is hot, so that advancing age has paved the way to cowardice, since fear in itself is a species of chill. They cling to life, and all the more as the latter end of it comes nearer; for, as the object of all desire is the absent, so the thing they most lack will be the thing they most desire. They are unduly selfish – another trait of the mean-souled. And through selfishness they live their lives with too much regard for the expedient, too little for honor; by expediency we mean what is good for oneself, by honor what is good absolutely. They are not shy, but tend to be shameless; because they have less regard for honor than for expediency, they do not care what people think of them. They are slow to hope; partly from experience – since things generally go wrong, or at all events seldom turn out well; and partly, too, from cowardice. They live in memory rather than anticipation; for the part of life remaining to them is but small, while the part that is past is large – and hope is of the future, memory of the past. Here, again, is the reason for their garrulity; they are for ever talking of bygone events, which they thus enjoy in recollection. Their fits of passion, though quick, are feeble; as for their desires of sense, these have either wholly failed, or are weakened. Accordingly, the old are not characterized by passion, and their actions are governed, not by impulse, but by the love of gain. And hence men in this period of life are thought to be temperate; the truth is that their desires have slackened, and they themselves are mastered by the love of gain. Their lives are rather lives of calculation than of moral bias; for calculation aims at expediency, whereas the object of morality is virtue. When they wrong others, the injuries are done out of malice, and not from insolence. Old men, too, as well as young men, tend to feel pity, but not for the same reason. Young men feel pity out of human kindness, old men out of their infirmity. Because they are weak, they take all possible sufferings to be near them; and this, as we saw, is the state of mind in which pity is felt. And hence they are querulous, not given to jesting or laughter;

for the querulous disposition is just the opposite of the mirthful.[43]

The bitter sentiments expressed by Stagyrus may appear excessive and suspect; we feel, however, that they come much closer than Plato's to the way the vast majority of Greeks thought about the old. It is undoubtedly relevant that Plato wrote the *Laws* at the age of 80, whereas Aristotle was scarcely 50 when he was discussing old age. However, the root cause of their opposite views was different still; Plato, speaking from the point of view of the Ideal, turned many aspects of the real situation upside down, whereas Aristotle, who simply described what he saw and heard, reflected both the objective situation and the prejudices of his age and civilization, which were clearly unfavourable towards the old.

THE OLD MAN IN GREEK SOCIETY AND INSTITUTIONS:
A DIMINISHED ROLE

The real place of the old man in classical Greek society can be glimpsed beyond the confines of literature, and it was not a favourable place. He generally seems to have attracted scorn, mockery and bad treatment: 'A decrepit old man, with only three teeth left, scarcely sighted, who leans on four slaves to walk, whose nose distills a permanent drip, whose eyes are filled with rheum, insensible to all pleasure, a living sepulchre, an object of mockery for the young'[44] is how Julian describes him, and many Hellenes seem to have viewed old age through similar eyes. The many precautions taken by Plato to protect the old allow us to discern how precarious their situation must have been. Lack of respect by children for their aged parents seems to have reached serious proportions, going from straightforward abandonment to physical assault and murder; some accused their fathers of insanity; 'the cause of such variance is commonly to be found in utter unqualified badness of character.'[45]

The history of institutions seems in fact to show that the authority of the family patriarch diminished in Greece from the seventh century BC onwards, apparently giving rise to lively conflict between the generations, favoured by the greater legal independence acquired by the children.[46] The many Athenian laws insisting on the obligation to respect old parents were constantly renewed, suggesting that they were not obeyed at all.[47] One of Solon's decrees had already declared, 'If any man neglects to provide for his parents, he shall be disfranchised. The same measure for him who has squandered the property of his fathers',[48] with this great legislator of the beginning of the sixth century BC emphasizing the obligation of respect due to aged parents. Examples of conflict between young and old may be discovered as far back as Alexander the Great: the young king of Macedonia and his companions were frequently irritated by the boasting of the veterans' old leaders, who embroidered on their exploits during Philip's reign. According to Robin Lane Fox, this was even the basic motive behind Alexander's murder of Cleistus.[49] The old were often treated like drivelling fools: 'You are giving me old men's talk', retorted Dionysius, tyrant of Syracuse, to Plato, who was instructing him in morals.

Old age was a defect in itself, which could be reproved just like other vices. Diogenes Laertius provides several instances of this, so it is no surprise that the Greeks feared the approach of great age. According to Strabo, the inhabitants of Chios practised suicide at the age of 60. Xenophon tells us that one of the reasons way Socrates accepted death was that it would deliver him from the infirmities and misery of old age: 'Now that he was already so advanced in years, that he must have ended his life, if not then, at least not long after, and in the next, that he relinquished only the most burdensome part of life, in which all feel their powers of intellect diminished.'[50] In the *Crito*, Plato makes him say: 'When a man reaches my age, he ought to consider the approach of death without sadness.' Funerary inscriptions provide the only texts where the Greeks appear to appreciate old age. B.E. Richardson, who has studied more than two thousand such inscriptions, concludes mistakenly that the Hellenes considered great age to be a pleasant time.[51] It is known, on the contrary, that funerary texts are the subject *par excellence* of pious lies and the very fact that they are alone in praising old age disqualifies their content.

It is paradoxical that Greece is the land where charitable institutions designed to support the needy old are mentioned unequivocally: Eschinus alludes in a law suit to the two oboli granted to old or infirm citizens who had been registered. In the Athens Prytaneum free meals were served to old citizens who had rendered services to the state, and they could even be fed there for the rest of their lives, as proven by a sentence in Aristophanes' *Acharnians*:

> We think its high time that someone spoke
> About the way you treat us older folk.
> Time after time our valour's saved the city
> In naval battles; yet you have no pity
> For our old age, but let the younger sort
> On trumped-up charges haul us into court . . .[52]

In Sardis, Vitruvius also mentioned the 'house of Croesus, which the Sardians have provided for those of the town inhabitants who, on account of their great age, have acquired the privilege of living at rest in a college of old men, which they call *gerousia* . . .'[53]

Sparta formed the great exception in the Greek world. Everyone remarked on the privileged place accorded to the old there. This anomaly, which Aristotle criticized and Plato praised, was indeed the exception which proves the rule. According to Plutarch, Lycurgus is supposed to have insisted in his legislation on respect towards the old, their role being to instruct and to advise the citizens. They are to be found in the gymnasia giving advice on matters of politics, war and sport. This city's great original feature was the *gerousia*, consisting of 30 old men chosen for life by acclamation from among citizens aged over 60. This council governed the whole of politics, especially foreign policy; it prepared drafts of laws to be presented to the assembly, and it could even overthrow the latter's decisions; it was supreme judge in criminal cases, able to condemn criminals to disfranchisement or to death; it was a high court before which even the two kings could be cited and judged; finally, it was not answerable for its decisions.

The *gerousia* already held enormous powers by the sixth century BC, and these seem to have increased in the fifth and fourth centuries BC when it could veto the decisions of the *ecclesia*, which had practically no formal power any more; the unanswerability of the gerontocrats was increasingly strengthened. This military gerontocracy constituted a peculiar feature, a city-barracks governed by old men, who, it is true, cannot have been very numerous. Sparta was always short of citizens, and very few can have survived the warrior hecatombs brought about by some heroic but costly tactic. Was their prestige due to their rarity, to the homage paid to the glorious survivors? This factor must undoubtedly have played a role in determining the respect given by the Spartans to old age. In any case, their attitude was proverbial in the ancient world.

Nothing remotely similar occurred in Athenian institutions, where, unlike Sparta, the role of the old seems to have dwindled. Simone de Beauvoir observed that in the Archaic period the terms *gera* and *geron* already designated both great age and the privilege of age – the right of seniority – which suggests that the old played a political role then. However, we have seen from the works of Homer that the council of the elders was merely consultative and that in fact the young made all the decisions. For a while, however, the evolution towards a conservative plutocratic regime must have favoured an increase in the powers of old age.

This trend was a general one; in the seventh to sixth centuries BC, *gerousia* were established in Ephesus, Croton, Cnidus, Corinth; their members were generally aged over 60 and they stayed put until their death. Landed wealth was concentrated in the same way; the oldest people were often also the wealthiest. Solon sanctioned this institution at the beginning of the sixth century BC. At that time, the power of the elders was concentrated in the *areopagus*, an aristocratic body made up of elderly archons, who could not be dismissed or held to account. As the guardian of the city it supervised the magistrates, judged all offences and crimes, participated in the executive, in the legislative and the judicial arms; it interpreted the laws, had the right of veto over the *ecclesia's* decisions and could assume total power, which it did during the Persian Invasion. To sum up, it played a similar role to the Spartan *gerousia*.

It was the coming of the Democrats to power which brought about its ruin; attacked in a series of law suits, it lost its political and judicial attributes following a law of 462 BC, and was left only with its honorific powers: the jurisdiction of religious crimes and the administration of the sacred places. The *Boule*, the *ecclesia* and the *helia* divided its political powers among themselves. The elders were never again to acquire an important role, and towards the end of the fourth century BC, Aristotle could study the constitution of Athens as a model freed from the ascendancy of old men. While access to the magistracy did entail conditions of age, these managed to favour mature men. Aristotle recapitulated them as follows: 30 years minimum to accede to the council under Draco; having a legitimate child aged ten for archons and treasurers: 40 years for participating in the Ten according to the constitution of 411 BC (the Rule of the 400); 30 years to accede to the *boule*; 40 years for sophronists and the childrens' *choregoi* after the Restoration and 30 years for judges. Only public arbitrators had to be over 60, but their powers were not very great; drawn by lot, they were obliged to accept their duty under pain of *atimia*, and they dealt with law suits in cases involving more than ten drachmas; if their arbitration was rejected by the litigants, the case would come before the tribunal again. In the same way, the exegetes, who were responsible for interpreting the Law, also had to be over 60.

Thucydides tells us that in their disappointment over the failure of the Sicilian expedition the Athenians raised older men to power for a while. But the trend did not last, and Athens remained faithful to youth.

THE OLD MAN IN THE HELLENISTIC WORLD: A DEGREE OF REHABILITATION

Hellenistic civilization was to produce a more broad-minded attitude, even indifference. The question of age no longer bothered the thinkers and writers of that period. As for its institutions, they were reduced to monarchy, a form of government whose only criterion for recruitment is loyalty to the ruler, irrespective of the subject's age. Macedonian tradition appears to have granted a special place to aged counsellors: it is significant that the word for 'counsellor' is derived from the word for 'grey-haired man'.

Alexander's epic illustrates the Conqueror's superb indifference towards age. The young ruler took account only of a man's value and usefulness and he placed his trust in many old people who played an eminent role during his reign. Having himself been educated by two old men, Lysimachus and Leonidas, Alexander nominated on his great departure Antipater, aged 60, as general-in-chief in the Balkans and he chose Parmenion, aged 65, as second-in-command of the expedition. This old man played a vital role and ended by offending the king; he extended his influence by using family members as intermediaries: his son Philotas commanded the Companion Cavalry, another son led the Shield-Bearers, a nephew led half of the mounted scouts, and a son-in-law was leader of the Elimiot foot brigade. The accounts of the expedition were written after Parmenion's disgrace, and they try to denigrate him and play down his role. However, he seems to have driven the soldiers on to win and to have shown splendid initiative during the great battles. Alexander nevertheless judged it more prudent to have him executed in 330 BC, in mid military campaign. Parmenion, who was then 70, represented the individual power which could be achieved by an old man through his own abilities and by making use of his large family in a patriarchal manner. Many Macedonian clans were similarly ruled by their oldest member, as in the case of a famous Illyrian chief of Philip's time, who was greatly feared until his death at the age of 90.

Alexander was to use further old counsellors: blind old Antigonus would be nominated satrap of Asis Minor; old Mazaeus, one of Darius' satraps aged over 60, who may have betrayed his master at Arbela, passed into the service of the king of Macedonia, who appointed him governor of Babylon. There was also the oldest staff officer, Coenus, who was chosen by his companions for the delicate mission of informing Alexander of the army's refusal to advance on India.

The Conqueror's troops presented one distinctive feature: they comprised an elite corps of 3000 Silver Shields (mostly veterans of Philip's corps of Shield-Bearers)[54] many of whom were over 60: throughout the campaign they performed extraordinary exploits, always the first to attack and always employed for the most difficult tasks, doing forced marches of 50 kilometres a day across desert. At the end of this campaign, when Alexander decided to send these élite veterans back to Macedonia, they were on the verge of mutiny. They refused to hand over their places and their share of future booty to younger officers, but ended by giving way before the king's determination. This unusual and a redoubtable troop of old men, led by the 70-year-old generals Craterus and Polyperchon, then crossed Asia from Babylon to Macedonia where they were greeted by the 70-year-old Antipater and were awarded places of honour in the theatres for the remainder of their lives. Their career was not yet ended; after Alexander's death many of them took up arms again and played an essential role in the battles between his Successors.

The Hellenistic period offered the robust and ambitious far more opportunities for demonstrating strength and achieving power than in the classical period. Like all cosmopolitan and open societies, the Hellenistic world, the melting pot of civilizations, was not encumbered by prejudices about race or age. Success was open to every forceful personality, young or old. This period, too often decried and qualified as decadent, in fact experienced an extraordinary surge of life and creativity; liberated from the trammels of institutions and the xenophobia of the classical Greek world, it was one of the few moments in history when national, racial and institutional barriers, as well as those separating the generations, were lowered.

This mental change was illustrated by the evolution of the arts. Classical Greece shrank from portraying old age: their old were always idealized, with only their bald heads and beards to distinguish them from mature men; ugliness and deformity were absent. This tradition was continued in some cases until the third century BC, as with the statue of Sophocles in the Lateran Museum, which portrays him in his prime. Old age was denied and rejected: the vases of the fifth and fourth centuries BC show it in the guise of a hideous, skinny and wrinkled woman, or appearing as a bearded and long-haired man, being fought and vanquished by Hercules.

The real old man, however, emerges in Hellenistic statuary under various forms. Art was not exclusive in those days. The artist studied and reproduced the world around him. He was certainly fond of picturesque, extreme, unusual, amusing and pathetic subjects, and old people, especially old women aroused his creative verve. Striking examples of such works are the drunken old woman, the grotesque head and body of the old woman in the Louvre, the fisherman and shepherdess in the Capitoline Museum and Aristodemus' hunchbacked old Aesop. These portraits do not contain an ounce of malice; at the most, curiosity mingled with sympathy. The old pedagogue in the Louvre is particularly touching: the gripping realism of this frail old man, thin, bent, bald and bearded, who smiles at his young master with his toothless mouth while carrying the child's knucklebones in his left hand. In the same vein, but nobler, is the head of Seneca, marked by age and experience, with his uneven beard, unruly hair and intense stare.

These works of art announced the reinstatement of old age. Whether pathetic or ridiculous, it was no longer ignored; it was no longer taboo; it was represented as it appeared, without being judged. Hellenist civilization described, counted and compiled, but did not reject. Nor did it turn old age into a curiosity, but was neutral, and is not neutrality the sanest possible attitude, better than degrading pity, than humiliating scorn and hypocritical praise? What a contrast, too, between the founder's youth (Alexander died aged 33) and his successors' longevity; Ptolemy II lived 62 years (308–246), Ptolemy III (284–221) and Antiochos

I (324–261) lived 63 years, Antipater lived 73 years (dying in 319), Attalus I 72 years (269–197), Seleucos I 75 years (355–280) and Antigonus Gonatas 80 years (319–239), Attalus II 82 years (220–138) and Ptolemy I a full 85 years (367–282)!

The men of this heroic age were fascinated by records. As Alexander's expedition plunged into Asia, legends were circulating in the army about the wonders of the east, particularly the extraordinary longevity of its inhabitants: 130 years in a region in Southern Iran and 200 years in India. One of the episodes the soldiers found most striking was the arrival of two wise Indian gymnosophists, who accompanied the troops on several stages of their journey, one of whom immolated himself on a pyre at the age of 79 in order to avoid becoming an invalid.

Age at decease and longevity in Greece

Precise figures about the age of individuals in the ancient world may appear justifiably suspect, given that births were not regularly registered and that its historians are notorious for their tendency to exaggerate numbers. Nevertheless, landmarks do exist. In Athens, for instance, when the public arbiters were recruited their ages were checked by the archons and eponyms; every year the ephebes' names were carved on a bronze stele raised in front of the palace of the council.[55] Children were inscribed on the registers of their phratry while their parents testified under oath that their ancestors had enjoyed full rights of citizenship. At the age of 17, the Athenian would be inscribed on the registers of his deme, but this could be refused him. The fact that, several centuries after the event, the archives of the island of Cos could produce Hippocrates' birth certificate, testifies to the seriousness with which the Greeks registered civil status. Let us add that censuses were taken from time to time in Athens, and that works of geography, a subject invented by the Greeks, included sections on descriptive statistics, as did the 159 monographs of Aristotle's treatise on *Politics*.[56]

Since most of these sources have disappeared, it is very difficult to acquire an idea of the longevity and the proportion of old people in the Greek population. B.E. Richardson has drawn up a table from the 2,022 funerary inscriptions collected by him. We reproduce as table 3.2 the part relating to deceased persons over the age of 60.[57]

In total 10.2 per cent of these 2,022 Greeks lived over 60 years. Given the relative importance of the sample, this result appears probable and it pinpoints fairly well the numerical importance of old men in the Greek population. A contemporary of Aristotle's would have had a one in ten chance at birth of attaining the age of sixty, which seems fairly poor odds. But because of the heavy infant and child mortality, an adult aged over 25 had a high probability of growing old. Of these 2,022

Table 3.2. Longevity according to funerary inscriptions

Age at decease	Number of cases	% of total number of deceased
61–5 yrs	45	2.23
66–70 yrs	48	2.37
71–5 yrs	29	1.44
76–80 yrs	35	1.73
81–5 yrs	19	0.94
86–90 yrs	16	0.79
91–5 yrs	5	0.25
96–100 yrs	6	0.30
101–10 yrs	3	0.15

Source: B.E. Richardson, *Old Age among the Ancient Greeks*, Baltimore 1933.

individuals, 233 died before the age of five, 147 between the ages of six and ten, 180 between 11 and 15, 294 between 16 and 20 and 268 between 21 and 45, that is 55.48 per cent of the total. Of the 900 survivors aged 25, 206 of them (22.8 per cent) would attain the age of 60, a large enough proportion to ensure that old age had lost the exceptional and miraculous character which invests it in more primitive societies.

Achieving old age had become common enough for people to take an interest in it. But while the old were sufficiently numerous to enable generalizations to be made about them, there were not enough of them for their own needs to be taken seriously. Numerous enough for their presence to be noticed, the proportion of old people did not yet constitute a social problem. Not rare enough to be precious, they were not numerous enough to be more than a curiosity. The demographic picture probably does play a part in society's overall view of the old. Thus, the two most advantageous situations are those at the two extremes; societies with a very small percentage of old people honour them; societies with a large percentage of old people, such as ours, are aware of the real problems of great age and of its economic significance; they start looking after the old. A society such as ancient Greece, where the old were relatively small in number, trivial yet not inconvenient, tended to neglect them. Other factors obviously came into play, but the demographic weight of the old cannot be neglected.

Maximum longevity has not evolved. Among the 2,022 individuals listed by B.E. Richardson, a certain Pancharius is the record holder, dying at the age of 110. As for famous men, the author cites 128 who lived beyond 60, all of them remaining active until the end. Thus, to the philosophers cited earlier, can be added poets such as Achaeus (74 years), Aeschylus (96 years), Anacreon (85 years), Apollonius of Rhodes (80 years), a comic author of 106 years, the rhetoricians Apollodorus of Pergama (82 years) and Lysias (83 years). From there it is only a step to the conclusion that most written works, especially literary ones, were written by old people, a step mistakenly taken by the author, who thus broaches the well-known argument especially well illustrated by Harvey C. Lehman's famous work *Age and Achievement*: does man achieve his full potential before or after 40?

Greek Medicine and Old Age: Research into the Causes of Ageing

Given that old age was felt to be an ineluctable decline and, at the end, a mortal illness, the Greeks looked for its physical causes. But, being less good at physiology than they were at philosophy, they reached only the most fantastical conclusions, which had little to do with science. Nevertheless their explanations led the field for the next 2,000 years, until the Renaissance and even beyond.

As is proper, the first medical hypotheses about the causes of ageing were formulated by Hippocrates, who himself lived to 83 (460–377). Following Empedocles (490–430), he developed the theory of the four humours, which, when balanced against each other, ensure good health. These four humours correspond to the four cosmic elements, and whichever of the four predominates produces one of the four temperaments governing mankind:

Cosmic elements	Their properties	Corresponding humours	Corresponding temperaments
AIR	hot and moist	blood	sanguine
EARTH	cold and dry	black bile	melancholic
FIRE	hot and cold	yellow bile	choleric
WATER	cold and moist	phlegm	phlegmatic

Hippocrates envisaged the process of ageing as a loss of heat and moisture; the body grows cold and dry. The source of heat resides in the left side of the heart, whence it spreads through the body:

> growing bodies have the most innate heat; they therefore require the most food, for otherwise their bodies are wasted. In old persons the heat is feeble, and therefore they require little fuel, as it were, to the flame, for it would be extinguished by much. On this account, also fevers in old persons are not equally acute, because their bodies are cold.[58]

This theory was to be adopted many times.

Hippocrates stated elsewhere that every individual receives at birth a certain quantity of energy, called internal heat, or vital spirit, or vital force, which would gradually be consumed during the course of his existence. There are various ways of periodically refuelling the body's vital spirit, but its reserves can never be reconstituted entirely at the previous level, so that its available energy never stops diminishing, and so ageing occurs. The initial reserves and the rate of consumption naturally vary with each individual, so that some age faster than others. Thus old age is a purely natural, physical and irreversible phenomenon; it is this statement, rather than in his description of the process that the principal merit of Hippocrates' theory resides.

Although he did not regard old age in itself as an illness, it predisposes the body, being less resistant, to illness. The great doctor considered the principal afflictions of old age to be respiratory problems, catarrh, coughing, difficulty with articulation, kidney trouble, apoplexy, dizziness, insomnia, colicky maladies, failing vision and hearing and nasal maladies.[59] All of which are in fact an amalgam of maladies and problems intrinsic to old age. Finally, in order to prolong the latter, Hippocrates recommended a moderate diet and physical exercise. He advised taking hot baths and drinking wine to counteract the loss of heat and moisture.

Aristotle adopted the basis of Hippocrates' explanation and pushed his conclusions further. His theory of ageing, which was described as 'visionary', was not challenged until the modern age.[60] He elaborated it in his treatise *On Youth and Old Age, on Life and Death, and on Respiration.* [61] Everything that lives has a soul, located in the heart, and which cannot survive without heat. The soul and natural heat are closely linked at birth, and life consists of maintaining this heat and its relation to the soul. It is like a fire which has to be maintained and fed with fuel, but which is destined to go out after a long period of weakening. Every organism has a certain quantity of innate latent heat at birth, which is progressively dissipated and ends by running out, giving rise to natural death.

This theory, which in fact prefigures the 'rate of living' theory recently propounded by Pearl, announced the discovery that the basal metabolic rate decreases with age in adults.[62] Aristotle thought that illness affected the old more seriously than the young and that it could accelerate the advance of death. The slightest thing can extinguish the little flame burning in an old man, and if no accident occurs, it will go out by itself.

The Greeks also inquired about the nature of certain deficiencies particular to old people. But the answers supplied by authors of lesser calibre than Hippocrates and Aristotle demonstrate a high degree of fantasy and are interesting only as curiosities. Plutarch echoed these erudite discussions when he himself joined in the debate, in *The Nine*

Books of Table Talk.[63] Here are, for example, two of the trivial questions posed during the discussion: 'Why women are least liable to intoxication and old men most quickly liable?'[64] That, Plutarch replied, is due to the fact that the female temperament is moist, so that wine is diluted by it and is quickly eliminated through the constant drawing down of fluids. The temperament of old men is on the contrary dry, their bodies like sponges which soak up wine and, in any case, they always look drunk: they are characterized by trembling limbs and stammering tongue, excessive talkativeness, irascible temper, forgetfulness and wandering minds.

Another question was: 'Why old men hold writing at a greater distance for reading?'[68] Plutarch reviewed the various answers produced until then: some people thought that the old have to hold books at a distance to allow more light between them and the script; others say that it's because when the book is too close, the two rays of light coming from the eyes do not fuse, making one see double. This opinion, which was based on the laws of optics and appears the most likely to us, seemed ridiculous to our author, who then mentioned the extravagant theory of Hieronymus, a philosopher of Rhodes in the Hellenic period:

> (He) expressed the opinion that we see by means of the forms which fall upon the vision from the objects viewed. These forms, when they first come off, are large and coarse, and so at close quarters they disturb old men whose vision is slow and stiff; but where they rise into the air and gain distance, their earthly parts are broken and fall away, while the light parts, as they approach the eyes, painlessly and evenly fit into the passageways, and thus old men are less disturbed and more readily apprehend the forms.[66]

Plutarch, for his part, took his stand on principle: vision results from the bright emanation which flows from the eyes and mixes with the light outside, fusing with it to form one body. But the luminous emanation from the pupils of old men is weak and powerless, so that instead of mingling with the light outside, it dissipates and vanishes. So a book has to be held at a distance, in order to reduce the brightness of the light coming from it, so that it can mingle correctly with the luminous emanation from the eyes.

PLUTARCH AND GERONTOCRACY

Thus, in Greek and Hellenistic society, the deficiencies of the old were the subject of debate because they constituted one of nature's curiosities. Plutarch, who died at the age of 75 in 125 AD, was the last Greek writer to dedicate an entire work to old age, at least if the essay called

'Whether an old man should engage in public affairs?' included in his *Moralia* is authentic. In it he picks up the great debate between Plato and Aristotle about the merits of the old and their place in political life. But his thinking was no longer exclusively Greek. Writing four centuries after Aristotle, he was able to reflect on the Latins' contribution to these questions. His treatise is interesting precisely because he reveals cases and practice in ancient Greco-Roman life, rather than because he tells us his personal point of view. As a historian and compiler, Plutarch was in possession of a great number of facts, which illuminate Greco-Latin behaviour towards old age.

His position was as follows: old men ought not to retire from political life, but should take part in it up to the end.

> Cato, for example, used to say that we ought not voluntarily to add to the many evils of its own which belong to old age the disgrace that comes from baseness. And of the many forms of baseness none disgraces an aged man more than idleness, cowardice and slackness, when he retires from public offices to the domesticity befitting women, or to the country, where he oversees the harvesters and the women who work as gleaners.[67]

Even for a man who has never been involved in politics, it is never too late to start.

Plutarch also accumulated references to old men who had remained active: the actors Philemon, who died in 262 BC at the age of 99, and Alexis, who died in 270 BC at 96, the politicians Cato the Elder and Agesilas. It is shameful, he continues, to retire from politics to engage in pleasures, as Pompey reminded Lucullus: 'Pompey said that it was more untimely for an old man to indulge in luxury than hold office.'[68] The old, being deprived of the pleasures of sex and of the table, ought to indulge in pleasures of the mind, especially those of government. Recalling the words of Euripides: 'Aphrodite with old men is wroth', Plutarch thought that the aged man, deprived of physical love, would find compensation in the pleasure of accomplishing noble actions. Furthermore, 'it is a man's duty not to allow his reputation to become withered in old age like an athlete's garland, but by adding constantly something new and fresh to arouse the sense of gratitude for his previous actions, and make it better and lasting.'[69]

The presence of old men in government also contributed to the good management of the institutions. The old were less subject to envy and blind criticism, because their reputations were already firmly established. They were harder to uproot than were the young, because they had acquired numerous relations during their careers, and rather than retreating before criticism, they had to try and increase their power. Plutarch then advanced an important argument, which evokes once again the general climate in Greece: society despises the old. Being active in political life would be an excellent remedy against this scorn: 'Just as an old man active in word and deed and held in honour is a sight to arouse reverence, so one who spends the day in bed or sits in the corner of the porch chattering and wiping his nose is an object of contempt.'[70]

The old possessed precious qualities which made them indispensible in politics: prudence, which runs the risk of being lost in times of inaction, experience and prestige. Plutarch recalled too how the Greeks established a council of elders around old Nestor, how the monarchy in Sparta was advised by elders, how the Senate in Rome means an assembly of elders, and how the term *geras* also means honour and reward. It is absurd, he says, to rush at honours when one is young, only to reject them when old. Old politicians can give the young the benefit of their experience; they are necessary to the state; their disinterest renders them more devoted to causes in the general interest, whereas the young seek personal glory. Soldiers must be young, but governors old: did Massinissa not remain a great leader until the age of 90?

Although he is a remarkable advocate of gerontocracy, Plutarch does advise avoiding excess. Old men who seek to amass duties, to take over every post, to set themselves forward at every election, are ridiculous and are detested by the young for whom they leave nothing. They must reserve themselves for matters of importance, leaving lesser matters to younger men. Plutarch here touches on a very sensitive point, which was to be one of the principal reasons for conflict between the generations in every age: the more the old monopolize power, the greater the impatience of the coming generations, developing into hatred and mockery of old age. The excessive authority of the Roman *pater familias* was obviously related to the bad image of old men in comic Latin literature, which provided an outlet for the accumulated resentment against old and oppressive fathers. Later on, the Italian mercantile republics, which were often controlled by their oldest and thus richest citizens, gave rise to a massive rejection of the concept of old age in favour of exalting the young and brilliant courtier.

Plutarch had felt this danger. So he requests that the old man refrain from avidly seeking posts, but that he accept them and retain them if he is offered them. If he wants to be respected, he should not assert himself unceasingly by his words and criticisms, but must keep himself for great occasions. Another reason for this is health. Old men must moderate themselves, lead healthy lives, take small amounts of physical exercise and not overload themselves with work: 'By swinging and walking and in some instances playing a light ball-game and by conversation, old men accelerate their breathing and revive the body's heat. Let us then neither allow ourselves to be entirely frozen and chilled by inaction, nor on the other hand, by again burdening ourselves with every office and engaging in every kind of public activity.'[71]

Plutarch ends by recalling illustrious examples favouring old age: Lycurgus telling the young to obey the old as if they were law-makers, because they are the state's natural counsellors; Solon replying to Pisistratus when he asked him what gave him the right to resist him: 'My age!' Plutarch concludes with a superb formula which should warm the cockles of every white-bearded tyrant's heart: 'Age does not so much diminish our power to perform inferior services as it increases our power for leading and governing.'[72]

Plutarch's other works contain further allusions to old age, which show up the subject's many nuances. He acknowledges the faults of the very old; their propensity to chatter interminably, their unstable temper and loss of memory,[73] their excessive attachment to this life and material possessions: 'Do not fancy that old age is vilified and ill spoken of because of the wrinkles, the grey hairs and the debility of the body. No, its most grievous fault is to render the soul stale in its memories of the other world and make it cling tenaciously to this one, and to warp and cramp it, since it retains in this strong attachment the shape imposed upon it by the body.'[74] The old are also vainglorious, exaggerating their former deeds of prowess, but they can be excused: 'Here old men especially go astray: once they have been drawn into admonishing others and rating unworthy habits and unwise acts, they magnify themselves as men who in the like circumstances have been prodigies of wisdom.'[75] Finally, old men are on the whole, less acquisitive and more reasonable: 'In old men the source of desire, which is seated about the liver, is in the process of being extinguished and becoming small and weak, whereas reason increases more and more in vigour as the passionate element fades away together with the body.'[76]

This is the reasoned opinion of a wise man who had assimilated his own personal experience and the many examples furnished by his erudition. As the heir to three cultures, Hellenic, Hellenistic and Roman, Plutarch is not a good witness for any of them, and his *Moralia* tell us most about himself. But it is not uninteresting to reflect on what he personally drew from ancient history. Was he not one of those best acquainted with it, even though he chiefly remembered its anecdotal side? After all that he had seen, heard and read, he envisaged old age in a fairly kindly manner, effecting a sort of synthesis between Plato's apologetic attitude and Aristotle's negative opinions. Does the equilibrium which he achieves reflect the general climate of the age? This would be very difficult to establish.

Given that he lived five and a half centuries after Pericles, he is not the best witness for classical Greece, since he was as far removed from Socrates as we are from Joan of Arc. So we should stick to our original impression that ancient Greece was not a land of welcome for the old, that she preferred youth and maturity to old age, which she rejected as a divine curse, that she gladly poked fun at the old, that she rarely trusted in aged rulers; that she limited herself to asking advice of her elders, without always following it, that it was only in Plato's Utopias that she took care of the old, that she experienced conflict between the generations, in the course of which aged fathers and mothers were ill-treated, that though she respected some old men, it was because they were great philosophers or writers of tragedies. With the exception of Sparta, neither the gods nor the men of Greece liked old people.

The Hellenistic period was more open to foreign influences, as it was to old people. Ostracism disappeared. The melting pot of cultures favoured those at the margins of age; from then on people's value was not affected by the number of years; in the political sphere, young and old rivalled one another in their exploits: Archimedes' 75 years and his master, Hiero II of Syracuse's 91 years had symbolic value. While the ordinary old man was doubtless no happier than his Hellenic ancestor, he was less despised, less ridiculed and less oppressed. He was regarded with amusement or sympathy.

4

The Roman World:

The Old Man's Grandeur and Decadence

Rome comprises more than eight centuries of history. She is a city which turned into a world, a small nation whose own values fused with those of Greece before it established itself over the whole of the Mediterranean basin. This was an exceptional achievement, in terms both of breadth and duration, and one which defies all attempts to sum it up. 'Roman man' was the inhabitant of the *urbs* of both the third century BC and the fifth century AD as well as being a Gallo-Roman, a Briton or an Egyptian, all citizens since the reign of Caracalla. The limited geographical character of the Greek world meant that it had been a relatively homogeneous milieu, in spite of its political fragmentation into cities. Here, the huge human and cultural mix which would result from the conquests of the second century BC onwards imbued Latinity with a previously unknown cosmopolitan character. With its Greco-Etruscan culture and Latin institutions, the Roman world was history's first melting pot, especially in the imperial world: Spanish African and Pannonian emperors, surrounded by Gallic senators, by Greek slaves and freedmen, commanding Germanic, Gallic and Breton armies, gave rise to a religion involving Egyptian and Asiatic divinities. Yet, as with the United States today, the Roman empire had its own civilization, with an essentially Greco-Latin base.

This dual origin combined to give the old a certain importance: in political and social life through the privileges conferred on them by Roman law, and in cultural life through the models derived from Greek literature and philosophy. As it happens, importance does not necessarily mean advantage or favour, but rather presence. The Romans talked a lot about the old, but rarely to praise them. And indeed they talked about them a lot because the problem of old age had arisen among them, under all its aspects: demographic, political, social, psychological and medical. These different aspects of reality are reflected in the attitudes adopted by writers.

The demographic weight of old age and its consequences

The Romans were confronted by the demographic problem of old age to a far greater extent than were the Greeks. This was not due to increased longevity. The extreme cases presented by the sources include an 84-year-old Etruscan man,[1] another man aged 110 in an Armorican tomb in Corseul[2] and around 30 aged 120 in African necropoli,[3] which is comparable with Greek norms. Centres for the study of historical demography feel obliged systematically to contest every evaluation of antiquity dealing with great age; it is well known that the writers of antiquity tended to exaggerate and that there was a competitive aspect to old age which sometimes induced relations and friends and the old themselves to inflate the figures. We come across this problem again in the Middle Ages. It is, however, the practice of rounding off numbers to the nearest tenth rather than actual exaggerations which can be observed.

When people of antiquity spoke of extraordinary longevity, it always concerned peoples in distant time or space, in foreign and exotic regions. In our contemporary world, the people with record longevity are always Siberians, Japanese or Peruvians; in the second century AD, Pliny set the oldest living people on the island of Ceylon, with an average life expectancy of over 100, and Trebellius Pollio referred to the Hebrew elders:

> The wisest astrologers reckon that the life of man can be prolonged to 120 years, and claim that it has not been granted to anyone to go beyond that limit. They add that Moses, who conversed with God, according to the writings of the Jews, was the only one to live 125 years and that, on complaining at dying young, he was answered by I know not what divinity, that no man would go beyond that.[4]

These curiosities are of little moment. What matters is that the Latins held a reasonable view of affairs with regard to the inhabitants of the *Romanitas*, and one which surely came very close to reality.

The remarkable development of the law certainly encouraged a realistic awareness of the extent of human life. In this respect, the *Table of Ulpian* constitutes a document of inestimable value. Dating from the third century AD, it has been transmitted by the *jurisconsultus* Aemylius Macer, and was included in the legal collections compiled in the age of Justinian. Its purpose was to evaluate the importance of the life annuities settled by legacy, according to the age of the beneficiaries. The estimates provided in this table, based on empirical observations, give a likely idea of the life expectancy of the Romans in each age group:

Aemylius Macer, book 2, *Commentary on the twentieth law on inheritance*. Ulpian writes that, according to the calculation he had to make for food pensions, the rule is that from the first to the twentieth year, the sum total of the pension is calculated according to a period of thirty years, and that the Lex Falcidia is applied on this basis; from the twentieth to the twenty-fifth year, according to a period of twenty-eight years; from the twenty-fifth to the thirtieth year, according to a period of twenty-five years; from the thirtieth to the thirty-fifth year, according to a period of twenty years. From the fourtieth to the fiftieth year, the calculation is made by subtracting one year each time, so as to find the difference between the age given and the sixtieth year; from the fiftieth to the fifty-fifty year, seven years; from the sixtieth year onwards, whatever the age, five years.[5]

If these estimates are to be believed, relatively few Romans in the third century BC lived over the age of 60. This view is contradicted by another great source which antedates statistics: funerary inscriptions, suspected of exaggerating old age.[6] They are notwithstanding of fundamental interest. Firstly because, if any exaggeration is present, it can only be a matter of four or five years at the most, because of the practice of rounding numbers off to the nearest tenth; secondly because this source is comparable from one civilization to another, which means that parallels can be established.

In the present case we are thus able to observe that the bulk of old people in the Roman empire was certainly greater than in the Greek world. This observation applies mainly to the later empire, since there are too few records dealing with the previous periods. Among the Etruscans, 113 inscriptions for Tarquinia and Volterra dating from 200 to 50 BC show an average age of decease of 40.88 years, with men enjoying a slight advantage; 41.98 years as against 40.37 years for women.[7] The most complete figures are provided by J.C. Russell in a famous article[8] based on the epigraphical inscriptions of the *Corpus Inscriptionum Latinarum* published by the Berlin Academy in the nineteenth century. Thirteen tables referring to 24,989 individuals living in Rome and in the different provinces of the late empire provide an appreciable quantitative base. We reproduce in table 4.1 the sections which relate to our theme.

This table requires a few comments. First of all on account of the consistently recorded fact that there were more old men than old women, the reverse of the situation in the contemporary world. This was principally due to the dangers of childbirth, which had important social consequences; there were in effect twice as many men than women aged over 60. In the first place, this may explain the rarity with which elderly female persons occur in literature. However, the frequency with

The Roman World

Table 4.1 Longevity within the Roman empire

	Still alive at the age of									
	60	65	70	75	80	85	90	95	100	105
In Rome										
of 4575 men	344		200		111		42		4	
%	7.5		3.4		2.4		0.9		0.08	
of 3490 women	138		75		34		10		1	
%	3.5		2.1		0.9		0.2		0.02	
In Italy										
Calabria, Apulia, Samnium, Sabina, Picenium (892 cases)	110		63		30		7			
Brutium, Lucania, Campania, Sicily, Sardinia (1913 cases)	199		105		42		13			
Aemilia, Umbria, Etruvia (631 cases)	82		45		14		6			
Cisalpine Gaul	85		53		29		10			
Latium	44		34		19		11			
Total	520		300		134		48			
%	10.1		5.8		2.6		0.9			
In the provinces										
Africa (6238 cases)	2389		1756		1030		441		177	98
%	38.2		28.1		16.5		7.0		2.8	1.5
Asia, Greece, Illyricum (2345 cases)	353		191		83		19			
%	15.0		8.1		3.5		0.8			
Narbonne in Gaul (422 cases)	41		24		14		5			
%	9.7		5.6		3.3		1.1			
In Egypt										
of 813 persons	107		58		30		10			
%	c.13.1		7.1		3.7		1.2			
In Spain										
Men (1111 cases)	269	195	163	100	70	39	23	12	10	
%	24.2	17.5	14.6	9.0	6.3	3.5	2.0	1.0	0.9	
Life expectancy (years)	13.7	13	10.1	9.9	8.1	7.5	6.0	4.2	2.5	
Women (885 cases)	120	82	66	38	23	13	7	5	2	
%	13.5	9.2	7.4	4.3	2.6	1.5	0.8	0.6	0.2	
Life expectancy (years)	12.3	11.9	9.2	9.1	8.4	8.0	7.6	4.6	2.5	

Source: J.C. Russell; 'Late ancient and medieval population', *Transactions of the American Philosophical Society*, vol. 48, part 3 (1958).

which men became widowers and the disproportion of the sexes towards the apex of the age pyramid were the reason above all for the high number of marriages between old men and young women, or at least for the great disparity between the ages of spouses. The literary type of the old lecher infatuated with the woman his son loves is more easily understood in this context, and Plautus' and Terence's audiences would have watched situations on the stage which were all the more piquant in that they were current. Old Romans lacked wives of their own age; few elderly couples grew old together. An old man would have to resign himself either to a wise and studious retirement on his own, if he had the means, or to a new conjugal life, disturbed by an excessively young wife who would deceive him with a string of lovers.

These figures also reveal strong differences between one region and the next, with the proportion of those surviving to 60 altering from 7.5 per cent in the city of Rome to 38.2 per cent in Africa. This distortion, due of course to the sources, also reveals that mortality was far higher in strongly urbanized regions and in the large towns than in the countryside; 60 years on, 7.6 per cent of a given generation would have survived in Rome; 10.1 per cent in the suburban belt; 13.1 per cent in Egypt; 15 per cent in Asia, Illyricum and Greece; 24.2 per cent in Spain; 38.2 per cent in North Africa. While there is undoubtedly an element of exaggeration in all this, in the Roman period, Africans had always had the reputation of being long-lived.

These figures should not be made to say more than they mean. They are not modern statistics and many of them should undoubtedly be treated with caution. Their value may only be indicative. Nevertheless, we can infer from them that the demographic weight of the old in the Roman empire was not negligible, a weight which doubtless increased as a result of the ruling classes' Malthusian outlook. The Roman world, from the second century onwards at least, probably experienced an ageing process, especially in Italy. A process which, we must remember, is also a feature of contemporary Europe, albeit in quite different proportions. Under these conditions, it is understandable that old men held an important role, in people's conversation and mentalities at least.

THE *POTESTAS* OF THE *PATER FAMILIAS*, ITS CONSEQUENCES AND EVOLUTION

Roman Law furthermore endowed the old man, in the person of the *pater familias*, with an authority peculiar to himself. This was a basic trait of Roman society. From the fourth century onwards the progressive disintegration of the *gens* gave birth to independent *familiae*, whose members were linked together by a legal tie, not a natural one; they were placed beneath the same *patria potestas*, either by being born to the same father, or by adoption or marriage. This was the *agnatio* system of parentage by males, because the power which characterized it was transmitted solely between males. The members of a *familia* were divided into two categories; the *sui juris* and the *alieni juris*. The *sui juris* was someone who was subject to no private power, and who obeyed only himself. In a *familia*, there was only one *sui juris*: the *pater familias*, who had *potestas* over the other members of the *familia*. These last were *alieni juris*: they were not responsible for themselves from the familial and private law point of view; they could not engage in contracts.

Thus the *pater familias* was absolute head of the family. Being himself subject to no one, he had exorbitant rights over the members of the *familia*: *dominica potestas* over the slaves, *mancipium* over the *alieni juris* integrated with the family through emancipation, *patria potestas* over his children, and *manus* over his wife. His authority was unlimited: he could reclaim in justice any *alieni juris* who had run away; he could sell his children as slaves in foreign lands or in Rome to another *pater*; he could exclude them from the family; he could hand a child over to another *pater* in compensation for a fault committed by that child; he could abandon newborn babies; could condemn a member of the *familia* to death after having conducted an inquiry and secured the opinion of the closest relatives. This *potestas* disappeared only with the father's death. It extended over his wife, his children and grandchildren. The father represented the whole family – in matters of justice, for instance. Although children could indeed be emancipated, this involved a sanction and not a liberation pure and simple: an emancipated son became *sui juris* but lost all his rights in the family, he was no longer protected by anybody and owned nothing. His situation was not an enviable one.

These enormous powers are enjoyed by the head of the family under the Republic explain the vital role of old men in society. As they grew older, they saw their family and goods increase and their power accrue correspondingly. Since they retained it until their death, it is easy to imagine their sons' growing impatience, forced as they were to remain subject to their old father until a relatively advanced age. The conflicts between generations which occur in every society were exacerbated by the fact that children retained the position of minors until their father's death. It is clear that this situation gave rise to real hatred towards such old men as took ages dying. Roman comedy was to echo these conflicts. In no other literature does the theme of opposition between father and son hold such sway. The odious old man, deceived by his children, was a subject which attracted an audience every time, one consisting of those men aged between 20 and 40 or 50, who were furious at having to submit daily to their old father and who found in comedy their only outlet.

The fate of the old is shot through with this permanent ambiguity: the more powers and power the law confers on them, the more they are detested by subsequent generations. Roman society illustrates this. Conversely, the more they are deprived of rights, they more they are despised; contemporary society witnesses to this. Being detested or despised: such appears to be the choice open to them. Legal systems do not have the power to crack this cruel dilemma, and its solution patently resides elsewhere; in peoples' hearts, not in the law.

Whereas the old Roman *pater familias* was feared and detested, the old woman, for her part, underwent a more obscure fate. The *mater familias*, while possessing only the same rights as her daughters, enjoyed in fact a degree of authority. She is sometimes portrayed as a shrew in comedies, but just as often as a more reasonable person than her husband, whose passions she ridicules. By conniving with her sons and servants, she succeeds in deceiving the *pater familias* and both writers and their public felt more sympathetic towards her. She was one of the *alieni juris*, subjected by the law, like her children, to the domestic tyrant, and she was frequently felt to share in the general resentment against her spouse. Her influence was not negligible, to such an extent that it was said that the Republic obeyed the senators and the senators obeyed their wives. On the other hand, old women were neglected and despised, and treated very harshly on account of their physical ugliness.

The *patria potestas* declined under the Empire. Those persons subject to it were henceforth able to complain to a magistrate about their *pater's* abuses. His right of life and death over his children was severely regulated, and if a father punished a child for no reason, he could be obliged to emancipate him. He was no longer able to hand him over as a pledge or to marry him against his will. Sales of children became rare. From the second century onwards, the father was obliged to contribute to the upkeep of his family members. From then on, a son was a legal person: he could own property and engage in contracts; he could appeal to the law in cases of prevention by his *pater*; he could assemble a separate patrimony to that of his father, with goods acquired during military service, for instance.

Finally, under the late Empire, paternal power lost its public character and became purely familial. From 319 a father could no longer condemn his child; from 374, he could no longer expose him; from 326 the family son holding a position at court could keep the goods acquired through the exercise of this function for himself. In 319, Constantine decided that the goods which accrued to the son as part of his maternal inheritance would form a lot separate from the family patrimony and that the father could not sell them. The son was able to engage in most legal processes. The mother's influence increased: a woman could become her children's guardian. Emancipation became easier. In the Hellenic provinces, emancipation took place without formalities and in the Orient all that was required was to produce a written declaration before a curia. Emancipation now presented the child only with advantages: he kept his sources of income; he acquired full ownership of two-thirds of his adventitious goods; he was no longer subject to his father's authority, and he retained his rights of succession in the family.

Thus was the father's power for life, and consequently that of the old man, gradually demolished. His moral authority remained great but he no longer had the legal means of applying it. Here, too, literature bears witness to this evolution; with the emergence of the Empire social criticism of the old man disappears. The theme of conflict between fathers and sons becomes exceptional. Plautus' and Terence's tyrannical, miserly and lecherous old man gives way to Juvenal's impotent, ugly and decrepit old man. Now that he could no longer frighten, he was mocked on account of his physical defects.

THE POLITICAL ROLE OF THE OLD. ITS CONSEQUENCES AND EVOLUTION. THE REPUBLIC

A parallel evolution may be observed in relation to the political role of old age.

The Roman republic put its trust in age. 'Having gathered a sufficient number of men together, Romulus decided to temper force with politics and turned his attention to the organization of society. He created a hundred senators, deciding on this number either because it was sufficient for the purpose he had in mind, or because there were not more than a hundred persons capable of becoming 'Fathers', as they were called, or Heads of Clans.'[9] 'The title of Fathers was undoubtedly derived from their rank, and their descendants were called patricians.'[10] This was how Livy described the creation of the senate, which was to direct Roman policy for centuries to come. Soon consisting of 300 members, heads of the *gentes* and former magistrates, they were all men of years, who ensured the continuity of its policy and respect for tradition. Although the senate's power was in theory only consultative, it was in fact a sovereign assembly, the incarnation of the power of age. As for the magistrates, if they were not old men, they were at least mature men, as required by the *cursus honorum*, that manifestation of distrust towards youth: it stipulated a minimum of 30 years for quaestors, 40 years for praetors, and 43 years for consuls.

The history of the Republic shows that in critical circumstances the Romans did not hesitate to entrust important powers to aged individuals, and some people's careers were remarkably long. Cicero had no trouble producing many examples: Paulus Aemilius, who died at the battle of Cannae; Curius, who defeated Pyrrhus; Coruncanius, high priest in 253; Appius Claudius, consul in 307 and 296; Cnaeus Publius Scipio; Lucius Metellus; Atilius Calatinus; Valerius Corvinus, six times consul during 46 years, who retired from political life when over 100. Fabius

Maximus was elected dictator at the age of 58 when Hannibal invaded: 'he was of an age', wrote Plutarch, 'in which the vigour of the body is sufficient to execute the purposes of the mind, and courage is tempered with prudence.'[11] His colleague, Minucius, despised him and considered him a timorous old man, but the Romans trusted in his wisdom. And indeed, his strategy of avoiding confrontation was successful in the long run. Several years later, however, when he was 71 years old, he opposed Scipio's policy, judging it dangerous. Many Romans 'now considered him as a captious and envious man; or as one whose courage and hopes were lost in the dregs of years and who therefore looked upon Hannibal as more formidable than he really was.'[12] At the same time, Marcellus was nominated consul for the fifth time when over 60 years old, and he found death at the age of 63 while fighting the Carthaginians.

The most illustrious example from the republican period is that of Cato the Elder, who died in 149 BC at the age of 85 having remained an active politician until the end of his life. Plutarch dedicated some famous pages to him: 'As for himself, indeed, by his strong make and good habit of body, lasted long; so that even in old age, he frequently indulged his inclination for the sex, and at an unseasonable time of life married a young woman.' He was accustomed to sleeping with a young slave girl, but since his son thought this unsuitable, he married the daughter of one of his clients.

> For he did not, like Lucius Lucullus, and Metellus Pius, think age an exemption from the service of the public, but considered that service as his indispensible duty . . . But, as one told Dionysius (Tyrant of Syracuse) that the most honourable death was to die in possession of sovereign power, so Cato esteemed that the most honourable old age, which was spent in serving the Commonwealth. The amusements in which he passed his leisure hours, were the writing of books and tilling the ground . . . he always invited some of his acquaintance in the neighbourhood to sup with him. With these he passed the time in cheerful conversation, making himself agreeable not only to those of his own age, but to the young; for he had a thorough knowledge of the world, and had either seen himself, or heard from others, a variety of things that were curious and entertaining.[13]

The Civil Wars were another occasion when ambitious men who were no longer very young clashed. Although Sulla preferred to retire from political life at the age of 59 in 79 BC, his adversary Marius clung to power until his death at the age of 71, when he had just been elected consul for the seventh time, in 86 BC. But his trials had broken him and, unable to tackle a new conflict, he sought for peace in drink and sleep:

The Consul himself (Marius), worn out with a series of misfortunes and distress, found his faculties fail, and trembled at the approach of wars and conflicts . . . Thus agitated, thus revolving the miseries, the flights, the dangers he had experienced both by land and sea, his inquietude affected him even by night . . . Thus, at the age of seventy, distinguished by the unparalleled honour of seven consulships, and possessed of more than regal fortune, Marius died with the chagrin of an unfortunate wretch, who had not obtained what he wanted.[14]

Juvenal was to cite Marius as an example of the type of politician who ruins his career by living too long and refusing to retire betimes.[15] In any case, the wars and assassinations of the first century BC succeeded in curtailing the destinies of political men: every member of the First Triumvirate died a violent death, at 62 years against the Parthians for Crassus, at 53 and 56 years under the blows of their assassins for Pompey and Caesar. Anthony committed suicide at 53. As Juvenal put it, 'For ages now, growing old has been something of a phenomenon, if one is a nobleman.'

THE EMPIRE

Augustus initiated a new era. As the sole survivor of the Civil Wars, he lived 76 years. His last years, however, were darkened by accentuated physical and mental decline. If Suetonius is to be believed (which is not always the case) the Emperor had become a vicious maniac and gambler:

as an elderly man he is said to have still harboured a passion for deflowering girls, who were collected for him from every quarter, even by his wife! Augustus did not mind being called a gambler: he diced openly, in his old age too, simply because he enjoyed the game – Not only in December, when the licence of the Saturnalia justified it, but on other holidays as well, and actually on working days. That this is quite true a letter in his own handwriting proves: 'My dear Tiberius . . . we had the same company for dinner, except that Vinicius and the elder Silius were also invited; and we gambled like old men all through the meal both yesterday and today.'[16]

Augustus was a fine old man, but his sight was much diminished; he liked to read his works in public, but this tired him and he would ask Tiberius to finish off for him. He used to indulge in weakminded forms of amusement:

Afterwards, he invited these men to a banquet at which he presided, and not merely allowed but expected them to play jokes, and freely scramble for the tokens he threw, entitling the holders to fruit, sweetmeats and the like. In fact, he indulged in every form of fun.[17]

Without picking up all the court gossip, Tacitus too admitted that Augustus had grown simple-minded in his old age.

From the first century AD onwards and throughout the Empire, the power of the elders, of the senate, lapsed. This august assembly was cajoled or terrorized by the emperors and no longer led politics. The old, as an institution, no longer ruled the Roman world. Nevertheless, many old men still held key posts as individuals, starting with the emperors. Tiberius was endowed with an exceptional constitution and ruled until he was 77; Claudius was assassinated at 64 years; Galba seized power at 73 years of age. Suetonius has left us a cruel portrait of this septuagenarian homosexual: bald, hooknosed, his hands and feet twisted by arthritis, his body bent to the right, walking with a crutch. Vespasian died at the age of 68 and 7 months. Nerva was chosen to be Emperor at the age of 70 and reigned two years; as for the Antonines, although Marcus Aurelius lived only 60 years, Hadrian 62, and Trajan 64, Antoninus' reign ended at the age of 75. From the third century AD onwards, the career of most *imperatores* was interrupted by the general political instability and the frequent assassinations. The luckiest managed to attain or even live beyond 60 years: Septimus Severus (65 years), Diocletian (68 years), Constantius Chlorus (81 years), Constantine (*circa* 65 years).

Within the imperial entourage, old politicians continued more often than not to be trusted for their experience and wisdom. Under the Julio-Claudians, the *consilium principis*, a sort of private council of the Emperor's, which controlled the finances, the army, foreign policy and legal business, and took all important decisions, was composed of 20 senators and 30 equites who remained in place from one reign to another and ensured the continuity of imperial policy.[18] In Rome, the office of town governor was for life, and was thus frequently in the hands of old men: under Tiberius, Lucius Calpurnius Piso exercised the office until the age of 80 to general satisfaction. His predecessor, Titus Statilius Taurus was also very old,[19] as was his successor, Lucius Aelius Lamia, who died in 33 and was granted a state funeral.[20] This being a particularly delicate function, it was voluntarily entrusted to old politicians above all suspicion.

Even under the reign of a young emperor like Nero, who was surrounded by a cohort of young people,[21] many of the leading roles were left to the old; apart from Seneca, with whose personality and ideas we will deal at greater length, we should mention Corbulo, a prestigious general, the leader of the eastern army, who took part in a conspiracy against the Emperor when nearly 70, and had to commit suicide. Another septuagenarian general, Lucius Tampius Flavianius, was governor of Pannonia in 69 AD. The famous Xenophon of Cos, the head of the court doctors under Claudius, was nominated by Nero to the department *a libellis*, which was run by Doryphorus, where he was directed to examine the supplications sent by Greek cities; he was then a very old man. Locusta, who dealt in poisons, was also very old, and yet she was employed fulltime by Nero, and Suetonius accuses her of having headed a school for poisoners.[22]

Many imperial freedmen passed unscathed through the hecatombs of his reign to enjoy a peaceful old age: although Pallas, who was immensely rich from ill-gotten gains, was perhaps assassinated in 62 AD on Nero's orders when he was long past 60,[23] Lucius Domitius Phaon, head of finance between 55 and 68 AD, who took in the fleeing Emperor while denouncing him to his pursuers, ended his days when very old under Domitian, in peaceful retirement on his estates. Epaphroditus, an arrogant and servile parvenu, who accumulated wealth, was minister of petitions from 62 AD onwards, and also betrayed the Emperor in 68 AD, retained his post until 95 AD, when he was executed at an age doubtless well over 70. As for Anicetus, he died of old age in Sardinia.

Among the opponents of the imperial regime, let us mention Musonius Rufus, a Stoic *eques*, exiled in 65 AD, who returned to Rome, was banished again by the Flavians, and died in his eighties at the end of the century. Others owed their longevity to their prudence, like Crispus, whom Juvenal mentions. He was consul for the third time in 63 AD at the age of 80. At the local level, finally, old persons are found in responsible posts: the Armorican *civitates* were governed by a sort of senate, consisting of a hundred members nominated for life and co-opted from among old magistrates.[24] Chance inscriptions allow us to discover old magistrates in various places, such as the mayor of Volterra, grandfather six times over, who remained in office from the age of 28 to 66.[25]

BETWEEN STOICISM AND EPICUREANISM

The history of Roman politics evolved generally speaking in the sense of a decline in the power of the old. Their golden age was the Republic. Under this aristocratic regime, old age, in which wealth and authority are concentrated, made the law, for the family as for the state. However, this excessive concentration of power earned the old unpopularity in the *Res publica* and hatred in the family. These excessively rigid frameworks were burst asunder by the Civil Wars and the Empire, times when fortune smiled on ambitious, bold and wily men of any age, as she did in the Hellenistic period. But whereas the Hellenistic monarchies which took over a gerontophobic Greece represented an improvement for old people, the Empire, which followed on a senatorial period, experienced a setback in the condition of old men. They lost their familial and political power, which had given them a reason for carrying on, and were left alone with their pains, their ugliness and frailty. Henceforth nothing would distract them from their misfortunes. Left to themselves, old men became the very incarnation of suffering.

Literature provides a pitiable picture of them, of which Juvenal's *Satire X*, written at the beginning of the second century AD, is a good example:

> Look at the most ugly, hideous thing
> of all, the face, unlike itself, the ugly hide
> Passing for skin, the sagging cheeks, and wrinkles of
> the kind that where Tabarca spreads unbrageous burst
> A mother baboon now scratches on her aged chops . . .
> The old, one aspect all: limbs quavering with the voice,
> A now smooth head, and the infancy of a drivelling nose.
> His bread the poor wretch has to break with gums unarmed.

He must be looked after by others; food no longer has any savour for him.

> while coition's long forgotten; or should
> You try, variocele and stunted nerve be limp,
> And though they be caressed all night, limp they remain.

He can no longer hear, he is no longer in his right mind.

> A's lame in the shoulder, B in the loins, C in the hips;
> That man has lost both eyes and envies those with one
> This man's pallid lips take food from other's fingers!

He watches every member of his family die:

> This is the penalty assigned to the long-lived;
> With ever renewed disaster in one's home, in much
> Mourning, constant grief and black clothes, to decay.[26]

This pessimistic vision of old age is not merely a literary device. The despair engendered by suffering and solitude, in conjunction with the growing influence of Stoicism among the wealthy classes, lay at the origin of a wave of suicides among old Romans in the second half of the first century AD and the beginning of the second century AD. Pliny the Younger echoes this in his letters. One of his friends, aged 67, who was crippled with gout and undergoing 'the most incredible and undeserved pain', had just killed himself, which, he says, 'arouses my admiration before his greatness of spirit'. In another letter, he mentions Titius Aristo, who 'carefully weighed up the reasons for living and for dying' and killed himself. He mentions elsewhere a man aged 75, afflicted with an incurable illness: 'tired of life, he put an end to it.' He also recalled the case of Arria, a Roman lady who sought to encourage her old and sickly husband to commit suicide by setting an example and killing herself in front of him (II.16). And again, the affecting case of an old couple of humble citizens: since the old man was afflicted with incurable ulcers, his wife 'urged him to take his life: she went with him, even led him to his death herself and forced him to follow her example by roping herself to him and jumping into the lake' (I.24).

Pliny, and with him the whole of Roman high society, approved and admired this behaviour, which was in direct line with the climate of Stoicism and which Seneca had justified magnificently in his letter LVIII to Lucilius:

> The man who awaits his doom inertly is all but afraid, just as the man who swigs off the bottle and drains even the lees is over-given to his liquor. In this case, however, we shall try to find out whether the last part of life is really less, or something extraordinarily bright and clear if only the mind's uninjured, the senses come unimpaired to the aid of the spirit, and the body isn't foundered and a prey to death in life . . . If, on the other hand, the body's past its duties, it may be (why not?) the right thing to extricate the suffering spirit. Old age, if it lasts very long, brings few to death unmarred: for many of the aged life collapses into lethargy and impotence. After that do you consider a scrap of life a more poignant loss than the freedom to end it? . . . I shan't cast old age off if old age keeps me whole for myself – whole, I mean, on the better side; but if it begins to unseat my reason and pull it piecemeal, if it leaves me not life but more animation, I shall be out of my crumbling, tumble-down tenement at a bound . . . I shan't lay hands on myself for pain: to die so is to be beaten. Still, if I'm assured that I can never be free of it, I shall make my exit, not because of the actual pain, but because its like to prove a bar to everything that makes life worth while. The man who dies because of pain is weak and craven; the man who lives to suffer is a fool.[27]

The high moral tone of these reflections is all the more remarkable in that they were no empty words. Seneca and many others demonstrated that they were able to keep faith with their philosophy until the end.

However, not every old Roman went to such extreme lengths. Pliny had other examples in reserve, the most comforting of which was undoubtedly that of his friend Spurinna, who retired to his lands at the age of 77, having held magistracies and governed provinces, where he led a comfortable, active and balanced life, without excess:

> Every morning, he stays in bed for an hour after dawn, and then calls for his shoes and takes a three-mile walk to exercise mind and body. If he has a friend with him, he carries on a serious conversation, if he is alone, a book is read aloud . . . Then he sits down, the book is continued, or preferably the conversation; after which he goes out in his carriage accompanied by his wife (a model to her sex) or one of his friends, a pleasure recently mine . . . After a drive of seven miles he will walk another mile, then sit again or retire to his room and his writings . . . When summoned to his bath (in mid-afternoon in winter and an hour earlier in summer) he first removes his clothes and takes a walk in the sunshine if there is no wind, and then throws a ball briskly for some time; this being another form of exercise which keeps old age at bay. After his bath he lies down for a short rest before dinner, and listens while something light and soothing is read aloud . . . Dinner is brought on in dishes of antique plain silver, a simple meal but well served . . . Between the courses there is often a performance of comedy, so that the pleasures of the table have a seasoning of letters, and the meal is prolonged into the night, even in summer . . . The result is that Spurinna has passed his seventy-seventh year, but his sight and hearing are unimpaired, and he is physically agile and energetic: old age has brought him nothing but wisdom.[28]

Spurinna embodied the Romans' ideal old man: rich, cultivated and in perfect health, he combined all the conditions for a happy retirement. It is obviously much harder to discover the fate of old plebeians, which did not interest our literati. We sometimes catch a glimpse of them in a snatch of text, whiling their time away at playing dice in the public places,[29] crowding to the circus games, even taking part in the spectacle, as a certain Aelia Catella did, who was still appearing in dances at the age of 80 in the time of Nero.[30] As for slaves too old to serve, they were either freed or abandoned, in the streets or around the temple of Aesculapius. From the third century AD onwards, Christian hospices were to start caring for the most unfortunate cases.[31]

THE OLD MAN IN LATIN LITERATURE. FROM SOCIAL SATIRE (THE
REPUBLICAN PERIOD) . . .

Given that the documents on the subject are few and uncommunicative,
we are obliged to turn once more to literature to see how old Romans
lived. Literature holds up a distorting, though indispensible, mirror to
life and a critical study of literary works allows us to elude its main
traps. We have already traced the connections between Latin literary
themes and social reality. Thus, the theatre of the first period, until the
second century BC, was marked by ferocious attacks against old men,
who acted as substitute objects of revenge against the tyrannical power
of the *pater familias*. Plautus and Terence were the bitterest playwrights.

Plautus (254–184 BC), who himself lived to be 70, was a plebeian.
He was able to meet the Roman public's demand for comedies in the
Greek manner. He borrowed the traditional figures of new Hellenic
comedy, such as the deceitful and ingenious slave, the parasite, the
braggart soldier or the slave dealer, but added a typically Roman element
to them, which suited his audience's taste: the detestable, tyrannical and
lecherous old man, who is mocked and cheated by his entourage. *The
Merchant* introduces Demiphon, an old man enamoured of his son's
mistress. He is helped by Lysimachus, another old man cast in the same
mould. The plot revolves around the theme of the conflict between
generations, with the father driven by his unbridled passions to plot at
depriving his son of his legitimate pleasures. Dorippa, the old woman
married to Lysimachus, is wiser. It is she who finally brings about the
collapse of the project; she berates her husband for entertaining desires
no longer appropriate to his age: 'Men's seasons, like the year's, should
have their different uses; why, if that's the proper thing – for oldsters
to occupy their old age with affairs of gallantry – what'll become of
our affairs of state?'[32] The play ends with the decision to draw up a
new law, one which certainly conformed to the wishes of young Romans
of the age: 'Whatsoever man, having attained his sixtieth year, be he
married or – yes, by gad! – be he celibate, shall be known to us to
wench, with such man we shall deal in accordance with this law: we
shall deem him a dotard.'[33]

Here 60 is considered to be the age of entry into old age and, in
accordance with the portrait of the ideal old man drawn by the
philosophers, the pleasures of the flesh are henceforth forbidden him.
The old man must dedicate himself to wisdom and the pleasures of the
mind.

This theme occurs again in the *Asinaria*, where Demetrius, an old
lecher, tries to sleep with his son's mistress. Here, too, it is his wife,
old Artemonis, who prevents him, being a shrewish woman, who rules
the household. She undoubtedly resembled many a Roman matron
whom the public would have recognized.

The same sort of hero reappears in *Casina*: Lysidamus, a lecherous old man, is in love with the same girl as his son. He sends the latter abroad and during that time he has the girl married to his farmer, whom he frees on condition he can sleep with the girl. Once again, it's the hero's wife who foils the whole project.

The other great fault of old age is avarice. As the sole proprietor of all the family property, the *pater familias* could dispose of it at will until his death, and his sons raged at not being able to get their hands on more money for their own needs, notably where girls were concerned. The comedy goes on to show how the required sums could be extracted by deceiving the old father. In *Epidicus*, the old man Periphanus, although wise, allows himself to be relieved of money by his slave Epidicus, who is at the service of his son's amorous adventures. One of Periphanus' friends, Apecidus, is also a victim of mystification. The same plot occurs in *Pseudolus*, in which the old man, Simon, allows himself to be cheated by a slave in the service of Calidorus, who needs money to buy himself a girl. The *Aulularia* also stages an old miser in the character of Euclion, who is hard and suspicious, as well as other old men and women: Megadorus and his sister Eunomia and the old slave Staphyla. In *Rudens*, the old man Demones is exceptionally sympathetic, and has been ruined on account of his excessive kindness.

In *Trinummus*, four of the nine characters are old men who grumble about their wives; Charmides has buried his treasure and leaves his friend Callicles to guard it while he goes off on a journey. In *The Brothers Menaechmus*, Plautus dwells for once on the miseries of old age; the hero's father-in-law complains that

> My body's a big heavy trunk, I've no strength.
> Oh, oh, old age is bad – no more vigor remains.
> Oh, when old age arrives, it brings plenty of pains.
> I could mention them all but I won't talk at length.

A good old man, Periplectomenus, finally turns up in the *Braggart Soldier*. He is portrayed as the exact opposite of the ordinary old man, whose behaviour is thereby once again castigated:

> I'm the perfect party guest – I'm quick with very clean quips
> And I never interrupt another person when he's talking.
> I refrain from rudeness, I'm restrained with guests and never rowdy.
> I remember to contribute just my share of conversation,
> And I also know to shut my mouth when someone else is talking.
> I'm no spitter, I'm no cougher and I'm not forever sneezing. . . .
> Never at a party do I screw around with someone's girl.
> Never do I filch the food or take the goblet out of turn.

Never do I let the wine bring out an argument with me.[34]

This swarm of old men in Plautus' comedies reveals the importance
of the social problem constituted by old age at the beginning of the
second century BC. Being all-powerful, the old man was hated. In
many families, his death was awaited with impatience, since it would
mean freedom for all his relatives. Terence staged this aspect of old age
in the *Adelphi*. Although too frequently classed in the same category
as Plautus, Terence (190–159 BC) in fact portrayed old age in a different
tone and from a different angle. As a former slave, freed by an
enlightened senator who had recognized his talent, he had received an
excellent education. Brought up among lettered aristocrats, he wrote his
comedies for them, and they are infinitely more subtle than those of
Plautus, as well as more sentimental and moralistic. The characters are
more virtuous, the masters more benevolent, the servants more devoted,
the young more respectful and the fathers more indulgent. His old men
are far less numerous and not such caricatures. Nevertheless, here too
we meet the problem of the conflict between generations.

In *Heautontimorumenos*, two old men, Menedemus and Chremes are
in conflict with their sons. Menedemus, who is passionate and violent,
is opposed to his son's marriage, but soon repents and turns generous,
whereas Chremes, who plays the sententious philosopher, is cheated by
his slaves. *The Adelphoi* is a serious comedy, which stages two methods
of education; gentleness, indulgence and flexibility, as practised by old
Micio, a bachelor who understands the young and is loved by all, and
severity, as applied by Micio's brother, Demea. The latter is unhappy.
He realizes that his entourage is just waiting for him to die; he is not
loved and suffers on account of this:

I too, wish my sons to love me, wish to gain their high esteem:
If that comes by gifts and humoring, I'll not second play at that.
Funds may fail, but, since I'm oldest, that concerns me least of all.

Terence aims at advising the old men of his age through the anguish of
this basically pathetic character, at teaching them impartiality:

In everything besides our wisdom grows with years,
But this one sole fault that old age brings to men,
That money matters fill our minds beyond what's fit.[35]

The manner differs from Plautus', but not the social reality underlying
these comedies: criticism of the omnipotence of aged fathers. Even the
old and serious Cato, a contemporary of the young and comic Terence,
admitted that the behaviour of the old was not beyond reproach, that
they were often miserly ('When riches abound to thee, in extreme old

age, see that you are bountiful, not niggardly towards your friends'); they tend to criticize the young too frequently ('When you are an old man relating the sayings and doings of many men, remember those things which you did yourself when you were young'); they tend to ramble on ('Do not mock old age though you be quick in your understanding: for a childish understanding is in him who lives to be old').[36]

Plautus, Terence and Cato were not alone in testifying to this, and it would be possible to assemble an anthology of criticism of old men consisting of innumerable extracts from the literature of republican Rome dedicated to this subject. Maria S. Haynes has collected a number of these and can demonstrate that the vocabulary dealing with the physical aspect of the old used the following terms in order of frequency: dirty; sallow complexion; stinking breath, smelling like a goat; grey-haired, pot-bellied, slanting-jawed, flat-footed; untidy; shabby; sickly; ragged and aged; bent-double, shaky, loose-lipped; groaning and of damnable shape . . . ugly old thing; a withered, worn-out, flabby old man; the old fossil; decrepit old frame and stupid old chatterbox.[37]

Avarice is the most frequently mentioned fault: 'A vice common to all mankind is that of being too keen after money when we grow old'. Weakness of mind recurs just as often: 'fool, blockhead, stock, donkey, and stupid . . . senile, decrepit' are among the most frequent epithets. Old men are equally choleric and bad-tempered; a nothing sets them in a rage. One of the most frequently formulated reproaches concerns their authoritarian manner of marrying off their children in a summary and irrevocable way: 'I found you a wife, you've got to get married today; go home and get ready' declares an old father. Their sons' resentment is one of the motor forces of comedy: 'How unjustly all fathers judge young men; they think that when we cease to be boys, we ought straightaway to turn into old men, and have nothing to do with the pleasures youth brings with it.' Lysiteles reminds his old father of how much he has always been subject to him: 'From my earliest youth all the way to my present age, father, I have always been subservient to your injunctions and your precepts . . . From the standpoint of your paternal control I deemed it proper that my inclinations should be subservient to your wishes.' On hearing these plays, one might well think that the *pater familias* had always ruled his family by terror: 'To think that he should have no regard for my authority, or fear of my anger!' thundered an old man in amazement at his son's disobedience.

The theme of the concupiscence of old men and women is among the most popular; the incongruity of physical love and ugliness has always provided a standard comic theme. Roman theatre swarms with old debauchers. 'I gave you my daughter to provide you with entertainment at night time. Now it seems but right that I receive a girl from you to pass the night with', one such declares to his son-in-law, who then mocks him: 'Even now the old rascal still takes himself for a youngster. He can have a girl to sing him to sleep at night. Frankly, I can't see what else he could do with one', because 'a senile decrepid old man is as good a lover as a mural.'

Maria Haynes concludes her retrospective of Latin literature in the republican period very concisely as follows:

> The reason for the Roman playwrights' tremendous concern with old men can easily be understood if one thinks of the sceptre and sword position held by the Roman paterfamilias. Open revolt or even resentment on the part of the young against this system was too risky; it might have resulted in a death penalty inflicted upon the daring son by the judge with unlimited powers, the paterfamilias. For this reason, it is only natural that the stage served as an outlet for all the pent-up feelings against the almighty paterfamilias. Therefore, a sober study of old men and their interplay with the young on the Roman stage which takes into consideration the playwrights' manipulations for the purpose of comic effects seems to be a rather reliable source of information for our understanding of the concepts about old age held by the ancient Romans.[38]

. . . TO PSYCHOLOGICAL STUDIES (CIVIL WAR AND EMPIRE)

People's perspectives changed during the first century BC, a period of instability when traditional values were overturned. The senate and the *pater familias* were being increasingly contested; their powers were diminishing. The revolutions led to the birth of individualism and strong personalities established themselves in the forefront. Plays disappeared; from then on, entertainments took place in the streets, often with tragic outcomes. It was the hour of political speeches, or, for the shy or disappointed, of intimist withdrawal into oneself, of romantic reflection on the vagaries of fortune, on the brevity of human life and on the transient nature of love and youth. The extrovert criticism of old people in comedy was succeeded by the poets' lamentations on their own fate and that of their love affairs, destined as they were to wither. As history speeds up it strengthens awareness of the passage of time, which brings redoubtable old age to everyone. This theme was most widely employed in classical literature during the Augustan age.

The young Tibullus (54–19 BC), who died prematurely at the age of 35, was obsessed with ageing: 'How fall'n when Fate brings on old age, and weakness, the horse that was Olympic winner once!'[38] a problem he was never to experience. This *eques* had been disappointed in his dreams of military glory by illness, and he passed his days between the worldly circles where he rubbed shoulders with Ovid and Horace and his country domain. Fearing 'the ills which weigh down old age', he proclaimed in his elegies his wish to enjoy life while still young, for 'The time will come when I as bearer of Love's message am attended in old age by troups of studious youths.'[40] When one is old:

> Too late alas is love and too late youth recalled
> when white-haired age has stained the head[41]. . . .
> Beauty then is studied. Hair is changed to hide
> the years with dye from a nut's green rind.
> Solicitude then turns to rooting out white hairs
> and recovers face by slack skin's removal.[42]

However, his fear of death was even greater than his fear of growing old:

> is not the true hero the man slow death surprises
> in a little hut with his children round him? . . .
> Such life be mine and with it leave to shine white-haired.
> Recounting in old age old memories.[43]

His friend Ovid (43–17 AD) did not live to a great age either, since he died at 60, but his mature years were darkened by his exile. This worldly poet, a fine wordsmith, but without depth, was aged around 55 when he wrote his *Tristia*, in which he was already deploring the signs of old age:

> My temples like the swans soft feather are
> And white old age doth cover my black hair
> Now idle age and weak years coming be,
> And now to bear myself doth trouble me.[44]

Pining away on the shores of the Black Sea, he regrets his inability to live to a peaceful old age:

> Now all my former labours I should end,
> And without fear my life in quiet spend:
> And now my mind should take her rest at leisure
> And in my study I should live at pleasure.
> To my house and gods some honour I should grant,
> And my fathers' lands, which now their Master want.
> That in my nephews or wives bosome,
> Within my Country might grow old and die
> Thus formerly I hop'd my age should end.[45]

Before he was exiled, Ovid had turned for a while to mythological

subjects in the *Metamorphoses*, in which Medea, Jason's wife, is described
in the process of rejuvenating Aeson, her father-in-law. Having cast
him into a lethargic sleep, she prepares magic juices and replaces the
old man's blood with them:

> and when Aeson drank,
> Through wound and lips, at once his hair and beard,
> White for long years, regained their raven hue;
> His wizened pallor, vanquished, fled away
> And firm new flesh his sunken wrinkles filled,
> And all his limbs were sleek and proud and strong.
> Then Aeson woke and marvelled as he saw
> His prime restored of forty years before.[46]

Rejuvenation is an old dream of mankind which recurs several times
in mythology: Bacchus rejuvenates his wet-nurses and Venus restores
youth to Phaon, the old sailor of Lesbos, with whom Sappho falls in
love. Until the sixteenth century, before resignation prevailed, men
sought passionately for the chimera of absolute knowledge, infinite wealth
and eternal youth, through the philosopher's stone, the transmutation of
metals and the fountain of life. Ignorance, poverty and old age were
among the sequence of nightmares which humanity nowadays is still
trying to exorcize.

As an Epicurian, could Horace (65–8 BC) have felt anything other
than revulsion for old age? This delicate and refined old man, who
enjoyed all worldly pleasures with moderation and who loved beauty,
was capable only of fastidiously rejecting decrepitude. He was revolted
by the ugliness of the old; that the female body, the symbol of beauty
in its youth, should become the emblem of absolute ugliness in old age,
was a veritable insult to the senses, especially when the woman persisted
in wanting to arouse love. Gentle Horace could lose all restraint under
these circumstances and lapse into the most indecent and cruel vulgarity:

> The idea that you should ask all this long time what it is that
> unnerves my strength – you stinking hag! – when you've got one
> black tooth, when old age furrows your forehead with wrinkles,
> when a shameful hole like a cow's with diarrhoea gapes between
> ugly buttocks. But what stirs me up is that flabby chest, those
> flabby breasts, like a mare's teats, and that spongy belly and
> skinny thigh perched on top of swollen legs. Bless you then, and
> I hope likenesses of triumphant men-folk will lead your funeral.
> May there be no wife who may walk along laden with rounder
> blobs of pearls than yours. There are little Stoic treatises which
> tend to lie among neat little pillows of silk; What of it? Surely
> those unlearned sinews stiffen no less? That poker doesn't droop

any less, does it? However, to stir that up from a proud groin one's got to work hard with one's mouth.[47]

The old woman in love was condemned to mockery and neglect:

> Less often now do riotous youths shake thy shutters with repeated blows; no longer do they steal thy slumbers from thee; and the door that once right willingly did move its hinges now hugs its threshold. Less and less often hearest thou such plaints as this: 'Sleepest thou, Lydia, while I, thy lover true, die throughout the livelong night.' Thy turn shall come, and thou, a hag forlorn in deserted alley, shalt weep o'er thy lovers' disdain, when on moonless nights the Thracian north-wind rises in its fury, while burning with love and passion, such as are wont to goad the stallion's dams, shall rage about thy wounded heart. Then shalt thou make moan that merry youths take more delight in my green and myrtle dark, consigning withered leaves to the east wind, winter's mate.[48]

Such bitterness about old women would recur only during the Renaissance, 15 centuries later, when the themes of classical antiquity came back in fashion and when the cult of earthly beauty would lead people to destroy all images of ugliness. Horace, while the cruellest, was not alone in attacking the old women of his age. Young Propertius (47–15 BC), who also belonged to Maecenus' circle, spoke of an old woman in his elegies: 'All her bones can be counted through her skin. Blood-streaked spittle seeps through the hollows in her teeth.' Later on, the sarcastic poet Martial (40–104 AD) wrote ironically in his *Epigrams* about 'Thais, who smells worse than an old jar of fuller's earth, than an amphora spoilt by rancid brine.'

Horace is less nasty about old men, without however flattering them. For him, they are timorous and drivelling misers:

> Many ills encompass an old man, whether because he seeks gain, and then miserably holds aloof from his store and fears to use it, or because, in all that he does, he lacks fire and courage, is dilatory and slow to form hopes, is sluggish and greedy of a longer life, peevish, surly, given to praising the days he spent as a boy, and to reproving and condemning the young. Many blessings do the advancing years bring with them; many, as they retire, they take away.[49]

One must know how to profit cynically from those old people who are rich and extract money from them scrupulously; this is the good counsel which Tiresias gives to Ulysses himself, who, wily as he is, is staggered by such moral indifference:

Tiresias: Let's not mince words. Poverty is what you're afraid of. So here's the way to get rich. Suppose you're given a thrush or something else for yourself, let it fly away to the glitter of a great household with an aged master. Your sweetest apples and the various kinds of tribute that come from your tidy farm – let the rich man taste them in preference to the god of your hearth, for he is more worthy of respect. He may be a liar or a man of no family, an escaped convict stained with his brother's blood; no matter. If he asks you to go for a walk, be sure to keep outside him.

Ulysses: What? defer to some filthy menial! I did not behave like that at Troy, where I always strove with my betters!

Tiresias: All right, you'll be a pauper.

Ulysses: I shall brace my heart to bear what you spoke of. I have endured even greater ills e'er now. So tell me, sir, with your prophet's insight, how to rake in piles of cash.

Tiresias: I've told you and I'll tell you again. You must fish cunningly around for old men's wills. If one or two are clever enough to nibble the bait off the hook and escape your clutches, you mustn't be so disappointed as to give up hope and abandon your craft . . . A further point: if the old dotard happens to be under the thumb of some scheming woman or freedman, make a deal: you praise them, they praise you when you're not there. That helps too. But much the best idea is to storm the main objective. If the idiot churns out doggerel – praise it. Is he a lecher? Don't wait to be asked – do the decent thing and hand Penelope over to your more deserving rival.

Ulysses: Do you think she can be prevailed upon, a lady so pure and proper, a lady whom the suitors have failed to tempt from the straight and narrow?

Tiresias: Of course! When those lads came, they were rather mean with their presents; it wasn't sex that enticed them so much as the palace cooking. That's why your Penelope is pure. But if you make her a partner and let her taste some cash at an old fellow's expense, there'll be no holding her. She'll be like a dog with a juicy bone.[50]

Are Tiresias' counsels Horace's own, or are they just a joke? Knowing what Horace thought of old age, one cannot be sure of anything. In any case his casual, to say the least, treatment of the characters in the *Odyssey* marks a mental evolution. Old age could expect no favours in an age when men behaved more than ever like wolves towards each another. In the *Aeneid*, Virgil flanks old age with Morbi and Metus, illness and fear of dying.

A century later still, Pliny the Younger, whom we have seen praising the ideal old age of his friend Spurinna, wrote a letter to Attius Clemens, in which he drew the portrait of another old patrician, who, being vain and boring, was courted only on account of his wealth;

It is amazing how he is now beseiged by people who all loathe and detest him and yet flock around him in crowds as if they really loved and admired him. To put it briefly, they court Regulus by his own methods. He will not stir from his gardens beyond the Tiber, where he has covered a vast area with immense colonnades and littered the bank with his precious statues; for he is extravagant for all his avarice, and vainglorious in spite of his notoriety . . . He says he wants to marry again, and is as perverse on this point as he is in everything else. You will soon hear that the mourner is married, the old man is wed – the one too early and the other too late.[51]

Seneca's view of old age was more balanced. As we have seen, one should not hesitate to commit suicide if it becomes wearisome. But old men are not always reduced to this extremity. His *Letters to Lucilius* reveal his main thoughts on the subject. The Seneca who wrote them was 64 years old and a disillusioned man. His plans for educating the young Nero had turned out to be vain: philosophy had failed when confronted by monstrosity. In 62 AD, using the death of his old friend Burrus as a pretext, Seneca gradually retired from public life and took his definitive retirement in 64 AD, embittered by the charges of excessive wealth and pride brought against him by the Emperor's new advisers. In his last works, the *De otio*, for instance, he discusses the possible existence of an autonomous spiritual universe. His *Letters to Lucilius*, which were written in this context, started off as a real correspondence, and were then adapted with a view to publication. In them, the old Seneca defended his right to retirement and spoke at length of old age. 'Old age is full of enjoyment if you know how to use it . . . Life's most delightful when it is on the down slope but not at the edge yet. Even when it trembles on the eaves it still has its pleasures. I opine, or else pleasures are compensated by freedom from the need for them' (letter XII). It behoves him not to remain idle; he must work for posterity (letter VIII) and continue his studies: 'You must learn as long as you don't know – and that's as long as you live' (letter LXXVI). Above all, he must not let himself go, neglect his physical appearance and his clothes, if he wants to keep his friends: 'One must watch over one's old age all the more carefully if one knows that a certain thing is pleasing, useful or desirable in the eyes of a person dear to us. One must abandon political ambitions or the field of business and seek for tranquillity, abdicate a career of honours, preferring rest to it.'

Old age ought to be spent meditating on the works of the philosophers, an occupation which will bring peace and felicity and will open the way to eternity: 'What happiness, what a good old age awaits him who has placed himself under their patronage! he will have confidants with whom he will be able to discuss the most trivial and the greatest matters, whom he will be able to consult every day about his interests, who will tell him the truth without oaths, will praise him without flattery, on whose likeness he will be able to model himself.'

Contrary to what Plutarch was to say a century later, Seneca despised those who threw themselves into public life when they were old: 'What is more shameful than preparing to live when one is already old?' The old man must renounce the pleasures of youth: 'Count your years, I cry, and you'll be ashamed to retain the desires and designs of your boyhood. Against the day of your death provide at least that your vices may predecease you' (letter XXVII). In letter XCIII, he takes up an idea previously enounced in his treatise *De brevitate vitae*: true old age does not wait on the number of years; the true old man is one who is wise, whatever his age.

This theme was to be adopted frequently by Christian writers. 'You ask what the utmost extent of life is. To live till you reach true wisdom'; 'Just because a man has white hair and wrinkles, don't go thinking that he has lived a long time; he had not lived long, but lasted long. What then! Do you think that he has done much sailing, who has been surprised on leaving port by a cruel tempest, and has been beaten here and there, always turning within the same space under the changing breath of the raging winds? He has not done much sailing, but lots of floating.' Ridiculous too are those old people who make up their faces in an attempt to pass as still young: 'Some decrepit old men beg in their prayers for an extra few years. They disguise themselves as young, they cosset themselves with lies, and abuse themselves with as much confidence as if they could simultaneously cheat destiny.'

At the beginning of the second century, another Stoic, Epictetus, when almost 80 years old, said that man must play his role imperturbably up to the end. Seneca, however, was less rigid. Firstly, if a man's sufferings become too painful, it would be stupid to go on living; next, the wise man must learn how to profit from the advantages retirement can bring him, without straining at his role. Finally, however much of a Stoic he was, he admitted in letter XII that old age sometimes made him bitter: on arriving in his country house, he was instinctively revolted at finding himself in an environment where everything reminded him that he was old: his old servant, his old trees, his old house in need of repair. Thus, even the most elevated form of philosophy could not shelter him from moments of depression about old age. It is greatly to his credit that Seneca acknowledged this, and his position is, in the last analysis, one of the most balanced known to history.

Juvenal (65–128) was the last to maltreat the old systematically and to caricature their weaknesses and ugliness. From then on, however, such abuse consisted of clichés or stylistic exercises. Since the old man was no longer feared on account of his power, he was no longer of interest to literature. His furtive shadow can only just be glimpsed on the parameters of an ode, and he can be heard, if at all, complaining timidly about his fate in Silius Italicus' *Punica* or Maximianus' *Book of Elegies*. The old man fell into oblivion and was forgotten for a long time to come. His passage through the Roman empire had not been any happier than it had been through the Hellenic world.

ROMAN MEDICINE AND OLD AGE

The old, with death looming before them, held no attraction for therapists. Theirs was an incurable sickness, at least if one considers its only remedy to be youth. So nothing could be done for them, other than drawing up a clinical list of their commonest illnesses. This is what Celsius did in the Augustan age, and his *De medicina* differs very little from the satirists' catalogues. The old are subject to chronic illnesses, to colds, to urinary and respiratory problems, to sinusitis, to problems with kidneys and with articulation, to insomnia and paralysis, to ear and eye ache and bowel pains, to dysentry and to colic.[52] All of which was more or less copied from Hippocrates and, in any case, anyone could have made the same observation. Celsius added that the old could not endure hunger, that their wounds did not heal easily. He also provided a few prescriptions: the old should bathe in warm water and drink undiluted wine; when their sight grew dim, their eyes should be anointed with honey or olive oil. Winter is the season they find most difficult to endure, whereas they tend to do better during summer and at the beginning of autumn. None of which went very far.

Galen (131–201) pushed his investigations a bit further. He was of Greek origin, having been born in Pergama, and he adopted Aristotelian theory and combined it with the Hippocratic method of observation to achieve fairly penetrating conclusions in his principal work *De sanitate tuenda*. He perfected a system explaining the process of ageing which used the doctrine of humoral pathology and the pneuma. His conclusions represented the summit of Greek thought on the subject, and remained authoritative right up to the Renaissance, because they were in accordance with Christian theology.

Galen considered that there were two sorts of illness: those which are unavoidable and incurable, whose causes are intrinsic and lie in the generative process, and those which can be avoided and treated, which are derived from extrinsic causes. Old age belongs to the first category and is explained as follows: the body's tissues are produced from the humid mixture of blood and semen, dehydrated by its interior heat.

By this means, then, the embryo is first formed and takes on a little firmness; and after this, drying more, acquires the outlines and faint patterns of each of its parts. Then drying even more, it assumes not merely their outlines and patterns, but their exact appearance. And now, having been brought forth, it keeps growing larger and drier and stronger until it reaches full development. Then all growth ceases, the bones elongating no more on account of their dryness, and every vessel increases in width, and thus all the parts become strong and attain their maximum power.

But in ensuing time, as all the organs become even dryer, not only are their functions performed less well but their vitality becomes more feeble and restricted. And drying more, the creature becomes not only thinner but also wrinkled, and the limbs weak and unsteady in their movements. This condition is called old age . . . This then, is one innate destiny of destruction for every mortal creature . . .

These processes, then, it is permitted no mortal body to escape.[53]

Galen thus affirmed the unity of the human individual's development and his decline; the same mechanism makes the embryo grow and makes the old man decline until his death. In modern terms, our body is programmed to grow, age and die, as Galen has clearly stated: 'Every mortal creature has in him from the beginning sources of death'[54]. His internal heat makes him lose substance, which is partly replaced by breathing, food and drink, but it is impossible to achieve a complete restoration of the previous state. A necessary decline takes place.

This is why we grow old, some at one age, others at another, sooner or later, because we either are from the beginning by nature excessively dry, or become so either from circumstances, or diet, or disease, or worry, or some such cause. For that which all men commonly call old age is the dry and cold constitution of the body resulting from many years of life.[55]

For Galen, illness was contrary to nature, and so old age was not an illness:

The impaired capacity of function determines health. Nor is weakness of function, strictly speaking, a sign of disease, but only what is contrary to nature . . . Such a man we should say has some disease, unless he suffers this on account of old age; and some say that this also is a disease . . . For all disease is contrary to nature, but such people are not contrary to nature, any more than the aged.

One ought not, therefore, to determine health and disease merely by vigour or weakness of function, but one should apply to the health the term 'in accordance with nature', and to the sick man 'contrary to nature', and disease a condition producing function contrary to nature . . .

For the present consideration it will suffice to have this much only, that the range of health is very wide, and that it does not exist with equal absoluteness in us all.[56]

In all, Galen's views appear remarkably modern; they offer the first complete and consistent theory of ageing. However this does not alter the fact that he was alone in studying the physical nature of old age over eight centuries of Roman history. Further, the passages quoted above must be set in context. Galen only mentioned old age incidentally, in a few lines lost in his immense work. It is only in the modern age that people have thought of treating the problems of great age specifically. For the Romans, an old man was an aged adult, just as a child was a young adult; old age was a miserable prolongation of life, just as youth is its radiant prologue. Only man in his adult phase was worthy of interest.

A suspect apologia: Cicero's *De Senectute*

Cicero's *De senectute*, the sole Latin work exclusively dedicated to the old, is all the more remarkable in consequence. It may seem strange that Roman civilization, which was so hard on the old, should have produced this remarkable and in many ways unique apologia for old age. Through the place it occupies in literature, through its qualities of style and argument, the work represents a vital milestone in the history of old people.

It takes the form of a dialogue (its first similarity with the works of Plato) between historical characters: Cato the Elder, 84 years old and still going strong and two young men, Scipio, son of Paulus Aemilius and his friend Laelius. The latter tell Cato how much they admire him for being so active at so great an age, and the old man then monopolizes the next nine-tenths of the work and lectures them about his concept of old age.

The dialogue opens however with an admission which undermines in advance what follows. Cato is an exception, because in normal life old men are unhappy:

Many a time have I expressed my admiration (for you), but above everything because I have noticed that old age never seemed a burden to you, while to most old men it is so hateful that they declare themselves under a weight heavier than Aetna.[57]

That's because, Cato replies, those who complain about old age are not
sensible; the wise man, for his part, knows how to accept all the ages
of life with good grace. Many complain about being obliged to renounce
the pleasures of the senses, but it is in fact a blessing to be freed from
this servitude:

> The fact is that the blame for all complaints of that kind is to be
> charged to character, not to a particular time of life. For old men
> who are reasonable and neither cross-grained nor churlish find old
> age tolerable enough; whereas unreason and churlishness cause
> uneasiness at every time of life . . . The arms best adapted to old
> age are culture and the active exercise of the virtues. For if they
> have been maintained at every period -- if one has lived much as
> well as long -- the harvest they produce is wonderful, not only
> because they never fail us even in our last days (though that in
> itself is supremely important), but also because the consciousness
> of a well-spent life and the recollection of many virtuous actions
> are exceedingly delightful.[58]

The whole of his introductory speech has simply been borrowed from
Plato, in particular from Cephalus' speech in the *Republic*, which, it
may be said in passing, looks peculiar in the mouth of this great
adversary of Hellenism, who only learnt Greek in the last years of his
life.

After this, however, Cato appears in a more Roman guise. He seeks
out examples from the history of the *urbs*, and develops the cases of
Quintus Maximus and Ennius, which he compares to those of Plato,
Isocrates and Gorgias, all of them venerable old men fully satisfied with
their old age, he assures us. And so he comes to the crux of the debate:

> When I come to think it over, I find that there are four reasons
> for old age being thought unhappy: First, that it withdraws us
> from active employments; second, that it enfeebles the body; third,
> that it deprives us of nearly all physical pleasures; fourth, that it
> is the next step to death. Of each of these reasons, if you will
> allow me, let us examine the force and justice separately.[59]

First argument:

> Old age withdraws us from active employments. From which of
> them? Do you mean from those carried on by youth and bodily
> strength? Are there then no old men's employments to be after
> all conducted by the intellect, even when bodies are weak? So then

Q. Maximus did nothing; nor L. Aemilius – your father, Scipio, and my excellent son's father-in-law! So with other old men – the Fabricii, the Curii and Coruncauii – when they were supporting the state by their advice and influence, they were doing nothing! . . . but, it is said, memory dwindles. No doubt, unless you keep it in practice, or if you happen to be somewhat dull by nature. Themistocles had the names of all his fellow citizens by heart. Do you imagine that in his old age he used to address Aristides as Lysimachus? . . . Did old age then compel (them) to become silent in (their particular) art . . . Is it not rather the case with all these that the active pursuit of study only ended with death?[60]

And Sophocles, who, at the age of 80, recited by heart *Oedipus at Colonus* before the judges in order to convince them that he had retained all his faculties, and Homer, Hesiod, Simonides, Stesichorus, Isocrates, Gorgias, Pythagoras, Democritus, Plato, Zeno, Cleanthes and Diogenes the Stoic: 'Has old age dimmed their intelligence to the point that they were no longer able to continue in their labours? Did their activity not continue as long as their life?'

But, it will be further objected, the old become odious to others. Nothing is more false:

Just as old men, if they are wise, take pleasure in the society of young men of good parts, and as old age is rendered less dreary for those who are courted and liked by the youth, so too do young men find pleasure in the maxims of the old, by which they are drawn to the pursuit of excellence. Nor do I perceive that you find my society less pleasant than I do yours. But this is enough to show you how, so far from being listless and sluggish, old age is even a busy time, always doing and attempting something, of course of the same nature as each man's taste had been in the previous part of his life.[61]

There are even old men who undertake new studies; Socrates took up the lyre, and Cato himself started learning Greek!

Second argument: Old age reduces our physical strength. Cato recalls the example, which he finds despicable, of Milo of Croton, who, having grown old, wept at the sight of athletes exercising: 'you trifler! As if life is measured by the strength of biceps! Is physical strength the only thing that counts?'

I am afraid an orator does lose vigour by old age, for his art is not a matter of the intellect alone, but of lungs and bodily strength. Though as a rule that muscial ring in the voice even gains in brilliance in a certain way as one grows old -- certainly I have not yet lost it, and you see my years. Yet after all the style of speech suitable to an old man is the quiet and unemotional, and it often happens that the chastened and calm delivery of an eloquent old man secures a hearing. If you cannot attain to that yourself, you might still instruct a Scipio and a Laelius. For what is more charming than old age surrounded by the enthusiasm of youth?[62]

Certainly, Cato continues, modesty not being his chief virtue.

> I am not indeed as vigorous as I was as a private soldier . . . but yet, as you see, old age has not entirely destroyed my muscles, has not quite brought me to the ground. The Senate-house does not find all my vigour gone, nor the rostra, nor my friends, nor my clients, nor my foreign guests.

Only those who have led a life of debauchery are physically broken. In any case, it is better to be resigned. It is said that Milo made his entry on the stadium of Olympia carrying a bullock on his shoulders. What of it? 'In fine enjoy the blessing when you have it; when it is gone, don't wish it back.' Cato here makes an involuntary admission which betrays yet again the general tenor of his speech: 'For I have never given in to that ancient and much-praised proverb: Old when young is old for long. For myself, I had rather be an old man a somewhat shorter time than an old man before my time.' Strange words in the mouth of one who claims to vaunt the merits of old age. He goes on to say:

> Bodily strength is wanting to old age; but neither is bodily strength demanded from old men. Therefore, both by law and custom, men of my time of life are exempted from those duties which cannot be supported without bodily strength. Accordingly not only are we not forced to do what we cannot do; we are not even obliged to do as much as we can. But, it will be said, many old men are so feeble that they cannot perform any duty in life of any sort or kind. That is not a weakness to be set down as peculiar to old age: it is one shared by ill health . . . What wonder, then, that old men are eventually feeble, when even young men cannot escape it? My dear Laelius and Scipio, we must stand up against old age and make up for its drawbacks by taking pains. We must fight it as we should an illness. We must look after our health, use moderate exercise, take just enough food and drink to recruit, but not to overload, our strength. Nor is it the body alone that must be supported, but the intellect and soul much more. For they are like lamps: unless you feed them with oil, they too go out from old age.[63]

. . .

The fact is that old age is respectable just as long as it asserts itself, maintains its proper rights, and is not enslaved to any one. For as I admire a young man who has something of the old man in him, so do I an old one who has something of a young man. The man who aims at this may possibly become old in body – never in mind. I am now engaged in composing the seventh Book of my origins . . . I frequently attend the Senate and bring motions before it on my own responsibility . . . For a man who is always living in the midst of these studies and labours does not perceive when old age creeps upon him. Thus, by slow and imperceptible degrees life draws to its end. There is no sudden breakage: it just slowly goes out.

Third argument:

The third charge against old age is that it lacks sensual pleasures . . . What a splendid service does old age render, it takes from us the greatest blot of youth!

Here the old moralist lets rip wholeheartedly. Our passion for pleasure drags us into shameful and criminal actions:

Nothing can be so execrable and fatal as pleasure; since, when more than ordinarily violent and lasting, it darkens all the light of the soul . . .

We should be grateful to old age for subduing an appetite we should not tolerate within ourselves. Pleasure hinders thought, it is a foe to reason . . . Not only should one not reproach old age for knowing how to do without pleasure, one should congratulate it. Old age does not want to know anything of 'the pleasures of the table feasts, the heaped-up board, the rapid passing of the wine-cup'; this is why headache, disordered digestion and broken sleep are unknown to it. Look at me: I have led a virtuous life, and that is why I am so well.[64]

The case is carried where the pleasures of the table are concerned, but what about love, or to be more precise, sex? The question was much debated in Cato's time, as we have seen in the comedies. The old man sidestepped the question with a scornful and ambiguous reply, lacking in clarity: 'But – you may urge – there is not the same tingling sensation of pleasure in old men. No doubt; but neither do they miss it so much. For nothing gives you uneasiness which you do not miss.' Yes indeed, but is he quite sure that they do not feel the need? According to the following words, this can be doubted:

In the first place, they are insignificant things to enjoy, as I have said; and in the second place, such as age is not entirely without, if it does not possess them in profusion . . . so youth, because it looks at pleasures at closer quarters, perhaps enjoys itself more, yet even old age, looking at them from a distance, does enjoy itself well enough.

Cicero would have been hard put to state the contrary, given that, at the age of 60, he had just divorced Terencia after 29 years of marriage in order to marry his young ward Publilia. In any case, he was eager to turn over this embarrassing page in order to tackle the pleasures of the mind: 'What pleasures are there in a feast, games or mistresses comparable to pleasures such as these?'

Then there were other pleasures the old could enjoy as much as other people: agriculture, for instance, meaning the satisfaction of a great landowner on seeing his crops growing and on directing the work. Cicero's Cato grows lyrical here, ecstatically happy about 'the good hard-working farmer's wine cellar (which the old man will never be able to taste) and oil store, as well as his larder, (which) are always well filled . . . abounding with . . . pigs, goats, lambs, fowls, milk, cheese and honey'; 'the rows of trees, the beauty of the vineyard and olive grove.' 'Nothing can either furnish necessaries more richly, or present a fairer spectacle than well-cultivated land. And to the enjoyment of that, old age does not merely present no hindrance – it actually invites and allures to it. For where else can it better warm itself either by basking in the sun or by sitting by the fire, or at the proper time cool itself more wholesomely by the help of shade or water.'[65]

But, it will be said, old men are fretful, fidgety, ill-tempered and disagreeable. If you come to that, they are also avaricious. But these are faults of character, not of the time of life. And, after all, fretfulness and the other faults I mentioned admit of some excuse – not, indeed, a complete one, but one that may possibly pass muster: they think themselves neglected, looked down upon, mocked. Besides, with bodily weakness every rub is a source of pain. Yet all these faults are softened both by good character and good education . . . But throughout my discourse remember that my panegyric applies to an old age that has been established on foundations laid by youth. From which may be deduced what I once said with universal applause, that it was a wretched old age that had to defend itself by speech. Neither white hairs nor wrinkles can at once claim influence in themselves: it is the honourable conduct of earlier days that is rewarded by possessing influence at the last.[65]

Fourth argument: old age means the approach of death. Dying? What a treat! Either there is nothing after death, in which case, there is nothing to fear, or death opens the way to eternal life, in which case it is to be desired. Cato then produces his classic couplets on despising death: death affects the young more than the old; the proof is that very few people achieve old age!

His conclusion is very worthy:

> Again, if we are not to be immortal, it is nevertheless what a man must wish – to have his life end at its proper time. For nature puts a limit to living as to everything else. Now, old age is as it were the playing out of the drama, the full fatigue of which we should shun, especially when we also feel that we have had more than enough of it. This is all I had to say on old age. I pray that you may arrive at it, that you may put my words to a practical test.

Assuredly this is a beautiful piece of writing. Everything that could be said at the time to console old men is gathered in it and maybe some wise old men and old *rentiers* did acquire serenity through reading its pages. It is probable, however, that Cicero could only convince the converted, old men already happy to be such, and such people doubtless did exist. The others, by far the most numerous, would not be affected at all by his rhetoric. Indeed, the author himself was not too convinced by it. Cicero, who was 60 at the time, dedicated his treatise to his friend Atticus, who was 63, admitting in the introduction that his purpose was to try to console himself at the onset of old age, whose burden he feared. 'For from the burden of impending or at least advancing old age, common to us both, I would do something to relieve us both.' He admits here that old age is not in itself a happy period, an opinion reinforced, as we have seen, by several allusions in the text. The very fact that Cicero felt the need to write this consolation is in itself sufficiently eloquent.

The old age he presents us with is an ideal old age, expounded by a legendary Cato; it is the great age of a rich and cultivated landowner, wellknown and respected, inspired in all his actions by the highest forms of philosophy. That this ideal was far from being achieved even by the author is easily established from the content of certain of Cicero's letters to Atticus. In these epistles, which were not destined for publication, Cicero expresses himself with the utmost spontaneity: 'Old age sets me in a bad mood, he confesses, the slightest thing puts me in rage.' In another instance, he tells how his sister-in-law's behaviour at a dinner party made him furious; 'I behaved like an ass' he admits elsewhere.[67] His treatise, like most of his other works, is an extension of Plato's ideas on the subject, and is situated in the world of ideas more than in the cavern where real old men of blood and bone were languishing.

The sole domain in which the Romans had always treated the old well was that of art: the old Etruscan couple of Volterra, whose lined faces are full of tenderness and contained emotion, evoke the grandeur of the aged spouses' fidelity. The sculptured portraits of old patricians, executed from their funerary masks, with their energetic faces, their high foreheads, like that of the famous patrician bearing the busts of his ancestors in the Palazzo dei Conservatori in Rome. The magnificent funerary group of *Cato and Porcia*, whose lined foreheads alone indicate their age, dates from the reign of Hadrian and expresses grandeur, nobility and affection. The pathos and spiritual anguish of the defeated old man in the relief sculpture of captive barbarians on the Aurelian column -- the beauty of these sculptures could almost make one forget the sarcasms of Plautus. A civilization which was capable of producing such masterpieces could not have been fundamentally hostile to the old: in any case, the Roman world was the first to allow them to talk about themselves and to have given us the first complete apologia of old age. But these contrasting visions prove primarily that this world was aware of the fundamental ambiguity of great old age, so nobly tragic and derisorily comic, so mean in all its faults and so sublime in its qualities.

The Romans had few prejudices; they managed to construct a cosmopolitan and tolerant world, where people fought for power, but not for religion, ideology or race; a world in which they admired what was great and noble, whether this was the work of Tiberius Gracchus at the age of 28, or of Cato, at the age of 84. Little inclined to generalization and above all practical, the Roman genius spoke about old men much more than about old age, and in this it differs from the Greek world. The *De senectute* itself is a web of individual examples more than a treatise on old age in general. By rejecting categories and concepts, the Romans rejected constricting simplifications and managed in the long run to preserve the dignity of old people. They criticized individuals, but not the age group, and so safeguarded the complexity, the contradictions and the ambiguity of old age, both its miseries and its grandeur.

5

The Early Middle Ages:

The Old Man as a Symbol in Christian Literature

The fourth century is one of the great turning-points in the history of the western world. While the barbarian menace was putting growing pressure on a Roman empire wracked by civil wars and periodically restored by energetic emperors – Diocletian, Constantine and Theodosius – Christianity was gaining strength. From Constantine onwards, most of the emperors were Christians. At the end of the century, Theodosius definitively imposed the new religion: paganism was prohibited, but the pulation as a whole was far from converted. The countryside kept faith with the old religions for many centuries, and bishops often did no more than alter terminology so as to cover age-old practices with a very thin veneer of Christianity. The towns were Christianized to a greater degree, but when the Roman empire in the west collapsed and the barbarians were installed, they retreated and even disappeared, dwindling into tiny kernels corresponding to the number of episcopal cities.

The new arrivals, Angles, Saxons, Franks, Alamans, Burgundians, Ostrogoths, Visigoths, Suevi, Vandals and finally Lombards, Aryans and Pagans, were rapidly converted to 'catholicism', while retaining their brutal customs. The fifth to the tenth century, the early Middle Ages, or the Dark Ages, constituted (despite the Carolingian renaissance) an age of brutality in its pure state, when justice was reduced to its simplest expression, as represented by such travesties as the Wergeld, the Ordeal and the Judgement of God. It was an age when the great were preoccupied above all with massacre and pillage, when art was limited to fabricating spears, belts and jewels, when literature was limited to copying manuscripts in monasteries, when trade had contracted to the level of the domain, when plague and famine had reduced the population to a bare minimum. Gregory of Tours has sufficiently described these barbaric times in his *History of the Franks*.

Charlemagne, Alcuin and Aix-la-Chapelle did of course happen, in a

40-year parenthesis between two-and-a-half centuries of Merovingians
and a century of Normans, Hungarians and Saracens. A parenthesis,
furthermore, which affected only the administration and a few intellectuals. In short, in spite of the odd glimmer of light occurring here and
there, the overall picture of the early Middle Ages is still very Dark.
The only law to have been definitively applied in this age was that of
the strongest, physically and militarily. The weaker elements curried
favour with the more powerful ones, who gathered a clientele of vassals
around themselves and who submitted only to those more powerful
than themselves. The only accepted form of arbitration was by the
sword. At the bottom of the scale, the most vulnerable elements lost
even their liberty. Slavery and serfdom characterized the peasant masses.

In such a world, what could the fate of old people be? Weakest
among the weak, inept at bearing arms, the value set on their lives by
the Wergeld was low, and killing them did not cost much. Among the
Visigoths, old men aged over 65 were valued at 100 gold solidi, the
same as children aged under ten, whereas the murder of an adolescent
of 14 was taxed at 140 solidi, that of a boy aged between 15 and 20
years at 150 solidi, and that of a man aged between 20 and 50 years at
300 solidi. The fine diminished from 50 years of age onwards: 200 solidi
for the murder of a man aged between 50 and 65. The Wergeld for
women was assessed according to their reproductive capacity: 250 solidi
between the ages of 14 and 40, 200 solidi after the age of 40, and almost
nothing after 60 years. Among the Franks, 'Where murders were
concerned, a pregnant woman and the mother of a family were worth
three times the price of a man until the menopause, and not much after
it.'[1]

Given that the old were cast aside in this brutal society, did they at
least find succour and comfort in the Church? It might be taken for
granted that Christianity, from the first the religion of the poor and the
oppressed, would become the protector of the old. And indeed, where
the Church was concerned, there was no specific problem about the
old. Mankind includes the poor, the widows and orphans, the infirm
and the sick, and the old, all muddled up together without any
distinctions of age or sex. The Church gathered them into her hospitals,
lodged them temporarily in her monasteries, but did not grant a specific
place to great age.

THE AGES OF LIFE AND OF THE WORLD, THE SYMBOLISM OF NUMBERS

Christian authors were clearly not interested in the problem of old age.
The old are almost entirely absent from their writings, and one has to

read hundreds of volumes in order to gather a meagre file on them. Bishops studied the human species independently of time, ageless humanity and its relationship with God. For them, enclosed as they were by abstract and systematic concepts, the number of years in a man's life had no more than symbolic significance.

This concept developed under the late Roman empire, as Philippe Ariès has already noted in his *Centuries of Childhood*.[2] The magical-scientific theories of this age adopted the ideas of the Ionian philosophers in the sixth century BC postulating the fundamental solidarity between all the elements of the universe, between the natural and supernatural worlds, between the cosmos and individual life. Viewed from this perspective, life appears to be divided into ages corresponding to the ages of the world. Christian writers, fascinated as they were by symbolism, very early on adopted these speculations, to which biblical interpretation so clearly lends itself.

At the beginning of the fifth century, St Augustine developed in his book *On Genesis against the Manicheans* the theme of the seven ages of the world, an extension of the seven days of creation, which correspond to the seven ages of life, of which the last, old age, is the image of renewal in man's spiritual life.[3] In his treatise on *The 83 Different Questions*, however, he reduced the ages of life to six, making old age begin at 60, and extending it to a maximum of 120 years. This too involved pure symbolism; thus, for instance, he stated that if John the Baptist had been born of old parents, it was to reveal to mankind that we are in the sixth age of humanity. There is constant correspondence between spiritual life, physical life and the age of the world:

> There are six ages in the life of a man; that of the cradle, of childhood, of adolescence, of youth, of maturity and of old age . . . The old man is extinguished by the corruption of old age, and the inner man is formed and renewed from day to day . . . Old age normally comprises as much time as all the other ages together. Given that old age begins around the sixtieth year, and can extend to 120 years, it is obvious that it can last as long on its own as all the other ages together.[4]

At the beginning of the seventh century, Isidore of Seville, another pillar of medieval thought, adopted in book V of his *Etymologies* the idea of dividing human life into six or seven parts; childhood (until the age of seven), *pueritia* (from seven to 14), adolescence (from 14 to 28), youth (from 28 to 50), maturity (from 50 to 70), and old age, which begins at 70, the last part of which, *senies*, corresponds to senility, the last stage of decrepitude. This master compiler was to exercise enormous influence right through to the Renaissance. Strange as it seems, this division of human life which extends youth to the age of 50 was to be adopted in its entirety in the thirteenth century by the *Magister de Proprietatibus Rerum (on the Properties of Things)*, who compiled a vast encyclopaedia in Latin of all the knowledge of the age, expressing: 'The fundamental unity of Nature, of the solidarity which exists between all the phenomena of nature, which could not be distinguished from supernatural manifestations.'[5] This work was translated into English in 1397, and printed by Wynkyn de Worde in 1495.[6]

Between Augustine and Isidore, came Gregory the Great, the first great medieval pope (590–604), who gave explicit expression to the idea of the interdependence of ageing man and ageing world:

> Just as we bear a body formed from the elements of this world, we should judge the end of the universe by that of this same body which is part of it . . . Our body is strong and robust in youth; when it begins to approach old age, it also begins to weaken through illness; and if it falls into a decrepit old age, these languishing remnants of life are no more than a continual weakening which tends towards death.[7]

In the fifth century, St Eucher, Bishop of Lyon, likewise also referred to 'this white-haired world'.[8] Likewise too, the Christian writings of the first centuries compared the Church, then in her infancy, with an old woman, 'because she has been created the first, before all other things', as the Pastor of Hermas said.

Speculations based on numbers were also derived from Pythagorean concepts, according to which order of ideas, age and the number of years were purely allegorical things. At the beginning of our era, the Jew Philo of Alexandria (20 BC–50 AD) engaged in high-flown discursions on the age of the patriarchs in his allegorical and platonic interpretation of the Bible. Thus, Genesis declares that Abraham left Haran at the age of 75, to show that he had then achieved the fullness of his being, the balance between his natural and intellectual forces:

> This number represents the border-land between perceptible and intelligent being, between older and younger, between corruptible and incorruptible. For seventy represents the principle of intellectual apprehension, of seniority and of incorruption, while the principle that corresponds numerically to the five senses is that of juniority and sense-perception.[9]

For many, the essential stages were represented by the multiples of seven, the perfect number. To achieve the age of 70 is already the sign of blessing; to go beyond it an exceptional phenomenon. This is what St Jerome affirms, relying not on personal observation but on the Book of Psalms.[10]

The *Manual for My Son* written in the ninth century (841–3) by Dhuoda, wife of Bernard Duke of Septimania, for their eldest son William, contains strange speculations about numbers of years. The ideal was to live to a hundred, which enabled one to reach paradise; we may find her reasoning disconcerting:

Expert calculators count to 99 on the fingers of their left hand, but when they reach a total of 100, the left hand ceases to intervene and they raise their right hand joyfully for the number 100 . . . What does the left hand signify, my son, if not our present life, during which each of us is constantly working? And what does the right hand signify, if not the holy and true celestial homeland? May you then achieve the blessed state of a hundred.[11]

TRUE OLD AGE IS WISDOM

This type of reckoning indicates that Christian thought in the early Middle Ages took no interest in actual old age. Old age was primarily a symbol, and the pagans were despised for their fear of dying: 'Is it not a great misfortune for you other pagans to grow old, and to be reduced to damning old age, after your youth has run its course without reaping any of the fruits of true happiness?' John Chrysostom preached, contrasting the old pagan's despair with the old Christian's joy at reaping the fruits of his virtue.[12] For his part, Lactantius, in the *Workmanship of God of Creation*, mocks philosophers for finding life too short. For him, wanting to live to a hundred is as utopian as wanting to live on earth for ever. The extent of terrestrial life is of no importance at all: 'Assuredly they wish that no man should die, unless he has completed his hundreth year.' Lactantius however thinks that seeking to achieve extreme old age is evidence of extravagance; if man is mortal, it is normal for him to die at any time.[13] In any case, it is not age which matters, it's virtue, as St Augustine says; given that old age is not in itself perfect, it does not necessarily bring wisdom with it.[14]

It is in fact with no surprise that we here encounter an idea from the Book of Wisdom, that physical old age is not true old age. The true old man is the wise man, whatever his age. All the authors agreed on this point: Gregory the Great, talking about St Benedict, declares that he 'from his younger days, carried always the mind of an old man.'[15] In the fifth century, St Hilary of Arles, in the *Life of St Honoratus* tells how he and his brother Venantius were treated while still young as old men because of their wisdom and virtue; when they decided to leave their country, people tried to prevent them:

For all their homeland felt that it was losing fathers in these youths. And indeed, they had attained to an old age that was not white-haired, but white with graces, and seen, not in withered limbs, but in lovely dispositions.[16]

And again: 'And what serious minds they had already acquired! and, with them, the mature wisdom of old men.'[17] At the beginning of the eighth century, the *Book of Sparks*, consisting of passages from Scripture and the Fathers compiled by Defensor, a monk of Ligugé, reminds us: 'Solomon has said: – old age will not be counted by the number of years. White hairs are the judgement of men; whereas the age of old age is a life without stain and which is pleasing to God . . . The crown of the old is great experience, and their glory is fear of God.'[18]

Origen, inspired both by Scripture, by Philo of Alexandria and by the pagan mannerism of the late Roman empire, reached the same conclusion. In his homilies on Joshua, when commenting on the verse 'Joshua was old and full of days', he recalled: 'In Scripture, the name of elder or old man is not given because of great age, but is granted in order to honour maturity of judgement and gravity of life, especially when the words "full of days" are added to the term "elder".'[19] He points out that this expression is never applied to sinners. Adam, Methuselah and Noah are never called elders, although they lived many centuries. Abraham was the first to bear this title, although he did not live nearly as long as the others. St Ambrose, in the *Treatise on the Gospel of St Luke*, took the same line: 'Thus even in childhood there is a sort of venerable old age of behaviour, and in old age a child-like innocence, because there is a form of old age which is venerable not by its duration, and which is not calculated by the number of years.'[20]

THE OLD MAN AS AN IMAGE OF SIN

Christian authors also made use of old age in the moral domain, always under allegorical form. Decrepitude, with its ugliness, furnished them with an excellent image of sin. The old man was the sinner who had to seek regeneration through penitence; youth, on the contrary, was the freshness of the new man, saved by Christ. Sin and evil were as hideous as old people, and like old age, they led to death.

The comparison was too pertinent to be neglected and it became a cliché common to all preachers. In his tenth homily on the Epistle to the Romans, John Chrysostom gave explicit expression this idea: the sinner's soul becomes as abject and hateful to people as an old man; it is 'led to the last degree of idiocy, speaking only of insignificant things, in the manner of old men and delirious persons; subject to phlegm, to stupidity, to forgetfulness, to rheum, hateful to men, easy prey for the demon.' He even goes beyond this image to establish a real physical link between sin and old age. Sin affects man in his flesh; each time it ages him more: 'After we have been restored to youth by grace, we become old men again by the effect of sin . . . In the ordinary way, every sort of sin ages him who commits it.'[21]

St Augustine did not contradict this in his first treatise on the Epistle of St John, in which he established the equivalence between the sinner and the old man, and between the child and the regenerate man. Elsewhere, in a commentary on a passage of Isaiah: 'And even to your old age I am he', he makes the following distinction: those who praise God will have the white hairs of wisdom, whereas the others will see their flesh wither.[22] The old man thus possesses both the signs of wisdom (white hair) and of the manifestations of sin (his withered skin). His white hair provides a further image; it is the mark of the venerable character of the old man, the immaculate aspect of his soul and, paradoxically, of his true youthfulness, of his innocence:

> As the old man's head is, so will our deeds be. See how his head grows white and hoary, as his old age approaches. If a man grows old in his natural span, you may search in vain for a black hair on his head, and you will not find one; in the same way, if our life has been sufficiently just, so that, on searching for the blackness of sin in it, one finds none, our old age will be a real old age, a verdant old age, an evergreen old age.[23]

For his part, John Chrysostom intones a hymn to white hair:

> Honour to white hair, not that we have a predilection for this colour, but because it is the colour of virtue, and because this venerable exterior leads us to conjecture that the inner man also has white hair! But the old man who gives the lie to his white hair by his behaviour, is only the more ridiculous.[24]

Apart from hair, all the other signs of old age are marked with the seal of ugliness. There is nothing to choose between the descriptions of the physical and psychological ills of old age by Christian authors and the portraits drawn by Plautus and Juvenal. One can even distinguish among some of them a degree of savage pleasure in accentuating the defects of decrepitude, which provided in their eyes an excellent picture of the vanity of worldly things. This theme, which was not new, was to be taken up again hundreds of times in the religious literature of subsequent centuries.

The old man was thus to serve as a repellent image in order to witness to the decrepitude of creation and to the vanity of the terrestrial world. Under these conditions, it was best for him to be as ugly as possible:

His eyes grow dim, his ears dull, his hair thins, his complexion turns pale, his teeth rot and disappear, his skin withers, his breath stinks, his chest is sunken, he breaks out in coughing fits, his knees shake and his heels and feet swell up; the inner man, who ages not at all, is himself affected by these signs of decrepitude, which show that his bodily dwelling is about to fall into ruin. What is there left for every old man to do, given that the end of this life is nigh, other than think on one thing only, how to reach the shores of the life to come in all happiness?[25]

We owe this portrait to St Augustine, who declares further:

Much as one would like to be able to combine beauty and old age, these two desires are contradictory; if you grow old, do not hope to preserve your beauty, which will flee before the advance of old age, and it is not possible for the strength of beauty and the lamentations of old age to dwell within the same person.[26]

You are not thinking if you wish for old age, you are wishing for something which you will complain of, when it has arrived.[27]

Consider man, how he is born, grows up and grows old. How much he has to complain of in old age! Cough and catarrh, dim vision, worries and weariness, they all afflict him at the same time. So a man who has grown old is a prey to every form of misery.[28]

St Augustine drew the following lesson from all this: reduced to this derelict state, the old man should think of nothing other than achieving salvation, fortifying his soul, aiming at perfection and at doing good works: 'It is more appropriate for old people than for all the rest to be concerned with religion, they for whom the flourishing years of this present world have passed by.' St Jerome also underlined the pitiable state of the old: 'For how few pass beyond the age of a hundred years, or attain it without regretting the attainment?'[29] Whereas Salvian, a German who was converted in the fifth century, becoming a monk at Lerins and then a priest at Marseille, classed the 'wretched old' in the category of those who must inspire us with pity, along with 'weeping mothers' and 'little children in tears'.[30]

OLD AGE, A CURSE AND A PUNISHMENT

Christian authors thus held a pessimistic view of old age. In this, they were heirs to the most recent writings of the Old Testament and of Greco-Roman civilization, whose mordant descriptions they re-employed. Given too that in their eyes every earthly event or phenomenon had a spiritual significance, old age, which was clearly an evil, could only be a form of divine punishment, a curse which weighed on man as a result of his sins. Like suffering and death, old age formed part of Adam's painful legacy. According to Ephraim of Nisbe, a doctor of the Syriac churches in the fourth century, old age was even the supreme punishment for original sin. One of his dogmatic hymns, which were sung by the faithful, proclaims this:

> Adam was young, fair, and joyful;
> But having spurned the commandment,
> He became unhappy, old, and fading,
> Bearing the weight of years
> And a load of miseries.[31]

Paradise, on the contrary, was the realm of eternal youth, where all the elect were to grow young again:

> Attach your thoughts,
> Old age, to Paradise:
> Its perfume will rejuvenate you,
> Its breath will give you youth,
> Your rags will be hidden
> By its splendid clothes!
> For you it drew
> This picture in Moses:
> His wrinkled cheeks
> Shone like the sun,
> Signs that old age
> Will find rejuvenation in Eden.[32]

In paradise happiness is complete, because 'nobody grows old there, nobody dies there.'

Ever since original sin, man has been 'harassed by the dual evil of old age and illness', explains the *Life of the Fathers of Jura*, a sixth-century work recounting the lives of the anchorites of the Burgundian period. These ancient fathers, like St Lupicin, St Oyend, St Roman, all lived to be very old and considered the evils of their great age as a divine punishment.[33] This notion is further illustrated by an anecdote told by Theodoret of Cyr in the *Philotheus* from the first half of the fifth century. In his life of St James we are shown young washerwomen busy treading linen, their skirts hitched up and bareheaded. When the saint came by, suitably harsh and grumpy, far from being charmed by the scene he took umbrage at it, the more so in that the impudent young girls watched him without even covering themselves and hiding their legs:

The man of God was incensed and wanted to take the opportunity to demonstrate the power of God to them in order to rid them of impiety by means of a miracle. He damned the source and immediately the current of water vanished; then he damned the girls by inflicting premature old age on their insolent youth, and his word was followed by the result: their black, hair changed colour, and they resembled young trees which have been arrayed in autumn leaves in springtime.

Old age is clearly seen as a divine punishment. However, can one not discern in this story a trace of envy and jealousy on the part of the venerable St James towards 'insolent youth'?[34]

As an image of sin, a symbol of terrestrial decrepitude, subjected to God's curse as a consequence of original sin, the old man was entitled to be miserable, ugly and ill. More often than not, as the authors observed with satisfaction, he did indeed conform to this stereotype. Any exceptions were suspect. An old man in good health did not conform with the divine scheme of things. This was a phenomenon which could be explained in only two ways: as the result of diabolical intervention or of God's special favour towards a particularly virtuous subject. St Jerome stated this explicitly in a letter to one of his friends, Paul, a remarkably well-preserved centenarian; a letter which must be compared with Pliny the Younger's letter to Spurinna.[35] Their perspectives are completely different: the flesh was henceforth to express only a spiritual reality; whereas Pliny felt that his old friend's good health was due to his hygienic way of life, St Jerome knew that it was the fruit of a virtuous life:

Here we have your years circling their orbits for the hundredth time, and you, ever observing the precepts of the Lord, bear in mind the blessings of the future life as you enjoy a foretaste of them in this life. Your eyes clear and full of life, your steps steady, your hearing unimpaired, your teeth white, your voice resonant, your body robust and full of energy. Your ruddy cheeks give the lie to your white hairs. Your physique protests your age. Extreme old age has not (as we commonly see) impaired the tenacity of your memory, nor has cooling blood blunted the sharp edge of your warm spirit. There is no furrowed brow to give a forbidding look to a face furrowed by wrinkles, and there is no trembling hand to cause an errant stylus to trace out crooked paths over the writing wax. The Lord shows us in you the flowering of the resurrection to come: He wants us to know that while it is by reason of sin that the rest of us, though still alive, die prematurely in the flesh, it is evidence of virtue practised that you counterfeit youth at an age alien to it.[36]

Thus healthy old age provided but another image, that of virtue. It is true, St Jerome observes, that depraved old men may also be well preserved, but in such cases, they are aided by the devil.

THE GUILTY AND INEXCUSABLE OLD MAN

If the Christian authors are to be believed, virtuous old men were in any case the exception. The number and gravity of their vices seemed to increase with years. Lascivious, miserly, choleric, greedy and egoistical, old men were hotbeds of vice, which was all the more unforgivable in that their experience and wisdom were supposed to direct them towards the good: 'Here is a vicious, corrupted, adulterous and immodest man, who glories in his disorderly ways, in whom the chills of old age have not quenched the fire of his passions', St Augustine said about an old man of 84 years, who, after living with his wife for 55 years, bought himself an actress in order to indulge his passion for her. For this man, the fact of having managed to live a long time while satisfying his desires had convinced him of his right to do this, and had hardened him in his vices, especially when he noticed that young people leading virtuous lives were dying all around him.[37]

Old people who engaged in debauchery were far more guilty than the young. Salvian of Marseilles was especially horrified to be present at the orgies into which old men of high society in Trèves threw themselves at the time of the Germanic invasions. The imminence of disaster and the collapse of the civilized world robbed them of all restraint:

> It is depressing to tell what I have seen: honoured old men and decrepit Christians enslaved to greed and debauchery while the city's fall was imminent. With what could I reproach them first? Their rank, their age, their title as Christians, the danger menacing them? . . . This is where I saw, I who address you, pitiable things: there was no difference at all between children and old men. They engaged in the same foolishness, the same frivolity. Every vice was indulged at once: luxury, drink and immorality. There was not one among them who did not practise all the vices, just like the others: they were gambling, drinking, debauching. Old men and men in high places were running wild at the feasting: they were already almost too weak to live, but still very strong at drinking wine, too puny for walking, but robust for imbibing,

shaky on their pins, but agile at the dances.[38]

Old age and poverty were two aggravating circumstances where sin was concerned.

> Furthermore, as I have already said, those who commit (these sins) have grown old, furthermore too, they have become poor: two circumstances which only serve to worsen their crime, for sinning in youth, sinning in wealth is a much less surprising matter. What hope, what remedy can there be for these men who are not turned away from their habitual impurity either by indigence or by declining age? . . . Is this not a new kind of monstrosity, that people should remain dissolute until death?[38]

The same idea crops up with St Ambrose, who had studied the question in his work on *Penitence*: the young have the excuse of their youth when they commit sins, but the old are inexcusable.[40] All the confessional manuals agree on this point, and John Chrysostom did not gainsay it when he castigated the pleasures he had observed among many old people in his sermons:

> What, you will tell men, does one not find old men who are more corrupt than the young? For when an old man has the ills of youth, it is a great evil. If, in our old age, our behaviour is still as shameful and as dishonourable, do we deserve the name of old men when we fail to respect our age? . . . Is not the behaviour of an old man who gets drunk, haunts the cabarets, goes to the races, who climbs onto a stage, who runs with the crowd like a child, ridiculous and inexcusable? It's a great shame and a very ridiculous thing to have white hair on one's head and the lightness of youth in one's heart . . .
> God, by giving you this crown of white hair has placed a diadem on your forehead. Why do you fail to acknowledge this honour? How can you expect youth to respect you when you are even more dissipated, more debauched than the young . . . What I say is not meant to accuse all old people – God preserve me from that! I accuse here only those old people who act as young men . . . My reproaches are not addressed to all old men, and I am not attacking old age in general. I am not angry enough for that; I am attacking the juvenile character who dishonours old age: I am addressing these bitter words not to old men, but to those who dishonour their white hairs. An old man is a king if he so wishes: he is more of a king than the ruler arrayed in purple, if he can command his passions, he tramples his vices underfoot like vile satellites. But if he allows himself to be dragged off, if he

degrades himself, if he makes himself a slave to avarice, to love, to vitality, to the refinements of the nobility, to wine, to anger and the pleasures, if he perfumes his hair, if out of his heart's gaiety he himself curses his old age, what punishment does he not deserve?[41]

According to the Patriarch of Constantinople, people in the high society of his age had an entirely profane notion of old age: 'One must not judge according to current opinion, and say that a beautiful old age is one which is spent in luxury and debauchery in the midst of immense riches, a crowd of courtesans and a troupe of slaves.'[42] The old men of the popular classes were not any better; they passed their days at the hippodrome and at performances. 'Some old men run there faster than the young people in the flower of their youth, with no respect for their white hairs (this symbolic thatch is always present!), without any fear of making a spectacle of their years or of exposing old age itself to public laughter.'[43] Their piety is shortlived indeed: in church, they cease not from complaining, while at the hippodrome they are ready to endure a thousand ills to see the races. His sermon turns picturesque in his effort to describe these contrasting attitudes:

> Here (at church), they have scarcely entered, when they succumb to boredom, they feel uncomfortable, they loll back to listen to the word of God, they complain about the lack of room, about the crowd and other such inconveniences. Over there, where their bald heads are exposed to the sun, they are rumpled, crowded and suffocated by the milling crowds, maltreated in every way, one would think they were lying nonchalantly in a meadow, so happy they are.[44]

Although he denies any desire to generalize, John Chrysostom does not appear to like old people. No other Father of the Church has criticized them as much as he has. He considers them much worse than the young:

> Old age has certain vices which youth does not have. It is lazy, slow, forgetful, its senses are rusty, it is angry . . . Yes, there are among the old even men who allow themselves to be overcome by fury and dementia, some as the result of drunkeness, other because of their grievances; because old age makes us pusillanimous.[45]

It also brings us drunkenness: 'because when age chills us, we love wine with passion . . . It is especially at this age that wine is needed, because old age is weak.'[46] The old give a bad example everywhere. Consequently they are not respected, but in spite of their faults, they still demand to be held in honour. They are indignant when a young man offends them, although they are only getting what they deserve:

> Should a young man manage to offend an old man, the latter will immediately take advantage of his age and will find a thousand persons to share in his indignation: but when it's a question of educating youth, of becoming a model of virtue for its sake, age is no longer taken into account, and it demonstrates more passion than even the young people for throwing itself at prohibited performances.[47]

Old men were thus to be punished more severely than the young.

After all, it would be so easy for them to be virtuous: age weakens the passions, blunts desire and extinguishes pleasure. John Chrysostomus here shares Sophocles' and Plato's opinion on this frequently debated problem: old age frees us from the desires of the flesh. His sermons on the Epistle of St Paul to the Hebrews dwell on this point: Old men are lucky in no longer being able to enjoy physical pleasure; let them take advantage of this to purify their souls and to raise them above the tumult of passion; for them, spiritual strength must take over from physical strength, on reaching their goal, they must redouble their efforts in the race for salvation: 'It's in old age that the soul is fortified; it's then that it has most strength; it's then that it leaps forwards.' In his *Commentary on Isaiah*, he returns to the same idea: 'Him to whom age has brought the most repose, who is no longer besieged by furious passions, but for whom it is easy to live in wisdom, and who can abstain from worldly things, will be justly punished with more severity if he demonstrates the same degree of licence at an advanced age as young men do.'[48]

St Augustine is more divided on this problem, and to a certain extent his confusion reflects that of Cicero. In some of his sermons, he appears to admit that old men can no longer enjoy the pleasures of the flesh:

> Old age brings many benefits and many evils with it; benefits, because it frees us from our passions, the cruellest of all tyrants; because it puts a stop to voluptuousness, tames vivacity, increases wisdom, provides mature advice, and, since the body's ardour is chilled, it sleeps without loss of virginity, scorning the pleasures offered by the Sunamite.[49]

Elsewhere, he makes up for this by confessing that, in spite of his great age, he is still assailed by the stirrings of concupiscence. For all that the temptation is not as strong as it is with the young, it is none the less redoubtable:

We ourselves, who have grown old in these battles, we have to struggle against less powerful enemies, but we still have to struggle. Our enemies seem themselves worn out by age, but weary as they are, they do not cease from troubling, by every possible means, our repose in old age.[50]

He considers that there are two parts within us which do not age and which lead us into sin: the 'heart', that is to say the seat of impure thoughts, and the 'tongue', which expresses them. Thus we are never sheltered from wrongdoing. Justinius, in the second century, appears on the the contrary to infer that from the ages of 50 or 60 onwards, no one need fear for their virginity.[51]

However this may be, old women who went on making up their faces in order to conceal the ravages of age drew Tertullian's wrath upon themselves:

> What's more one may also see those women who regret having lived to old age trying to pass from black to white. O temerity! age is summoned back from its vows and blushes: a felony is being committed; they sigh for youth, the age of sin; they spoil the opportunity for *gravitas* which is theirs. Such foolishness is far removed from the daughters of wisdom. The more old age attempts to conceal itself, the more it betrays itself . . . You are truly eager to approach the Lord! You are truly keen to quit this world of iniquity, you who think it ugly to be at the end of your lives.[52]

Lastly, taken as a whole, the Christian authors reproached the old with a variety of faults. According to Cyril of Alexandria, 'an old man is a being inclined to telling lies and who tries assiduously to have his additions to what he could wish and say were he worthy of belief accepted'; 'old age is always morose: it is very reluctant to go out, especially when it's raining'; hesitation 'is always natural to old age'.[53] Old people's great age and experience often render them presumptuous. Gregory the Great thus tells in his *Dialogues* how some nuns entrusted a child possessed by a demon to the care of St Eleutherius, then very old. When the demon did not dare manifest itself, the saint took all the credit:

> Whereupon the old man, seeing him to continue so well, was immoderately glad thereof, and therefore, in the presence of the monks, he spake thus: 'The devil did dally with those sisters: but now he hath to do with the servants of God, he dare not come near this boy.'[54]

Lactantius writes further: 'And old men, when they have lost their teeth, so lisp that they appear to have returned afresh to infancy.'[55] They are found in all depraved circles, including among the worst bandits. John Moschus, a monk living near Jerusalem at the beginning of the seventh century, recounts the story of the old brigand who committed murder and denounced his young accomplice. Being hardened in crime, he refused to repent, unlike his companion, and was strung up in front of the temple of Kronos.[56]

Is there yet time for an old man to alter his behaviour? Opinions were divided on this. St Patrick thought in his *Confessions* that it was useless to try to acquire in old age what one failed to master in youth.[57] On the other hand, a ninth-century sermon affirms that one ought not to despair of attaining sanctity, even if one has sinned right up to extreme old age; for one can be summoned to God's vineyard at any age.[58] St Augustine, in a letter written to St Jerome in 415, when he was 61 years old, also declares:

> Although you are much older than me (St Jerome was then 68, which demonstrates these authors' precise awareness of their age), it is already as an old man that I am addressing you. But when it is a matter of learning what is necessary, one is never too old; for if it is more suitable for old men to teach than to learn, it is nevertheless better to learn than to ignore one's own teaching.[59]

As it is, the facts appear to support Augustine; his period was particularly rich in late conversions, the most resounding being that of the famous Roman rhetorician, Marius Victorinus, who became a Christian at a very advanced age in *c*.355.

GREGORY THE GREAT: A FRIEND OF OLD PEOPLE

Seen as a whole, Christian literature provides a very negative view of old age. This being the case, it is in direct line with Greco-Roman thought. The few manifestations of sympathy towards the old are not sufficient to alter this picture. Of all the Christian authors of these iron centuries, Gregory the Great seems to have had the greatest regard for old age. He reminds us of this frequently in his *Dialogues*: 'A certain poor old man was brought unto me (because I loved always to talk with such kind of men).' He feels real friendship for old Fortunatus, whom he honoured with the title of *pater*, enjoyed by abbots, bishops and priests, though he was but a simple layman. 'Venerable Fortunatus, a man that doth much please me for his years, life and simplicity', told him stories from the life of his namesake, St Fortunatus. On occasion, he was felt to be rather too talkative: 'When the old man had told me this strange story, ready he was to proceed unto another', but the holy

Pontiff did not always have time to hear him, and would tell him so kindly, making sure he came again the next day.[60] Such tact was most unusual in those days. Gregory felt that old men were also the agents of the next world; he tells us how a young and very sick monk had a vision in which an old man appeared and touched him with a wand, saying that he would not die of this sickness.[61] When retracing the miracles of St Boniface, St Fulgentius and St Eleutherius, he always appealed to the testimony of old clerics, and the central place in his stories is generally taken by 'venerable old men'.[62]

Gregory the Great was exceptional in this. When they are not denigrating them, other writers considered them only as symbols and attributed purely formal qualities to them. In his *Sermons on Numbers*, Origen, when speaking of the 70 old men among whom Moses distributed the Spirit, attributed them with 'purity of heart, sincerity of soul and ready understanding: such are the qualities of the old'.[63] One detail from the *Life of St Honoratus* also shows that, in spite of the scorn lavished on the old, their reputation for wisdom had not been completely obliterated: while still young, Honoratus and Venantius had decided to join company with an old man before leaving their country, in order to give their escapade a more serious air:

> They did not wish, however, to be thought to have undertaken anything out of mere youthful foolhardiness and therefore took with them an old man who had attained to the very summit and perfection of weight and dignity. This was the holy Caprasius, whom they had always regarded as their father in Christ and who is still living the angelic life upon the islands.[64]

IS OBEDIENCE DUE TO PARENTS OR TO GOD?

The first-generation Christian authors broke with Latin tradition on one basic point: the authority of the *pater familias* was obliged to give way to divine authority. Writing as they were in a world where the majority were still pagan, they encouraged the conversion of young people whose parents opposed this. In such cases, they turned disobedience towards the parents into a duty. God has to be obeyed over and against parents. St Hilary of Arles relates the exemplary case of St Honoratus who drove his father to despair by converting to Christianity: 'Thus the father took the youth's renunciation to be a censure on his old age.' Coming from an illustrious family, St Honoratus' father despised the Christian religion, whose adherants were mostly of plebeian origin, and he did his best to distract his son, even trying 'to renew his own youth in a kind of comradeship with his young son', and leading him into earthly pleasures to make him forget his destiny. But Honoratus 'shrank from what his elderly father enjoyed and constantly plied himself with good advice',[65] and Hilary praises him for having held firm in his disobedience.

St Jerome was even harsher. In his letter to Heliodorus the Monk, he recommends total indifference towards the pleadings of parents if they try to turn him away from the monastic life:

> although your mother, with dishevelled hair and torn garments is displaying the breasts with which she nurtured you, although your father lies on the threshold, trample your father underfoot and set forth, fly with dry eyes to the standard of the cross. Cruelty is a kind of dutiful conduct in these circumstances, and only then, is it a sort of piety to be unfeeling . . . Now too, your onetime nurse, already old, and her spouse – second only to your own father in claims on your affection – exclaim: 'Wait a little for us to die, and then bury us.' Perhaps your foster mother, with pendulous breasts, her brow furrowed with wrinkles, recalling an old lullaby, may repeat it for you. But (you say) we must obey our parents. But whomsoever loves parents more than Christ loses his own soul.[66]

Later on, when European society was entirely Christianized, the writers firmly re-established the principle of filial obedience, which was however only moderately respected. In her ninth-century *Manual for my Son*, Dhuoda was particularly anxious to ensure the submission of her son, William, then aged 16, towards his father, Bernard of Septiminia, who must have been about 60. Given the high incidence of female mortality in childbirth and of subsequent remarriage with young women, especially among the nobility, the age differential between fathers and sons could be very great, creating a gap which was not conducive to good mutual understanding. Dhuoda was aware of this and she cited passages from Scripture for her son's benefit: 'Uphold old age; do not grieve it during its life and in your strength, do not despise it; honour your father, that you too may achieve old age.' Writing two years after the wars which characterized the revolts by the sons of Louis the Pious, she appears obsessed by the likelihood of a rift between father and son, 'an offence actually committed, as we know, by many people'.[67] In the same period Hincmar and Rabanus Maurus were also composing treatises on the obedience due to parents.

OLD MONKS

A flagrant example of the lack of consideration shown by the Church towards the old is provided by monastic life, the attempt to realize the

City of God on earth. Monastic rules set little store by old monks. The most famous rule is that of St Benedict, and it relegates them to the rank of children, recommending a degree of indulgence towards them:

> Although human nature itself is drawn to feel sympathy to those in these stages of life, namely the old and children, yet it is right that the authority of the Rule also should have regard to them. Their weakness should at all times be taken into consideration, and the letter of the Rule should by no means be applied to them in matters of food. Indeed they should always be thought of compassionately, and they should have their meals before the prescribed times.[68]

It was, however, quite out of the question to confer the slightest privilege on old age, for instance, where choosing the deans was concerned: 'Of the deans of the Monastery: They should not be chosen according to seniority but for their merits and their wisdom in teaching.'[69]

Among the Fathers in Jura, the least old were assimilated among the ill and were often the objects of scorn on the part of the young. Nevertheless, when the devil wanted to tempt St Romanus, he produced an old monk to advise him, thinking that he would thus be better listened to. When too, in the life of St Lupinus, the bursar wanted to tell the abbot something, he got five elders to accompany him to give his words greater weight.[70] In eastern monasticism, at Seridos, south of Gaza, the heads of the monasteries were given the title of 'great old men'. But in these last cases, old age was again respected for its symbolic value, because the actual situation of these old monks was in no way to be envied.

The *Rule of the Master* is a collection of monastic rules of the beginning of the ninth century based on the *Rule of St Benedict*, and it relegates old men to employment as gate-keepers: 'For two brothers made decrepit through age a lodging shall be constructed within the monastery gates and close to them.' They are to be entrusted with small manual jobs and will act as foils for the abbot's humility: 'These old men will eat with the abbot, on account of their age, according to the example of perfect humility provided by St Eugenia, when she said that she did not want to show herself superior even to them.'[71] The *Custumal of Chartreuse*, compiled at the beginning of the twelfth century by the Prior Guigues I mentions the old only to observe that they had been obliged to increase the number of conversi brothers: 'Some of them, in effect, were old and frail, and they could no longer work.'[72] Some communities even wanted their aged monks and nuns to return to their families; Salvian of Marseille was opposed to this idea.[73]

Trained as they were to see traces of sin and the marks of punishment in everything, Christian authors managed to discern them in premature death as well as in advanced old age. If human life is so brief, St Jerome wrote, this was firstly Adam's fault, who lost us our immortality, then that of our antediluvian ancestors, who lived longer than 900 years, which is 'semi-immortality'. Since Noah, we can no longer hope to live longer than a hundred:

> The brevity of human life is a punishment for our sins, and the fact that frequently on the very threshold of life the newborn child is overtaken by death is clear proof that the times are lapsing daily into wickedness. For when the serpent had dragged down to earth the first inhabitant of Paradise, entangled in its shaky coils, eternity was exchanged for mortality, but one of nine hundred and more years. The sentence of man's life had been deferred for so long that it amounted to a quasi-immortality – then, as sin gradually burst out anew, the impiety of the giants brought on the shipwreck of the entire world. After that baptism – if I may so call it – of the world thus cleansed, the life of man was contracted into a brief span of time.[74]

In spite of the puny span of his present existence, man is soon afflicted with the marks of decrepitude and he often experiences a miserable old age. However, Christian authors were not interested in flesh-and-blood old men: 'The inner man also has white hair', as John Chrysostom used to say, and it was this inner man who interested the Fathers, whose attitude was normative rather than objective. Old age constituted an abstract and symbolic problem. It is clear that in the last analysis Christianity did nothing to improve the position of old people. The old man was simply a weakling, and in the hospices no distinction was made between him and the beggars, the infirm and the sick. As far as the Church Fathers were concerned, old age did not present a specific problem, and they were interested in old people's ugliness simply as a fine image of sin, of which it was in any case the consequence. On other occasions, physical old age would be rejected in favour of a wholly abstract old age which bore no relation to age, and which was held to be synonymous with virtue and wisdom.

6

The Early Middle Ages:

Indifference to Age

From the sixth century onwards, the Church was the sole unifying element in the youthful Western Europe emerging chaotically from the ruins of Romanitas. However, although she managed to salvage the shreds of the civilization of antiquity in the episcopal towns and monasteries, and although she brought about the slow penetration of the new moral values and forms of piety characterizing Christianity, she contributed nothing new concerning the place of old people in society. At the very most, she restricted herself to trying to limit brutality towards them, in so far as they belonged among the weak. Apart from the symbolic role she attributed to the old, the Church never considered them as a specific group. Consequently, the condition of the old was to be determined by pagan customs and was to be arbitrarily modified according to how this troubled period evolved.

It was a period of conflict, of diversity, of contrasts and contradictions. The invasions stripped off the veneer of institutional and legal unity imposed by the Roman empire. It was replaced by young, sometimes ephemeral and always fluctuating barbarian kingdoms. Social relations juxtaposed or combined some pre-Roman, mainly Celtic, customs, which had never disappeared and which re-emerged in the westernmost regions, among the wreckage of the *jus romanorum*, and the newcomers' Germanic traditions, themselves very diverse. Nothing could be more ill-defined than this legal cocktail of the Merovingian and Carolingian periods and the attempts at clarifying it by modern lawyers, while worthy, should not hide the truth. The only universally accepted principle in these societies, whatever its various disguises, was the law of the strongest, or the most cunning, which is the same thing. And the old are seldom the winners at this game.

However, as we shall see, their situation was not as deplorable as one might imagine *a priori*. Barbarian societies were not the worst where the weak were concerned. The constant presence of supernatural elements, the multitude of taboos and belief in the immanence of punishment all acted as obstacles to pure brutality. Everything that seemed to touch the divine world from close to or from afar, from the madman to the epileptic, passing via the old man, was the object of superstitious respect, although there were no general rules. Theirs was a world basically characterized by contrasts and contradictions, as flagrantly illustrated by the condition of old people.

THE AMBIGUOUS SITUATION OF OLD WARRIORS

In this intensely brutal period, an old man might often be a former warrior who had not found death in combat and who was obliged to wait for illness and weariness to finish him off. There ensued a primary ambiguity; if death in battle was glorious, was it not more so to kill one's opponents and so achieve decrepitude, unvanquished and covered with scars? Such was the misfortune of the Anglo-Saxon hero Beowulf, whose story is told in a famous epic poem, composed in the eighth century in England, and which enjoyed a level of renown in the British Isles comparable to that of the *Song of Roland* at a later date.[1] The action takes place in the fifth and sixth centuries in southern Scandinavia: the invincible hero, after having triumphed over numerous dragons, returns home to tell of his adventures. His account of the banquet given in his honour by the 'Scylding king' anticipates his own inevitable old age and retirement.

> We took our seats at the banquet-place.
> There we had story telling, there we had music:
> The old Scylding, time-schooled, told over the past;
> Now the hero of battles awoke the harp's sweetness.
> Plucked the happy strings; now sang a poem
> Heartbreaking and true; and the great-spirited king
> Recited after tradition a narrative of marvels;
> And then again the warrior in chains of old age
> Would begin to bewail his youth and his war-strength --
> His breast was vexed within him, while the crowding memories
> came to him from so many winters.
>
> (*Beowulf*, ll. 2104–14)

Of course, an old chief enjoys the wisdom age brings, and Beowulf will rule for 50 years yet; like his long-lived father Ecgetheow, the old king of the Geats, before him:

> Well known was my father among the peoples,
> A princely battle-chief, Ecgetheow his name;

Many many years he lived before he left us.
Went from our courts: him every counsellor
Happily remembers far and wide.

(Beowulf, ll. 262–6)

After the war came the time of wisdom, and the old warriors formed
a group whose duty was to read the marks of Fate:

Immediately the wise-hearted men who were looking
With Hrothgar at the water saw that its waves
In their streaming tumult were all stirred turbid.
That the flood was blood-flecked. The grey-streaked heads.
The old men, drew together speaking of the good warrior.
How they thought the prince would never return
Come back in victory to visit again
The illustrious king.

(Beowulf, ll. 1591–8)

But resigning themselves to this passive role was hard. Nothing
matched up to fighting, and becoming wise men was but meagre
consolation to those who could no longer hold a spear. When it came
to choosing between strength and wisdom, they did not hesitate and
old Beowulf, albeit loaded with years, longed to do battle once more:

Beowulf spoke, uttered his vows,
For the last time: many are the battles
I dared when I was young; yet old as I am
And guardian of this folk, I shall still join fight,
Still deal with glory if that fiend of wickedness
Comes out to attack me from his hall of earth.

(Beowulf, ll. 2510–15)

When all was said and done, the warrior could decide between dying
by the sword, the dagger or the lance, and experiencing the ugliness of
old age. For Beowulf, old age presented a false ambiguity, because it
was not a choice: an old man is wise or otherwise; he acquires his
experience through necessity, but preferable by far is the strength of
his muscles!

This false dilemma is also to be found among many other peoples.
Tacitus had already observed it among the ancient Germans who
appeared to make a great fuss of old age. In their assemblies, the chiefs
spoke in order of age, beginning with the oldest; young warriors would
often receive their weapons in a form of dubbing from the hands of the
chief's father; the ritual of precedence put age before birth, military

glory and eloquence. But in peacetime none of this prevented the idle warriors from leaving domestic and distasteful work to the women and old men.[2]

Many Roman historians even stated that the Germans used to kill off their old. According to Procopius, an old man of the Herulae would himself ask his family to put him to death, which would be done by swordstroke before placing the body on a pyre.[3] Caesar hinted at an identical practice among the Gauls. The Scandinavians had a rite which involved marking an old man with the point of a javelin, thus dedicating him to Odin, evoking (perhaps) the actual putting to death which used to take place in ancient times.[4] Pliny the Elder speaks of old people committing suicide among the Hyperboreans. A Norwegian law post-dating the introduction of Christianity stated that old people and those incapable of supporting themselves were to be put in a hole in the cemetery and left to die.[5] For these people, dying in battle was certainly preferable to dying of old age.

The same opinion was prevalent among the Alans, according to Ammianus Marcellinus: 'They regard it as the height of good fortune to lose one's life in battle; those who grow old and die a natural death are bitterly reviled as degenerate cowards.'[6] The *Saga of Gautreks* mentions old people committing suicide by throwing themselves off a cliff, and the Venerable Bede testified to a similar practice in Sussex during a famine.[7] In any case, such events occurred only seldom, and were restricted to periods when the survival of the group was threatened. In normal circumstances, the old were cared for out of family solidarity.

Some folklorists think that the Celts used to practise putting old people to death during the Druidic period. P. Sebillot relies on oral tradition to claim that in Armorica excessively hardy old people were finished off by being forced to climb Mane Guen, the White Mountain of Guenin. In Scandinavian, Germanic and Slav mythologies features reminiscent of those we studied concerning the Greeks may be found: the old, aged gods have all perished during a battle against the young gods. Extreme prudence is required, however, before mooting the possibility of a link between the existence of a real generation clash and of a rejection of the old among these peoples of the remote past.

THE FIRST FORMS OF RETIREMENT

In any case, it does appear that, as with primitive peoples, finishing off the old was an exceptional measure relating to the prehistoric phase of these peoples, except in the situation reported by Bede. The Celts and Germans and the Scandinavians entered history during the early medieval period. They were engaged to varying degrees in a process of stabilization. Efforts were being made to introduce Christian morality, and murder, whether legal, ritual or customary, was no longer accepted, whatever the victim's age.

So what happened to old people? In general they were assured of subsistence by family solidarity. Among the wealthy, however, individuals began to take steps to ensure a peaceful retirement for themselves, one which would be safe and comfortable and at the same time would guarantee eternal salvation. The Church had in fact created an additional preoccupation for mankind. To the already tricky problem of survival in this world was now added the anxiety of having to merit eternal felicity in the next. While the family was in most cases able to assist in the first need, it was powerless about the other one. Although the concept of solidarity, and of collective punishment and rewards, was still well-entrenched in the population, individualism was already insinuating itself among the dominant categories, the moneyed and educated élite, which was beginning to envisage salvation as a personal matter between God and oneself. And indeed, a wealthy old man had the means of ensuring his salvation while living out his old age sheltered from disregard: by retiring to a monastery.

This practice, which was born in the sixth century, marked a turning point in the history of old age. Firstly because it introduced the idea of a fundamental break in human life and thus induced awareness of the specific nature of old age. Secondly, because old age became synonymous with ceased activity and breaking with the professional world. The term 'retirement' was gradually to acquire these different meanings. While the old Roman patricians certainly might also retire to their estates in order to end their lives in peace there, theirs was only a partial retirement. They kept in touch with their friends and family, they continued to lead a social life, they managed their own farms, and they stayed at home in their own villas, surrounded by their families or else frequently visited by them.

This in no way compares with the isolation represented by a monastery, even if the life led there was not that of a recluse. The break with the world was here much more radical. And then, since they were all old men, the monastery represented a far-distant blueprint for the old people's home, being both a refuge and a ghetto. Thus was the modern idea of setting the old apart first mooted, initially as a voluntary process. The segregation of the generations was germinating, as too was the specific nature of old age, but in a negative sense. Old men, being cut off from the life of this world, were in transit; they were preparing for eternal life. They were no longer completely of this world, but were not yet of the next. As the antechamber to life everlasting, retirement to a monastery provided old age with its chief preoccupation: that of ensuring its salvation.

Of course, these trends appeared only in draft form during the early Middle Ages, when retirement affected only a very meagre minority of great personages. Cassiodorus (480–575), counsellor to Theodoric and friend of Pope Agapit, was to provide the first illustrious instance. He was favoured with exceptional longevity – 95 years – and spent his last years in Vivarium, his Calabrian monastery. His was also a studious retirement; he installed a workshop of editors and translators and compiled encyclopaedic treatises, working, along with his companions, for posterity; 'scribantur haec in generatione altera.'

The fashion was extended in the eighth and especially the ninth centuries, in the Carolingian period, with the multiplication of the great monasteries Fulda, Corvey, St-Gall and Reichenau, all of which included lodgings for old men. The monks, who benefited from generous donations by their wealthy retired members, encouraged this trend. Two different régimes were permitted; some lived a quasi-monastic existence, participating in the offices of the community and living with the monks, whereas others were lodged apart and received an alimentary pension. In the monastery of St-Gall, one contract specified the conditions of keep for a retired layman. He was to enjoy a heated room of his own, a new habit every year, and the revenues of a life-prebend equal to that of two monks. Some did indeed practise humility, such as the wealthy landowner Willibald, who gave the abbey an estate in return for being received in the poor hospice. His contract stipulated simply that his daily nourishment be the same as that of the monks, that he be provided annually with a woollen and a linen robe, with a mantle every three years, with shoes and everything similar to that of the monks. At Cysoing, near Lille, the canons undertook to lodge an aged layman, to provide him with two loaves like their own every day, with a portion of stew, a pint of beer and two litres of wine, and to give him five *sous* for his clothing every year.[8]

THE MISFORTUNES OF THE INDIGENT OLD

There was no question of the indigent old enjoying a voluntary retirement. This was to remain the prerogative of the privileged categories until the twentieth century. The poor man had to go on working for as long as his strength permitted, after which his communal family would support him -- after a fashion. But if he was unlucky enough to be on his own, he was immediately relegated to the ranks of the beggars, this wholesale category which embraced the infirm, the sick, orphans, madmen, old men and cripples of all kinds. Once included among the mass of the poor, the old man cannot be distinguished from his companions in misfortune. He belongs to the more general history of poverty.[9]

During the early Middle Ages, the number of poor people increased following the invasions and the deteriorated condition of the peasantry.

Christianity was still superficial and the clerics predominantly understood poverty to be evidence of man's sinfulness and fall from grace, which did nothing to encourage organized charity. Even a man as remarkable as the Venerable Bede expressed no regret at the existence of so many poor people.[10] Alms-giving was certainly a duty, but one destined to ensure the salvation of him who gave; people did not as yet talk of loving the poor and even less about their eminent worth.

Is it possible to know what sort of place the old occupied in this world of wretches? They were listed alongside others, in no particular order; they were frequently even omitted. When Rather, Bishop of Verona (890–974), evoked the unfortunate inhabitants of northern Italy in the tenth century, he mentioned 'widows, orphans, captives, defeated, infirm, blind, crippled and weak'.[11] While the old were undoubtedly included in each of these categories, nobody thought of turning them into a distinct category, because this classification was determined by the causes of poverty. The poor were to remain ageless for a very long time. This was one of the important differences between them and the well-off categories, among which the notion of retirement, and thus of classes of age, began to emerge. In this sense, no history of old age in the peasant world of the Middle Ages is possible.

Nevertheless, the very occasional comment reveals that within the mass of poor people, the old were among the most wretched. We can glimpse them in the institution of the poor register, first mentioned in the second half of the fifth century in Gaul. Each church and monastery drew up 'a list on which were inscribed the poor people to whom was distributed a reserved portion'. These privileged persons among the wretched, the *matricularii*, were lodged, given provisions and clothes. Their number was obviously very restricted compared to the multitude of beggars in the mid seventh century, for instance.[12]

From the eighth century onwards, following the confiscation of Church lands by Charles Martel and his successors, people's chances of finding succour were further reduced and in the Carolingian period, according to Hincmar, the *matricularii* were chosen from among the most wretched of the wretched, the old men and the infirm, excluding the healthy poor. The number of those chosen became symbolic: they were 12 at Corbie, St-Gall and St-Paul of Lyon. The mutual help associations, which can be glimpsed in the *Capitulary of Herstal* of 779 and in England, were not any more effective. Some texts even suggest that public charity was directed towards the infirm rather than the old. Thus we read of an old blind man in Aix who refused to pray for the return of his sight, since he would then lose his alms, which he owed to his blindness and not to his old age:

> Why do I need the vision I lost so long ago? It is worth more to me to be deprived of it than to have it. Blind, I can beg and none will repulse me. Rather, they hasten to attend to my needs. But

if I got my sight back, it would seem wrong for me to beg alms even though I am old and weak and cannot work.[13]

The Church found it hard to accept that old age in itself justified preferential treatment and a specific attitude towards it. In the *Books of Timothy to the Church*, Salvian of Marseille pronounced that the old should be content with a sufficiency and that they should not use their weakness as a pretext for demanding more.[14] A sermon of the ninth century stipulated that old people should not plead their age to obtain a dispensation from attending matins every Sunday, even though they might live far from the church.[15] Under these conditions, an old man could not expect much sympathy from those around him, which explains the advice given by the author of *Beowulf*: while you are young, be open-handed and make friends, so that when old age comes and your enemies are gathering, your loyal companions will keep close by your side.

A PRECARIOUS FAMILY SITUATION

For even if one were not alone, little could be expected of one's children. Firstly, Celtic and Germanic custom put a legal term to a father's authority once he had become physically incapable of instilling respect. An old man was thus at the mercy of those around him. However, Caesar and the *jurisconsultus* Gaius had observed that, among the Celts, the father of the family was master in his own home, of his house and his family, and that in Gaul he exercised a form of *patria potestas* like the Romans, with the right of life and death over his children.[16] Irish and Welsh laws testify to the same powers, but they fixed a limit to them: in Ireland this was incapacity on the father's part, and in north Wales the son won his emancipation on taking up military service, that is, at the age of 14. This was when the son left the tutelage of his father in order to enter the service of his chief, to whom he had been presented.[17]

The old man thus lost control over his family fairly early on, and his authority over the woman of the household was far from being as absolute as in Rome. He was in any case only the caretaker of the family property, for which he was accountable. The nuclear family was integrated into a much wider group, which, while ensuring material support for the old, did not confer any particular power on them. In Ireland, the group consisted of the *gelfine* (father, son, grandson and great-grandson), of the *derbfine* (grandfather, uncle, first cousin), the *iarfine* (great-grandfather and great-uncle) and the *indfine* (great-grandfather, great-great uncle, and two degrees of cousinship). Family solidarity was tight, but the head of the group, who played a political, legal and military role, was chosen on account of his popularity, his wealth and strength, which practically excluded the old. They were entirely dependent.

In the Germanic world at the time of the invasions, those who did not bear arms were subject to the *mundium*, their father's authority, but his power ceased once his children had assumed arms. It was perpetual only where women and slaves were involved.[18] The Merovingian kingship perpetuated this practice. The *mundium* of the family father, which included the right of correction, as well as the death penalty, over his children, the right to consent to their marriage and to their entering the priesthood, the right to represent them in contract and private vengeance, and to administer family property, ceased as soon as his son reached the age of 14, when he was given his arms. This ceremony was gradually neglected and the boy then became responsible for himself at the age of 15. As for the wife, she left her father's *mundium* only to enter under that of her husband. From then on, she could not act without her husband's consent, from which only widowhood would free her. Old widows were undoubtedly entitled to act in justice on their own behalf.[19] What does emerge from all this is that old men, having no authority over anyone, had to rely on the goodwill of the group.

Did not this fact alone contribute towards encouraging elderly landowners to retire to a monastery, in exchange for donating part of a domain, in order to provide for their old age? This is all the more probable given that filial piety does not seem to have been a dominant quality among Merovingian and Carolingian ruling circles. Among the latter, a father's authority does not appear to have been respected once he was no longer physically capable of maintaining his rank. The legal code of the Bavarians stated explicitly that the son of a chief must not seek to replace his father as long as the latter is powerful, can assist the king in person, lead the army, ride on horseback, bear arms and is neither deaf nor blind,[20] which suggests on the one hand that generation clashes and revolts against fathers must have occurred frequently, and on the other hand that old men no longer able to hold their own were excluded from power.

Other texts imply much the same. In the tenth century we saw how anxious Dhuoda was to keep her son loyal to his father. Rabanus Maurus testified to this type of preoccupation in his *Liber de reverentia filorum erga patres et erga reges* (book about the reverence of sons towards fathers and towards kings), while Einhard insisted in his *Life of Charlemagne* on the merits of the great Emperor who had always honoured Bertha, his mother. People in high places provided plenty of bad examples. Gregory of Tours provides a few rare instances of kings attaining old age, only to be murdered by their sons in their impatience to rule. Clovis was thus supposed to have written to Chloderic, the son of old Sigebert the Lame, King of the Ripuarian Franks: 'Your father is old and lame. Were he to die, his kingdom would fall to you by right and you would be my ally.' So Chloderic killed his father, before being himself murdered by envoys of Clovis. In the Carolingian period, the revolts by the sons of Louis the Pious provide an illustrious instance of this sort of behaviour.

On the whole, the early Middle Ages seem to have provided old people with little security on the family level. The law did not favour them. Depending as they did on the goodwill of their family, they had no safeguards. It can be deduced from the very brutal customs of the age, which a superficial Christianity had done little to alleviate, that the fate of its weaker elements was unenviable. Their mediocre value in the eyes of their contemporaries is well expressed by their value in terms of the Wergeld. It is revealing that the hagiographical accounts of the saints of that period never allow grandparents to feature. The great amount of recent research into the structure of the family in the Merovingian world shows that the role of the extended family has hitherto been exaggerated by historians.[21] In fact, the restricted nuclear family seems to have been predominant everywhere; where grandparents are concerned, we are met only with silence.

This silence augurs ill for them. Where did the old go? Nowadays it can no longer be maintained that they were practically non-existent. A good proportion of those who reached the age of 20 had a fair chance of living into their sixties. If they do not appear in the records, it is not because they did not exist, it is because they did not matter. In Rome, the old were talked about because they played a role. In the early Middle Ages, when they are estimated to have formed a negligible quantity, they were left out of the texts, already so rare, out of the legends and out of religious literature. The poorer ones joined the troupes of beggars; the wealthier ones took refuge in the monasteries. Many were undoubtedly supported by their families, but they were without power, without a defined position, and were condemned to vegetate while waiting on death.

Celtic poems and legends portray the degrading condition of the old with pathos. An epic Welsh poem tells the story of Llywarch hen, the old chief who lived in the sixth century and fought against the Saxons. He had 24 sons, all of whom had died in combat. On growing old, he saw his last child, Gwen, leave him in his turn to go to do battle. 'The old man was not weak when he was young!' Gwen says to his father to console him by reminding him that he has had his hour of glory. But Gwen too is killed, and Llywarch laments: 'Gwen, misfortune to him who is too old and who has lost you.' Left on his own, the old warrior intones the extraordinary *Can yr Henwr*, the 'song of the old man', a bitter complaint about the weakness, the infirmities, the solitude and the end of pleasure, friendship and love which characterize the old man. In its intensity his plaint rivals that of Ptah Hotep, 3,000 years distant:

Before I had a back like a cross,
I was fleet and fast talking. My exploits were admired.
The men of Argoet always came to my help.

Although I have a back like a cross
I was strong, I was welcomed in the beer houses;
O Powys, Paradise of Wales!

Although my back is bent crooked,
I was handsome; my stroke was the first; it met the first blow.
My back is bent; I am heavy, I am pitiable.

. . .

Staff of wood, familiar branch,
May you support a nostalgic old man
Llywarch the Dotard!

What a mockery is old age,
And myself, from the hair to the teeth and the ankles
Which women love.

. . .

What I loved as a young man
I now hate; a girl, a stranger and an unbroken horse
Now I can no longer match them.

. . .

I am old, I am alone,
I am cold and misshapen, The glory of my progeny gone,
I am pitiable, I am bent double.

I am old and bent double:
I am inconstant and demented, I am mad, I am wild.
All who loved me love me no more.

The young girls love me no more;
Nobody visits me. I cannot move from here, alas.
O death, which comes not.[22]

    The poetic soul of the Celts found its only possible remedy against
old age in dreams and imagination. Beneath the sea, beneath the lakes,

are to be found marvellous countries, the lands of eternal youth; no one grows older in certain distant islands where goddesses rule. As is the case on the Isle of Avalon in the legend of the Round Table, or on the isle of the apple trees, where time is abolished. The hero Bran spent two months there which were two centuries in the ordinary world, thus anticipating relativity in truly poetic fashion. 'We are without old age or cemetery since the beginning of creation', as its inhabitants said.[23]

Until the nineteenth century old men were considered in Celtic tradition as the harbingers of the Beyond. Clear traces of this concept can be found in the *Legends of Death* by Anatole Le Braz. 'The old woman of Ker Is' appears at night time to the two young men and asks for their help; had they accepted, the town of Is would have been resuscitated. 'The old man of Tourc'h' returns to play tricks on his servant and to give his widow a child. 'The old hemp-spinner' returns to his room to spin until a mass is said for him. In *The Three Women*, a mysterious old man can tell the past and the future and knows what happens in the Beyond. In several accounts, old women come to help a woman in labour: if the child is born at night time, the oldest woman goes to the threshold to read the new born baby's future in the stars.[24]

THE DEMOGRAPHIC PROBLEM: WERE THERE OLD PEOPLE DURING THE EARLY MIDDLE AGES?

Generally speaking, the presence of the old in these pagan practices, superstitions and recitals contrasts with their near absence from Christian stories. And this although these same hagiographical recitals, which kept quiet about the old, often made their heroes live to an advanced and even an improbable old age. This was the case in the 'Lives of the Breton Saints', which have been studied by Bernard Merdrignac.[25] Alone among all these venerable persons, Meloir and Salomon, who were murdered, and Goulven and Suliac, who died of a fever, led a brief existence. For his part, the Anglo-Saxon chronicler Nennius, did not hesitate in his *Kentish Chronicle* to attribute St Patrick with 85 years of preaching in Ireland before his death at the good old age of 120. In his *Welsh Annals* he even came close to antediluvian biblical models when he attributed the Bishop of Ebur with 350 years.[26] Nor indeed did Frankish historians, when retracing the origins of the Merovingian dynasty, demonstrate a greater sense of proportion:[27] the legendary Pharamond, whom they claimed was one of Priam's sons, lived to be 300, as did his sons and grandsons. His descendant Clodion died at the age of 170, and his son, Merovius, at the age of 146. Some historians managed, by combining several generations within one individual, to attribute Pharamond with 2,000 years of life.

These exaggerations did not necessarily indicate that old age enjoyed any prestige in real life. In many cases, the authors took their inspiration from the Book of Genesis and their extraordinary sums were only intended to enhance the epic, heroic and supernatural character of their recital: it can even be said that over the age of 100, these old men were no longer old men, but mythological heroes who had been released from the human condition. Far from testifying to the admiration of contemporaries for actual old age, such fabulous accounts of longevity were rather a means of allowing the heroes to escape the weaknesses and limitations of human decrepitude. Such fabulous forms of old age were a negation of actual and real old age. This is confirmed by inverse forms of exaggeration. Childeric, at the age of eight, was leading armies, raping women and girls, and enjoying an unbroken sequence of debauchery and orgies; he already possessed all the qualities required by a good adult Merovingian. None of this enables one to state that a glorification of childhood was involved. Like Hercules strangling the serpents in his cradle, what was involved was simply an illustration of the hero's fabulous character. The need to exaggerate people's ages, in one direction or another, is a sign of dissatisfaction with things as they really are. If real old men enjoyed so much prestige, why would the need to multiply their longevity by a factor of two or three be felt at all?

If we now descend from the level of fable to that of demography, we will obviously encounter the problem of source material. How many old people were there in sixth to tenth century Europe and how long did they live? Both these questions elicit merriment among demographers for the very good reason that serious quantitative records are completely lacking for this period. If Caesar is to be believed, however, the inhabitants of Gaul were not incapable of keeping a tally: 'A roll was found in the Helvetian camp, written in Greek characters, and brought to Caesar. It contained a list of all who had set out on this expedition capable of bearing arms, likewise of the children, women and old men.'[28]

It is a great pity that Caesar has not communicated these figures to us. Consequently, we are reduced to estimates based on reports by a few individuals, a dozen skeletons from scattered Merovingian cemeteries, from funerary inscriptions, from rare references by the chroniclers and from many guesses and deductions *a priori*. Many historians have concluded from these meagre findings that there must in fact have been very few old people in that brutal and primitive world. How many men and women could have slipped through the tight meshes of the net cast by death, meshes woven of malnutrition, famines, epidemics, wars, lack of hygiene, medical ignorance and high infant mortality? Given that human life in those days involved such a fearful obstacle race, how many combatants were able to complete it without accident and live

The Early Middle Ages

Table 6.1 Age at death of Merovingian rulers

Rulers	Date of birth (presumed)	Date of decease	Age at decease
Clovis	467	511	45 yrs
Thierry I	486	534	48 yrs
Clodomir	492	524	32 yrs
Childebert	495	558	63 yrs
Clotaire I	497	561	64 yrs
Caribert	521	567	46 yrs
Gontran	545	592	47 yrs
Sigebert I	535	575	40 yrs
Chilperic I	539	584	45 yrs
Childebert I	570	596	26 yrs
Clotaire II	584	629	45 yrs
Theodebert II	586	612	26 yrs
Thierry II	587	613	26 yrs
Dagobert I	604	639	35 yrs
Caribert	606	632	26 yrs
Sigebert III	631	656	25 yrs
Clovis II	632	657	25 yrs
Dagobert II	650	680	30 yrs
Clotaire III	652	673	21 yrs
Childeric II	653	675	22 yrs
Thierry III	654	691	38 yrs
Chilperic II	670	721	51 yrs
Clovis III	682	695	13 yrs
Childebert II	683	711	28 yrs
Childeric III	714	751	41 yrs
Dagobert III	699	715	16 yrs
Clotaire IV	700	719	19 yrs
Thierry IV	713	737	26 yrs

Source: Maurice Bouvier-Ajam, Dagobert, Tallandier, 1980, pp. 44–5.

into their sixties? Only a tiny minority, according to Pierre Riché, who has paid particular attention to these questions.[29] He has investigated the inscriptions of the necropolis of Choulans at Lyon, which date from the seventh century, and those of Grigny, and has discovered that they do not include anybody over 60. The literary texts appear to convey the same information. Gregory of Tours, for instance, considers the age of 70 to be exceptional.[30]

Merovingian rulers generally died young, either murdered or killed in battle or worn out by debauchery. Maurice Bouvier-Ajam[31] has provided the dates in table 6.1, which reveal the age of death for each of them.

Of these 28 kings, only two lived longer than 60 years, and then only by a margin: Childebert I (63 years) and Clotaire (64). Three of the latter's sons died young, as did two of Chilperic's sons. Caribert's son died at the age of three, Clotaire's at the age of six. Nantilde, Dagobert's legitimate wife, died at the age of 33, while Ragnetrude, one of his concubines, died aged 43. The only member of the dynasty to reach the age of 70 was its foundress, Clotilde (475–545), wife to Clovis. According to Gregory of Tours, 'Queen Clotilde died at an advanced age and rich in good works, in the city of Tours, in Bishop Injuriosus' time.' Her record was perhaps matched by Queen Ingoberg, King Caribert's widow. The same author, who knew her well and had conversed with her shortly before her death, declared: 'I think that she was in her seventieth year.' However, there was also the famous Brunehaut, still a great beauty when over 50, who died aged around 80 at the end of a troubled life after three days of torture and stoning, dragged behind a galloping horse. Going by the royal family, it does indeed seem that people very seldom achieved old age in that period. Is their example significant, however? One has only to read Gregory of Tours to be convinced that political assassination played a primary role in determining the average age of decease among the great.

There are records which indicate the opposite. Take for instance Khindaswintz, who was elected king of the Visigoths at the age of 79 in the seventh century. If we stay with the ruling families, it becomes flagrantly apparent that the Carolingians, who did not inherit their predecessors' mania for murder, lived to a much greater age. Their ancestor, Pepin of Landen, who died in 640, was touching 90, and his wife Induberge lived to over 60. The Duke of Adaglise, father of Pepin of Heristal, was 84 years old at his death, and his brother Clodulf, Bishop of Metz, was 92. Although Pepin of Heristal, Charles Martel and Pepin the Short did not live to 60 (56, 55 and 54 respectively), Bertha of the Big Feet lived 61 years and her famous son, Charlemagne, 72 years.

He was indeed an exceptional person from many points of view, and it behoves us to dwell a while on his case. Thanks to Einhard, we are relatively well-informed about this great Emperor's last years, and we can assist at his progressive decline, punctuated by extraordinary bounds of energy. It was the image of the old man *à la barbe fleurie* which legend was to retain, and history too sometimes. Charlemagne was to become the incarnation of a glorious and vigorous old age, and popular imagination, influenced by the *Chanson de Roland*, was to represent him as a perpetually old man, the antithesis of Alexander. With Charlemagne, old age penetrated the world of prowess, where he kept company with Arthur, another greybeard and one much more legendary than himself. Charlemagne entered legend much later on, however, as will be seen further on in the book. For the moment, let us follow the ageing emperor's last historical years.[32]

Charlemagne made his last will only at the age of 64, on 6 February 806. He was still very active, as the numerous reforms dating from that period prove. He was, however, sensitive to signs. The following year, an eclipse of the sun and Mercury in a changing phase made him fear that his end was nigh. This did not prevent him from going to Baden, north of Verdun, in 808, to meet the King of the Danes, and in 810 at the age of 68, he called up the army to meet the Scandinavian threat. For the first time, however, the chronicler shows him indecisive about the question of whether to launch the campaign in Frisia or Danemark. The year 810 boded ill in other ways. The Emperor saw his eldest daughter Rotrud die, and then Gisela, his youngest: the country was ravaged by an epidemic: defections multiplied and he suffered a bad fall from his horse. He was felt to be more hesitant than ever before and overwhelmed by fear. His anguish over his salvation caused him to effect a general confession of his sins in a letter to the clergy, and he thought seriously about abdicating in order to retire to a monastery. He did not do so, but the spring was broken. From then on the old man's decline was rapid. In 811 he drew up a second will and, tormented by gout, once more considered retiring to a monastery. Only one of all his sons was left to him, the weakest, Louis, 32 years old, whom Charlemagne officially designated his successor in 813. In the autumn, he still hunted for a month, before working on the correction of the Vulgate. He died in the following year of pleurisy.

Arthur, whose legend antedates that of Charlemagne, also owed his fame in part to his longevity, which turned him into the wise and respectable type of king who is still redoubtable in spite of his age. This British hero's reign occurred between 475 and 515, and he must have been around 65 or 70 at his death.[33] It is in any case remarkable that the Anglo-Saxons' wergeld, unlike that of the Visigoths and the Franks, did not set different rates according to age. Does this imply that the Anglo Saxons had more respect for the old?[34]

However, it was not only among the rulers that old people were to be found. Although the cemetery at Choulans did not include any sexagenarians, that on the island of Lavret, on the coast of Trégor, dating from the seventh century, contained many septuagenarians. And the precious cartulary of the Abbey of St-Victor of Marseille, which enumerates the serfs on the abbey's domain in the ninth century, shows us that even among this category of poor peasants, more than 11 per cent of the adults were aged over 60:[35]

56 serfs were aged between 20 and 24 years
50 serfs were aged between 25 and 29 years
80 serfs were aged between 30 and 39 years
58 serfs were aged between 40 and 49 years

37 serfs were aged between 50 and 59 years
17 serfs were aged between 60 and 69 years
6 serfs were aged between 70 and 79 years
4 serfs were aged between 80 and 99 years

Robert Étienne has studied the family demography of the Bordelais poet Ausonius between the chronological limits of the late Roman empire and the early Middle Ages, using his *Parentalia*, a compilation of funerary verse effected in 384.[36] The author addressed his text to the dead members of his family, giving the age of decease of each one of them. The results are astonishing: of the 14 men mentioned, Iulius Calippio died aged 65, Paulinus aged 72, Flavius Sanctus aged 80, Ausonius himself aged 84, Iulius Ausonius aged 88 and Ceacilius Argicius Arborius aged 92 years. Masculine longevity was far greater than that of the women, of whom only three out of 12 reached the age of 60: Iulia Dryadia (60 years), Aemilia Corinthia Maura and Aemilia Hilaria (63 years). The average age for men can be set at 44 years, and for women at 33.7 years. This difference is confirmed by other research into the demography of the Bordelais area and into slave and freedman circles.[37]

Thus the old were, if not excessively numerous, in no way an unknown species. They consisted mostly of men, given that the number of women was severely reduced by the dangers accompanying childbirth. Once they had survived to their twentieth year, the men of the Merovingian and Carolingian ages could expect to live as long as we do, and if the sources do not mention them, this was basically because they played only a negligible social role and were dependent on the care of their families.

THE IMPORTANCE OF OLD MEN AMONG THE CLERGY

There was, however, one circle where the old were particularly numerous: the Church. Although ecclesiastics dedicated, as we have seen, scant space in their writings to old age, nevertheless they knew what old age meant in the flesh. Innumerable bishops and monks attained a very advanced old age, which is easily understood: the sacred nature of their person generally protected them (though not always) from the murders which decimated the political world. Enjoying a standard of living superior to that of the rest of the population, they were fed a more balanced diet and were less affected by the epidemics and famines. The monasteries were the sole havens of peace, relatively sheltered from massacres. The asceticism of many monks and hermits testifies to their frequently uncommon physical toughness.

Looked at from this angle, it is less surprising that longevity was thought to signify a divine reward for a virtuous life. St Anthony, the father of monasticism, was the very type of those hermits who were protected from contamination by their healthy and ascetic lives in the desert: 'Then, for the first time, those who had come saw him. They were struck with admiration: his appearance had stayed the same; he had neither grown fatter through lack of exercise, nor emaciated by fasts and struggles with demons, but was just as they had known him before his retreat.'[38] What a splendid old man of 105 he must have been, as described by St Anthasius, Bishop of Alexandria (251–356)!

How many other eastern monks also lived to an extreme old age, like Simeon 'the Young' who died on top of his column at the age of 75 in 592. In the west, the hermit Patroclus in the Berry region lived over 80 years; St Genevieve over 90; St Benedict of Aniane over 70 (750–821); the Abbot St William of Volpiano died at the age of 69 (962–1031); Theodore of Tarsus, who was chosen in the seventh century by the Pope to become the Archbishop of Canterbury at the age of 67, remained active until the age of 88. Venantius Fortunatus was also nominated bishop when aged 67 at Poitiers, and he died three years later. Salvian of Marseille lived 94 years (390–484); St Germain of Auxerre lived 70 years (635–705), as did the chronicler Einhard (770–849), and most of these venerable personages were remarkably active right up till the end, like Boniface, who was murdered while performing his ministry.

What's more, there was also St Columban, who died at the age of 75 (540–615), Walbert, Abbot of Luxeuil, who died at the age of 66 (604–70), Isidore of Seville, dead at the age of 76 (560–636), St Eucherius, who was elected Bishop of Lyon at the age of 65 in 435, and who remained in office until the age of 80 (370–450). Let us add Ephraim of Nisibis, who lived 67 years (306–73), Anathasius, Bishop of Alexandria, who lived 78 years (295–373), John Chrysostom who lived 62 years (345–407), Cyril of Jerusalem, who lived 74 years (313–87), St Jerome, who lived 73 years (347–420), St Augustine, who lived to be 75 (354–430), St Ireneus, who lived 78 years (130–208), Origen, who lived 67 years (185–252), Eusebius of Caesarea, who lived 75 years (265–340) and St Bernard of Menthon, who founded the Petit and the Grand-St-Bernard hospices and lived 64 years (923–1009), as well as Narsai, who organized the Persian Nestorian Church and lived to be 100 (402–502), Rather, Bishop of Verona, who lived 84 years (890–974), St Patrick, who lived 70 years (390–460), Maximus the Confessor who lived to be 82 (580–662), John Moschus who lived 79 years (540–619), St Benedict of Nursia who lived 67 years (480–547), and finally Lactantius, who lived to be 80 (245–325). Whenever St Augustine wrote to the primates of the Church, he was always addressing old men, such as Primate Aurelius, Primate Donatian and the Primate of Numidia, all of them holy old men.[39]

Even more significant than their longevity was the age at which bishops and missionaries were chosen. Their recruitment could occur in the most various ways, proving yet again that both in theory and in practice the Church took no account of age. St Germain became Bishop of Auxerre at the age of 40, while his namesake became Patriarch of Constantinople at 81! This variety is found at the papal level too, since popes could be elected at any age, from John XI (931–36), who was scarcely 20, and according to some as little as 15 or 16 years old, to Agathon (678–82), who was, it has been claimed, 103 years old. In this period, the nomination of a pontiff often involved no more than an arrangement between the Roman clans, in which the emperor intervened from the ninth century onwards. This means that we are unable to draw any conclusions about the attitude of the Church towards age, but may simply observe that the tendency was to entrust the highest responsibility to men who had on the whole reached middle age.

Of the 20 popes reigning in this period whose ages are known, the average age at the beginning of their pontificate was 54.3 years, which completely contradicts Simone de Beauvoir's assertion that the popes of the Middle Ages were young men.[40] Of these 20 pontiffs, seven were 60 or more at their election; Siricus was 76 years old (384–98), Silverus was also 76 (536–8) and Agathon, who is mentioned above, was over 100. The average age of decease can be established at 65.2 years. Damasus I (366–84) and Sixtus III (430–40) were 80 years old. while it would be an exaggeration to speak of 'pontifical gerontocracy' in the early Middle Ages, it is none the less clear that already in this period the popes were the oldest persons in the religious and political world. Kings and emperors were much younger. With the exception of Charlemagne, they seldom achieved 70 years, Louis the Pious died at the age of 62, and Charles the Bald at the age of 54. Ecclesiastical dignitaries were, as they still are nowadays, definitely older than the political figures of their day.

Is this one of the reasons why the character of the Church is always more conservative? It is undoubtedly too early on to answer this question. Let us simply note the tendency within the episcopate to attribute responsible tasks to the oldest individuals. In Numidia the bishops recognized as their Primate not the titular holder of a particular see, but the *senex*, the oldest member of the episcopacy.[41] Further, the early Church gave old men a special place in the order of widowers, recruited from among those over the age of 60, who had been married only once, and had exercised hospitality and practised good works. Their role combined ascetic, contemplative and catechizing elements.[42]

The link between old age and conservatism has however yet to be established. At the Council of Constantinople in 381, according to Gregory of Nazianzus, the old men were not the least excited members: 'The bishops were chattering like a gathering of magpies. They were as noisy as a group of children, the din was like that in a new workshop,

Table 6.2 Ages of popes, 314–1003

Popes	Dates of pontificate	Age at election	Age at decease
Sylvester I	314–35	44 yrs	65 yrs
Julius I	337–52	57 yrs	72 yrs
Damasius I	366–84	62 yrs	80 yrs
Siricius	384–94	60 yrs	74 yrs
Sixtus III	432–40	62 yrs	80 yrs
Leo I	440–61	50 yrs	71 yrs
Simplicius	467–83	47 yrs	63 yrs
Silverus	536–8	76 yrs	78 yrs
Gregory the Great	590–604	50 yrs	64 yrs
Theodore I	642–9	62 yrs	69 yrs
Martin I	649–55	59 yrs	65 yrs
Agathon	678–82	103 yrs?	107 yrs?
Leo III	795–816	45 yrs	66 yrs
Sergius II	844–7	44 yrs	47 yrs
Leo IV	847–55	47 yrs	55 yrs
Nicholas I	858–67	58 yrs	67 yrs
John VIII	872–82	52 yrs	62 yrs
John IX	931–6	20 yrs	25 yrs
Gregory V	996–9	24 yrs	27 yrs
Sylvester II	999–1003	64 yrs	68 yrs

raising clouds of dust, a real whirlwind . . . They were discussing without any order and, like wasps, aiming straight at each others' faces, all at the same time. The venerable old men, far from calming the young ones down, were following hard on their heels . . .'[43] Heterodox or heretical streams of thought were often launched by old men, thus providing evidence of their remarkably hardy thought processes. Although Nestorius was only in his fifties when he broached the debate about the natures of Christ, it was an old monk of 70, Eutychius, who raised the heresy to a higher level when he stated that the divine nature of Jesus had absorbed his human nature, thus providing the Monophysite doctrine with its basis. Apollinarus of Laodicia was the same age when he found a compromise solution to this same argument, stating that Christ did not have a human soul. Arius was around 65 when he began denying the divinity of Christ in 320; Narsai was almost a centenarian when he disseminated the Nestorian creed in Persia at the end of the fifth century. These few examples will suffice for the moment to introduce an element of doubt concerning any assumptions about conservative attitudes and lack of openness in old age. Was it not an 81-year old pope who summoned Vatican II, the most revolutionary council in modern history?

THE POLITICAL ROLE OF THE OLD

The world of politics in the early Middle Ages was equally capable of making use of the resources of old age. Some of the barbarian kingdoms had a council of elders. In Britain, Nennius mentions such a council several times in his *Kentish Chronicle*. When Hengist, King of the Angles, decided to grant his daughter in marriage to Vortigern, the King of the Bretons, he summoned his council of elders to decide on what to demand in exchange; Vortigern did the same, but his 300 elders were massacred in a surprise attack by the Angles.[44] Among the Merovingians, the old played an essential role in the judiciary, if one may speak of a judiciary for that period. When the count held a law court, he would be assisted by 'honourable people', notable ecclesiastics and laymen, who were in fact the oldest people in the region. In northern and eastern Austrasia, these assessors were nominated for life; they were called *rachimbourgs* and were automatically the village elders. The oldest among them, the *thungin*, necessarily an old man, was empowered to preside over the tribunal in the count's absence. 'The *rachimbourgs* were real jurors, who had voting rights when sentence was determined and who could interject an appeal to the king or the mayor of the palace if they considered that the count had exceeded his rights, notably by neglecting their majority advice.'[45] In every village, the law court would be presided over by the oldest member of the community.

Finally, the royal entourage consisted of a surprising number of old counsellors. Behind the facade of young kings decimated by debauchery and assassination were to be found relatively elderly individuals who guaranteed a degree of continuity to royal policy; as in the time of Dagobert (629–39), about whom more is known. During his childhood, the king had been brought up in contact with old noblemen and women of quality who watched over his well-being. During his reign, his entourage included Landri, the mayor of the palace of Neustria, Fredegond's former lover, who was now over 70 years old; the seneschal, a sort of superior major domo who was the king's oldest servant; the referendary Bobbo, who was so old that he was immediately given an assistant secretary called Ouen, the future Bishop of Rouen, who died at the age of 79 in 698; Pepin of Landen, the mayor of the palace of Austrasia, who remained active until his death at the age of 89 in 640; Warnachaire, the mayor of the palace of Burgundy, who was also very old, but was dominated by his son Godin; Arnoul, Bishop of Metz, who died a year after Dagobert at the age of 60; Faro, Bishop of Meaux, who died in 672 when more than 70 years old; Omer, Bishop of Thérouanne, who lived 73 years (597–670); Wandrille, count of the palace, who also lived over 70 years; Duke Adalgise, who ended his life at the age of 84 (601–85); and Clodulf, Bishop of Metz, who lived into his nineties (604–96). While some of these individuals belonged to Dagobert's generation, his three principal counsellors were decidedly older than him; the famous Eloi, who was born in 588, was 51 years old when the king died and went on to live a further 21 years; Didier, Bishop of Cahors, who was born in 580, was 24 years older than the king and died at the age of 75; above all, Ega, the prime minister and great man of the reign, who was appointed mayor of the palace in 637 by Clovis II on account of his competence both as a remarkable administrator and as a strategist, was 64 years old when that king died.

It thus emerges, albeit not without some surprise, that behind the disturbed and anarchic front presented by the Merovingian period, with its troubles, rumours, massacres, pillages and assassinations, stirred up by its young and ferocious tyrants, lay a solid backing of old politicians, most of them churchmen, who ensured the continuity of administrative life. The fact that the dynasty endured for 250 years was due less to the praises heaped on the young blood-letters who occupied the throne from Clovis to Childeric III, than to their elderly servitors.

ART: THE STEREOTYPE OF OLD AGE

The early Middle Ages were thus a period of strong contrasts. The old were not absent, although the sources do not mention them. Among the humbler classes, they were at the mercy of the young, but they had a role to play concerning the supernatural. Among the great, they enjoyed no legal privileges, but they held many important posts, especially in the Church. Although killing them was not a costly undertaking in law, they often presided over the law courts. They were treated harshly in ecclesiastical discourses, but they governed the Church. They did not have any value in a warlike world, but they represented evidence and experience in an illiterate age.

The early Middle Ages were in fact not aware of old age as specific entity. In an extremely arid, rural society where nobody, except the great, had any precise idea of their age and where, given the extremely harsh living conditions, people looked old prematurely, there must have been much less difference between people of 40 and those of 60 or 70 years old than there is nowadays. In a world where no one, apart from a few great individuals, retired, there was no distinction between adults and old adults.

The art of the period witnesses to this lack of differentiation. It was basically a Christian art, one which was unfavourable from the start to any form of realism. Symbolism held a very great place in it, and man was relatively seldom represented. During the first centuries, Christ was frequently represented in frescoes as a young man very similar to Orpheus. The Coptic and Syriac Gospels of the sixth century were the first to portray old men, such as Eusebius of Caesarea and Ammonius of Alexandria in the *Gospels of Rabula*. The marks of old age are however stereotyped: long hair and long white beards, sometimes with the addition of wrinkles, as with two of the evangelists on Bishop Maximian of Ravenna's ivory throne (mid sixth century), or on the ivories of the Hellenistic school of Antioch. The famous mosaic in Sant'Apollinare Nuovo, Ravenna, which dates from the same period, is also interesting in that it suggests a difference in age between the three Magi bringing their offerings. The first, Caspar, is visibly an old man, with his beard and white hair, whereas the second is beardless and the third has a beard and black hair. It provides a clear indication of the precedence enjoyed by old age, since the old man is the leader, rather than of total indifference towards the old, since these three Wise Men include a young man, a mature man and an old man.

Merovingian art did not go in for such refinements. It was extremely stylized. As for Carolingian portraiture, it was also stereotyped; the old had white beards and were sometimes bald. St John, in the *Godescalc Gospels* (c.781–3), has a small beard and short hair. Nothing about him suggests old age, which the early Middle Ages were decidedly not concerned about.

7

The Eleventh to the Thirteenth Century:

The Social and Cultural Diversification of Old People

The first years of the eleventh century undoubtedly marked the start of a new era in Europe. Apart from its legendary terrors, the millennium and the years around it really and truly established a fundamental milestone in the history of Christianity. Looked at in depth, it marked the end of the great epidemics and famines, the beginning of demographic growth and of the clearances, the stabilization of the feudal régime and the renewal of trade and the towns. Looked at superficially, it marked the emergence of the new Capetian and Ottonian dynasties, the first stonebuilt keeps, the churches' 'white coats', the pilgrimage to Compostella, and soon the first currents of religious reform. The year 1000 was a new departure, introducing 250 to 300 years of the 'classical' Middle Ages. These high Middle Ages ended, according to region, between 1270 and 1330, with the Black Death of 1348 providing the death stroke.

The Middle Ages thus achieved their summer between the beginning of the eleventh and the beginning of the fourteenth century, when a relative equilibrium was achieved, producing some magnificent blooms: cathedrals, castles, dialectics and scholasticism, Cistercians and mendicants, St Bernard and St Francis. Let us not idealize the age: these flowers grew on the immense sump that was peasant poverty. All that is left to us of medieval civilization is the thin veneer: its art and literature.

Behind this mask lay the sufferings of rural society and, whatever may be said, the Middle Ages remained the Middle Ages, a period when it was not good to be a serf or a villein. At the dawn of the eleventh century, Archbishop Adalberon revived the concept of a society divided into *oratores*, *bellatores* and *laboratores* (that is, priests, warriors and peasants). The latter, who formed the immense majority, enabled the first group, a tiny minority, to educate themselves and to pray; they made it possible for the second group to fight. The façade of the Middle Ages, as grandiose and symbolic as that of a cathedral, was built thanks to their labour; but how many people did these refined Middle Ages, with their cloisters, episcopal palaces, frescoes and gothic statues, their universities and their castles, actually involve? How many people could understand them and profit from them?

The Middle Ages were a harsh period, neither better nor worse than preceding or subsequent ages. A period in which great things were achieved by its clerical élites, but which remained profoundly poor. It was an age of contrasts, one which produced both Francis of Assisi and Simon of Montfort and approved of them both. Both of them won the Pope's blessing, the one in order to serve his brothers, the other in order to massacre them. An astonishing world arrayed in black and white, where the sublime and the bestial rubbed shoulders, sometimes within the same character, and which apparently knew neither the average nor the mediocre.

THE OLD AGE OF THE WORLD AND THE AGES OF LIFE: A GAME FOR INTELLECTUALS

This was a world which was considered old by its élites, who were the only people capable of self-expression. Starting with the birth of Christ, considered as a central point in history since Denis the Little was writing in the sixth century, humanity had entered into its decrepit state and was moving towards the end: 'We are seeing the world failing and exhaling, so to speak, its last breath in extreme old age', wrote Otto of Freising in his *Chronicle*. According to Honorius of Autun, the world had lived through its childhood, youth, adolescence, maturity and old age, with these different stages being marked by the creation of Adam, Noah's law, the calling of Abraham, the kingship of David, the Babylonian exile and the birth of Christ. The end was nigh, and Hugh of St Victor interpreted the shift of the centre of civilization to the west as a sign of this. 'Divine Providence has ordained that the universal government which had been in the East at the beginning of the world, was shifting to the West at the same rate as the coming of the end of time, in order to warn us of the arrival of the end of the world, because the course of events has already reached the end of the universe.'

For many, this idea of an ageing world was accompanied by a pessimistic vision of their own age. Being old, the world was shrivelling up like an old man; men were diminishing. In the thirteenth century Guiot of Provins stated that: 'The men of the past were handsome and tall. They are now children and dwarves.' People lamented the misfortunes and the decadence of present times: 'Youth no longer wishes to learn anything, knowledge is in decay, the entire world is walking on its head, the blind leading the blind and casting them into the shallows . . . What was formerly despised is now respected. Everything has lost its way.'[1] Time was frequently envisaged in its portentous aspect, as a winged and emaciated old man, bearing a scythe, who appears among cathedral statuary. Time is the cause of decline and decay. The world's old age can only increase its ills, and cannot bring any improvement. Saturn, the Roman name for Kronos, is the furthest and slowest planet, which was imagined to be cold and desiccated. It was associated with senility and death and was represented as an old man bearing a crutch or a scythe.

However, old age could entail some advantages for the world. St Bonaventure stressed the growth in human knowledge resulting from it and Bernard of Chartres drew this now famous comparison: 'We are dwarves perched on the shoulders of giants, but we see further than they do.' In spite of everything, pessimism predominated. The world was old and decrepit, and everything was going wrong. The end was nigh.

It was this which boded so ill for the idea of old age in the medieval imagination. The classical scheme of the ages of life effectively endowed the last age with a sombre image. Dividing life up into four, six or seven parts was, as we have seen, a very ancient idea, which Isidore of Seville brought back into fashion. From then on, it crops up at every opportunity. In the thirteenth century, it was refined and made more precise, especially in the famous Latin encyclopaedia called *De Proprietatibus Rerum*, by Bartholomew de Glanville, which became famous following its translation into French in 1372 and into English in 1397. In it can be found the classical concept of the fundamental unity of the universe, its spiritual and material, supernatural and natural elements. Everything is interdependent; the cycle of the seasons, the movement of the planets, history, the course of human life, the humours, the elements and the symbolism of numbers. Everything is interconnected and affects everything, everything is in the image of everything: everything in this world is both reality and symbol. The ages of life illustrate this. According to Bartholomew de Glanville, there are seven ages, corresponding to the seven planets: childhood, *pueritia*, adolescence, youth, *senecte*, old age, and *senies*. Their characteristics are described as follows in the 1397 translation, in Wynkyn de Worde's edition of 1495:

Isidir seith and Constantyn also, that there ben mony divers ages. The firste hatte *infancia* 'the firste childhode', withouten teeth and neulich igete and bore, and dureth seven monthis, and is yit ful tenere and neische, quabby and gleymy. Therefore in that age a child nedith alwey tendre and softe kepinge, fedinge, and norischinge. And childehood that bredith teeth strecchith and durith seven yere. And suche a child hatte *infans* in Latyn, that is to mene 'nought spekynge'. . .

Hereaftir cometh ye secounde age, that hatte *puericia*, anothir childehode that dureth and lastith othir seven yere, that is to the ende of fouretene yere, and hath that name *puericia* of *pubertas*, ye age of fouretene yere, that is yit a tendir age, other of *pupilla* 'ye blak of the eye' so seith Isidre.

Hereaftir cometh the age that hatte *adholoscencia*, the age of a yonge stripelinge, and dureth the thridde seven yere, that is to the ende of on and twenty yere. So it is saide *in viatico*.

But Isidir saith that it dureth to the ferthe seven yere, that is to the ende of 28 yere. But ficicians strecchen this age to the ente of 30 yere or of 35 yere. This age hatte *adholescencia* for it is ful age to gete children, so seith Isidre, and able to brnische and encrece, and fonge myght and strengthe. Isidre seith yet in this age the membres ben neische and tendre, and abil to strecche and growe by vertue of hete that hath maistrie therinne anon to the perfeccioun of complement.

Aftir . . . cometh the age that hatte *iuuentus*, and this age is in the middil amonges ages, and therefore it is strengest. Isidir seith that this age lastith and durith to be 45 yere or to be fifty yere, and endith in that yere. Isidir seith that this age *iuventus* hath that name of *iuvare*, that is 'for to helpe', for a man of that age is isette in the ende of his ful encresinge, and therefore he is strong to helpe at nede. Isidir saith that aftir this age *iuventus* cometh the age that hatte *senecta*, as is ye middle age bitwene the age that hatte *iuventus* and *senectus*, the secounde elde that Isidir calleth 'hevynes'. This age acordith to olde men and sadde, for to clepe *iuventus* 'youthe' (in the firste elde men drawen from youthe) to the seconde age. For such men ben naught in the seconde elde, but here youth passith. So seith Isidre. And (aftir) this age *senecta* cometh (the age that hatte *senectus*) ye second elde. And som men wolde mene that this age endith in the 70 yere, and some wolen mene that it endith in none ceteyne nombre of yeres . . . (Isidre seith that elde hatte *senectus* for passing and failyng of wittes, for bycause of elde olde men doten.) . . . The laste partye of elde hatte *senium* for it is rulende of age and of lif. This age hath with hym mony damages and also propirtees bothe goode and yvel. So seith Isidre.

. . . Alle men dispisen the olde man and ben hevy and wery of him. The olde man is itraveiled and greved with coughynge and spettyne and with othir greves, for to asschen to falle and turne into aschen, and poudre into poudre.[2]

It can be seen that what we currently know as old age here occupies three of the seven parts of human life. This reflects the importance accorded it in the Middle Ages. Far from considering old age as a rarity, it was given a vital place, and was made to begin at around 50 years, thus following directly on youth. We have grown used to this characteristically medieval idea of contrasts, which left no room for the average; one was either young or old; young so long as one retained one's physical strength, old as soon as it started to decline. Medieval people do not appear to have been aware of transitional periods. Just as they passed directly from good to evil, from the sublime to the beastly, from laughter to tears, so they fell brutally from youth to old age. And, just as their bodies were prematurely worn out in that brutal world, so too did they grow old very early on.

The old were very numerous in the eyes of medieval man. Old age is a totally relative notion and modern classifications are totally inappropriate to the thirteenth century. Whereas we make old age begin around 65, this would leave the Middle Ages with very few old men indeed. Such an arbitrary limit is valueless for past centuries. What counts is the way medieval man envisaged life, and it is certain that he saw many old people among those men and women aged over 50. Like us, he undoubtedly felt that he was rubbing shoulders with a great number of old people, and the notion of old age was as familiar to him as it is to us, to the extent that he could distinguish between *senecte* and *senies*, anticipating our categories of the third and fourth ages. Other treatises were even more detailed, dividing human life into 12 parts according to the 12 months of the year: in this case old age still comprised three parts, beginning with October, so that it occupied on average a quarter of man's life:

> From the month which comes after September
> Which is called the month of October
> If he has LX years and no more
> He then becomes an old man and hoary
> Who must then remember
> That time is leading him towards death.[3]

Or again, in another poem:

> In October coming after
> Man must sow the good wheat
> On which everyone must live;
> So too must the good man
> Who has reached LX years:
> He must sow to the young folk
> Good words by his example
> And give alms, that's what I think.[4]

Some authors arranged the months into seasons, thus dividing life into four parts, which corresponds more closely to our present-day divisions into childhood, adulthood and the third and fourth ages. Thus the Italian Philip of Novara, who wrote his treatise *Des quatre tenz d'aage d'ome* (Of the four ages of man's life') around 1265 when aged over 70, felt that existence was composed of four periods of twice ten years each, setting the onset of old age at 60 and the end of life at 80 years old. After which age, 'man ought to long for death.' We find this four times 20 schema with Arnold of Villanova, where it is equated with the four humours and the four elements.[5]

Medieval art adopted these concepts and illustrated them. In the thirteenth century the capitals in the baptistery in Parma established the connection between the workers of the eleventh hour and old age, man's *senectus*.[6] In the fourteenth century the capitals in the Doges' Palace and a fresco in the Eremitani in Padua portrayed the ages of life according to the characteristic occupations of each. After the ages of school, of love, of hunting, of war and of chivalry comes the time of old age, symbolized by a learned old man with a beard studying his book by the fire; learning and study were the functions of the old.[7]

Were such concepts as generalized as Philippe Ariès maintains? This was probably not the case in the Middle Ages. From the eleventh to the thirteenth century, they appeared only in works of learning, and generally in Latin, as in *The Properties of Things*. As for frescoes and sculptures, their symbolic meaning was apparent to only a tiny minority. It was only from the seventeenth century onwards, and more so in the nineteenth century, that the ages of life became a popular theme, thanks mainly to the huge numbers of engravings and almanachs. However, it wasn't necessary to possess a complete theory of the division of life into four, six, eight or 12 periods to be aware of ageing and its manifestations. The medieval peasant did not divide life up into slices, and there was no question of his having specific occupations for each age of his life. For him there was no time for school and no age for hunting, war or studying. From start to finish, he worked the land and everything was arranged around his work, which only allowed three periods to subsist: babyhood, when the individual could contribute nothing, adult life, which began as soon as he could help in the fields and ended when he was too worn out and decrepit to sow or reap. This was when true old age began, doubtless later than in the aristocratic theories. When 60 tolled, the warrior might perhaps retire, but the reaper certainly did not. Old age in the sense of retirement was initially a feature of aristocratic and literary circles only.

The diversification of social functions undoubtedly encouraged awareness of the specific nature of great old age, a feeling which had disappeared during the early Middle Ages, as we have seen. From the eleventh century onwards, the documents begin to refer specifically to old age and to describe it, to research its causes and also its remedies. This led to certain aspects of antique thinking being revived, especially in the thirteenth century. By searching painstakingly through the chronicles and theological treatises of remote ages, the old man was rediscovered as a literary figure. People took an interest in the old, dedicated books to them and concentrated on their situation.

This fact on its own is significant: in the Middle Ages, old age was experienced as a reality which was truly present, both through the existence of numerous old persons and as the very probable future state for most adults. Stephen of Fougères, Henry II's chaplain and Bishop of Rennes, wrote a poem 'On Old Age' in *c.*1175; Philip of Novara dedicated a good part of his book to the subject in *c.*1265; at the end of the thirteenth century Arnold of Villanova published *The Defence of Age, and Recovery of Youth*; in the 1280s Roger Bacon, the 'doctor mirabilis', composed his *The Cure of Old Age, and Preservation of Youth*; as we have seen several books took an interest in the ages of life and in the Muslim world Avicenna wrote a treatise *On Weariness and Old Age*. It is thus certain that literate people at least were interested in old age. Theirs was a personal interest, since most of these authors were around 70 years old when they compiled the works in question, but it was also a more general interest, testifying to the relative importance of the old in medieval society.

Old age in the imaginary world: an unfavourable point of view

They approached the question from every angle: descriptive, normative, medical, moral and symbolic. On the whole, their vision remained pessimistic. In *The Properties of Things* old age is a burden and old people wither; they talk drivel and they are full of coughs, spit and filth, before returning to dust. According to *Le Grant Kalendrier*, the old man has only to think about death and to give alms. Philip of Novara, who knew what he was writing about, said that for the old life was but pain, and that one must above all avoid asking them 'Vous dolez?' (Are you in pain?).

Summing up his personal experience, Philip observed that current opinion taxed the old with talking drivel and loss of reason: 'There are some who say that the old have grown foolish and forgetful, and that they are changed and have lost what they were accustomed to knowing.'[9] The young despise them and do not hesitate to interrrupt them in the council chamber; when they do so, however, they are rebuffed by their colleagues (which provides a precious indication of the general level of respect shown the old). Old men, Philip continues, should thank God for having left them so much time for repentance; they should concentrate on saving their souls and should despise life. Above all, they should avoid marrying a young girl, because they are invariably cuckolded. However, marrying an old woman is not to be recommended either, because 'two decaying bodies in one bed can never be endured.' So it is best to renounce marriage from a given age onwards, since in any case God abhors elderly sensualists. Let the old concentrate on giving alms in order to gain Paradise. Old women are generally full of vice. They paint their faces to conceal their ugliness and reminding them of their age makes them angry. Philip's traditional misogyny is however tempered by his recognition of the usefulness of old women: they manage the home and property, they bring up the grandchildren and arrange marriages. In *The Book of Manners*, written around 1170–5, we can observe the old Countess of Hereford spending her time founding chapels, caring for the poor, educating children and receiving church-men.[10]

Romances and poems emanating both from clerical and lay milieux agree in decrying the vices, the ugliness and the horror of old age. The tale of Aucassin and Nicolette, composed in the first half of the thirteenth century, reserves its antipathetic roles for the old. In contrast with the youth, freshness, loyalty and beauty of the hero and heroine, we have Aucassin's tutor, the old seigneur Garin de Beaucaire, who is involved in dubious transactions, dishonest dealings and who does not keep his promises. 'The Count Garins de Beaucaire was old and frail, he had lived his life';[11] beyond a certain age, one is no longer good for anything. Aucassin reproached him in particular for not keeping his word, a grave fault at that time: 'Truly, said Aucassin, it grieves me much when a man of your age lies.'[12] As for Nicolette, she was placed by the Vicomte de Beaucaire, one of Garin's vassals, in the care of a disagreeable old woman.

The *Roman de la Rose* in the mid thirteenth century drew an unflattering portrait of old age, retaining only its ugly features. The passage in question is interesting in more ways than one. The cruel portrait drawn here already announces the bitter reproaches and portraits of the Renaissance. Above all, however, this vision of old age passes rapidly to a meditation on the passage of time, as rendered by Chaucer's translation:

> The Tyme, that eldeth our ancestours
> And eldeth Kynges and Emperours.
> And that us shall overcomen
> Er that Dethe us shal have nomen.

The sad cortege of ymages and peyntures which decorate the garden wall shows us old age (Elde) following behind Hate, Felony, Vyllany,

Covetyse, Avaryce, Envye and Sorrowe, and preceding Hypocrisy and
Poverty, good company all.

Elde was paynted after this,
That shorte was a foote, iwys,
Than she was wonte in her younghede;
Unneth herselfe she migh fede,
So febel and eke so olde was she.
That faded was al her beaute,
Ful salowe was waxen her colour,
Her need for-hore was, whyte as flour.

Iwys, great qualme ne were it noue,
Ne synne, although her lufe were gone.
Al woxen was her body unwelde,
And drie and dwyed al for elde.
A foule forwelked thyng was she
that whylom rounde and softe had be.

Her eeres shoken fast withall
As from her heed they wolde fall.
Her face frounced and forsyned.
And bothe her hondes lorne, fordwyne.
So olde she was that she ne went
A foote, but it were by potent.

The Tyme, that passeth nyght and daye,
And restlesse travayleth aye,
And steleth from us so prively,
That to us semeth sykerly
That is in one poynt dwelleth ever,
And certes, it ne resteth never,
But gothe so fast, and passeth aye
That there nys man that thynke many
What tyme that nowe present is:
Asketh at these clerkes this:
For (er) men thynke it redily
Thre tymes ben (y) passed by.
The Tyme, that may not soiourne,
But go the, and may never retourne
As water that downe renneth aye,
But never droppe retourne maye;
There maye nothyng as Tyme endure,
Metal, nor erthly creature.
For al thing it frette and shal:
They Tyme eke, that changeth al,
And al dothe waxe and fostred be,

And al thyng distroyeth he:
The Tyme, that eldeth our auncestours
And eldeth Kynges and emperours,
And that us al shal have overcomen
Er that Dethe us shal have nommen:
The Tyme, that hath al in welde
To elden folke, had made her elde
So inly that, to my wetyng,
She might helpe herselfe nothyng,
But turned ayen unto chidhede;
She had nothing herselfe to lede,
Ne wytte ne pyth in her holde
More than a chyle of two yere olde,
But nethelesse, I trow that she
Was fayre sometyme, and fresshe to se,
Whan she was in her rightful age:
But she was paste al that passage
And was a doted thyng becomen.
A furred cappe on had she nommen;
Wel had she clad herselfe and warme,
For colde might els done her harme.
These olde folke have alway colde,
Her kynde is suche, whan they ben olde.[13]

INDIFFERENCE TO TIME AND TO OLD AGE: THE CHURCHMEN'S PREROGATIVE

'The Tyme, that passeth nyght and daye', 'The Tyme, that may not soiourne', 'There may nothyng as Tyme endure', 'Tyme eke, that chaungeth al', 'Tyme, that eldeth our ancestours', 'Tyme that hath al in welde': Guillaume de Lorris does not appear to have shared the 'vast indifference to time' with which the Middle Ages have been credited. Neither did Rutebeuf, who warned the young in his *Chanson de Pouille* (Song of the Louse): 'When you are old . . .' From the end of the twelfth century onwards, the monk Helinant of Froidmont saw the image of death in the faces of the old:

> Morz, qui est a veue escrite
> en la vielle face despite.[14]

> (Death, who is written clear
> in this miserable old face.)

While one may certainly agree with Jacques Le Goff's statement that

time 'is fixed in eternity, it is a bit of eternity . . . For the Christian in
the Middle Ages . . . his sense of existing was a sense of being, and his
sense of being was a sense, not of change or of undergoing a process
within himself, but of subsistence. His tendency towards nothingness
was compensated by an opposite tendency towards the primary cause.'[15]
As the same author states elsewhere, however, 'it seems to me that, far
from being indifferent to time, the men of the Middle Ages were
strangely aware of it. When they fail to be precise, it is simply that
they do not feel the need so to be and that the frame of reference of
the event under discussion is not that of numbers. However, they very
seldom omit a reference to time . . . The truth is that there is no unified
time or chronology. For the medieval mind, temporal reality consists
of a multiplicity of times.'[16] Relativity was a familiar notion to medieval
man, and consequently his awareness of growing old varied according
to his socio-economic circle and to circumstance. It is logical that
indifference to time was the prerogative of the churchmen. The liturgical
calendar was a vast enterprise aimed at abolishing time through a cyclical
and mystical process: Christ is born and resuscitated every year and
every day, and is eternally present to the mankind He has saved. This
cyclical time and the myth of Christ's eternal return are illustrated by
the wheel of fortune which decorates every cathedral: 'I am without a
kingdom, I have ruled, I am ruling, I will rule . . .'

The millennarians looked to the future for the Golden Age of the
past. Scholasticism glossed the texts of the past. The prayers, hymns
and canticles tirelessly repeated the same inexhaustible and eternal words,
permanently reliving the past. History became a chronicle of present
times. Thomas of Aquinas thought that there was no point in studying
successive schools of philosophy; all that counted was what each school
could offer in the way of universal and eternal value. And when some
individuals dared to retrace the history of the world from the Creation,
they were horrified by their vision of its decrepitude and of its
approaching end. This horrible movement towards the future had to be
stopped. The ideal was immutable and incorruptible: medieval thought
was 'a desperate attempt to petrify history', as Gilles Lapouge has put
it.[17]

Monastic life enabled the Church to sow islands of eternity in the
world. Within those ageless buildings, ageless men recited litanies
without beginning or end to a frozen melody. Apart from their prayers,
which were a re-enactment of 'the order of words of the primordial
discourse', there was silence, and thus timelessness: the word, which is
the act of becoming, was abolished. Monks were not born; they did
not die; they subsisted eternally, because they were no longer individuals,
they were a community. They lost their names and 'with their name,
what they left behind was their childhood, their family, their father and
mother, and all the lineage preceding them, just as that moment in time

when the child came into the world is also abolished.'[18] They took the name of a saint, whose image they then perpetuated, and this name would subsist through those brothers who assumed it in their turn. The name was immortal, as was the community, as were the monks. No one grew old in that world. The Monastic Rules do not mention old age, nor the ages of life. The Cistercian abbot Isaac de L'Étoile, who died c.1168–9, speculated in his sermons about the symbolism of numbers, which abolished the reality of time: seven designates the present and this is the perfect and eternal number.[19] Philo, St Gregory, Rabanus Maurus, Isidore of Seville and John of Salisbury all said the same thing.[20]

Given such a vision, the act of retiring to a monastery at the end of one's life also came to mean leaving time and entering eternity. It was a way of escaping old age, of prolonging and perpetuating oneself. Having started in the early Middle Ages this trend now expanded. At the beginning of the twelfth century Eustace of Boulogne (brother to Godfrey of Bouillon), who had been elected King of Jerusalem in 1118 by the Frankish barons of the Holy Land, renounced his title and his journey to retire at the age of 60 to the abbey of Rumilly, where he died in 1125. Cluniac, Cistercian, Carthusian, Premonstratensian and soon Franciscan and Dominican houses all became refuges where ageing nobles could shelter from time. Many bishops imitated them. In 1120, Marbode, Bishop of Rennes since 1096, retired at the age of 80 to St-Abin d'Angers, where he died in 1123.[21] Arnoul, Bishop of Lisieux for 40 years and counsellor to Henry II, entered the abbey of St Victor in Paris in 1181 at the age of 81; he died there aged 84. Alain of Flanders, Bishop of Auxerre between 1152 and 1167, retired to Clairvaux where he died at the age of 80 in 1186. The theologian Alan of Lille, (Alanus Magnus), who taught at Paris and at Montpellier, entered the Cistercian order towards the end of his life and died in it in 1203, aged 89.

As in the preceding period, theologians took little interest in the old. St Thomas has said very little about old age, merely commenting that it is not a natural phenomenon. Physically, it is characterized by the exhaustion of the vital functions resulting from the exudation of animal heat, because life can survive only when heat and moisture are mingled. Physical collapse and ensuing death are the effects of the destruction of original justice, according to which man's soul was allowed to preserve his body from all faults. Before the advent of original sin, man was eternal through the gift of grace, and he would become so again.[22]

Cistercian spirituality scorned both earthly and corporeal things, and was unable to accord old age any special importance. It did not deny the existence of old age, however, but tried to use it for a moral and eschatological purpose. St Bernard assigned to old people the role of spiritual guides for the young, in a master–disciple relationship which recalls Greek practice:

it is safer to keep company with old men; by their authority and
experience, they form the young people's morals and endow them,
so to speak, with the hue of probity. If those who do not know
their way attach themselves, before setting out, to those who are
firmly set on the direction ahead, how much more sensible is it
for young people to start on a new journey in the company of
old men, so as to be less exposed to error and to missing the path
of virtue? There is nothing finer than having elders as the leaders
and the witnesses of one's progress. The mingling of young and
old has many charms. Some are there to teach, others to console;
some entertain and others give honour.[23]

However, the old had above all to think of themselves, since they
were approaching death:

The time of man is short: to the old man death is at the door.
You have a short, a very short time with those who say to you
'Well! Well!' . . . you are even now ready to be brought before
the scrutiny of the angels: and, unhappy man that you are, are
being hastened by the very failure of nature before the dread
tribunal of Christ.[24]

It is thus ridiculous for an old man to launch himself into new
enterprises, such as the man who, on becoming a widower, entered the
monastery, and then left it 'to contract a second marriage, (which) is
indecent and dishonourable',[25] or Eustace who, at a very advanced age,
usurped the episcopal see of Valence:

How can such an old age, which ought to be spent quietly in
fruitful deeds of mercy, wipe out the punishment due to all your
past days, or blot out their guilt? Why, alas! Should your hoary
head alone, which should be reverenced, be robbed of its
accustomed veneration; why should it sink unhonoured into the
grave, when it should have been especially respected?[26]

For all that, there was nothing particularly specific about old age; the
virtues and vices of the old were the results of their whole lives. It was
generally too late for them to alter their behaviour in their later days:
'It is extremely difficult for the old to correct themselves and to abandon
the vicious habits engrained in them.' They are as capable of presenting
a good example to the young as they are a bad, and their responsibility
in this domain is great:

Their wisdom shines all the more in that old age is herself instructed
by age, is fortified by experience and becomes more prudent in

the course of time. It is old age which produces the sweet fruits of preceding efforts, and which renews and builds the future. Since many old people are full of days and make no progress, because they have amassed no riches in the good times, and the corruption of their guilty lives infects the spirit of young people who are destitute of all virtue. Religion, in fact, is as effectively destroyed by a vicious and foolish old man as by a bold and shameless young man.[27]

Age thus has nothing to do with virtue and wisdom:

I do not say that there is any age too youthful or too advanced for God's grace; on the contrary, one can see many young people surpass the old in intelligence . . . These young adepts of virtue are worth more than men who have grown old in sin. A man is still a child when he can number 100 years of existence and is worthy of all kinds of scorn; but there is on the contrary an old age worthy of every respect although it does not number a great many years and does not go very far back.[28]

St Bernard thus established his links with a theory familiar to the religious thought of the Middle Ages: true old age is wisdom and virtue, to which the number of years is completely secondary, even if, nowadays, a wise young man is 'a prodigy of grace which must strike one with astonishment'. The old man was thus not singled out for aiming at perfection, because he who does not advance falls back; in the race towards the goal, every notion of giving up or retiring from the fray is excluded: 'For however far you may have run, if you do not persevere even unto death, you do not obtain the prize.'[29] No relaxation is allowed, because the demon goes on tempting man for the rest of his life and one sees only too many of those 'stubborn and hardened old men who abound in these days full of perils'.

Old age's opportunity lay in its bodily decrepitude which allowed a man's soul to rise more easily towards the celestial realities. The weaker the body grows, the stronger the soul becomes. This is what William of St Thierry, the biographer of St Bernard, observed about the saint: 'He is always full of vigour and strength, and as his body grows weaker, he shows himself stronger and more powerful, and does not cease from doing things worthy of remembrance.'[30] Although he lived only 63 years, St Bernard was in fact assailed by a series of illnesses during his last years, but his spiritual activity remained prodigious until the end.

St Bernard himself observed an identical phenomenon in his friend Guérin, abbot of Sainte-Marie-des-Alpes, who undertook the reform of his monastery at a very advanced age. He congratulated him on this:

Rest is due to you in your old age, you have won your crown
. . . And there is no fear that the enemy will overcome one who
has not yielded to old age. The mind is stronger than time, and
even while the body is growing cold in death a holy zeal glows
in the heart, and while the limbs grow helpless, the vigour of the
will remains unimpaired and the ardent spirit feels not the weakness
of the wrinkled flesh. And this is no wonder. For why should it
fear the destruction of its old home when it sees a spiritual building
daily rising on high and growing for eternity. For we know that
if this earthly house is dissolved we have a building of God, an
house not made with hands, eternal in the heavens.

. . .

For in a robust and active body there always dwells a more
effeminate and lukewarm soul; and, again, in a weak and infirm
body a stronger and more vigorous soul flourishes. And this the
Apostle testifies that he found true in his own case: 'when I am
weak', he says 'then am I strong.'[31]

St Bernard would consider as nonsense the modern notion that mental
strength is dependent on physical well-being. In his *Book on the manner
of living well* he declares on the contrary that 'A healthy body, which
leads man to infirmity of soul, is a bad thing: but an infirm body,
which leads man to the health of his soul, is a good thing.'[32]

The Church's splendid indifference towards age is further revealed in
the timeless stylization of Romanesque statuary, in which old men are
chiefly identified by their beards. Evidence of a first attempt at
individualization appears, however, in Moissac in the first third of the
twelfth century, if not in the 24 old men of the Apocalypse on the
lintel, at least in the two great old men on its pier, one of whom has
plenty of hair, and the other is bald with a lined forehead. Man was
still being represented in a timeless manner in the thirteenth century, as
Georges Duby remarks;[33] as a type, an idea or an ideal incapable of
bearing the deforming marks of old age. Men and women are eternally
young and beautiful. The venerable character of old saints and prophets
is symbolized by a magnificent beard, as on the cathedral portals of
Chartres and Rheims. Wrinkles are exceptional; they furrow the forehead
of St Paul, who is also bald, at Chartres, and that of St John the Baptist
on his statue at the College of Rieux.

Kings and princes on their tombs were just as timeless. Their effigies
were ageless, like that of Robert, Duke of Normandy, who died in
1134 at the age of 80, which lies in Gloucester cathedral; the coat of
mail covering his forehead and chin effectively conceals any trace of old
age. At Fontrevaud, the octogenarian Eleanor of Aquitaine and the
septuagenarian Isabelle of Angoulême are represented as young women.
There is no difference in this between east and west: a few wrinkles, a

long beard and white hairs confer wisdom on the bishops who cluster around Emperor Constantine XI in the miniatures of the Chronicle of John Skylitzes, of the eleventh century.

Giotto remained faithful to these precepts. In his famous scene representing the reconciliation between St Anna and St Joachim, in the Scrovegni chapel in l'Arena in Padua, Anna has grey hair and Joachim a beard and white hair. However, art critics are mystified by the presence of a mysterious woman, her head covered by a fold of black cloak, who watches a smiling young woman with a penetrating and jealous gaze. Some see in this a symbol of old age's envy of youth. In any case, it was in Italy in the thirteenth century that a more realistic representation of old people first appeared, in the frescoes of the upper church in Assisi, the work of the Roman Pietro Cavallini: Jacob serves a meal to his old father Isaac, who is lying down, his face a picture of collapse and suffering.

MEDIEVAL MAN'S AWARENESS OF OLD AGE

We should not be misled by the relative indifference to age which characterizes the work of the moralists, theologians and artists of the classical Middle Ages. In fact, the men of that period paid great attention to the passage of time and to ageing. Nevertheless, their lack of precision about the age of individuals, especially among the chroniclers, has been noted often enough. Villehardouin, for instance, when referring to Enrico Dandolo, the Doge of Venice, who led the Fourth Crusade at the age of 97, tells us simply that 'The Doge of Venice (was) a very wise and able man.' He does indeed mention elsewhere that he was an old man, but what he found most striking was his blindness: 'For he was very old and although his eyes appeared bright and clear, he was none the less totally blind, having lost his sight through a wound in the head.'[34] Even with great men, the principal problem is that we don't know their date of birth. According to Christopher Brooke, Henry I's daughter Matilda was the first English princess since the seventh century whose date of birth is known.[35] William Marshal, whose chivalric exploits filled the chronicles at the beginning of the thirteenth century, was born *c.*1145; more often, one has to be content with rounding the numbers off to the nearest tenth.

A flagrant instance of this is provided by canonization proceedings, which involved hundreds of witnesses stating their age and profession. The proceedings for St Yves in 1330 involved the appearance of 216 witnesses at the enquiry held at Tréguier in front of the Bishops of Limoges and Angoulême and the Abbot of Troarn; ages were recorded with the qualification 'as he appears according to his physical aspect'.[36] Physical appearance remained the sole and very approximate means of

Table 7.1 Age declared by the witnesses in the canonization proceedings for St Yves (Tréguier 1330)

15 yrs: 1	30 yrs: 12	+50 yrs: 1	70 yrs: 5
16 yrs: 1	35 yrs: 7	55 yrs: 13	+70 yrs: 1
18 yrs: 1	37 yrs: 1	+55 yrs: 1	72 yrs: 1
19 yrs: 2	38 yrs: 1	60 yrs: 50	75 yrs: 2
20 yrs: 5	39 yrs: 1	62 yrs: 1	78 yrs: 1
22 yrs: 1	40 yrs: 42	63 yrs: 1	80 yrs: 4
25 yrs: 6	45 yrs: 2	65 yrs: 1	+80 yrs: 1
28 yrs: 3	50 yrs: 45	66 yrs: 1	90 yrs: 4

Source: Monuments originaux de l'histoire de saint Yves, Saint-Brieuc 1887.

verification of advanced numbers of years. Of these 216 persons, 162 gave their age as a multiple of ten, and 191 as a multiple of five. The ages of only 25 people fell in between these. Nor were the young any more precise. This generally depended on their social status: churchmen and knights seem to have been more aware of their exact age; one knight was 62 years old, another 72; a cathedral chanter was 63 years old; one noble was 28 years old, and another 32.

Did these men round off their ages to the higher or lower tenth? Some, like Georges Duby, think that individuals, from a certain age onwards, happily exaggerate their age, and that a 76-year-old will, for instance, call himself 80. This is matter of prestige for people who can in any case no longer claim to be young. While this may well apply nowadays, it did not necessarily do so in the Middle Ages. T.H. Hollingsworth, in his great work on the demography of the Middle Ages, shows on the contrary that the tendency was to round off figures to the lower tenth. He made use of the Inquisitiones post mortem and the proofs of age concerning the vassals of the king of England between 1250 and 1450. These documents show the date of decease of the feudal tenants and the age of their heirs: thus, when the latter's date of decease can be found, we know how old he was, and it is frequently the case that these individuals tended to make themselves out to be younger than they were.[37] Another set of figures seems to tend in the opposite direction: during canonization proceedings, several witnesses would attest to being over 50, 60 or 70 years old; they never claimed to be less than 50 etc. years old!

Modern historians have often exaggerated this tendency towards approximation among medieval people. It corresponded, where numbers were involved, to a conscious desire to amplify, to simplify and to apply symbolism. This is flagrant in cases where multiples of seven or 12 were used by the learned authors. They themselves, however, were not dupes.

At the beginning of the twelfth century, even a chronicler as prone to recording marvellous events as Ordericus Vitalis knew his age. Towards the end of his work, he wrote:

> Now indeed, worn out with age and infirmity, I long to bring this book to an end, and it is plain that many good reasons urge me to. For I am now in the sixty-seventh year of my life and service to my Lord Jesus Christ.[38]

Born at Attingham in 1075, he died in 1145 at the age of 68.

The frequent absence of references to numbers does not mean that medieval man was unaware of age. Everyone possessed a reference system linked to familiar, social or liturgical events which allowed him, when required, to locate himself precisely in time. The proof-of-age procedures in England amply demonstrate this. On 1 October 1304, several, generally elderly, witnesses came to Skipton in Craven to give evidence concerning the date of birth of a certain John Tempest, in an inheritance case. Each one used his personal references, with astonishing precision: William de Marton (aged 60) 'recollects the day and year because on the day of the Exaltation of the Holy Cross following a son Patrick was born to himself who was 21 at that last feast.' William de Cestrunt (aged 50) also recalled the date, because his own mother was married again on the St Martin's Day following the birth of John Tempest, which was 21 years ago; John de Kygheley's (age given 60) grand-daughter Alice was born to him on that day; Henry de Aula (age given 40) recollected that his father married again on the following day of the Decollation of St John the Baptist; Robert Buck, then 41 years old, was still smarting over his particular point of recall: on the morrow of the Nativity of St John the Baptist next before the said birth, he was so badly beaten by his school-master that he left school for home; this took place, as he well remembered, 21 years ago. Robert Forbraz (age given 50) had crossed to France that year; Elias de Stretton (age given 70) had become a widower; Adam de Brochton (age given 65) had been John Tempest's godfather; Robert de Bradely (age given 80) had that year been engaged in a lawsuit over some land; Richard de Bradley (age given 60) had had a son, as had Henry de Marton; William de Brigham, aged 44, had entered the service of Sir William de Paterton.[39] They were all formally agreed; it happened 21 years ago. This did not prevent them from giving their own ages rounded off to the nearest tenth. They could be approximate here, because this was not the issue. When necessary, however, they were capable of precision.

REMEDIES FOR OLD AGE

Everyone thus knew very well what stage of their life they had reached. The absence of figures is due to medieval man not being as conscious as we are of the importance of keeping meticulous statistics. However, this did not prevent him from keeping tally of the number of his years for himself. The sense of passing time and its irreversible nature was firmly anchored in his mind, which is why he worried about growing old. Far from being indifferent to time, medieval man feared ageing, and he searched for a means of escaping decrepitude, through dreams or through science.

On the popular folklorist level, age has always been associated with the idea of death and suffering. German tradition holds that all old women are evil: they are witches who symbolize the association between evil and old age. In some villages the effigy of an old woman would be burnt in order to drive away old age. A well-known folk tale declares that at the beginning, God fixed the span of life for men and animals at 30 years; the donkey then asked to have removed 18 years, the dog 12 years and the monkey ten years, at which man demanded these supplementary years for himself, thus obtaining a lifespan of 70 years. But he did not realize that these would be years of pain and decrepitude. Once past 30, he has to work hard, like a donkey, for 18 years: for the next 12 years, he drags himself from one corner to the next like a dog, growling but with no teeth left for biting; finally, during his ten last years, from 60 to 70, he no longer makes sense, and people make fun of him, as of a monkey.

In the Roussillon, Lent, a time for repentance, was symbolized by an old woman, the *patorra*, who was burnt on Easter Day. In Italy and Spain, the rite for driving off death featured the custom of 'sawing the old woman'. It involved sawing in half a very ugly effigy representing the oldest woman in the village. In Palermo, they pretended really to saw the old woman; in Florence the effigy of the old woman was stuffed with nuts and dried figs which the crowd picked up after the sawing. In central Europe, the last sheaf of the harvest was called the Old Woman, the Old Man, or the Grandmother, and the person who bound it was laughed and jeered at.[40]

More than ever before, the fountain of youth now formed part of the collective imagination. In John de Mandeville's *Book of Wonders*, it lies hidden in the middle of the Indian jungle. In the *Fabliau de Coquaigne*, from the mid thirteenth century, it is well-placed in this marvellous town where all sorts of good things are found in abundance. In the *Alexandrecite*, it is more than a fountain, it is a whole lake which rejuvenates those who plunge into it. Elsewhere it is a matter of the elixir of long life and of the island where no one grows old. The famous elixir was, like the philosopher's stone, the object of alchemical research. Here and there magical recipes against ageing are suggested: drink the blood of a child, or, more pleasant but less effective, the milk from the breast of a young woman; otherwise, take a blood-bath.[41]

Some of the great names in philosophy sought for the causes of ageing and especially for an eventual solution to them. Avicenna (980–1037) picked up the question where Galen had left it, and insisted on the influence of climate, of diet, and of physical exercise on the ageing process. 'In old persons', he wrote in his *Canon*, 'and in the decrepit, the earthly element is more predominant than in the other ages.'[42] Maimonides (1136–1204) recommended moderation in sexual matters and advised taking wine and medication. Arnold of Villanova (1135–1211), in his treatise *The Defence of Age, and Recovery of Youth*, a complicated mish-mash of astrology, alchemy, medicine and theology, declared:

> The conservation of youth and withstanding of age, consysteth in the manytenynge of the powres, the spyrites and the naturall heate of the body in theyr state and temperancy: and in the comfortyng and repayrynge of theym beynge defectyve. For so longe as the powres, the spyrytes and the naturall heate of the mannes body are not debylitate nor wekened, so longe (I saye) neyther shall ye skynne wrynkle, for the debylyte of ye natural heate declynynge to coldenes and drynes through the which the fode and norisshement of the body is corrupted and hyndered; is cause of corrugacyon or wrynklyng of the skynne.[43]

In other words, he adopted the classical theory according to which ageing is caused by the body's growing cold and dry, which must be combated by eating good food, drinking wine and taking baths. He went on to edit the *Regimen Sanitatis* in the school of medicine in Salerno and undertook research into the elixir of long life.

The most important works on the process of ageing and its remedies were those of the astonishing Franciscan known as Roger Bacon. Born in Dorset *c.*1210, he studied at Oxford under the great theologian Robert Grosseteste, and then went to Paris, returning to teach in Oxford from 1251 to 1257, when he entered the order of St. Francis. He divided his time between Paris and Oxford, but encountered numerous problems with the ecclesiastical authorities, who were worried by the unorthodox nature of his writings. He died after 1292, aged over 80.

In spite of his fragile health, this perceptive and tormented man took the original step of stressing experience as the main factor in scientific knowledge. Experience would enable man to prolong human life, to construct flying machines, ships with neither sails nor oars, automobiles and submersible engines. His thinking was exceptional for his age, but it remained entrenched within a religious and even ecclesiastical scheme.

The prodigies of science could be used to triumph over unbelievers and would allow the reorganization of the world by the Church under the direction of the clergy. Consequently, he considered his scientific works to constitute real military secrets, as exemplified by his treatise on *The Cure of Old Age, and Preservation of Youth*. In this he provides advice on how to prolong life and to keep old men healthy, and since he wanted to limit these salutary precepts to Christians in order to make them superior to the Muslims, he chose to couch his instructions 'in obscure and difficult terms, which I judge requisite to the Conservation of Health, lest they should fall into the hands of the unfaithful,'[44] which does not make his text easy to understand, even for good Christians. He was keen on this subject, and returned to it in his treatises *On the Retardation of Old Age* and *Of the Wonderful Power of Art and Nature*.

His thinking was not, however, as revolutionary as it has been considered. In his search for the causes of ageing and man's mortal nature, he made use essentially of Greco-Latin medicine, within a Christian theological framework:

> The Possibility of Prolongation of Life is confirmed by this, that Man is naturally immortal, that is, able not to dye: And even after he had sinned, he could live near a Thousand Years, afterwards by little and little the Length of his Life was abbreviated. Therefore it must needs be, that this Abbreviation is Accidental: therefore it might be either wholly repaired, or at least in part. But if we would but make Enquiry into the accidental Cause of this Corruption, we should find, it neither was from Heaven nor from ought but want of a Regimen of Health. For in as much as the Fathers are corrupt, they beget Children of a corrupt Complexion and Composition, and their Children from the same cause are corrupt themselves: and so Corruption is derived from Father to Son, till Abbreviation of Life prevails by Succession. Yet for all this it does not follow, that it shall always be cut shorter and shorter: because a Term is set in Humane Kind, that men should at the most of their years arrive at Fourscore, but more is their Pain and Sorrow. Now the Remedy against every Mans proper Corruption is, if every Man from his Youth would exercise a complete Regimen, which consists in these things, Meat and Drink, Sleep and Watching, Motion and Rest, Evacuation and Retention, Air, the Passions of the Mind. For if a Man would observe this Regimen from his nativity, he might live as long as his Nature assumed from his parents would permit, and might be led to the utmost Term of Nature, lapsed from Original Righteousness: which Term nevertheless he could not pass: Because this Regimen does not avail in the least against the old Corruption of our Parents.[45]

Table 7.2 Population growth in
England, 1234–1299

Period	Annual growth (%)
1234–9	+ 2.06
1240–4	+ 0.99
1245–9	+ 0.94
1250–4	+ 0.62
1255–9	+ 1.1
1260–4	+ 0.98
1265–9	+ 0.48
1270–4	+ 0.35
1275–9	+ 1.1
1280–4	+ 1.97
1285–9	+ 0.18
1290–4	− 0.15
1295–9	+ 0.32

Source: T.H. Hollingsworth, *Historical Demography*, London 1969.

So there was no question of rendering man immortal, but of extending his longevity so as to render it similar to that of the patriarchs. All in all, his was an optimistic vision, coloured by his confidence in the progress of science: man, by improving his way of living, would gradually extend his existence and would limit the sufferings of old age. Bacon broke with the theory of the universal solidarity of the elements in his *Cure of Old Age*, and attributed ageing solely to natural causes:

So the World waxeth old. Men grow old with it: not by reason of the Age of the World, but because of the gret Increase of Living Creatures, which infect the very Air, that every way encompasseth us, and through our Negligence in ordering our Lives, and that great Ignorance of the Properties, which are in things conducing to Health, which might help a disordered way of Living, and might supply the defect of due Government.[46]

When man ages, his body temperature diminishes due to the Decay of Natural Moisture and to the increase in external moisture. Atmospheric pollution was an important factor of decay, which is provoked by the proliferation of living beings. Can we interpret this as Bacon's intuition of the strong demographic growth in Europe at the period when he was writing? Table 7.2 shows this growth as demographers have calculated it for England.[47]

Bacon's foreboding was indeed remarkable: as the population grows, it creates more pollution and so endangers the environment and public health. His reflections on the psychological causes of ageing are no less remarkable: black thoughts and anxiety dry up and diminish our natural moisture, and cause us to age prematurely. Roger Bacon next proceeds to list the clinical features of old age:

> The Accidents of Age and Old Age are, Grey Hairs, Paleness, Wrinkles of the Skin, Weakness of Faculties and of natural Strength, Diminution of Blood and Spirits, Bleareyedness, abundance of rotten Phlegm, filthy Spitting, Shortness of Breath, Anger, Want of Sleep, an unquiet Mind, Hurt of the Instruments . . .[48]

He attributes to each of these features a cause, whose extravagance contrasts with his reasonable general causes; 'Greyness ariseth from putrid Phlegm coming out of the Regions of the Brain and Stomach'; 'Wrinkles of the Skin are contracted either from the Flesh extenuated . . . or from the Want of Flesh . . . This comes through the Putrefaction of the Humour.'

'Man's beauty reaches its peak' at the age of 40, after which comes decline, which can be slowed down by various means, which Bacon claimed he had tried out himself. Had he not succeeded in passing the fatal age of 80? The main thing was to lead a carefully regulated life and to follow a diet which maintained moisture, based on meat, wine, egg yolk and vegetables. He provides a lengthy dissertation on the problem presented by meat: Pullets, Kids, sucking Calves, young Geese, Lambs, Partridge, and Pheasants are especially recommended. 'Old mens meats ought to be of good juice, hot and moist, that they may quickly and easily be digested, and descend from the Stomach.'[49] Also to be avoided are putrid vapours, drugged sleep, wakeful nights and effort. While good humour preserves energy, excessive laughter disperses it and is consequently not advisable.

> Whence in Conclusion it is made manifest, that Mirth, Singing, Looking on Humane Beauty and Comeliness, Spices, Electuaries, warm Water, Bathings, some things lying in the bowels of the Earth, others lying hid among the Waves of the Sea, some living in the Air, others taken from the Noble Animal, well tempered and prepared, and many more such things are Remedies, whereby the Accidents of Age in Young men, the Infirmities of Old Age in Old Men, the Weaknesses and Diseases of the Decrepit Age in very Old Age, may be restrained, retarded and driven away.[50]

Table 7.3 Age at death in medieval cemeteries

| | Number of dead | | |
Age interval	Males	Females	Total
14–19 yrs	144	308	452
20–39 yrs	1107	1365	2472
40–59 yrs	1664	951	2616
60 yrs and over	414	305	719

Source: J.C. Russell, 'Population in Europe, 500–1500', in Carlo M. Cipolla, ed., *The Fontana Economic History of Europe, The Middle Ages*, Harmondsworth 1978.

THE NUMBER OF OLD PEOPLE AND LONGEVITY

The men of the Middle Ages were thus preoccupied with age, both in the world of learning as well as that of ordinary people. This fact on its own shows that the old were relatively numerous. People would not have attributed so much importance to a phase in life achieved by only a tiny minority. Hitherto, however, the lack of precise figures, coupled with the slightest reflection about the sanitary, alimentary and medical situation in the Middle Ages, has caused almost all historians to state that medieval old men were exceptional phenomenons. We are not so presumptuous as radically to contradict such a generally held opinion, which has been supported by eminent medievalists, but we have nevertheless formulated a few reservations.

Firstly, serious research, as distinct from any prejudice or vague feelings, based on the examination of skeletons from medieval cemeteries, tends to show that a great number of people died aged over 60. J.C. Russell, in the *Fontana Economic History of Europe*,[51] has built up statistics from a hundred such cemeteries, bearing on 6,259 skeletons of persons aged at least 14. The results show that 719 individuals (414 men and 305 women), 11 per cent of the total, lived longer than 60 years (table 7.3).

By using the same type of source material, Eric Fugedi has been able to provide a demographic analysis of medieval Hungary in the period from the tenth to the twelfth centuries, which reveals that 13.7 per cent of all deaths (including those of children) occurred between the ages of 50 and 59, 8.7 per cent between 60 and 69, 3.1 per cent between 70 and 79 and 0.3 per cent at the age of 80 or over. Of 100 births, 25.9 persons survived to the age of 50, 12.2 per cent to 60, 3.5 per cent to 70 and 0.3 per cent to the age of 80.[52] This means that, if one disregards the enormously high infant mortality rate, a significant number of adults was able to reach the age of 60. For our purposes, it is not the purely statistical point of view which matters but the effect on people's mentalities of the fact that a good number of adults did achieve old age. Medieval man could observe that once he had left childhood behind, he had circumnavigated the most perilous rocks and could hope, or fear, to grow old. The fraction of old people, when compared with the adult population, was not negligible : a state of affairs which did indeed deserve some attention, the more so in that anyone might be called to take part in it.

The old were thus not accidental:

Comparatively speaking, the medieval expectation was excellent. It seems better than the Roman, except for the unexplained North African data, better than for undeveloped countries until a few years ago, and even better than for early modern Europe. This is, of course, for the non plague periods.[53]

According to J.C. Russell, who bases his claims on a very illuminating table using English demographic data for the period between 1276 and 1300.[54] According to this table, it may be observed, among other things, that of a group of 1,000 boys whose births were recorded, only 650 were still alive by the age of 20, 381 at the age of 40, but still 144 at 60, and 56 per cent of those who reached this age lived longer than 64 years; 60 per cent of these survivors reached the age of 70 (table 7.4).

Other tables have been compiled using the *inquisitiones post mortem* in medieval England. These enquiries were set in motion in questions of inheritance, and obviously only involved landowners, the great majority of whom were men. The life expectancy of this social group was around ten years at the age of 60, and five years at the age of 70, with fairly significant variations according to the period. Very old men were not as rare as one might have thought: Alina de Marechale inherited his lands at the age of 90 and died aged 97; a Reginald de Colewyk was said to have lived a century; his son probably lived a long life and his grandson passed the 80 mark.[55] It is more difficult to discover the proportions in the peasant world. Nevertheless, according to the same author, a comparison between the life expectancy for landowners and for certain peasant groups in England between 1280 and 1340 does not reveal any significant differences. The diet in the manor-houses, with their excessive consumption of meat and wine, was in any case no healthier than that of the peasants.

Within every social category old men were more numerous than old women, many of whom died prematurely from the effects of childbirth. Robert Fossier has established that Picardy enjoyed a favourable period after 1225–50, a period when obstetrics are supposed to have begun to

Table 7.4 Generation life table of males born 1276–1300 in England

Age interval (yrs)	Mortality rate within interval(%)	Likelihood of survival (%)	No. of individual survivors	Life expectancy (yrs)
0	15	85	1000	31.3
1–4	11	89	850	35.75
5–9	4.35	95.65	756	35.65
10–14	4.65	95.35	723	32.16
15–19	5.68	94.32	689	28.62
20–4	12.6	87.4	650	25.19
25–9	13.66	86.34	568	23.47
30–4	11.01	88.99	490	21.8
35–9	12.7	87.3	436	19.19
40–4	16.67	83.33	381	16.61
45–9	25	75	311	14.78
50–4	25.66	74.34	194	10.52
55–9	18.44	81.56	381	16.61
60–4	43.86	56.14	144	8.3
65–9	39.39	60.61	81	7.81
70–4	45	55	49	6.29
75–9	69.56	30.44	27	4.37
80–4	71.43	28.57	8	3.75
85–9	100	0	2	2.5

Source: J.C. Russell, *British Medieval Population*, Albuquerque 1958.

Table 7.5 Life expectancy for men in medieval England

	Men born between							
Age	1200 and 1275	1276 and 1300	1301 and 1325	13426 and 1348	1348 and 1375	1376 and 1400	1401 and 1424	1425 and 1450
0	35.3	31.3	29.8	27.2	17.3	20.5	23.8	32.8
10	36.3	32.2	32	28.1	25.1	24.5	29.7	34.5
20	28.7	25.2	23.8	22.1	23.9	21.4	29.4	27.7
30	22.8	21.8	20	21.1	22	22.3	25	24.1
40	17.8	16.6	15.7	17.7	18.1	19.2	19.3	20.4
60	9.4	8.3	9.3	10.8	10.9	10.0	10.5	13.7
80	5.2	3.8	4.5	6	4.7	3.1	4.8	7.9

Source: J.C. Russell, 'Population in Europe, 500–1500', in Carlo M. Cipolla, ed., *The Fontana Economic History of Europe, The Middle Ages*, Harmondsworth 1978.

improve.[56] This does not appear to have been the case in other regions.

The epidemics do not seem to have affected the general proportion of old people in society. They even seem to have been less affected than the other age groups, as will be seen in the next chapter, which deals with the Plague. From the eleventh to the thirteenth century, however, there were relatively few great epidemics and the deadliest illness in that period was probably tuberculosis, which is particularly lethal for those aged between 15 and 35.

More important, given its effects on their material, psychological and social condition, is the fact that many old men lived on their own, and for three reasons. First, the low rate of marriage: 28 to 34 per cent among the serf population in the early Middle Ages, 32.8 per cent at Basle, 34.6 per cent at Ypres, 38.7 per cent at Fribourg, 35 to 45 per cent in England in 1377.[57] This led to a high proportion of celibate people, especially men. Further, the greater female mortality considerably increased the number of widowers and, by introducing an imbalance between the sexes, made it even more difficult to get married. According to the calculations quoted above, of 719 individuals who reached the age of 60, there would be a surplus of 109 men, and the remaining 610 men and women would not all have been couples. Robert Fossier reckons that in thirteenth-century Picardy a third of all married couples were childless, which meant that the survivor was condemned to solitude. It was also frequently the case that where an old man was married again to a young woman the old husband would die first, which explains the relatively high number of widows, whose situation was often tragic; widows and orphans have long been symbols of distress. The canonization proceedings show widows of all ages shuffling past. During the proceedings for St Yves, 18 of the 51 women who made depositions were widows, one aged 30, two aged 40, five aged 50, three aged 55, four aged 60 and one aged 66 and two aged 80.

THE CLERGY: A STRONG PROPORTION OF OLD MEN

Medieval old man was thus no myth. He pulled significant weight in society and each of the three orders which, according to Adalberon of Rheims, constituted the Christian population, had its particular group of old men and women. The place they occupied and the role which devolved on them varied, of course, from one category to another.

The order which comprised the strongest proportion of old men was still, and by a long margin, that of the clergy. The age requirements for entry into holy orders excluded the excessively young, although dispensations were not rare. The sacred nature of the clergy protected them to some extent, as in the preceding period, from the brutality of the age. Maintained by their order or by their prayers, they did not need to fear food shortages or lean times; the isolation of the monks also served to protect them from epidemics. Finally, their essentially tertiary functions allowed them to avoid violent or dangerous physical labour: celibate as they were, nuns did not fear the pangs of childbirth either. So it comes as no surprise to find the most cases of longevity within cloisters and among the ranks of the churchmen. Inquiries into canonization proceedings throw up venerable monks, both regular and secular, among their witnesses. At the proceedings for St Yves, which serve as our reference, there appear John de La Vieuville, a 90-year-old cleric, and two others aged 80 and 70, as well as the rector of La Roche Derrien, himself aged 70 years. The chronicler Matthew Paris tells how, at the beginning of the eleventh century, when excavations were made into the ancient city of Verulanium (St Albans), they had to call on a decrepit old priest to decipher the inscriptions found there.[58] The monasteries were full of old monks who remained very active.

In the same way, the Cistercian order was so popular at the beginning of the twelfth century that thousands of recruits flowed to it, who, 30 or 40 years later, were to form a generation of old men more numerous than the younger generation of monks who joined after the spate of vocations had subsided. In the 1150s, those monks belonging to St Bernard's generation were aged over 60, and although the famous abbot of Clairvaux did not, as we have seen, grant any special privileges to old age, he did however talk about it a lot and advise on the role the old were to play. Can it not be assumed that the appearance of old people in his last writings was above all due to the fact that he encountered a strong proportion of elderly monks in every monastery of his order that he visited? His father, whose own vocation came late in life, had become a monk and had died 'in a happy old age'; his religious correspondents were often old men, such as Guérin, the abbot of Sainte-Marie-des-Alpes, or like Robert, who had stayed a monk for 67 years.[59] His biographers were old; the chief one, William of St Thierry (1085–1148), was 63 years old when he undertook the work, which was interrupted by his death. In his preface he declares:

> Even now the sands of my life are running out, and my body, in the grip of illness and weakness, will soon be answering the call of death. I am certain that the time is not far off when I must leave this life and appear before my Creator. I fear that I may already be too late to start and finish a book that I dearly want to complete before my life ebbs out.[60]

His work was continued by Arnaud de Bonneval, and then by Geoffrey d'Auxerre, who died at the age of 68 and who had been St Bernard's secretary (1120–88). Alan, a former Bishop of Autun (1153–61), who retired to Clairvaux where he died in 1181 when over 70, wrote a second life of the saint. After 1180, John the Hermit, a septuagenerian and one of St Bernard's former disciples, wrote another biography at the request of the Bishop of Frascati. All these accounts depict the abbot of Clairvaux in frequent contact with old monks, who were often favoured with the gift of prophecy and with visions: 'an old and very pious monk' from the monastery of Clairvaux heard demons rejoicing at having dragged off the soul of one of the conversi brothers with them. The latter also appeared to him to tell him about his torments. Following St Bernard's intervention, the old man had a third vision in which the departed brother told him how he had been saved.[61] The saint often employed the services of old monks, whose wisdom he valued. In 1127, in a letter to Thibaud, Count of Champagne, he recommends one of them, who is to go and find the king: 'He is aged, as you see', he remarked discreetly.[62]

With every monastic order, its period of decline is marked by a clear ageing of its residents. When recruitment ceased, the number of young monks fell dramatically and their average age rose spectacularly. This may be observed of the Templars at the beginning of the fourteenth century. The records of the 1307 trial tell us the age of those monks who were interrogated and give the impression that their strongholds were old people's homes. Jacques de Molay, the Grand Master, was 64 years old at the time, and died at the age of 71 (1243–1314); Geoffroy de Charnay, the Preceptor of Normandy, was over 60; Hughes de Pairaud, Visitor to the Order in France, was 66, and Geoffroy de Gonneville, the Preceptor of Aquitaine and Poitou, was around 50 years old. Of the 40 friars ordinary who were interrogated, ten were over 60 and only 12 were less than 40 years old. Since the order had lost its military function, it could sometimes be joined at an advanced age. Gilles d'Encrey, from the diocese of Rheims, took his vows at the age of 50, Albert de Rumercourt was however 67. According to his testimony, he had not had to spit on the cross on account of his great age: 'Since you are an old man'.[63] He was 70 years old at the time of the trial and another friar was 72. The average age of the deponents was 47.4 years.

The founders of monastic orders and the abbots of monasteries were often vigorous old men. Robert d'Arbrissel (1047–1117), the Archdeacon of Rennes who retired to live as a hermit in the forest of Craon, was nominated Apostolic Preacher by the Pope in 1096 and travelled around eastern France, barefoot, in rags, practising draconian fasts, between the ages of 50 and 70; he founded the Abbey of Fontevraud. Blessed Gerard (1040–1120) was a contemporary who died in his eighties having founded the hospital of St John in Jerusalem, whereas a similarly-named saint, who died aged 79 in 959, founded the abbey of Brogne. Herluin, who founded the abbey of Bec and died at around 83 years of age in 1078, remained active until the end. He was seen in 1070, when over

75, arriving in Boulogne and embarking for England, having miraculously summoned a favourable wind. St Bruno, who founded la Chartreuse, was born before 1030 in Cologne. In 1090 he was sent for by Urban II, who had known him when he was a canon at Rheims, and ordered him to leave his hermitage and become his adviser. However, the old hermit proved incapable of adjusting to the papal court and retired to Calabria where he died in 1101, aged 71. Reginald, veteran of St Aignan d'Orleans and a former master at the University of Paris, where he had taught canon law, was miraculously cured in 1217 by St Dominic when aged over 60, and did not shrink from undertaking a pilgrimage to Jerusalem and then entering the Dominican order. He next taught in Bologna, before being sent once more to Paris by St Dominic.

The chroniclers, many of whom were monks, often began writing late in life, as was the case with St Bernard's biographers. The feeling of having lived for a long time and of having been present at important events unknown to younger generations was the main motive driving them to write. The old man thus gradually became aware of his only element of superiority over the young – that of being the living witness to a glorious past which his juniors would never know in person. Nobody will ever be able to remove this advantage from the old, and the ancient combatants of all wars always constitute irreplaceable living records, in the image of Joinville, who spent five years, from the age of 80 to 85, writing his *Life of St Louis*, which records his memories of the Seventh Crusade when he was 60. The seneschal of Champagne, who was to die in 1317 at the age of 93, symbolized the essential role of medieval old men as witnesses to the past. At the end of his book, he alludes discreetly to his pride in his position as a living archive:

> I wish to make known to all that I myself actually saw and heard a great part of what I have told you here concerning the saintly king. Another considerable portion of it is based on what I found in a certain book, written in French, and which I have incorporated in this Chronicle. I am drawing your attention to this so that those who hear this book read may have full confidence in the truth of what it says I saw and heard. As for the other things recorded here, I offer no guarantee of their truth, because I did not witness them myself. This work was completed in the month of October, in the year of Our Lord 1309.[64]

When William Le Breton (c.1150–1225) composed his *Gesta Philippi Augusti*, there was certainly less of a chronological gap between the events he reported, but the author nevertheless benefited from the prestige conferred on him by his 70 years.

The Benedictine Guibert de Nogent was writing at more or less the same age (1053–1130), as was Gerald of Wales (1146–1223); we have already mentioned Ordericus Vitalis, who composed his chronicle at the age of 67 (1075–1143) and William of Malmesbury, who compiled his own at the age of 60 (1080–1142).

Whether testifying during canonization proceedings, or writing chronicles, telling stories in the evening, or transmitting their knowledge, old men in the Middle Ages fulfilled an essential function as links between the generations. In the event of argument over a point of law, in the absence of written proof, they were the ones to be consulted. In 1252 a conflict over tithes arose between the serfs of the chapter of Notre Dame of Paris. This led to an enquiry. The oldest men of the region were questioned concerning the tradition: Simon, Mayor of Corbreuse, who was more than 70 years old, 'old and sick', and Archdeacon John, a former canon, who declared that he had in his time known of 'old rolls' in which were written the chapter's rights, and who had heard those even older than himself talking about them, stated that the rights had been levied since 'earliest antiquity' and that the value of these rolls was confirmed 'with regard to the antiquity of the script'. Everything old determined the law, and the older the testimony, the greater its value. In Picardy, Robert Fossier reports the presence of three witnesses aged between 70 and 85 at a trial in Bethune in 1316, and in Montreuil in 1236, three deponents were between 50 and 60, three between 60 and 70, one of 76 and four of over 80 years of age. During the proceedings for the canonization of St Dominic, Sister Cecilia, a nun aged over 80, provided a very precise description of the saint.[65] Since the old were well versed in the law, they used to be consulted about its application; this was the case with Philip of Novara and also with Joinville.

Given the number of old people in the ranks of the ordinary clergy, both regular and secular, it stands to reason that the hierarchy comprised a strong proportion of aged persons. Christopher Brooke has shown that the eight bishops whose ages are known in England in 1158 were all aged over 70.[66] There is no shortage of individual examples of illustrious prelates and theologians: Robert Grosseteste, born in 1175, was elected Bishop of Lincoln at the age of 60 and died in 1253 at the age of 78; St Anthelm, born in 1107 in Savoy, was Bishop of Belley between the ages of 56 and 71 (1163–78); Arnold of Rochester, born in Beauvais in 1040, was first a monk then prior of Canterbury, then Abbot of Peterborough, was elected Bishop of Rochester at the age of 74 in 1114, and died at his post at the age of 84; Diego Gelmirez, the first Archbishop of St James of Compostella, died in 1140 at the age of 70; John of Salisbury was elected Bishop of Chartres at the age of 61 in 1176; Otto, Bishop of Bamberg, who converted Pomerania to Christianity died at the age of 79 in 1139.

The archbishops of Canterbury present a magnificent succession of intractable old men, who passionately defended the rights of the Church in the teeth of the monarchy. The most remarkable of these were Lanfranc, Anselm and Stephen Langton. Lanfranc was born in 1005, became Abbot of St Étienne in Caen in 1060 and was appointed Primate of England at the age of 65 by William the Conqueror, who trusted him completely. He acted as regent on several occasions during the king's absence, and it was due to this old 82-year-old man's prestige that the crown passed to William Rufus without incident in 1087. The new king bore reluctantly with his remonstrances and he died two years later, respected by all. He was succeeded in 1093 by Anselm, Abbot of Bec and one of the most remarkable thinkers of the Middle Ages, who was then 63 years old. He clashed at once with the king, who hated him, and had to go into exile. He returned in 1100 at the beginning of Henry I's reign, and soon quarrelled with the new king over lay investiture. In 1103, at the age of 70, he travelled to Rome on a mission, remained in exile in Lyon, and returned to England in 1107 after a compromise had been reached. He exercised his functions until his death at the age of 75 in 1109. Cardinal Stephen Langton was elected Archbishop of Canterbury in 1207 at the age of 57, and had the weighty task of confronting John Lackland, who forced him to stay with the Cistercians at Pontigny for ten years and drove the monks out of Canterbury, although they were all old and infirm.[67] In 1215, he played a vital role in drawing up the Magna Carta, after which he ruled his clergy firmly until the age of 78. The see of Canterbury was occupied by another septuagenarian, the Dominican Robert Kilwardby, between the years 1272 and 1279.

Old theologians were legion in this period. Among the most famous were William of Champeaux, a master at the cathedral school of Paris, who founded the school of St Victor, where Abelard attended his lectures. He was elected Bishop of Chalons-sur-Marne in 1113 at the age of 63, and died aged 71 in 1121. William of Conches was tutor to Henry Plantagenet at the age of 60 and he died aged 74, after 1154. William of Saint-Amour was professor of theology at Paris and died aged 70 (1202–72). Alan of Lille, the Universal Doctor, retired at the end of his life to Citeaux, where he died in 1203, aged 75 according to some, or 88, to others. Albertus Magnus, a Dominican, was Thomas Aquinas's master, and became Bishop of Regensburg in 1260 at the age of 54; he went on teaching until his last years and undertook an enormous *Summa Theologica*, before dying at the age of 74, leaving a gigantic opus behind, the scientific part of which was devoted to the elixir of long life. His pupil Gilles de Lessines was to imitate him im everything including his longevity (1230–1304).

While most churchmen exercised their functions until the end, some of them were constrained by their frailty to retire from the ministry, resulting in the appearance of several hospices for old priests in the thirteenth century, proof that the number of very old men among the clergy must have been high. In 1251, Bishop Walter of Marvis opened one of these hospices at Tournai, which was reserved to priests whose benefices had been withdrawn on account of their age.[68] The dignity of the priestly state and concern for simple justice demanded that these old priests were not reduced to mendicancy.

There was no retirement for popes, however, and whatever may have been said to the contrary, the pontiffs of the Middle Ages were old, and indeed the most energetic among them were not always the younger ones. Think of Gregory VII (1073–85), actively opposing the Emperor at Canossa, who was elected at the age of 60 and who died in exile aged 73. Think of Calixtus II, who signed the *Concordat of Worms* at the age of 62; of Celestine III (1191–8), elected at 85 years of age, who was an energetic adversary of Frederick Barbarossa, who himself experienced a thousand tribulations and died aged 97 while Rome was being besieged; think of Gregory X (1271–6) who presided over the Council of Lyon, was elected at the age of 61 and died aged 66; of Celestine V (1294), who was elected at the age of 79 but sat only a moment on Peter's throne; of the irascible Boniface VIII (1294–1303), that megalomanic old man, the author of the papal bull 'Unam Sanctam', who treated Philip the Fair, King of France, as a young ne'er-do-well and threatened 'to depose him like a naughty boy', and who died aged 86 shortly after the episode at Agnani. Finally, think of his successors, Benedict XI (1303–5), who was pope between the ages of 63 and 65, or of John XXII (1316–34), who was elected when aged 72 and died aged 90.

Even these few names make it difficult to subscribe to Jacques Le Goff's statement that bishops and popes 'were often elected when young'.[69] In fact, apart from the scandalous period of the 'pontifical pornocracy' in the tenth century and the beginning of the eleventh century, the Church put her trust in age and experience, a tradition which has not been belied even in our day. But the old men who were chosen as pontiffs were energetic types cast in an exceptional mould.

Old warriors: respected as long as they remain active

The attitude towards old age of the feudal world of *bellatores*, warriors and knights posed a different problem. While one might assume *a priori* that this milieu, which prized physical prowess above all else, would have been unfavourable towards the old, a more careful examination shows that in reality knights were not at all concerned about the number of their years. Once their helmets were on their heads, there was no difference between young and old. There were only strong and weak men, men of prowess and cowards. Chivalric literature itself vacillates between the emperor *à la barbe fleurie* and the youthful Lancelot of the Lake.

The defence of a fief certainly required a master in full possession of his faculties, and Girard of Vienne's *chanson*, composed at the beginning of the thirteenth century, retraces the drama of an old knight, Garin of Montglane, whose lands in Gascony were ravaged by Moorish raiders because he was too old to defend them, and his sons too young. One of them, Girard, has quarrelled with the emperor over a point of honour, and Garin, mindful of the solidarity due to his lineage, sides with him and becomes a rebel, thus drawing the sarcasms of the barons upon himself: 'Look at this intractable old man! His hand shakes, his head is hoary, and he is challenging the emperor, he is rebelling! Look at this hero whom one could knock down with a feather!'

Chivalry was not kind to old men once they had grown too weak for fighting. But it was not old age so much as weakness which was derided, because any young and inept squire would be treated just as harshly. Chivalry did know how to respect old age, whether in the form of an old warrior who had retained all his vigour, such as the Charlemagne of legend, or confined to the role of counsellor, the man of experience whose advice was all the more precious because he had enjoyed a brilliant career. In this, the knights thought along the same lines as the theologians: everyone reaps in his old age what he sowed during his life; an old man is the product of his whole existence; the saint is the fruit of a virtuous life, the old knight is honoured according to how glorious he once was. These men were forged all of a piece and they did not dissociate the adult man from the old man. A gallant knight's exploits would win him the respect of his peers for the rest of his life. He would definitely become a legend.

This is perhaps one of the basic differences between then and the modern age, in which men never acquire heroic status. Our age cannot compete with Arthur and Charlemagne, the authentic heroes, the supermen of the Middle Ages, who were still achieving great things well after their seventieth year. Their historical longevity, amplified by the troubadours, turned them into eternally young men with white beards. Arthur, who in fact died in 515, between the ages of 65 and 70, lives on to a hundred years of age in *La Mort d'Arthur*, in the company of perky octogenarians such as Gawain. As for Charlemagne, who died in 814 at the age of 71, one of his tenth century 'lives' attributes two hundred years to him. This was also the age given him by the *Chanson de Roland*, an astonishing epic which runs along briskly after its timeless old men: Marcile's wise counsellor is the old Blancandrin, whereas the 200-year-old Charlemagne listens to the advice of Richard the Old. His terrible adversary, the Amiral Baligant, is an 'ancient old man, who has survived Virgil and Homer', which did not prevent him from having preserved an impressive physique:

This gallant knight is of very high stature,
Slim his hips and broad his flanks,
His chest is strong and well formed,
His shoulders are large, his face is bright,
His expression proud, his hair curly,
And as white as the flowers in Summer.

In the Frankish army, Anseis le Vieil (the Old) and Gerard de Roussillon le Vieux (the Old) manage to distinguish themselves, and 100,000 vigorous old barons of France line up for the decisive battle:

Their bodies are hardy and their countenances proud.
Their hair is hoary and their beards are white.

They all accomplish extraordinary athletic exploits. This is an admirable document which witnesses to a period, the eleventh and twelfth centuries, when old age had not yet attained autonomy, when it was still indistinguishable from adulthood, whose prestigious finale it still constituted. These old warriors had lost nothing of their strength and daring, but their white beards conferred prestige, experience and wisdom on them. It was an essential attribute of the epic hero; Charlemagne strokes his unceasingly while thinking, and he pulls at it when anxious (the recital mentions it 17 times). The narrator's very last verse refers once more to it: 'His eyes weep tears and he pulls at his white beard.'[70]

In the quite different context of the Scandinavian world, the sagas of the thirteenth century similarly reflect Icelandic society's respect for its old leaders, but they also show how this attitude evolved as a result of sedentarization. These recitals form exceptional source material about old age in warrior societies, and are thought to tell of events and to describe a situation going back 300 years to the ninth century. Far from being despised, the old leaders, like the French feudal nobility, enjoyed a prestige proportional to the importance of their past exploits. Once retired, they lived on their lands; people came to consult them, and the young benefited from their experience. One such was Olaf Feilan, who 'became a mighty man and a great chieftain. He lived at Hvamm to old age.'[71] Before they died, they gathered their children and their associates around them to impart their final advice and last wishes to them. The *Laxdale Saga* also tells of chieftain Hoskuld, who died in 964, and of Snorri the Priest, who died in 1031 at the age of 67.[72] Thordinn Karlsefni, an Icelandic merchant, returned to Iceland after a great many adventures at sea to set up as a farmer and live to a very advanced age, honoured by all.

Some indeed continued to feel the pull of the sea and went on sailing until old age, deliberately seeking death on their last voyage. *Njal's Saga* recounts of old Flosi Thordarson:

This is how men say that Flosi died: when he was an old man he went abroad to fetch himself some house-timber. He spent the winter in Norway, and next summer he was late in getting ready to sail. People warned him that his ship was not seaworthy, but Flosi replied that it was good enough for a doomed old man. He boarded the ship and sailed out to sea. Nothing was ever heard of that ship again.[73]

Old women were held in just as much respect and they exercised an authority comparable to that of men when head of the family. Old Unn, in the *Laxdale Saga*, exercised a real matriarchal rule, and distributed her lands between her children and grandchildren.

The tone of other sagas, however, is different: they show us deposed old chieftains being maltreated without any consideration. The finest of these stories is that of *Egil Skallagrimsson*, an epic poem telling the life of this famous hero who died at the age of 80, in 990. Egil's exploits had been numerous, but his old age was rendered difficult because of his infirmities. The tale of his collapse is pathetic in its simplicity:

Egil Skallagrimsson became an old man, and in his age he grew infirm, and was enfeebled in both hearing and sight. He grew stiff-legged too. Egil was now at Mosfell with Grim and Thordis. It happened one day that Egil was walking outside by the wall and stumbled and fell. Some women saw this and laughed at it, saying: Its all over with you now, Egil, when you fall of your own accord. The women took us more seriously, said farmer Grim, when we were younger.
Then Egil chanted:

> Neck halter's steed falters.
> I fall dread on bald head;
> Love limb's left limp, and
> Last, hearing fails fast.[74]

Having grown blind, Egil goes to warm himself by the fire, but being clumsy and in the way, the housekeeper scolds him:

Be easy, said Egil, though I toast myself by the fire, and let us give and take a little here.
Stand up, she ordered, Be off with you to your place, and let us get on with our work.
Egil stood up and went to his place and chanted:

> Blind towards brand's blaze turn I.
> Patch-goddess ask for pity;
> So ail I where my eyelids

Alight on eyesight's meadow.[75]

Egil did all he could to make people talk about him in spite of everything: he wanted to attend the Thing in order to throw handfuls of his money around and hear the people kicking and clouting for it. Such was the old chief's tragic decline. But Egil was an exception. It was because of his infirmities that he was reduced to this pitiable state. In the same saga, old king Harald Fair-Hair, having reigned over Norway for 70 years and having retired in favour of his son Eric, now led a peaceful and honourable retirement, although he was paid tribute less regularly than before.

The prestige of the old warrior in Iceland was definitively toppled by the transition from an economy based on war and rapine to a pastoral economy. Under the old system, the old man was the living witness to warrior exploits; he embodied the honour of the family, which he protected by inciting its younger members to inflict bloody revenge. The new society, being peaceful and agrarian, no longer admired this bravado and the realistic style of saga of the thirteenth century made fun of such belligerent old men. Thus, in the tale of *Thorstein Staff-smitten*, old Thorarin, a retired viking, encouraged his son, a peaceful and hard-working man who had many weapons, to undertake a bloody vendetta. He was a fossilized relic of the viking past, who could not integrate with the peaceful rural community of which he was an unwilling and useless member.[76]

The account is clearly critical:

> There was an old man called Thorarin, who dwelt in Sunnudale, an old man and feeble of sight: he had been a red-hand viking in his younger days, nor was he a man good to deal with though he were old.

On speaking to his son Thorstein, he reproached him for his cowardice:

> Time has been when I would not have budged before such as Biarni, yet he is the greatest of champions. Now would I rather lose thee than have a coward son.

The subsequent fight resulted in a draw, but Biarni reported back to Thorarin that his son had been killed. The indomitable old man then tried to avenge him and addressed Biarni as follows:

> Come thou on to my shuttle-bed floor and draw very nigh, for the old carle tottereth on his feet now with eld and feebleness: nor deem it so but my dead son yet runneth in my head.
> Biarni came close and found the old man fumbling with a sax

which he had a mind to thrust into Biarni, who avoided the
blow.[77]

Horarin's lamentable failure was that of all old men of the older
generation, of the old warriors who were no longer respected.

In the *Saga of Hrafnkel*, a washerwoman expresses the old ideal in a
derisory manner, when she reminds her aged master of his obligation
to take revenge:

> The old saw is mostly true that 'who grows old, grows afraid'.
> Little is that honour which is got early, if a man afterwards puts
> up with disgrace, and has not pith enough ever to push his rights;
> and such is a great wonder in a man who has been doughty.[78]

As demonstrated by the Icelandic example, old men were held in
greater respect by warrior societies than in agricultural circles. Whereas
the old warrior bathed in the glow of his exploits, what could an elderly
peasant pride himself on? As long as he was not infirm, an old warrior
retained all his power, and his experience only served to enhance his
prestige. The feudal system did not in any case include an age limit:
the act of homage committed both partners until death, in conformity
with the prevailing monolithic vision of human life. A vassal was
responsible for his fief right up to the end, although facts might indeed
bely the law. Impatient sons might revolt against their old fathers, and
Henry II Plantagenet also underwent this cruel experience. Such examples
are, however, astonishingly few. The type of the old knight who
voluntarily handed power over to his son is more literary than actual.
The story of *El Cid* was derived from the traditions of the eleventh
century, and is one of the exceptional cases: Don Diego entrusted his
son, Ruy Diaz de Bivar, with wreaking revenge against Count Lozano,
'knowing that he lacked the strength for vengeance and was too old to
handle a sword, he was unable to sleep at night and could not taste his
food.'

More often than not, the knight would continue to fulfil his obligations
in person for as long as he had strength to ride. Not even loss of sight
would stop him, as with John the Blind of Luxembourg, whose life
was spent in one battle after another until he met his death at Crécy.
He was 52 years old at the time, whereas Philip Augustus was 49 at
Bouvines, where he fought like a young lion – to no one's surprise.
But what about Frederick Barbarossa, who died while on Crusade at
the age of 68? And Raymond VI, Count of Toulouse, who reconquered
his fief by force of arms when over 60 (1156–1222)? And Raymond of
Saint-Gilles, one of the leaders of the First Crusade, who was taken
seriously ill during the march across Asia Minor, but recovered to
participate in every battle and to die during the attack on Tripoli at the

age of 63 (1042–1105)? And William the Conqueror, a warrior down to his fingertips and until the very last moment, who died at the age of 59 when returning from an expedition to pillage Mantes in 1087, and whom a monk of Caen described at the time as being as robust as a young man? And, again, what about the famous William Marshal, whose exploits have been told by Georges Duby?[79]

A professional contestant in tournaments, Marshal married for the first time at the age of 50. As the King of England's marshall he was given the regency of the kingdom at the age of 71, on the death of John Lackland. William led the charge in person at the Battle of Lincoln, although aged 72, and he was more than a figurehead; he seized the Count of Perche, the leader of the opposing army and lieutenant to the Dauphin Louis. Three months later, he was restrained with difficulty from joining the expedition against the French fleet. Nevertheless, the early thirteenth-century poem which tells the story of his life pays scant tribute to his age. A knight was not old so long as he could fight, and no one seems to have been surprised when the care of the kingdom was entrusted to a septuagenarian. When he asked his friends for their advice, John of Early was the only one to feel any dismay: 'I see your body weakened by fatigue and old age', he told him, but no more was made of this. That the marshall was old was apparent, not through his greater vulnerability in battle, but through his adherence to a bygone chivalric code: after the Battle of Lincoln, he escorted his vanquished enemy, Prince Louis of France, to the coast. Such respect for the adversary was no longer appropriate in a society where realism had begun to oust the chivalric ideal, and his fine gesture was equated with betrayal. Furthermore, the author of the poem, himself very old, bitterly regretted the disappearance of the old ideals.

William Marshal was not the oldest warrior still active at that time. The Venetian Enrico Dandolo, born around 1107, was employed several times on diplomatic missions, which led to his partial blinding in 1171 by order of the Byzantine emperor Manuel Comnenus. He was elected doge on 21 June 1192 at the age of 85. Twelve years later, when 97 years old, he decided to take part in the Fourth Crusade in person. According to him, his great age was an additional reason for his departure, because his experience would be of value to the expedition, as he pointed out in a speech to the Crusaders:

> Sirs, you are associated with the best and bravest people in the world in the highest enterprise anyone has ever undertaken. Now I am an old man, weak and in need of rest, and my health is failing. All the same I realize that no one can control and direct you like myself, who am your lord. If you will consent to my taking the cross so that I can protect and guide you, and allow

my son to remain here in my place to guard this state, then I shall go to live or die with you and with the pilgrims.[80]

The Crusaders cheered him and saluted his prowess, his great valour. When the decisive moment came, the Doge, bearing helmet and breastplate, threw himself at the head of his men into the assault on the walls of Constantinople, arousing the admiration of all: 'Let me tell you here of a deed of outstanding valour. The Doge of Venice, although an old man and completely blind, stood at the bow of his galley, with the banner of St Mark unfurled before him. He cried out to his men to put him on shore, or else he himself would deal with them as they deserved. They obeyed him promptly, for the galley touched ground and the men in it leaped ashore, bearing the banner of St Mark to land before the Doge . . . Then began a grand and marvellous assault on the city (as) Geoffroy de Villehardouin, author of this chronicle, here affirms.'[81]

Dandolo's case is undoubtedly unique in the annals of war. The Doge survived the attack and died the following year in 1205, aged 98 years. However, many other old men made the journey to Jerusalem among the anonymous crowds of Crusaders: 'Children, old women and old men got ready to leave; they well knew that they would not fight but they hoped to become martyrs,' Guibert de Nogent tells us about the Peasants' Crusade. Geoffrey of Bouillon's expeditions also included a number of old knights.[82] William the Conqueror's oldest son, Robert, took part in it; he was made prisoner at Tinchebray on his return, and died in prison at the age of 80.

Thus old age does not appear to have had any influence on chivalry. Those valourous knights who survived tournaments, battles, hunting accidents, feasting and apoplexy, constituted forces of nature who would never be obliged by old age to cede the care of their fiefs to younger men. Not many of them chose to retire to a Templar garrison. As for women, although they entered convents more frequently than men, once they had reached a certain age, many noble ladies also continued to lead very active lives. In an age when giving birth was more deadly than participating in battle, only the strongest mothers would reach the menopause, and they would then expend their surplus energy in politics.

The case of Eleanor of Aquitaine is still well known. After having given her two husbands a total of ten children and being twice widowed, she was still a fine woman when aged over 70, as William Marshall testifies, and she spent her old age travelling around Europe, between England and Aquitaine, in Spain, in Italy and Germany, in order to safeguard the power of her beloved and hairbrained sons. During her final 15 years, between the ages of 69 and 84, she travelled thousands of miles, moved heaven and earth for Richard and John, wove intrigues, arranged marriages, signed treaties and conducted sieges. Life for her began in 1189, at the death of Henry II, her tyrannical husband, who had kept her locked up. She was then 69 years old. Eleanor assumed control at once, organized Richard's coronation and went over to France in the following year to prepare his crusade. She also found a wife for him, Berengar of Navarre, and, in order to arrange the marriage, she went to Aquitaine, in spite of her 70 years and the bad roads of the age, and from there via the Mount Geneva pass, to Pisa, Naples and Brindisi, where she boarded ship to rejoin her son in Sicily. On her return journey, she was in Rome on 14 April 1191, and, recrossing the Alps, in Rouen on 14 June. Once installed in Bonneville-sur-Rouques, she learnt of the return of Philip Augustus and immediately undertook the fortification of the Norman strongholds, leaving for England on 11 February 1192, where she summoned the barons to Windsor, Oxford, London and Winchester, and kept a close watch on John's moves in his attempt to usurp Richard's place. When the latter was made prisoner, Eleanor deployed an extraordinary degree of diplomatic activity to get him released, thwarting John's ploys the while. In December 1193, she embarked for Germany at the age of 73, in order to pay over the ransom in person. She spent a while in Cologne, secured Richard's release at the beginning of February 1194 and returned to England via Antwerp and Sandwich (12 March 1194). Two months later, she was to be found in Barfleur with her royal son, while the people in her entourage muttered that she 'forgot her age'.

Nevertheless, it was probably during this same year that she decided to retire to the abbey of Fontevraud. This was, however, a false exit. Five years later, in April 1199, at the age of 79, she went to Chalus, in the Limousin, to be near her dying son. Once again, she assumed the role of lieutenant and mother hen, securing the loyalty of the vacillating towns and lords of the south-east towards John. A fantastic journey on horseback in the spring of 1199 took her to Loudun (29 April), to Poitiers (4 May), to Montreuil-Bonnin (5 May), and then to Niort, Andilly, La Rochelle, St-Jean-d'Angély, Saintes, Bordeaux, where she arrived on 1 July, and Soulac (4 July). Everywhere she went, she issued charters and received homage, before going on to pay homage herself, in her son's name, to Philip Augustus. And she was back in Rouen by 30 July.

The winter of 1199–1200, the winter of her eightieth year, was spent crossing the passes of the Pyrenees to travel to Castile to seek a wife for Philip Augustus' son, the Dauphin Louis. She brought her grand-daughter Blanche back with her, the child of her daughter Eleanor's marriage with Alphonse VIII of Castile. Finally, in the spring of 1200, she retired once more to Fontevraud, this time definitively, as she thought. In 1202, at the beginning of the war between Philip Augustus and John, she fled to Poitiers. Arthur of Brittany, her own grandson, ambushed her on the way and she retreated to the fortress of Mirabeau and withstood a siege until her deliverance by John Lackland. This very ancient lady then returned to Fontrevaud to die on 31 March or 1 April 1204, at around 84 years old. Her effigy in the abbey church is, however, ageless.

Hers was indeed an exceptional destiny, but there were other women, albeit in less spectacular guise, such as Queen Matilda, wife of Henry the Birdcatcher (890–968), Ida of Burgundy, Godfrey of Bouillon's mother, who died in 1113, Countess Matilda of Tuscany (1046–1115), Queen Blanche of Castile (1188–1252), Empress Mahaut (1102–67), and many more, who were models of strength and energy up to an advanced age. Although feudal law generally subordinated the widow to her male children, her personal status could still ensure that she played an eminent political role. Queen Blanche of Castile's ill-treatment of her daughter-in-law, Queen Marguerite, is well known. She had inherited her grandmother Eleanor's temperament, and Joinville has given a famous account of the subterfuges St Louis had to employ in order to meet his wife in secret:

> Queen Blanche had treated Queen Marguerite so harshly that, in so far as she could help it, she had not allowed her son to be in his wife's company except when he went to sleep with her at night. The palace in which the young king and his wife had most liked to live was at Pontoise, because there the king's room was on an upper floor and the Queen's room just below it. They had so arranged matters that they had managed to meet and talk together on a spiral staircase that led from one room to the other. They had also arranged that whenever the ushers saw Queen Blanche approaching her son's room they would knock on the door with their rods, and the king would run quickly up to his room so that his mother might find him there. Queen Marguerite's gentlemen of the bedchamber did the same when Queen Blanche was going to her daughter-in-law's room, so that she might find the young queen safely installed within.
>
> The king was once by his wife's side, at a time when she was in great danger on account of the injuries she had suffered in giving birth to a child. Queen Blanche had come to her room, and taking the king by the hand, had said to him: 'Come away; you're doing no good here'. Queen Marguerite seeing that the Queen Mother was taking the King away, had cried out: 'Alas! Whether I live or die, you will not let me see my husband!' Then she had fainted, and they had all thought she was dead. The king, convinced that she was dying, had turned back: and with great difficulty they had brought her round.[83]

None of this prevented Marguerite from presenting the king with 11 children or from living 74 years (1221–95).

This famous couple has also inspired genealogists. In 1949, Forst de Battaglia published an ancestral table of the 64 quarterings of St Louis, going back seven generations to the second half of the eleventh century.[84] We know the ages of 82 of the 128 kings, queens, princes and princesses mentioned, sometimes not very precisely, but within two or three years. The result is clear and should moderate the hasty and gloomy assertions of many historians; people did not always die young in the princely world of the Middle Ages. Of 82 persons, 30 (36 per cent) lived to be 60 or over, and the oldest, who died when over 70, numbered six women and five men, the longest-lived being Douce of Provence, wife of Raymond Berenger III, Count of Barcelona, who died in 1190 at the age of 95.

While this does not suffice to establish the medieval states as gerontocracies, and by a long way, it does however serve to point out that old rulers were not as rare as has sometimes been stated. Some medieval writers even became their advocates, one such being Bruno Latini. He was born in Florence in 1230 and, as a leader of the Guelf party, had to go into exile in France between 1260 and 1269. He subsequently played an important role in Florentine politics, as secretary, syndic and then prior, until his death in 1294. His political experience was important to the magistrates elected, since it involved above all the management of a republic. In his *Book of the Treasure*, his magnum opus, he advised the members of government, as his compatriot Machiavelli was to do two centuries later on. Unlike the latter, however, he clearly favoured government by the old, who offered greater guarantees of wisdom.

> Aristotle says that by long experience of many things man becomes wise: and no one may have long experience if he has not a long life. Consequently it appears that a young man cannot be wise, although he may have a good brain. And Solomon has said that unhappy is the land which has a young king. Nevertheless, he can indeed be very old and have little intelligence; for being young in mind is equal to being young in age. On account of this the burghers must elect a lord who is young neither in the one nor the other, it is better that he should be old in both.[85]

In accordance with this principle, monarchic governments often put their trust in old counsellors, who were appreciated on account of their experience. Since it was preferable that they should also be educated, they were often churchmen. Louis VI listened frequently to the Benedictine Abbot Geoffrey of Vendome's advice, which he provided until his death in 1132 at the age of 62. Louis VII was fortunate in having Suger, the Abbot of Saint-Denis, to assume the regency during his 1147–9 Crusade, between the ages of 66 and 68, and who died at

Table 7.6 Ancestors of Louis who lived to or beyond the age of 60

Name	Date of birth	Date of decease	Age at decease
Blanche of Castile	1188	1252	64
Louis VII	1120	1180	60
Alix of Champagne	1140	1206	66
Eleanor of Aquitaine	1120	1204	84
Thibaud IV of Champagne	1085	1152	67
Baudouin IV of Hainaut	1110	1170	60
Thierry of Flanders	1108	1168	60
Adela of England	1062	1137	75
Englebert II, Duke of Carinthia	1075	1141	66
Uta of Passau	1080	post 1140	60+
Godfrey of Namur	1068	1139	71
Ermesinde of Luxembourg	1080	1143	63
Douce of Provence	1095	1190	95
Henry I of England	1068	1135	67
Gertrude of Saxony	1035	1113	78
William I of Burgundy	1025	1087	62
Thibaud III of Champagne	1011	1089	78
William the Conqueror	1027	1087	60
Hedwig of Eppenstein	1050	1112	62
Clemence of Gleiberg	1065	post 1129	64+
Albert III of Namur	1030	1102	72
Hermesind of Longwy	1058	post 1129	71+
Fulk IV of Anjou	1043	1109	66
Alphonse of Castile	1030	1109	79
Geoffrey de la Perche	1040	1110	70
Malcolm of Scotland	1031	1093	62
William VIII of Aquitaine	1026	1083	60
Hildegard of Burgundy	1045	post 1114	69+

the age of 70. Philip Augustus had two old and antagonistic bishops in his entourage: the Cistercian William, who became Archbishop of Bourges in 1200 at the age of 80, and sided with the Pope against the King over his divorce, and died at the age of 89. His adversary, another William of the White Hands, a son of Thibaud II of Champagne, was

Bishop of Chartres and then Archbishop of Sens, then of Rheims, and then Cardinal. He headed the royal council between 1184 and 1202 when he was 67 years old. As the sovereign's uncle, he was called 'the king's eye and hand', or 'the second king'. During the Crusade, he managed the regency along with the Queen Mother, Adela of Champagne, who was around 60 years old.

Nor should we forget the Hospitaller Guerin, a man whom the King trusted, whom Louis VIII retained as his chancellor in 1223, when he was 66 years old, and who died four years later. St Louis was surrounded by counsellors senior to him by ten to 15 years and who were, by the end of his reign, relatively aged. The Archbishop of Rouen, a Franciscan called Eudes Rigaud, was 70; the Dominican Geoffrey of Beaulieu, the king's confessor and friend, was also a septuagenarian, and Simon of Clermont, Lord of Nesles and one of the most respected advisors, who sat in council and in the Parlements, was over 60. St Louis was to appoint him one of his regents in 1270. As for Blanche of Castile, her confessor was William of Auvergne, Bishop of Paris, until his decease in 1249 at the age of 69. Old men were thus not absent from the higher political spheres, where experience constituted a major asset.

OLD PEASANTS: AT THE MERCY OF THEIR FAMILIES

It is more difficult to distinguish the place of the old in the world of the *laboratores*, amid the throng of humble folk, and especially in the peasant masses of the Middle Ages. Such documents as might allow us to study the daily life of a rural community, such as the registers of Jacques Fournier, are all too rare. So let's take as our starting point the unique case of Montaillou, an Occitan village at the beginning of the fourteenth century.[86] Let us however avoid generalizing: Cathar society did not represent that of all Europe and many of its features appear to have been quite particular to it.

There were few old people in this village and their situation was not an enviable one. The adult son was master of the household and he treated his old parents roughly: 'As for Bernard Rives, the old father of Pons, he does not have much to say in the house where he is living, but which is henceforth ruled by his son'.[87] When someone tries to borrow something from him, he answers: 'I don't dare do anything without my son's consent.' Old mothers could also be tyrannized and live in complete dependence on their children. 'I am ruined. I have sold my goods and mortgaged my dependents; I live humbly and miserably in my son's house; and I don't dare move', complains old Stephanie of Chateauverdun.[88] Le Roy Ladurie points out that 'the few senescent pachyderms who still survived at Montaillou' were in a situation of total dependence, with no power or prestige. 'Truly, making old bones was not enjoyable in the land of Aillon, around 1300–1320.'

A situation whereby old fathers are dependent on their sons is common to every age, and the relationships which emerge depend largely on the personalities present in each case. Medieval literature broached the problem, most notably in the thirteenth-century tale of *La Housse partie* (The divided blanket): A widowed merchant has made his property over to his son, who has married the daughter of a ruined knight. During the next 12 years, the old father lives with his son and daughter-in-law; on growing very old, he becomes a burden to them and is despised and finally driven away: 'Father, go away. You are just a nuisance: go and punish yourself somewhere else! For the last twelve years, you have been eating our bread. So now go and lodge wherever the fancy takes you!'[89] However, the tale has a moral ending: when the unworthy son sends his own son to fetch a blanket to give to his departing grandfather, the child cuts it in half, declaring that he will keep the other half to give to his own father when he drives him away in his turn. Full of repentance, the son then agrees to keep his old father on.

Reality was not always as moral, and it was probably in this period that the conjugal family triumphed over the patriarchal family, to the disadvantage of old parents. Robert Fossier has studied this evolution in Picardy.[90] In this region, the extended family prevailed until the tenth century, imposing a strictly defined role on each member and thus ensuring the support and survival of the old. From the eleventh century onwards, under the influence of the Church and also because of improved security in the countryside, these links between the group members were relaxed, the authority of the father weakened and the conjugal family gained its autonomy. From then on, some of the adult children left the home, and those who stayed had to look after the old, who were no longer considered as an integral part of the family unit but as a more or less parasitical supplement. This sort of evolution appears to have been fairly general. Far from viewing the communal family as the norm between the eleventh and the thirteenth centuries, historians nowadays consider it to have been the exception.

Mediterranean Europe appears to have been the first to favour the conjugal family. Research concentrating on Catalonia, Languedoc and central Italy has shown the overwhelming predominance of the conjugal group from the tenth century onwards.[91] Northern Europe followed suit rather later. Patriarchal groupings involving the father of the family and his descendants survived only in south-eastern France, in response to the particular conditions prevailing there. Even in Montaillou, the conjugal family was clearly dominant, frequently resulting in old parents, or the surviving parent, cohabiting with the son and daughter-in-law who had taken over the home. In the case where an old mother remained a widow, she benefited from her status as widow-matriarch, with her own room and the right to control the household; she was generally held in respect. Her influence over her son and daughter-in-law was often equivalent to a *de facto* matriarchy. But an old father, once his physical strength had left him, was soon despised, although he was still theoretically head of the family. As soon as he had designated which of his sons was to inherit the house, he was relegated to a subaltern position. Contrary to the aristocratic world, the law in this instance was still very theoretical. Normally, a father's power was extinguished only by his death, and he remained the sole master in his home. However, this paternal power, known as *mainbournie* in traditional parts of the countryside, no longer applied to those children who had left the paternal hearth. The practice was in reality extremely diverse, and each family regulated its problems in the light of the group's main interest.[92]

Within the family, relations between the generations, quite apart from any question of law, depended mainly on their affective rapport. Thus, the grandparents' interest in their grandchildren is reported on several occasions in Montaillou, as Emmanuel Le Roy points out: Beatrice de Planissole is an attentive grandmother, careful of her grandson's health; a dead grandmother, now a ghost, returns to kiss her grandchildren in their bed; Raymond Authie takes an interest in his granddaughter's marriage.[93] The progressive appearance of the family name between the eleventh and the thirteenth centuries is supposed to have helped to reinforce solidarity between the generations and conflicts seem to have been rare. Every family supported its aged parents. In Ireland, a room was kept for them, the 'west room'. In some regions the local hospital granted a pension to the poorest families supporting an aged ancestor at home.[94] But, apart from the fact that this system was extremely rare and was intended rather to limit the growing number of beggars, it does seem to hint at a distressing tendency to throw old parents out into the street.

Practices thus varied according to resources and circumstances, with more old people being abandoned in times of crisis. St Bernard's *Book of Miracles* mentions several such miserable beings. He cures paralytic old men in Frankfurt and Meurville, near Clairvaux, and blind old men at Fribourg, Constance, Mons, at the monastery of Trois-Fontaines and in Cambraisis, and a lame old man at Cambrai.[95] Manifestly, old people with no resources formed a large battalion in the army of indigent in the Middle Ages: both childless old folk and those rejected by their families.

Their number was sufficiently important to justify the foundation of several charitable establishments specifically for the old. The Council of Mainz (1261) required that each monastery be equipped with an infirmary for old people.[96] At Passau, at the beginning of the thirteenth century, the burghers founded the hospital of St John, with the Chapter's agreement, to take in old men and women no longer capable of work. At Trèves, the old pensioners of St Elizabeth's Convent performed little tasks according to their strength: gardening and tending vegetables for the men, and spinning, knitting, sewing and laundry work for the women. The small religious houses of Venice, Florence and Lille took in widows or old men of good conduct, but these were preferably formerly wealthy persons who had fallen on bad times. In some places retirement homes appeared.[97] In the East, the Church's tradition of charity had resulted since very early on in the creation of *gerontachia*. In the West, some landowners supported their old rural workers, notably in England, where an old man sometimes concluded an agreement with his heir, whereby he made over his estate to him in exchange for a pension.[98] Such measures were inadequate, but they reveal a real need.

The sociable village life of the Middle Ages did however allow an old person to play a significant role. We can see him during those long evenings acting as an intermediary between the generations and telling his timeless stories. As the depository of family and village culture, he constituted for the group an indispensible link with their past. In Montaillou, as doubtless elsewhere as well, people were separated according to their sex and age during this evening ceremony, as at Mass, which to some extent it replaced, and in Catholic countryside complemented. During these moments of reunion around the fire, which represented a true form of lay liturgy, the old man discovered his essential function, his real dimension, one justified solely by his age. As high priest on account of his years, he was irreplaceable, unique and precious. The solemnity of the occasion and the mystery of the night contributed to enlarge and amplify his personality and his words. Such an assembly would have been smaller and doubtless more attentive than one in church. At such a time, for one evening every so often, the old man would become great and even slightly supernatural, because he came from a period no one else knew about, and had emerged from the mists of time.

His temple was the village square, in the Midi at any rate, as in Montaillou, where the old men and women came to gossip, to 'scratch for lice' in the sun and to comment on small and great events past and present. Their opinions carried considerable weight on account of their age, even in such serious matters as religious belief. In Montaillou, Raymond de l'Aire was to believe for the next ten years that God and Mary were none other than the visible world, simply because an aged peasant had told him so: 'Since Pierre Rauzi was older than me, I thought that he had told me the truth'; a fine example of the prestige enjoyed by elders! Some time later, the same character was also convinced of the fact that animals possess a soul similar to man's: 'I believed all that because Guillaume de l'Aire was older than me.'[99] His case is certainly not that of a halfwit who believes all he is told, but, as

Emmanuel le Roy points out, it illustrates the cultural authority enjoyed by the elders of the rural community. 'Culture flows from the older member to the younger', and never the other way. In this Cathar milieu, the sons never managed to undermine their parents' convictions. 'Male peasants might, at a stretch, allow their wives or their mothers-in-law to lead them by the nose but never their sons.'[100] It is clear that the clergy in Catholic regions insisted likewise on the exemplary role to be played by the old and their responsibility in educating the young. The old man represented a moral authority whose co-operation the Church herself deemed useful to secure.

The old man's *de facto* prestige would appear to designate him as a natural member of the village assembly. However, the documents are so few and imprecise that this is difficult to verify. Old people, including widows in charge of their households, undoubtedly did attend the general assembly, whose functions were to pay homage and to bear witness. The rare name lists which have come down to us reveal total heterogeneity where ages were concerned and there is no evidence that the old played a special role. On the other hand, in smaller gatherings, the village 'parlements', made up of the *major et sanio pars*, the *prud'-hommes*, whose role was more active and was defined by deed of franchise, consisted of the wealthiest and the oldest members. Given that this assembly's principal role was to allocate taxation, wealth was a more important criterion than age regarding recruitment, the more so in that intellectual competence was increasingly required in order to sort out the collective budget. They had at least to be able to read and count. It is here that the limits of the social role of old age in the village community are apparent. Although the cultural prestige of old age and its importance in relation to the development and continuity of the collective mentality were recognized, it was however denied any decision-making power. The domain of the old person was that of traditional knowledge not of effective power, that of the cultural not the practical sphere. What made a village *prud'homme* was in fact wealth and learning, not age.

COMMERCE: A NEW OPPORTUNITY FOR OLD AGE

From the eleventh century onwards, the growth of the towns presented the old with new possibilities. Within these new fortified spaces, as Jacques Le Goff has amply demonstrated, there appeared a different mentality, one based on calculation involving time and money. People within the merchants' sphere were numerate: they counted the years as they did their coins. While this did not constitute a discovery of time, to which no one in the Middle Ages was indifferent, it did at least mark the appearance of an awareness of the irreplaceable value of time, which even assumed a monetary aspect with the emergence of interest-paying loans. People's awakening to the notion of time as money generated an ambiguous and contradictory attitude towards old age, which, more than the other social categories, was presented under the aspect of a two-faced Janus.

Unlike the warrior, who reached his culmination at the prime of life, it was in old age that the merchant's career attained its apogee. For him, whose success was proportional to his wealth, his value depended fairly and squarely on the number of his years. Age brought him accumulated profits and, more than in the countryside, those profits were his own. Movable property was essentially individual, whereas landed property belonged rather to a particular lineage. Harpagnon's treasure was his own, as were Jehan Boinebroke's loans, and they belonged to no one else, not even their sons; the fief, however, belonged to the family, the lineage. Consequently a merchant grown old remained the sole master of his fortune, which ensured him prestige and authority. An old peasant could be supplanted by his son, but an old merchant could not be shifted for as long as it pleased him.

Although old age might be synonymous with wealth in the commercial world, the onset of death brought remorse. Even though a merchant might continue his commercial operations, his dealings with exchange and loans, well into his old age, he felt the finger of the Church pointing at him, and this bothered him in his search for profit. In his accounts, the Italian trader did not forget to attribute part of his profits to God in the shape of substantial alms. He who spent his time doing accounts envisaged God as the great Accountant, in whose book it behoved him to keep a solid credit. He was held in bad repute by the Church and this weighed on his conscience; in his old age, he would often be overcome by fear, and he would make restitution in his will. Even so pitiless a man as Jehan Boinebroke played the game. He called to a woman dyer, whom he was exploiting in a most dishonest manner: 'Gossip! I owe you nothing that I know of, but I will put you in my will.' In Prato, the grasping Francesco di Marco Datini nevertheless left almost his whole fortune, 75,000 florins, which he had accumulated soldi by soldi, to the poor.

Others went to even greater lengths. Not content with such posthumous distributions, which cost the donor nothing, they would in their old age retire from business to a monastery. It is a surprising fact that old merchants tended to renounce the world more frequently than old knights. Money was more easily abandoned than the sword, and the Church's teaching had greater weight in the world of commerce than in that of war. Was this not because merchants, being better educated and more 'evolved', believed in a more personal, more thoughtful and more profound manner, which drove them to put into practice the ecclesiastical concept of old age as a preparation for salvation?

Living in town, a merchant would frequent many monasteries, where the religious ideal was more elevated than in parish churches, and where he was influenced by the monks' teaching to a greater extent than has been thought. It was in a merchant circle, after all, that was born the mendicant monks' ideal of absolute poverty in the mind of Francesco Bernadone.

Long before him, at the beginning of the twelfth century, a merchant called Godric of Finchale had been canonized, as had been Homobonus, the great trader of Cremona, in 1197. Without going quite so far as sanctity, many old merchants felt the need to draw closer to God and retired to a monastery at the end of their lives. At the beginning of the twelfth century, Werimbold of Cambrai had his marriage annulled, and both spouses entered religious houses; their goods were distributed to the abbeys of St Aubert and St Croix. In 1178, Sebastiano Ziani, whose wealth was proverbial, retired to the monastery of San Giorgio Maggiore and bequeathed some of his houses to it, the rest going to the Chapter of St Mark. His son, Pietro Ziani, did likewise in 1229. At the beginning of the fourteenth century, Baude Crespin, an old banker of Arras, became a monk in the abbey of St Vaast. In 1344, another great Siennese banker, Bernardo Tolomei, retired to the congregation of the Olivetans, which he had just founded; the Church later declared him Blessed.

Not all old merchants retired. Those who were left were among the town notables, and were influential in public affairs. In the twelfth century, according to André Chédeville, age was one of the dominant factors in determining the recruitment of aldermen and goodmen in the Midi towns. The large towns of Flanders had recourse to old patricians for delicate missions: in 1127, when they sent a delegation to the King of France, it was composed of 20 knights and 12 'of the oldest and wisest citizens'.[101]

All this means that we cannot agree with Jacques Le Goff's statement in his 'Civilization in the Medieval West':

> It appears that the class of old men – the elders of traditional societies – did not play an important part in medieval society, a society of people who died young, of warriors and peasants who only pulled their weight for as long as they retained their full physical strength, of clerics led by bishops and popes, who (to pass over the scandalous adolescents of the X century – John XI ascended Peter's throne in 931 at the age of 21; John XII in 954 at 16) were often elected at a young age (Innocent III was around 35 in 1198). Medieval society knew no gerontocracy. At the very most, its sensibility may have been aroused by very old men with white beards – such as may be seen on church portals: the old men of the Apocalypse and the Prophets, and in works of literature

such as the *Chanson de Roland*, which attributes Charlemagne with a 'hoary beard'.[102]

Medieval society was certainly not systematically gerontocratic, but old people were numerous within the civil and above all the ecclesiastical hierarchies. Although age never appears as a positive criterion as such, it did in fact play a considerable role. The notion of old age, like that of childhood, was relatively confused in medieval minds. So long as physical incapacity had not totally paralysed the individual, no difference at all was made between the mature man and the old man, who retained his place in society until he went into retirement, which he did only in the last extremity. Dividing up the 'ages of life' was an intellectual game which did not correspond to any reality in fact or in law. Human life was one and indivisible. It began at baptism and ended with the tomb.

Its very precariousness was the cause of its unity. The great stages whose rhythm governs modern man's existence, school, coming of age, marriage, professional promotion, retirement and widowhood, did not exist for medieval man, or were viewed in strongly relative terms. He had no schooling, no legal coming of age, his active life began as soon as he was strong enough; his repeated marriages and widowhoods attenuated their importance; there was no promotion in a world with little social mobility, there was no official retirement, except for a minority of merchants and knights. The real stages were constituted by the seasons, family events, shortages, local catastrophes and religious feasts, events too numerous and frequent to act as rites of passage. Ageing occurred imperceptibly. Entry into the third age was not marked by any ceremony; there was in fact no third age; there was life and death.

A person's activity was limited only by his physical incapacity. An old man went on playing his role for as long as he could hold an aspergillum, a sword, a hoe or an accounts book. In fact, old age was seldom commented on, for it was concealed more easily than in our days. People's faces and their whole bodies aged sooner, reducing the gap between maturity and old age, which only attracted attention when it was very advanced; and when the man concerned was still active, it conferred wisdom and experience on him in the eyes of others. Old age was not dissociated from the rest of human existence; the old man was what he had been and he sowed what he had reaped. It was only when his physical decrepitude prevented him from carrying out his functions, when he had become 'slow and dull, shivering and somnolescent, not recalling past things well',[103] as Brunetto Latini puts it, that his condition really deteriorated.

The peasant world was the most merciless, because everyone there lived primarily from his physical and personal labour and, unlike the clergy who took care of their old men, the gentry who kept theirs in their manors, and the monasteries which took in retired merchants, old peasants could count only on their children, if they had any, who were not always gentle to useless mouths. In such cases, an old man was left with his risky role as the group's memory. Ageing in the thirteenth century was not a dramatic process, provided that those concerned could continue to keep their place or were able to provide some form of retirement for themselves.

8

The Fourteenth and Fifteenth Centuries:

Old People Assert Themselves

In 1348 the bubonic plague virus disembarked at Genoa. Within three years it had killed off more than a third of the population of Europe. Such an unprecedented demographic catastrophe was to have a fatal effect on the economy, on society, politics, the arts, literature and on mentalities. There was a constant feeling of insecurity fuelled by recurrences of the epidemic right up to the 1450s. Abandoned villages, retreating towns, a greater mingling of peoples, the return in force of fallow lands and savagery, urban uprisings, a constant state of war, murder and mayhem at the hands of bandits, *écorcheurs* and mercenaries, shortages and famine, unbridled extravagance in princely circles and royal courts, weird and worrying flourishings of flamboyant art: the Middle Ages were burning themselves out in a fascinating pyre whence the stench of death mingled with the odour of incense. It was a crazy time, with man and nature working together to destroy life, creating hell on earth in the hope of building paradise. Burnings took place as had never been seen before: Templars, Jews, sorcerers, Moors, Hussites, Joan of Arc and Savonarola. This waning of the Middle Ages, as described by Huizinga, did indeed mark the end of an era, in an apocalyptical climate.

It was a time of paradoxes, of extremes, of unbalance and contradiction, exemplified by that peculiar pair Gilles de Rais and Joan of Arc who entered the service of the equally peculiar Charles VII. One of them was 29 years old, the other 17 and the King 26: people blossomed young soon to disappear, or so it seems. The influential ones had their heads chopped off or were burnt at the stake; plague or famine put paid to the anonymous masses.

This was, however, no more than a romantic, glittering and misleading facade. In fact, the fourteenth and fifteenth centuries witnessed a considerable strengthening of the role of old people, not the least of the age's paradoxes. Hardly spectacular but incontrovertible, this trend had an important effect on relations between the generations and on art, literature and mentalities, in the broadest sense of the term.

THE PLAGUE SPARED THE OLD

One demographic fact supports this assertion, which struck contemporaries at the time, but which has until recently evaded historians: these killer epidemics of the fourteenth and fifteenth centuries, and the plague in particular, tended to single out children and young adults, leaving a momentary imbalance between age groups in favour of old age. From 1350 onwards, there was a marked increase in the numbers of elderly people, which was remarked upon at the time. In 1383, the Italian chronicler Marchionne Stefani noted: 'Many good people died, but the plague killed more young people and children than mature men and women.'[1] In 1418, the Burgher of Paris noted in his journal, 'This epidemic of the plague has, so the old say, been the cruellest since 3 centuries. Nobody it touched escaped, young people and children in particular . . . Out of four or five hundred deaths there were less than a dozen old people, they were nearly all children and young people.' He noted the same thing in 1445, with regard to smallpox: 'It struck the children most.'

Contemporary demographers confirm these observations. J.C. Russell notes that tuberculosis mainly killed those aged between 15 and 35 and that after the first wave of the plague, the second, coming about four years later, concentrated on the young: 'After the first plague epidemic, the children were particularly vulnerable to further outbreaks as they had been less exposed, or not exposed at all, beforehand . . . The second plague was called the plague of the children: the young who had grown since the last plague provided the greater part of the victims.'[2] Generally speaking, the life expectancy of the survivors increased with each epidemic: 'Presumably, the plague eliminated at earlier ages many who would have died of other diseases in earlier life.'[3] The least resistant ones were taken, many of the survivors reaching a ripe old age.

All the local studies point the same way. In the Comtat during the first half of the fifteenth century, the proportion of elderly people increased appreciably after mortality crises: 24 per cent of heads of families were over 54 years old, 21 per cent were over 57 and 12 per cent over 62.[4] In c.1380–1400, the mortality rate in Chalon-sur-Saône clearly decreased with age.[5] In 1400 most of those affected by the Plague in Périgueux were middle-aged adults. The case of the kingdom of Navarre, studied in detail by Maurice Berthe, is particularly illuminating.[6] Each recurrence of the Plague was marked by a brutal increase in the numbers of isolated old people. In the village of Oteiza in 1422, the Plague spared six dwellings inhabited by old women; in Larrainzar,

Martin Migua was 'dead, along with all his family . . . save an old woman called Orchanda', according to the registers. 'Families have been almost entirely destroyed, apart from the old people and the very young children, but more often than not it has killed only the father.'[7] At San Martin d'Unx it was the old people, the elders, who survived. In 1429, ten out of 12 farms at Marcalain were decimated and populated entirely by old people. 'The only hypothesis that can be summoned to explain this phenomenon is the immunity conferred by the disease on those that have been cured', declares the author.[8] In 1433, there were only 13 hearths left in the community of Baigorri and two of the heads of household were aged over 70, nine between 50 and 70, with only two under 50.

The emigration of the young following these crises led to a further increase in the proportion of older people: in this community, two hearths were composed of single old people, the children having left, and the sons and daughters had also left three other households. In the Navarre fiscal listings, the hearths of the *mugeres* (women) were those which had no adult males capable of work; they mainly consisted of elderly people living alone or elderly couples without children. Their total number was considerable, between 24 per cent and 36 per cent hearths, according to area, and between 21 per cent and 31 per cent in the Pamplona valley between 1360 and 1445. The records frequently reveal that hearths were being classified in a lower grouping on account of their physical falling-off due to ageing,[9] and that other hearths were disappearing as a result of sales or gifts made by elderly men and women alone,[10] notably after 1365.

The survivors were often reduced to begging. One poor old woman at Olondriz was forced by scarcity to abandon everthing to go begging; a 70-year-old woman, Gracia Garcia, lived alone in her hut. In the community of Sesma in 1433, 29 hearths out of 163, or 18 per cent consisted of old people like Martin Sacristan and his wife, 80 years old and living alone, with no animals, or like Theresa, a 75-year-old widow, helpless and living on charity. These old folk whose families had disappeared often regrouped to survive, forming complex households with the remnants of other hearths which had been cut down by the Plague. In Zudaire in 1433 two elderly widows were living together with three orphaned grandchildren and a married son; Pero Periz, a 40-year-old, had taken in his widowed 80-year-old aunt, together with two nephews. The same impression predominates everywhere: a deficit of young and middle-aged people and an increase in the numbers of elderly people.[11]

A HEAVY INCREASE IN THE PROPORTION OF OLD PEOPLE DURING
THE YEARS 1350–1450

A pre-statistical approach to the phenomenon is made possible thanks
to the growing accuracy of the sources dealing with age and an increasing
number of documents providing figures. The problems of the age
accentuated the need to count, leading to hearth-counts and records of
in-goings and out-goings, of victims and survivors. Measurement of
time became more precise; there were more clocks, chronology began
to take off and people made greater use of numerical dates. Parish
registers, so indispensable to demographic research, began to appear.
As early as 1232 a marriage register was in use at Rimini, followed in
1281 by a register of deaths at Cividale in Friuli and by baptismal
registers at Arezzo (1314), at Cremona (1369), Sienna and Gemona
(1379). The register at Givry (Saône-et-Loire) in France provided details
of burials from 1334 onwards; in 1406 the Bishop of Nantes ordered
registers to be kept in his diocese, and his neighbours of Saint-Brieuc
followed suit in 1421, as did those of Dol and Saint-Malo in 1446, and
those of Rennes in 1464. The oldest register of deaths in Florence dates
from 1398, and the baptismal register from 1450. In Germany, baptisms
were recorded in Rhein from 1345 onwards, in Munster from 1403 and
in Endersdorf from 1415. Milan kept registers of deaths from 1452
onwards, Barcelona from 1457 and Mantua from 1496, with some of
the records supplying the age at decease.

The first population censuses were recorded at roughly the same time,
in Dresden (1430), Ypres (1431), Nuremberg (1449), Basle (1454),
Strasbourg (1470) and Pozzuoli (1489). On the level of kingdoms and
principalities, there was the famous hearth count in France of 1328, as
well as the poll tax in England of 1377, the Catalonian levies of 1359
and 1378, and the one in Brittany in 1427.

People now had a more accurate grasp of their ages. The upper-class
Florentine families of the fifteenth century were meticulous about noting
down the day, hour and minute of birth.[12] This did not, however,
prevent the chroniclers from attributing 80 years to John Talbot, who
was killed at the Battle of Castillon at the age of 65, or Froissart from
making the Duke of Berry 60 years old at the time of his second
marriage, when he was in fact only 49. But these literary exaggerations
should not cloud the issue, which is that the last two centuries of the
Middle Ages marked a considerable advance towards the civilization of
figures. We owe our first statistics to this evolution, and they confirm
the extent of the growth in the number of old people at the time of the
great epidemics.

The greatest quantity of figures relate to England and to Italy. In
England, T.H. Hollingsworth and J.C. Russell's calculations have

Table 8.1 Distribution of Tuscan town-dwellers according to age

Place and age group	Inhabitants	% of total
Pistoia		
0–19	6,904	43.8
20–59	6,677	42.3
60 plus	2,194	13.9
Arezzo		
0–19	1,598	40.2
20–59	1,729	43.6
60 plus	644	16.2

demonstrated a marked increase in the life expectancy of old people following the Black Death in 1348 until the end of the fifteenth century. Their research, which involved some 3070 landowners, shows that average life expectancy at birth, which had been 35.3 years for men born between 1200 and 1275, had already decreased to 27.2 years for those men born between 1326 and 1348, falling to 17.3 years for the generation born in 1348–75 before gradually increasing to 32.8 years for the 1425–50 generation. On the other hand, the life expectancy of 60-year-old men climbed from 9.4 years for those born between 1200 and 1275 to 10.8 years for those born between 1326 and 1348, 10.9 years for the 1348–75 generation and 13.7 years for the 1425–50 generation. The life expectancy of 80-year-old men in the same periods climbed from 5.2 years to 6 years, 4.7 years and 7.9 years respectively.[13]

Studies dealing exclusively with the English peerage confirm this trend. During the fourteenth century, the mortality rate increased rapidly up to the age of 50 but decreased thereafter. Before 1325 18 per cent of peers died before they reached the age of 50; the ratio increased to 66 per cent between 1350 and 1370 before decreasing to 34 per cent during the first half of the fifteenth century. However, those who did turn 50 lived much longer.[14]

In Italy, studies of Tuscan demography during the first half of the fifteenth century by Christiane Klapisch and D. Herlihy[15] demonstrate with certainty the existence of a heavy proportion of old people: 13.95 per cent of the inhabitants of Pistoia in 1427–30 and 16.2 per cent of the inhabitants of Arezzo were aged over 60 (table 8.1).

For Tuscany as a whole, the proportion of people over 60 can be established at 14.6 per cent in 1427. As always during the Middle Ages, there was a preponderance of elderly males: a study of 1,000 families in Arezzo gives a male:female ratio of 103:100 aged between 58 and 67, of 97:100 (this is an anomaly) aged between 68 and 77 and of 138:100 aged 78 and over. The number of widows was, however, proportionally much higher than that of widowers, since men remarried more often than women: of 1,000 men aged between 60 and 69, 894 were still married, 42 were widowers and 64 in unknown circumstances; amongst those aged 70 and over, 739 in 1,000 were still married, 193 were widowers and 68 unknown. Where women were concerned, however, there were already 474 widows among 1,000 cases aged between 60 and 69, and 561 widows among 1,000 women aged 70 and over. This situation is further illustrated by the tax records of the Florentine 'catasto' of 1427, which cites a great many households such as that of Agostino di Bartolo at San Giminiano, which included the two grandparents (Agostino, aged 86 and his wife Caterina, 60), the children (Piero, 26, and his wife Cristofana, 26), and the grandchildren Mariana and Benedetto.[16] The age gap between spouses increased with remarriage. Scarcely discernible in the first marriages, it often increased considerably the second time round, when the new widowers married younger women.

In the case of heads of households alone, there was naturally a far greater proportion of elderly people. In Arezzo, of a total of 832 male heads of family, 341 were aged over 55; 160 were between 55 and 64 years old, 106 were aged between 65 and 74, 75 were over 75; the average age was just over 50. As far as women were concerned, of 168 heads of family, 92 were aged over 55: 47 were aged between 55 and 64, 29 between 65 and 74 and 16 over 75. Altogether, of a sample of 1,000 heads of family, 432 were aged over 55, 205 were aged between 55 and 64, 136 were aged between 65 and 74, and 91 were over 75.

Jacques Heers cites another instance of the urban Italian family – where the father was often elderly and married to a woman at least 20 years younger than himself – that of Matteo Chorsini, who died in 1402 aged 80, three years after the birth of the last of the 20 children his wife bore him over a period of 25 years. The latter, who was particularly robust, outlived her husband; her age is unknown, but calculating from the time of her last pregnancy, she must have been 25 to 30 years younger than her husband.[17] Of the 20 children, only five reached adulthood, so that towards the end, Matteo's family consisted of an old man of 80, who might well have been his own children's great-great-grandfather, a woman of about 50 and five children. Quite an unusual situation, hardly auguring well for good relations between the generations. The age gap between father and children was so huge that it became an impassable gulf; the father, isolated by his age, became a patriarchal figure, dominating a family in which the mother felt closer to her children than to her husband.

By killing off both youngsters and adults and sparing the old, the plague certainly accentuated this age gap, notably in France. In Rheims, the 'mouth count' of 1422, after the epidemics of the beginning of the century, shows a net deficit in the 0–10-year-old sector as compared to

Table 8.2 Longevity in Périgueux at the
end of the fourteenth century

Age at death	No. of deaths
15–19	1
20–4	3
25–9	4
30–4	18
35–9	12
40–4	43
45–9	50
50–4	62
55–9	73
60–4	77
65–9	42
70–4	37
75–9	18
80–4	15
85–9	6
90–4	2
95–9	1
100+	1

Source: Arlette Higounet-Nadal, *Périgueux aux
XIVe et XVe siècles. Étude de démographie
historique*, Paris 1977.

the 35–45 sector, which made for a heavy percentage of old as opposed
to young people in the 30 years to come.[18] As in Italy, the age gap
between spouses increased with remarriage: in Dijon 30 per cent of men
aged between 30 and 39 had wives between eight and 16 years younger
than themselves; 15 per cent of 40-year-olds were 20 to 24 years older
than their wives.[19] Given this state of affairs, the wife effectively became
an eternal minor, whom her elderly husband tended to treat as he did
his children.

The case of Périgueux has been studied in detail by Arlette Higounet-
Nadal, who has clearly shown an increase in longevity after 1350, and
particularly after 1400, an indubitable consequence of the Plague
epidemics. The records are full of old people, and according to the
author, the ages given were always minimum ages, which may be
increased by at least five years. As they stand, they are already
remarkable. Of 465 cases where the age at death is known (table 8.2),
199, or 42.8 per cent, referred to people aged over 60.[20]

The 26 witnesses present at a trial concerning comital rights in Puy-
Saint-Front were all 60 or over: two were about 60, five were 70, 16
were 80, one was 90, one 100 and one claimed to be 140. Disputed as

this last case may be by local historians, research on each of the other individuals proves that their ages were not exaggerated and that if there was any rounding-off done, it was down to the nearest ten. Some women, whether unmarried or widows, lived to over 80, as in the cases of Anthéa de Barrant, only daughter of the merchant Élie Barrant, who died unwed in 1415, and of Marie Peyroni, married once only, who died aged 88.

'The effect of selective mortality could make towns buckle under the weight of the elderly', Jacques Roussiaud observes in his study of urban environment at the end of the Middle Ages.[21] He adds: 'Perhaps more than at any other time, there was a greater awareness of the vulnerability of youth during the epidemics. The Black Death was horribly cruel, sparing those who had already lived and cutting down the young . . .' The old people's revenge aroused much bitterness among the young: 'Many of them had a father who had crossed the threshold of old age just as they were reaching their twenties, or a stepmother who might well, by a few years, have been their own wife. They were well aware that a notable proportion of marriageable girls were being carried off by established men; finally, that they were all excluded from civic life, the assemblies, offices and the bourgeoisie.'[22]

In the country, the ageing of the heads of family was just as obvious during the first half of the fifteenth century. The registers pertaining to the reform of the hearths in Brittany of 1427 which we studied with regard to the diocese of Tréguier reveal that over five per cent of the men were aged over 70. Within 22 parishes, 62 heads of family were 70 and 77 were 80 years old: four were classed as centenarians.[23] This situation is magnificently illustrated in *Les Très Riches Heures du duc de Berry*, illuminated in about 1413: the old man with the white beard working in the fields during the month of March is not an invention of the monks of Limbourg, who might well have seen thousands of similar old men working in the French countryside at the beginning of the fifteenth century. All their work is characterized by the importance of old age and the *Très Riches Heures* is full of old men: 24 in the Apocalypse, all bearded (folio 17 recto), St Matthew, in the guise of an old man (folio 18 verso), as are the Emperor Augustus (folio 22 recto) and Zacchary (folio 43 verso). David, who is illustrated many times, is always represented with white beard and hair; St Elisabeth is an old woman with hollow cheeks (folio 38 verso). God the Father is invariably depicted as an old man: in the Earthly Paradise (folio 25 verso), watching the Building of the Temple (folio 35 verso), in the Nativity (folio 44 verso), or watching several scenes from the Psalms (folio 45 verso, 46 verso, 49 verso).

The elderly father-patriarch figure is an illustration of what was a striking reality during the lives of the artists, rather than a conventional artistic form. The *Très Riches Heures* also shows that this was a transient state of affairs, given the difference between the way in which the Limbourg monks (in about 1413) and Jean Colombe, who was responsible for the decoration of the manuscript between 1485 and 1489, illustrated paternity. The former all portray fathers as old men, whereas the latter shows them as middle-aged adults. The difference is striking where St Joseph is concerned. Take the Nativity by the Limbourg monks (folio 44 verso): opposite a very young fair-haired Mary is Joseph, a shrivelled old man with a long white beard. They present a strange couple, with the father looking more like a great-grandfather. This picture illustrates a typical social reality. Equally, in his *Adoration of the Shepherds*, Hugo van der Goes depicts St Joseph with a lined face and tousled hair; he appears again in the *Très Riches Heures*, on the Day of Purification, leaning on a staff (folio 54 verso). Three pages further on, Jean Colombe has illustrated the Flight into Egypt (folio 57 recto): Joseph has grown younger by at least thirty years; he may look rather lumpish but he has traded his white beard for a short reddish one and looks a much more reasonable age. By the same token, in all his miniatures, Jean Colombe has made David much younger and, in the Presentation of Mary at the Temple, Ann and Joachim were not nearly as old as one might have expected (folio 137 recto). This was because Jean Colombe did not live through the same period: the effects of the Plague epidemics had begun to fade, youth was surging ahead once more and the proportion of old people had begun to diminish. Whereas C. Klapisch has established a proportion of 14.6 per cent of people over 60 in 1427, by 1545 they accounted for only 5.7 per cent of the population in the countryside and 6.4 per cent of the urban population.[24]

THE CONSEQUENCES: A WIDENED FAMILY CIRCLE

This increase in the proportion of old people during the years 1350–1450 had an important effect on social mores and mentalities. To start off with, it appeared that the partial disintegration of households beneath the repeated blows of the Plague epidemics caused the survivors to regroup and form extended families or communities allowing those worst hit to survive. The elderly could only benefit from this trend, whereas, during the previous period, the predominance of conjugal families had condemned widows and widowers to solitude.

This trend seems to have been general. In Trégor in 1427, only 181 of 16,368 hearths belonged to widowers or widows living alone, that is 1.1 per cent.[25] In 1481 in the same area, the proportion had risen to 6.7 per cent. Seen from this point of view, the epidemics favoured the elderly, since they were looked after by the decimated family groups, whereas in normal times the limited conjugal family had often excluded them. Cases of isolated old folk in tragic circumstances may indeed be found, such as the widows of the Perros-Guirec sailors in 1457 'whose husbands were drowned in three or four vessels, 26 men belonging to the same parish, and that the said widows are so very poor that they can pay no more than ten deniers of the 20 sous hearth tax, each supporting the other'.[26] Of the 849 households in Trégor which were classified as incapable of paying the hearth tax, 125 were composed of old or elderly people, such as that of Alain Quiener, 'a poor sickly old man who lived in great poverty and misery', or that of Alain Todic, 'a poor old man of 100 years, sick in bed, whose wife earns his bread', or that of Jean Leguen, '80 years old, poor and crippled who goes hunting, and his wife is just as old and they live on charity', or that of Jean Pratezer, an 'old and miserable person, unmarried and practically blind, who has become a beggar', or that of Jean Madec's widow, a 'poor woman of 70 years, racked with ill-health and physical weakness and lives on charity'.

The countryside around Navarre provided the same picture as in Trégor. Although there were many old people living in miserable conditions, the increase in the number of complex or extended families was just as obvious during the epidemics. Researchers faced with elderly people living alone always stress the abnormal nature of this situation. On the other hand, the 1427–8 census counted 1,983 complex families in a total number of 8,620, that is 23 per cent, which is not a realistic figure since people often forgot to mention the presence of an elderly mother or father within the household. In most cases, these extended families comprised three generations, and sometimes four. Occasionally one finds three generations of married couples surviving in households where the grandparents, the son and his wife, the grandson and his wife as well as two or three little great-grandchildren all cohabit.

The proportions were as follows:

Families consisting of parents and married son	846
Families consisting of parents and married daughter	718
Families consisting of parents and two married children	120
Families consisting of parents and three married children	5
Families consisting of parents and children and married grandchildren	16
Families consisting of parents and married grandson	12

In the Bordelais region during the same period there was an increase in the number of groups of *parsonniers* and *consorts* practising a form of communal life. In Anjou, families of brothers and sisters drew up agreements concerning the support of their aged parents.[27] Similar examples occurred in the regions of Limousin and the Pyrenees, and also in towns, as in Rheims, where grandparents sometimes lived with their children or grandchildren. It was, however, more of a rural phenomenon than an urban one, as C. Klapisch noted with regard to Tuscany: 'An old man seldom lives alone in a Tuscan *popolo* and he continues to be part of a household run by other generations more often than is the case in town.'[28]

Although this more frequent provision for the old by their children ensured their material survival, it is not certain that it conferred the same degree of prestige and power on them. Cohabitation has various effects. There were undeniably some advantages: old men sometimes reverted to their positions as patriarchs, which is what happened in the Italian towns where the family clans chose a 'head', who was generally the oldest member of the main branch of the family,[29] or in the Limousin region and in the Pyrenees, where the ancestor retained control of the *frèrêche*. The role of the elderly in the transmission of knowledge was often recognized and accepted. Take Navarre for example, where the disappearance of adults could indeed invest the grandfather's knowledge of cultural mores with a new importance: 'if he disappears without having been able to transmit this, a whole patrimony of minutely detailed practices is lost to use without ever having been exploited.[30]

This was even more flagrantly the case where artists were concerned, especially those whose techniques were particularly refined, such as goldsmiths. One may sometimes find whole dynasties of several generations working together in the same workshop, with the oldest teaching traditional techniques to the rest of the group. This was the case in Brittany between 1486 and 1515 with regard to the Le Bellec family at Morlaix 'and Saint-Jean-du-Doigt, and the Floch family at Tréguier: Olivier, Guillaume and Jean, grandfather, father and son all worked for the Duchess. The Lapous at Morlaix, and the Ploiber family at Tréguier are further examples. With regard to the architects of Tréguier, Beaumanoir le Vieil worked with Philippe and Étienne during the 1500s. At Rieux, the old potters worked alongside the young ones.[31]

On the affective level, the coexistence of several generations had the effect of bringing grandparents closer to their grandchildren and of forging new ties with them. The fifteenth century was certainly important as far as the art of grandfatherhood was concerned, in spite of its silence on the subject. The painters have fortunately made up for the writers' lack of interest. Take for example, Domenico Ghirlandaio's splendid painting of *An old man and his grandson* which hangs in the Louvre. The two are looking at each other with poignant intensity. The old man, balding, with short white hair and a bulbous nose, whose massive face contrasts with the child's youth, has been given a brooding, soft and disillusioned look by his heavy eyelids; a life which is ending watching a life that is just beginning, without bitterness but with nostalgia and resignation. His grandson, on his knee, looks up at him questioningly, as if trying to pierce the mystery of this sadness. Outside, a restrained symbolic scene: the path of life winds past a verdant hill towards an arid, steep and solitary rock, travelling from youth towards old age.

INTER-GENERATIONAL CONFLICTS WORSEN

Over and above the tenderness that brought together the two extremes of life, the lengthening lifespan of the old and their presence in the households of the younger members of the family accounted for renewed tension and a rebirth of the old conflicts between the generations that had diminished since the disappearance of the Roman empire. In 1405, Christine de Pisan described the relationship between the old and the young of her period in *The Treasure of the City of Ladies*: 'There is quite often argument and discord, as much in outlook as in conversation, between old people and young ones, to the point that they can hardly stand each other, as though they were members of two different species. The difference in age ensures a difference in their attitudes and social positions.' With reference to women in particular, she gives them some advice as to how to end this 'war'. The spirit of relationships between young and old at the beginning of the fifteenth century is revealed through her recommendations:

> It is seemly for any older woman to be sensible in her actions, her clothing, facial expression and speech. It is said that old people are usually wiser than the young, and it is true for two reasons. First because their understanding is more perfect and is to be taken more seriously; second, because they have greater experience of past events because they have seen more. So therefore, they are likely to be wiser, and if they are not they are the more reprehensible. Inevitably nothing is more ridiculous than old people who lack good judgement or who are foolish or commit the follies that youth prompts in the young (and which are reprehensible even in them). For this reason the elderly woman ought to see to it that she does nothing that looks foolish. It is not seemly for her to dance, frolic about or to laugh uproariously. But if she is of a happy disposition, she ought always to see that she takes her pleasure sedately and not in the manner of young people, but in a more dignified way. She should say her words calmly and indulge in her amusements with decorum and without any rowdiness. Although we say that she ought to be wise and dignified, we do not mean, however, that she should be snappish, bad-tempered, fault-finding or rude, hoping to make people think that those are all signs of wisdom. She ought rather to guard herself against such passions as generally come to old people, namely being wrathful,

spiteful and surly . . . The elderly woman ought to be dressed in well-cut and respectable garments, for there is a true saying: an overdressed old woman makes a laughing-stock of herself. Her face should have a fine and honourable expression, for truly, although some may say that it is fine clothing that denotes great honour and respect, this expression is characteristic of an elderly person who is wise and has an honourable manner in all things. The speech of this wise elderly woman ought to be entirely controlled by discretion. She must be careful that foolish, vulgar words do not issue from her mouth, for foolish and crude language in old people is extremely ridiculous.

But to return to what we were saying earlier, namely the disputes and disagreements that generally exist between old and young people: the wise woman ought to reflect on this matter so that when she feels like criticizing young people because of some intolerable fault of their youth, she should say to herself, 'My Lord, but you were young once; cast your mind back to the things you got up to in those days!' . . . One ought to correct young people and reprove them firmly for their follies, but not however hate or defame them, for they are not aware of what they are doing. For this reason you will put up with them tolerantly and gently rebuke them when you have to . . . If those particular vices have left you, other worse ones have taken their place, like envy, covetousness, anger, impatience and gluttony (especially of wine, in which you often over-indulge). You, who ought to be wise, do not have the power to resist them, because the inclinations of old age attract, tempt and encourage you. And you want these young people to be wiser than you and do what you are unable to do yourself, that is, to resist the temptations that youth puts into their heads. So leave the young people in peace and stop complaining about them, for if you examine yourself well, you have enough to worry about. If the vices of youth have left you, it is not because of your virtue, but because nature no longer inclines you to them, and for that reason they seem to you so abominable that you cannot bear them.[32]

As for the young, Christine de Pisan asks them not to despise the old, rather to respect them, just as the Spartans and then the ancient Romans did: 'Do not displease them or find fault with them, as some wicked young people do who are very much to be reproached for it.' You should obey them because they are wise, you should stand in awe of them even if they are physically frail because they always have ways of correcting the young; you should help them, out of charity, because they are fragile and 'there is no worse disease than old age.' They are to be respected because society owes many good things to them: 'Every day the elderly also uphold in all lands, countries and kingdoms the fine laws and ordinances of the world. For in spite of the great strength of the young, if it were not for the wise elderly people the world would be in chaos.' The young should earn the favours of their elders through their good manners, and young girls in particular should allow themselves to be chaperoned by the old women, who will guard their honour: 'If the elderly have this attitude to the young, and the young treat the elderly in this way, the peace can be kept between these two groups, who often are in great discord.'

These excerpts clearly show that relations between the generations at the beginning of the fifteenth century were quite bitter, and confirm the growing place occupied by the elderly at that time. The mere fact that Christine de Pisan felt it worthwhile dedicating two chapters to the subject proves that she was particularly sensitive to the 'great discord' between the old and the young. The increased longevity of the former and the great vulnerability of the young in the face of the Plague can only have exacerbated the impatience of the young when confronted with their elders' monopoly of authority and property. A situation not dissimilar to that in republican Rome.

THE GROWING AGE GAP BETWEEN SPOUSES: THE THEME OF THE OLD HUSBAND

Christine de Pisan is herself a good example of another characteristic feature of the end of the Middle Ages: the growing age gap between spouses. Married at 15 to Etienne du Castel, a nobleman from Picardy, in 1380, she was widowed at the age of 25 with three children and had therefore experienced at first hand what it was to live with a husband much older than herself. Her mother had been placed in the same situation through her marriage to Thomas de Pizzano, a colleague of her own father's. There were many cases of old men marrying again with very young women. In the famous Paston family, the mother, Agnes, forced her young daughter Elizabeth to marry a 50-year-old who was both ugly and the worse for wear; since she was unwilling, she was 'beaten once in the week or twice, sometimes twice one day, and her head broken in two or three places over a period of three months.'[33] In Florence during the fifteenth century, half the children less than one year old had fathers of over 38, and the age gap between spouses was 14 years for the rich and 11 years for the poor.[34]

The greater female mortality due to childbearing and aggravated by the ravages of the epidemics in the fourteenth and fifteenth centuries, was the reason for the dearth of marriageable women. In response to matrimonial needs, girls married younger and younger: the average age in Florence for first marriages was 17.6 years. This had the immediate effect of intensifying the rivalry between young and old males. The latter, who were richer, were frequently preferred by the parents of the young girls; the former, frustrated in their nuptial desires, began to loathe the old fogeys who were monopolizing the young beauties. The reverse was also true, albeit rarely: a rich older widow might well be chosen as their daughter-in-law by the parents of a young man. Christine de Pisan, who herself did not marry again, in spite of her 25 years, disapproved of this practice: 'The height of folly is an old woman taking a young man! After a while she is singing a different song! It is difficult to feel very sorry for her because she has brought her misfortune upon herself.'[35]

The extreme age differences between married couples also affected relationships between parents and children within the family. As D. Herlihy observes for Florence, a too-old father could see his influence diminish; the age gap rendered communication and understanding between fathers and children difficult, and the mother's role became correspondingly more important. Second marriages only served to increase the confusion and made for problems and ambiguous relations between young stepmothers and their stepsons. It was a paradise for mock Oedipus complexes, a repeat of the situations in the Latin comedies where father and son share the same woman.

It is hardly surprising, therefore, that the old literary theme of the elderly cuckold was revived once more, fed by the social realities of the fifteenth century. One of the most successful illustrations of this theme is the little satirical treatise on 'The Fifteen Joys of Marriage' by Gilles Bellemère, Bishop of Avignon from 1390 to 1407. This is a very misogynous work, one of several malicious depictions of households where a vast age gap between spouses existed. Apart from the exaggerations required by the literary genre, the work's recurring theme emphasizes just how often the situation occurred at the end of the fourteenth and beginning of the fifteenth centuries. Its lively and vivid style has led us to reproduce several lengthy extracts. As far as the author was concerned, the man is always the victim: be he a young man married to an old woman or an old man married to a young woman, the wretched husband is always prematurely aged by worry:

When he who is married has lived a married life, and stayed in it six or seven, nine or ten years, whether more or less, and has five or six children, and has experienced all the dreadful days, the bad nights, and the above-mentioned misfortunes, or any of them suffered many times: and his youth is already extremely chilled, so much so that it were time for him to rest, if he were able: for he is so exhausted, so tired, so worn by work and the torments of family life, that he no longer minds anything that his wife tells him to his face, but he is hardened like an old donkey who through very habit has learnt to endure the goad, and goes no faster than he is used to going.[36]

Certainly, declares our bishop, women have to endure pregnancy, but this does not merit our sympathy: do not hens lay an egg every day 'through a channel which you would not have been able to put your little finger in beforehand'? And this does not prevent them from being fatter than the cocks. These little feminine worries do not add up to much: 'They are nothing compared with the cares of a reasonable man when he is thinking profoundly about any important matter in which he is involved.' Worn out by his cares, the husband is exhausted while making love and no longer manages to satisfy his wife, who remains 'as strong as she was beforehand'. Also, 'there is a general rule in marriage: that each woman believes tenaciously that her husband is the nastiest and least potent man in regard to the secret business.' Consequently, the wives 'probably start investigating whether other men are as impotent as their husbands'.

All the more reason, then, for an old man who marries a young woman to be unhappy!

I consider most idiotic any old man who wishes to play the fool and gets married to a young woman. When I see such things happening, I laugh, thinking of the inevitable end. For you ought to know that if an old man takes a young woman it would be a great bit of luck if she were to hasten to satisfy his needs: consider whether she, being young and tender and sweet of breath, would be able to endure the old man, who will cough, spit and complain all night, who stinks and sneezes: it would be a wonder if she did not kill herself. And his breath is sour, on account of his liver, or other accidents which happen to old people. So consider whether it is well done, to put two such contrary things together? It's comparable with putting a cat and a dog in a sack: there will always be war in it till the end . . . And when the courtiers see a lovely young girl married to such a man or to a cretin, and they see that she is pretty and gay, they will press their suit: for they are sure that she will give better ear to them than another, who has married a young and capable man.[37]

If the old man has the bad luck to become impotent, he will suffer hell:

Should it happen that as a result of excessive suffering and work or on account of old age, the good man falls into the languour of illness, gout or other things, so that he cannot get up when sitting, leave a room, or loses an arm or a leg, or has suffered several accidents, such as one sees happening to many. When the war is over, and luck has turned against him, it's the lady, who is in fairly good shape and probably younger than him, who will maybe now do just as she pleases. The good man is caught, he who had fought well in the war in all sorts of ways. The good man's children, whom he had kept docile and disciplined, will be badly brought up from now on, for if the good man wants to tell them off, his lady will be against him: consequently, he feels great sorrow in his heart. Furthermore he is in danger from all his servants on account of the service he needs, which is very great. And however much intelligence he may have had once, they will make him believe he is a fool, because he cannot move anywhere. And his oldest son will probably want to take the management over from him, with his mother's support, as from one who is taking too long to die: there are plenty such. And when the good man sees himself thus overruled, and that his wife, his children and his servants take no account of him and do nothing he says, and probably don't even want him to draw up his will, because they feel that he does not want to leave his wife what she asks him to, and they sometimes leave him in his room for half a day without going to him: and he endures hunger, thirst and cold. And since the good man, who has been discreet and wise, and is still very intelligent, succumbs to a great desolation of thought, he tells himself he will deal with everything, and he summons his wife and his children. The said lady probably starts sleeping away from him, for her comfort, for the good man can no longer do anything and complains and suffers. Alas! All the pleasures he once gave his wife are forgotten, but she well remembers the times he scolded her, and tells her neighbours that he has been a bad man, and has led her such a hard life that were she not a very patient woman, she would not have been able to stay married to him.[38]

The mother and son agree to isolate the old man and pass him off as mad, to prevent him from disinheriting them:

And the lady and son talk together and say that he is out of his mind: and since he had threatened the son, they say that he is in process of squandering his inheritance, which he would never agree to, and they both conclude that no man of the world will talk to him any more. The son wants to take over the management more than ever, because his mother supports him. They go about and tell everyone that the good man has reverted to childhood: and the son tries to have the good man placed under his guardianship, and they make him believe he has lost his mind and memory, although he is as wise as he has always been.[39]

Should it happen that the age relationship is the other way round, with a young man marring an old woman, he will still be the victim.

> because there is no serf in greater bondage than a young, simple and carefree man who is subject to and ruled by a widow . . .: he who falls into this state can do nothing beyond praying to God to give him patience to endure and suffer all . . . and it often happens, because he is very young compared with her, that she grows jealous: for her enjoyment and lechery with the young man and his young body makes her lustful and jealous, and she would like to have him between her arms at all times, and she would always like to be close. She is like a fish in water, and on account of the great summer heat which has lasted a long time, the water grows stagnant and stale. Consequently the fish in it desires to find new water: it follows it and swims until it finds it. Thus is it with the aged woman, when she finds a young man with a young body who renews her. And know too, that there is nothing more displeasing to young men than an old woman, nor which harms his health more. And just as a man who drinks fusty wine, as long as he drinks it and is thirsty, he will put up with it; but once he has drunk it, he has a very nasty aftertaste, on account of the sourness, and he will not drink it so long as he can tap another wine. So it is with a young man who has an old wife, for he will certainly never love her, and a young wife will love her old husband even less. There are some men who marry old wives out of avarice, but such women are foolish indeed, because their husbands, however kind they are to them, will never keep any promise made to them.[40]
> And should it happen that an old woman takes a young man, the young man does it only out of avarice: since it so happens that he will never love her: and he will beat her very hard and ensure that she is very harshly treated, and sometimes she will fall into poverty. Know too that carnal knowledge of an old woman shortens the life of a young man, according to Hippocrates *non vetulam novi, cur moriar?* And indeed such old women married to young men are so jealous and so lustful that they are quite maddened, and wherever the husband goes, whether to church or elsewhere, it seems to them it is only for wrongdoing. God knows what tribulation and torment he suffers and how he is assaulted. A young woman would never be as jealous for these reasons, and she would also find a cure when she needed one. He who is in the situation I speak of is so brow-beaten that he dare not talk to any woman, and he must serve the lady who is old: because of

which he will age more in a year than he would have done in ten years with a young wife. The old woman will squeeze him dry, and he will live on in vexation and pain, in constant torment, and he will end his days miserably.[41]

CHAUCER'S ACCOUNT

Whereas Christine de Pisan told of conflicts between generations and Gilles Bellemère ridiculed marriages with old men or women, Geoffrey Chaucer, between 1385 and 1390, introduced many old men into his *Canterbury Tales*. Old age was clearly the order of the day, and particularly the problem of husbands who were too old. Chaucer provides a whole litany of them, veering from the ridiculous to the odious, against a background of animosity between generations. In the Miller's Tale, an old carpenter marries again, this time to an 18-year-old girl:

> She was a girl of eighteen years of age
> Jealous he was and kept her in the cage,
> For he was old and she was wild and young;
> He thought himself quite likely to be stung.
> He might have known, were Cato on his shelf,
> A man should marry someone like himself.
> A man should pick an equal for his mate.
> Youth and age are often in debate.
> His wits were dull, he'd fallen in the snare
> And had to bear his cross as others bear.[42]

He is inevitably cuckolded and ridiculed and eventually passed off as mad. The Wife of Bath, five times married, three times to an old man, regales the pilgrims with tales of how her elderly husbands laboured and sweated to satisfy her appetites:

> They could indeed with difficulty hold
> The articles that bound them all to me;
> (no doubt you understand my simile).
> So help me God, I have to laugh outright
> Remembering how I made them work at night.
> And faith I set no store by it, no pleasure
> It was to me. They'd give me their treasure.
> I had no need to do my diligence
> To win their love or show them reverence.[43]

She too spends her time heaping insults on her husband and picking fights with him:

Now, sir, old dotard, what is that you say?
Why is my neighbour's wife so smart and gay?
She is respected everywhere she goes.
I sit at home and have no decent clothes.
Why haunt her house? What are you doing there?
Are you so amorous? Is she so fair?
What, whispering secrets to our maid? For shame,
Sir, ancient lecher! Time you dropped that game.
And if I see my gossip or a friend
You scold me like a devil![44]

'Old traitor', 'old dotard crow', 'old barrelful of lies', 'dear sir shrew'
– this is what the husband has to listen to all day long, since according
to his wife 'bacon never gave me much delight.'

The Merchant's Tale describes the ridiculous efforts of the elderly
husband in bed with his young wife:

He lulled her, sought to kiss away her trouble;
The bristles of his beard were thick as stubble
Much like a dog-fish skin, and sharp as briars
Being newly shaved to sweeten his desire.
He rubbed his chin against her tender cheek . . .

But no caresses were enough to revive his flagging virility.

And so he laboured until the break of day.
They took a sop of claret-sodden toast,
Sat up in bed as rigid as a post,
And started singing very loud and clear . . .

God knows what May was thinking in her heart
Seeing him sit there in his shirt apart.
Wearing his night-cap, with his scrawny throat.
She didn't think his games were worth a groat.
At last he said, 'I think I'll take a rest;
Now day has come a little sleep were best.'
And down he lay and slept till half past eight.[45]

As the old Reeve admits in his *Prologue*:

The strength to play that game
Is gone, though we love foolishness the same.
What we can't do no more we talk about
And rake the ashes when the fire is out . . .
Desire never fails, and that's the truth
For even now I have a coltish tooth,

Many as be the years now dead and gone
Before my tap of life began to run.
Certain, when I was born, so long ago,
Death drew the tap of life and let it flow.
And ever since the tap has done its task,
And now there's little but an empty cask.
My stream of life's but drops upon the rim.
An old fool's tongue will run away with him
To chime and chatter at monkey tricks that's past;
There's nothing left but dotage at the last![46]

The merchant thinks that the only attraction an elderly husband can have for his young wife is his money. And after all, he states, how often nowadays does one see old men trying to find a young girl to marry! Like the knight of Lombardy whose story he tells and who, at 60 plus, wants to get married. But he requires a girl under 20, as he explains to his friends, charged with finding him a fiancée:

'My friends', he said, 'I am no longer young:
God knows I'm on the threshold of the grave.
I ought to think I have a soul to save . . .
I have resolved to be a wedded man . . .
The woman must on no account be old.
Certainly under twenty and demure . . .
Old beef is not so good as tender veal . . .
God knows these ancient widows know their trade
They are as tricky as the boat of Wade
And can be irritating when they try,
I'd never have a moment's peace, say I. . . .
A man can still control them with his tongue
And guide them should their duty seem too lax.'[47]

Disparagement of old women

The opposite situation, as depicted in 'The Fifteen Joys of Marriage,' was always viewed with repugnance, with the notion of carnal intercourse with an old woman considered as monstrous. The knight in the Wife of Bath's Tale has to marry an old woman as a result of an oath and is horrorstruck. The marriage takes place without any celebrations:

He married her in private on the morrow
And all day long stayed hidden like an owl.
It was such torture that his wife looked foul.

Great was the anguish churning in his head
When he and she were piloted to bed . . .

His wife tries in vain to console him and his reply is merciless:

Nothing can ever be put right now!
You're old, and so abominably plain . . .[48]

   As the precursor of one of the sixteenth century's favourite themes
of the ugly duchesses and hideous old women by Baldung Grien, the
old woman, the incarnation of evil, assumed the appearance of a witch;
according to Chaucer, one could never imagine a more hideous creature.
Villon contributed to the genre with his 'Lament of the Fair Heaulmière'
(helmet-maker's girl):

And I am left here, old and hoar
When I bethink my days of pride
What I am now, and was of yore.
Or when I hold a glass before
My naked body, how so chang'd,
Wrinkled and shrunken, frail and poor,
My wits with grief are nigh estrang'd.
. . .
The forehead scowls, the hair is grey
The brows are gone, the eyes are blear
That were so mocking and so gay
They fill'd the passers-by with cheer;
The nose is hooked and far from fair.
The ears are rough and pendulous,
The face is sallow, dead and drear.
The chin is purs'd, the lips hang loose.
Aye, such is human beauty's lot!
The arms are short: the hands clench tight;
The shoulders tangle in a knot;
The breasts, in shame they shrink from sight;
Nipple and haunch, they share their plight,
The twat – ah, bah! The thighs are thin
As wither'd hams, and have a blight
Of freckles, like a sausage-skin.

Thus we mourn for good old days,
Perch'd on our buttocks, wretched crones,
Huddled together by the blaze
Of some poor fire of forest cones,
That dies as quickly as our moans,
A briefly-lit, brief-living flame –

> We who have sat on lovers' thrones!
> With many a man 'tis just the same.[49]

According to Olivier de La Marche, the 60-year-old woman was the personification of ugliness:

> If your life runs true to nature,
> For whom LX years is a very great number,
> Your loveliness will turn to ugliness,
> Your health to some dark malady,
> And you will be no more than an encumbrance.
> If you've a daughter, you'll be her shadow,
> She'll be claimed and taken from you,
> And each one's mother abandoned and alone . . . [50]

In popular circles, the lonely and poor old woman was at the bottom of the social scale; held in contempt, insulted, exploited and defenceless. At least this is how Chaucer presented her in the Friar's Tale: a group of undesirables take against an old widow, 'an old tiddee, and ancient wreck'; they go to find her and call 'Come out you old inebriate; I'll bet you've got a friar or a priest inside.' Inventing a false injunction to appear before the archdeacon, they extort 12 pence from the 'poor old hag'.

The assimilation of the old woman into the ranks of malevolent powers was characteristic of the religious art of the fourteenth and fifteenth centuries. In representations of the Passion, an old woman appears as the incarnation of evil, leading the soldiers to the Mount of Olives and forging the nails for the Crucifixion. She can be seen in English miniatures shortly after 1300, in a French miniature of the 'Pilgrimage of Jesus Christ' of 1393, in the 'Hours of Étienne Chevalier' by Jean Fouquet, in a fifteenth-century mystery play, and in 'The Mystery of the Passion' by Jean Michel, in which she is called Hédroit, is ugly and loathes Jesus.[51] In many respects Pieter Bruegel's *Dulle Griet* was her direct descendant.

Chaucer thought that the only advantage in marrying an old woman was that there was no risk of being cuckolded. Thus the wife of the unfortunate knight in the Wife of Bath's Tale reassures her husband:

> You say I'm old and fouler than a fen
> You need not fear to be a cuckold then
> Filth and old age, I'm sure you will agree.
> Are powerful wardens upon chastity.
> . . .
> You have two choices: which one will you try?
> To have me old and ugly till I die.

But still a loyal, true and humble wife,
That never will displease you all her life,
Or would you rather I were young and pretty
And chance your arm what happens in a city
Where friends will visit you because of me,
Yes, and in other places too, maybe.
Which would you have? The choice is all your own.[52]

It is such a cruel choice that the knight ends by letting his wife make the decision and she resolves it in the best possible way: she becomes young again by magic and stays faithful to him.

In many ways, the problem of the strong age differential between spouses was greater at the end of the Middle Ages than it had been in the preceding years. The increased number of texts on the subject shows that contemporary writers were aware of the situation, of its novelty and its consequences, if not its causes. Like Boccaccio, they could sometimes still appear surprised by it. In the *Decameron*, written during the worst outbreaks of the Black Death, between 1349 and 1351, he presents the character of 'Charles the Old', that is Charles d'Anjou, King of Naples and brother to St Louis, who falls in love with the daughters of Messer Neri, a Neopolitan nobleman, and wants to carry them off. His adviser, Count Guido, is amazed: 'I find it so novel and extraordinary that you, who are already old, should fall passionately in love, that it almost seems a miracle.' The old are past loving and Old Charles presents a rare case within the exclusively young and licentious society portrayed in the *Decameron*. In any case, the King of Naples abandoned his project. Guillaume de Machaut, a one-eyed, gouty sexagenarian canon, made no secret of his affair with Peronnelle d'Armentières, a young girl of 18. In his *Livre du Voir-dit* he exposed their liaison uninhibitedly. It is true that there were advantages on both sides: the vain poet was flattered by being loved at his age by a young girl and she owed her emergence from anonymity to her lover's notoriety. This famous couple's very incongruity was, however, symbolic of a new social situation.

THE CONCENTRATION OF WEALTH AND POWER IN THE HANDS OF OLD MEN

The Black Death's selective ravages also had the effect of strengthening the economic and political power of old men. A father, if spared by the epidemic, would remain in charge much longer and then sometimes hand over his business directly to his grandson. He would have had time to accumulate more wealth and monopolize all the decision-making more than previously, a situation which led in some towns to serious generation clashes.

Arlette Higounet-Nadal has well demonstrated the decisive role of old age in the social ascendency of families in Périgueux. In 1254 an immigrant, Bernabé Joy de Dieu, moved into the town; he bought a house, and then ten years later another; in 1276 he was put in charge of the mint; his grandson, Hélie Bernabé, a goldsmith, became a consul in 1323, when just over 25; he went on performing his civic duties right up to the age of 90, and fulfilling several missions while continuing to acquire assets; he died after 1393, aged over 95. His son Arnaud, who died aged about 90 in 1436, married the daughter of a rich merchant of Limoges, sat in on the council of the wise (*prud'hommes*) between 1388 and 1432 and was elected mayor ten times between 1387 and 1420. There is no doubt that the exceptional longevity of these three men contributed greatly to their prestige and wealth. The most influential men in Périgueux at the time were mainly over 60, many having pursued a career in public service for over 25 years until their death. 'Generally speaking perhaps, but certainly in Périgueux, longevity was a trump card as far as social life was concerned. Power, influence, action were the lot of those who lived long.'[53]

In the south west of France, Barthélemy Bonis, a merchant of Montauban, was also doing well; enriched by the trade in cloth, silks, haberdashery, leather, jewels, weapons and spices, he became a local banker, lending money against bond or deposit until the age of 70 (1300–70). On a higher level, Francesco Datini, born in Prato in 1335, expanded his business after the age of 50, building up companies in his native town, then in Florence, Pisa, Genoa, Barcelona, Valencia and Majorca, which meant that he was able to bequeath 75,000 florins to found a hospice in Prato by the age of 75.

Posts and benefices were often for life, the most important jobs frequently being given to the elderly. This was the case in the countryside for the petty officials of great landowners, and even more so in the towns, where conditions of age governed access to civic appointments. In Avignon, in 1450, a citizen had to prove that he had been on the tax lists for at least ten years to be allowed on the council; in Tarascon, between 1370 and 1400, a citizen had to have served on the council for at least 17 years before becoming mayor: 'Rules such as these ensured that certain municipal élites were minorities on account of their age.'[54] Where there was a choice between equally qualified persons, the elder was always preferred.

In Italy, where municipal appointments had far greater significance, the concentration of power in the hands of the elderly was even more obvious, and led to a direct confrontation between old and young at the beginning of the fifteenth century. Thus Lucca was controlled by nine old noblemen and one gonfalonier. In Venice, the lengthy *cursus honorum* led to the more important jobs being reserved for older men and the doges produced the most remarkable series of aged heads of state of the fourteenth and fifteenth centuries, breaking all records of political longevity – an average of 78 years at death for the main seven, who were active to the end: Tommaso Mocenigo (1343–1423), elected at the age of 72; Francesco Foscari (1373–1457), elected at the age of 46, who remained in power for 34 years, until he was deposed; Pietro Mocenigo (1406–76), elected at the age of 68; Giovanni Mocenigo (1408–85), elected at the age of 70; Agostino Barbarigo (1419–1501), elected at the age of 67; Andrea Gritti (1455–1538), elected at the age of 68.

It is true that the doges were not the real instigators of Venetian policy, but their role was nonetheless not negligible, and the systematic choice of such elderly men constituted a fine homage to old age. Some of them produced veritable lineages of old men, thus amassing considerable power for themselves. The most remarkable instance of this was that of the Mocenigo family. Tommaso (1414–23) extended Venetian control over Trentino, Friuli and Dalmatia; his nephew Pietro, a famous admiral, defeated the Turks at Smyrna at the age of 66 in 1472, and again at Scutari, before being elected doge at the age of 68; his brother Giovanni was doge from the age of 70 to 77 (1478–85). The latter's grandson, Andrea, was a man of letters who died in 1542 aged 69; whereas a nephew, Alvise I, was doge from the age of 63 to 70 (1570–77).

The city's corporations were all run by old men too. In 1544 the statute governing the ruling on age at the Scuola della Misericordia stated that its Guardiani Grandi had always been 'noble men, respectable in rank and age', and they were often aged over 70; in any case the minimum age allowed by the statute was 50.[55] People were aware of the opposition between old and young: Doge Mocenigo made several impassioned speeches against youth and in 1433 several young men were known to have been plotting to seize power.[56]

It was in Florence that the rivalry between the generations reached its peak. Already rife during the first half of the fifteenth century, it became marked in every sphere: in one monastery, the old monks were driven out by the young ones; young noblemen tried to grab the electoral urns. Bernardino of Sienna criticized both sides, mocking the physical decline of the old on the one hand and jeering at the 'angelic' young governors on the other. In a city where 12,000 of the 20,000 male adults were under 30, unsuited to politics and classed as 'idiots', the Medici epoch witnessed a serious confrontation between generations, with the young backing the Medicis and the old favouring the traditional gerontocracy. Lorenzo il Magnifico's reign was characteristic in this respect: surrounded by young men and women, *il Principe*, the self-styled brilliant and splendid model 'courtier', would have been quite incapable of accepting the rule of stern old men, although, in the street, he would ostentatiously cede them passage.[57]

Several historians maintain that the political events are better explained in terms of the generation gap than by the economic and social rivalries taking place in Tuscany at the time: 'The most basic division in the *Res Publica* was the division between the old and the young', states Richard C. Trexler.[58] Piero di Medici would thus have fallen from power in 1494 because he 'supported the young and the minor noblemen and preferred them even in the face of opposition from some of the old *principali* and mature men. It seemed to these old men that Piero did not appreciate them.'[59] Savonarola tried to exploit this rivalry; he mistrusted the old men who still hankered after the days of Lorenzo il Magnifico, and he wanted to educate a virtuous youth to supervise society. 'Savonarola used the young as a weapon in the battle for his civil and religious reforms.'[60] During the sixteenth century, these conflicts between the generations, whose origins went back in part to the effects of the Black Death, were to develop further.

The theme of old age in poetry: a pessimistic vision

A natural consequence of the trend towards gerontocracy was the resurgence in cultured circles of criticism against the old. The image of old age in the literature of the time clearly deteriorated. The more that old people were playing important and active roles, the more they were seen as obstacles, as rivals, to be both despised and feared. Faced with their actual wealth and power, emphasis was laid on their ugliness, physical weakness, their faults and their grievous condition so close to death. Being more numerous and stronger politically, the old were disparaged; they were submerged in a general pessimism; the ransom extorted for the growth of their power. Old women, as we have seen, became witches and the incarnation of evil. Old men were, at best, objects of pessimistic meditation on the passage of worldly pleasures, an aspect tackled by all the great names of poetry in the fifteenth century.

The only discordant voice among these recriminations against old age is that of an obscure Scottish poet, about whom very little is known, except that he died when very old around 1500. In 'The Praise of Age' he declares his happiness at no longer being young, because the older he grows, the closer he comes to eternal bliss:

> For to be yong I wald not, for my wis
> Off all this warld to mak me lord and king:
> The more of age, the nerar hevynnis bliss.
>   . . .

> I am content that youthede is ago:
>
> . . .
>
> The state of youth I repute for na gude,
> For in that state sik perilis now I see
> Bot full smal grace . . .
> The more of age, the nerar hevyniis bliss.[61]

In 'The Ressoning betuix Aige and Yowth', he insists on the vanity of the advantages of youth, which passes so swiftly. His praise of old age is purely academic, since its sole advantage is that of having nothing to lose in this world. The other poets do not see things the same way, and they all weep, with greater or lesser felicity, for the springtime of their lives.

Charles d'Orléans, who dragged out his unhappy life for 71 years (1394–1465),[62] spending his last years in the Loire valley, sick and withdrawn from public affairs, was able to express with grace and melancholy the regrets inspired in him by the loss of his youth:

> For now that I have grown old,
> When I read in the book of poetry
> I take my spectacles to see better
> By which the letters are enlarged
> And I don't see what I wish for
> I didn't use to have this weakness
> In the hands of my Lady Youth.[63]

Elsewhere, he deplores his loss of memory; what used to take him one-and-a-half hours to learn by heart 'in the flower of youth' now takes him twice as long 'in the evening of my life'; he is obliged to leave the pleasures of gallantry to the young:

> I have been commanded and scolded
> Henceforth by Lady Old Age
> To leave prowess to the young men.

All that is left him is the memory of the past,

> for, upon my faith,
> nothing that I now see warms me:
> For old age is handed to me
> Like devalued money.

'Le vieil Briquet' is resting, and pining, on his own:

> And Old Age wanted to
> Emprison him in a locked room . . .
> Time and time has robbed my youth

And left me in the hands of Old Age.

The old poet is assailed by evils of all kinds: 'soussy, vieillesse et deplaisance' (worry, old age and vexation) turn his retreat into 'the house of pain':

> Deafened by not mattering,
> Blinded by vexation,
> With a taste for complaining,
> I don't know what I'm good for.

He concludes that 'Ung vieillart peult peu de chose!' (an old man can do very little!).

François Villon expressed more or less the same sentiments, but in quite a different context. His obsession with growing old began very early on; he already mentions the 'entrée de la vieillesse' (the entry of old age) in 'The Testament', written when he was 30. He points out that old men are everywhere despised and that they can do no good in the eyes of the young, 'toujours viel cinge est desplaisant':

> Though many would applaud his japes
> In youth, yet now they have no place.
> Men hate an aged jackanapes
> And cannot brook his least grimace.
> And if, to please, he hold his peace,
> They scorn him as an empty fool;
> And if he speak, they bid him cease
> Or take his prattle back to school.[64]

Old age means ugliness, especially horrifying for women: 'old I will be; you ugly and grey.'

> A time will come which will make
> Your flowering beauty grow yellow and fade.

In his 'Mirror of Marriage', Eustache Deschamps expressed the same ideas more pettily, but his systematically whinging attitude robs his evidence of much of its value, as Huizinga pointed out: 'In old age the poet sees only evil and disgust, a lamentable decline of the body and the mind, ridicule and insipidity.' For him, women were old at 30, men at 50 and they could not hope to live beyond 60. 'Tout va mal' was what his poems taught. The world is like an old man who has reverted to his childhood:[65]

> Now the world is cowardly, decayed and weak,
> Old, covetous and confused of speech:
> I see only female and male fools . . .

The end approaches, in sooth . . .
All goes badly.

Faced with this basic pessimism, one might well prefer the next ballad by Jehan Régnier, composed in 1460, although his message is much the same. The poet is 68 and his wife, Ysabeau Chrestienne, has asked him to compose a poem, reminding him of their long married life together:

My friend, we have been together a long time and have always lived happily and out of love for me you used to compose songs and other poetry, but because we are now in our old age, you no longer compose anything, and I beg you at least to make one out of love for me.

A touching witness to the fidelity and love of this married couple, contrasting with Charles d'Orléans' or Villon's frivolity, Jehan Régnier composed a little ballad on old age for his wife, charming in its sincerity, simplicity, melancholy and gentle resignation:

Since I feel that Old Age is coming to me
And youth has left me and forgotten me,
It behoves me to take leave of arms,
Because my strength has all dwindled away . . .
I seek nothing more than ease and repose.
When I recall the good times past,
When we went hunting with you riding pillion . . .
And now I have a drip on my nose,
Toothless, I eat milk broth,
Wrapped in furs, sitting in my dressing gown
Near the fire, with wine and water in two flasks.
With trembling hands dribbling my drink;
I seek nothing more than ease and repose.
Ah, my love! Those times will not return,
If we expect them to, its very foolish of us,
We must go on without knowing what will become of us,
We must cry Forget, forget, forget . . .
Prince, old age had reduced me
To studying calendars and dates,
Feeding on the medicine of my deeds,
I seek nothing more than ease and repose.[66]

The romances of the fifteenth century joined with poetry in decrying old age. We are far removed from the valiant old men of the *Chanson de Roland*. In the *Roman de Jehan de Paris*, written at the end of the fifteenth century, the old king of England 'who was already very old and broken' could not rival the young and handsome king of France. During war, old men were 'useless mouths' to be driven from the besieged towns. Chaucer, whom we have seen attacking the practice of marrying young people to old, slid a few positive portraits into his gallery of old men, such as this 'old and choleric and thin' Reeve, with his beard shaved close, full of experience and subtlety, wily and redoubtable:

> And he could judge by watching drought and rain
> The yield he might expect from seed and grain.
> . . .
> No one had ever caught him in arrears
> . . .
> Feared like the plague he was, by those beneath.[67]

But what are not the misfortunes of great old age! The Wife of Bath laments that: 'Age that comes to poison everything/Has taken all my beauty and my pith.' And the clerk points out that age gradually invades one, as silent as stone. If the pilgrims' stories are to be believed, old people everywhere were despised and insulted. When an old man greets a troupe of riders they reply:

> Old fool, give place!
> Why are you all wrapped up except your face?
> Why live so long? Isn't it time to die?
> The old old fellow looked him in the eye
> And said 'because I never yet have found,
> Though I have walked to India, searching round
> Village and city on my pilgrimage,
> One who would change his youth to have my age.
> . . .
> Not even Death, alas, will take my life:
> See how I wither, flesh and blood and skin!
> Alas! when will these bones be laid to rest?
> . . .
> But it dishonoured you when you began
> To speak so roughly sir to an old man
> Unless he had injured you in word or deed,
> It says in holy writ, as you may read,
> "Thou shalt rise up before the hoary head
> And honour it."[68]

A precept which appeared to have been quite forgotten, even by knights, according to the Wife of Bath:

Lastly you taxed me, sir, with being old.
Yet even if you never had been told
By ancient books, you gentlemen engage
Yourselves in honour to respect old age.[69]

At the beginning of the fourteenth century Dante revived the classical theme of the stages of human life in his *Convivio*, displaying a more elevated opinion of old age. But he attributed it with nothing more than the role of preparing us for death. The values of old age were all negative. He divided life into four stages; adolescence, characterized by warmth and humidity; adulthood, a period of warmth and dryness; maturity, which he extends generously from 45 to 70 years, cold and dry; and decrepitude, from 70 to 80 years, cold and moist. Life resembles an arch, with an ascending phase, a peak, at between 30 and 40 years old, and a descending phase. Each age has a role to fulfil: that of maturity is to help others achieve perfection, because its qualities are prudence, due to its memory of past events, justice, which should serve to give others a good example, liberality and affability. The age of decrepitude is one of preparation for death, which should take place peacefully, like a boat slipping quietly into harbour after a long journey. We are returning to our natural harbour, which is God; the old must renounce all earthly pleasures and adopt a religious way of life, blessing God for all their past life. Eighty years is the limit. Even Christ's body, had he not been crucified, would have been transformed into a glorified body at the age of 81.

Other writers remained loyal to the tradition of dividing life into 12 parts, but they too left the task of preparing for death to the last years of life. The artists of the end of the Middle Ages, taking their inspiration from a poem of the fourteenth century, used to illustrate human life by means of 12 scenes corresponding to the 12 months of the year: 48 years was the end of the August of life – youth is ending, it is harvest time; at 54, the end of September, the grain must be stored, because anyone entering old age without any property will be very miserable, and the miniatures show a beggar to illustrate this age; at 60, the end of October, he becomes an old man, with nothing to do but think on death; at the end of November, at 66, he no longer has any reason for living, everything shrivels up and dies, his heirs are getting restive – the miniatures show us an old man in his dressing gown with his doctor; at 72, the end of December, his life ends too: the wretched man expires.[70]

So old age, as portrayed in literature and art, is a tragic time of life, especially if one is alone. The agony of separation experienced by old married couples is poignantly expressed in Piero della Francesca's *Death of Adam* (in the Church of Saint Francis in Arezzo), painted between 1452 and 1459. Ancient Eve, wrinkled, sad and resigned, grandmother to us all, places her hand on Adam's shoulder in a silent and tender gesture in a drama which has universal relevance.

So people went on dreaming of perpetual youth, of the myth of rejuvenation. The fountains of youth flowed even faster in manuscript miniatures: in the *Roman de Fauvel* (beginning of the fourteenth century), in the *Histoire d'Alexandre le Grand* (fifteenth century).[71] Treatises were written on how to delay the physical degeneration of old age: Marsilius Ficinus himself dwelt on the question,[72] and Alviso Cornaro thought that it should be possible to extend life to its natural limit of 100 years, because it is on account of their dissolute morals that men have become decrepit at the age of 40.[73] In 1389, Gabriele Zerbi published his *Gerontocomia*, a work dedicated to the hygiene of the old.

ELDERLY POLITICIANS, CLERICS AND ARTISTS

The growth in the number of elderly men and in the importance of their role was also expressed by the growing recognition of the importance of retirement, signalling a new recognition of the particular conditions and specific requirements of old age. They were specific requirements which were still viewed negatively but which heralded a growing awareness of the problems of the third age.

Of course, the more vigorous of them continued to fulfil their roles and remained active right up to the end. The fourteenth and fifteenth centuries had their share of elderly statesmen, soldiers, merchants and artists, who did not retire and who died while still in office. There were many such knights and soldiers of all ranks. Although we don't know what became of Bérenger de Roquefeuil during the last years of his life – he built the fantastic Chateau of Bonaguil and died in 1530 aged 82 – we do know that Gaston Phoebus, Count of Foix, died in 1391 at the age of 60 returning home from a bear hunt, that Robert d'Artois died aged 56 of a wound received during the battle of Vannes, that John Hawkwood, the *condottiere* in the service of Florence who fought in Italy for the last 30 years of his life, was still taking part in tournaments in Bologna in 1392 when he was 72, that his brothers-in-arms, Federigo da Montefeltro, Francesco Sforza and Erasmo Gattamelata, were all still active until the age of 60 for the first two, and until 69 for the latter, that John Talbot, appointed Constable of Portchester at the age of 64, and who then became captain of the fleet and lieutenant in Aquitaine, was shot through the heart at 65 while leading an attack on the entrenched French encampment at Castillon (1453). We know that the armies of Philippe VI and Jean le Bon were led by old soldiers such as

Constable Gaucher de Chatillon and Marshalls Baudrain de La Heuse and Arnould d'Audrehem. In 1356, Jean le Bon did not shrink from calling up the *ban* and the *arrière-ban* of men aged between 18 and 60.

There were also a good many elderly people among the kings and queens, princes and princesses and royal counsellors: Philippe VI of Valois died at the age of only 57, whereas Jeanne d'Évreux, Charles VI's wife, lived for 61 years; Blanche, Philippe of Valois's wife, lived 64 years; Marguerite, the wife of Louis I, Count of Flanders, died at the age of 72; Isabelle of France, Queen of England, was 68; Isabelle of Portugal was 65; Jean, Duke of Berry, was 76 – at 60 he wrote a ballad about the number of his mistresses: 'Not just one, but three or four pairs.' René d'Anjou died in 1481 aged 71; Jean de Brienne, 'Bouteiller de France' for 40 years, died in 1296 aged 90; his similarly named father died in 1237 aged 89, and was Emperor of Constantinople between the ages of 83 and 89; Arthur III, Count of Richmond and Duke of Brittany, died aged 65 in 1458; Dunois followed him at the same age ten years later. Kings and queens often preferred experienced counsellors: in 1388 Charles VI recalled his father's 'marmousets': Jean Le Mercier, Bureau de La Rivière and Jean de Montagu.

The clergy held the record for longevity and tended not to retire. Following tradition, the popes were elected at an advanced age, often over 60: Urban VI was pope from the age of 60 to 71 (1378–89), Benedict XIII from 60 to 81 (1394–1415), Innocent VII from 66 to 68 (1404–6), Alexander V from 60 to 61 (1409–10), Calixtus III from 77 to 80 (1455–8), Sixtus IV from 57 to 70 (1471–84), and Alexander VI from 61 to 72 (1492–1503). The latter was said at the time to have been 70 years old and was described as growing 'Younger every day: his cares never last the night through; he is always merry and never does anything he does not like.'[74] Many ecclesiastics of all ranks and moral standards were very active during their declining years, from Philippe de Marigny, Archbishop of Sens, adviser to Philippe IV and prosecutor of the Templars, who died at the age of 70 in 1350, to the humble Jeanne Marie de Maille, who led a life of poverty wandering around Touraine and who died aged 83 in 1414; not to mention the Spanish Dominican Vincent Ferrer who died aged 64 in Vannes while on a preaching tour in 1419. The collegiate and cathedral chapters all had their share of old people: the cathedral of Laon had in 1409 one canon aged over 80, one aged between 70 and 80, eight aged between 60 and 70 and 11 aged between 50 and 60.[75]

However a new category began to threaten the supremacy hitherto reserved for ecclesiastics: that of the artists. Their creative urge seemed to carry these men through to an advanced age whilst preserving all their mental faculties. A glance at Vasari's *Lives of the Artists* confirms the above. Of the 47 Italian artists from the fourteenth to the sixteenth

Table 8.3 Longevity of artists in Vasari's *Lives of the Artists*

Name	Born	Died	Age at death
Arnolfo di Lapo	1226	1302	78
Cimabue	1240	1302	62
Niccolo Pisano	1220	1284	64
Giovanni Pisano	1250	1317	67
Giotto	1266	1337	71
Andrea Pisano	1270	1348	78
Andrea Orcagna	1308	1368	60
Duccio	1255	1319	64
Spinello Aretino	1346	1410	64
Jacopo della Quercia	1376	1438	62
Luca della Robbia	1400	1482	82
Paolo Uccello	1397	1475	78
Lorenzo Ghiberti	1378	1455	77
Filippo Brunelleschi	1377	1446	69
Donatello	1377	1466	82
Piero della Francesca	1416	1492	76
Giovanni da Fiesole	1387	1455	68
Leon Battista Alberti	1404	1472	68
Fra Filippo Lippi	1406	1469	63
Benozzo Gozzoli	1420	1497	77
Jacopo Bellini	1404	1470	66
Gentile Bellini	1429	1507	78
Giovanni Bellini	1430	1516	86
Antonio Pollaiuolo	1429	1498	69
Sandro Botticelli	1444	1510	66
Andrea Mantegna	1431	1506	75
Pietro Perugino	1450	1523	73
Francesco Francia	1450	1517	67
Vittore Scarpaccia	1455	1526	71
Luca Signorelli	1441	1523	82
Leonardo da Vinci	1452	1519	67
Bramante	1444	1514	70
Titian	1477	1576	99
Michelangelo	1475	1564	89

century that he cites, 34 (72 per cent) of them lived more than 60 years: 19 were over 70 and six over 80 at their death.

Very few of these artists retired, and the self-portrait of their doyen, Titian, at the age of 90 (Museo di Prato) gives us an idea why. The thin old man with his long beard has eyes which shine so fervently that it would be difficult to imagine such a man ceasing to work. He went on working for a further nine years, and died a few months before his hundredth birthday. Luca Signorelli died aged 82 whilst painting a fresco of the baptism of Christ; Giovanni Bellini painted his greatest pictures between the ages of 75 and 83; Andrea Mantegna was finishing his *Madonna of Victory* at 65 and his *Parnassus* at 70; Tintoretto painted his self-portrait at 70 and Leonardo da Vinci his at the age of 60; Michelangelo painted himself as Saint Bartholomew in his fresco of the *Last Judgement* when aged over 65. Jean-Paul Sartre and Simone de Beauvoir thought they could discern despair in these self-portraits. With regard to Tintoretto's, Sartre wrote that he had fixed on the canvas forever

> an ancient exhausted amazement, frozen like his life, hardened like his arteries . . . In this picture he gives himself the loneliness of a corpse . . . he pleads guilty: if he did not, would he have this haunted look of an aged murderer? . . . there is something about him that compels us to keep our distance – the austere pride of his despair.[76]

Did they experience despair at ageing? To some extent undoubtedly they did.

Michelangelo claimed to be tormented by the physical suffering caused by his advanced age:

> My long-drawn-out labours have broken, undermined and dismembered me, and the inn to which I am travelling, the inn at whose common table I shall eat and drink is death . . . I cage a buzzing wasp in a leather bag full of bones and sinews, and I have three balls of cobbler's wax in a tube. My face is a scarecrow's. I am like those rags they hang out in times of drought and that frighten away the birds. A spider runs about in one of my ears and in the other a cricket chirps all night. Weighed down by my catarrh I can neither sleep nor snore.[77]

Could it not be said that his sufferings spurred him on to his extraordinary activity until the age of 88? His output was colossal during his last 20 years and would have been enough to fill the life of any first-rate artist. He undertook the enormous fresco of the *Last Judgement* at the age of 65, an exhausting task involving lying on his back on scaffolding for hours on end, and even falling off it, injuring himself badly. At the request of Pope Paul II he started next on the paintings for the Pauline Chapel, dogged as always by constant money worries. In 1544, when he was 69, he fell gravely ill while continuing work on Julius II's colossal tomb. He worked on plans for fortifying Rome, for the Farnese palace, and for the Capitoline piazza and palazzi when aged 70. He was appointed architect for the rebuilding of St Peter's in 1547 and was persecuted by the followers of Sangallo, whose rival he had been. He sculpted the bust of *Brutus* in 1548. From 1555 onwards, after the death of his pupil Urbino, of whom he had been very fond, he grew weaker and lost interest in everything. He was tormented by the idea that he had wasted his life in the vain activities of painting and sculpting, when he should have dedicated himself entirely to God. He carried on working, nonetheless, overseeing the work on St Peter's, finishing the *Rondamini Pietà*, and continuing to stand up to his enemies who were trying to remove the management of the building projects from him. He suffered a heart attack at the age of 86 in 1561, and died three years later.

On a more modest level, the French painter Jean Coste is supposed to have worked until a very advanced age in the service of Jean le Bon during the fourteenth century in order to finish the frescoes in the Chateau du Vaudreuil.[78] In Flanders Hans Memling began his huge triptych for Lübeck Cathedral in 1491, at the age of 61.

The artist is unique and irreplaceable; his genius and originality can never be passed on. This is undoubtedly why the painters and sculptors of the Renaissance, a time when the demand for beautiful things reached unprecedented heights, continued working until they died. The Maecenes gave them no peace and there was no question of them retiring. Politicians may be replaced, but a Michelangelo never. These men were constrained to give humanity the benefit of their genius right up to the last moment, and even today they constitute the only category for which the word retirement has no meaning.

RETIREMENT: THE IDEA CATCHES ON

This term began to become more widespread among the wealthier strata of society towards the end of the Middle Ages. When Jean le Bon created the chivalric Order of the Star in 1351, he founded a retirement home for the old knights where they were to be treated with respect and served by two valets each; this was the first draft for the Hôtel des Invalides for elderly ex-servicemen. It was a project that was to affect only a very limited number of people, but it had symbolic value: it was the first time politicians had conceived the idea of supporting their former servants. Incidentally, such a measure was an indication of the relatively high number of knights who reached an advanced age, a fact which probably motivated the king's decision.

At about the same time, the merchants and artisans in some of the towns were getting together to secure their own retirements by taking out life subscriptions to a rest home. In Lyons, labourers and artisans pledged their assets to the hospital against the assurance that they would be looked after in their old age; charitable institutions were turning into retirement homes.[79] In 1488 an institution destined to accommodate 12 'feeble and listless' old women and 30 old nuns was founded at Roubaix; in London a vintners' almshouse was established in 1446 and a salters' almshouse in 1454. The Bishop of Milan set up a refuge for old women in the fifteenth century.[80] In Paris, Jean de Hubant opened a hospice in the Rue des Amandiers which took in ten old women and ten old breadwinners. A growing number of corporations was already able to provide help for their elderly members. Hospital beds were reserved for elderly people, even in county towns like Tréguier, Lannion and Guingamp.

It is laughable to think how few these institutions were and how limited the number of beds they offered. The great majority of the aged poor was obviously reduced to begging. However, the mere idea of retirement was clearly gaining ground, the main obstacles being material and financial. The need for and the legitimacy of a time of rest during the final years of life were beginning to be accepted.

This awareness stemmed partly from the increased proportion of old people following the Plague: they were now so frequently encountered that their particular problems began to be given some consideration. It occurred more and more often that those who had the means allowed themselves the luxury of retirement. Cosimo de Medici, for example, withdrew gradually from business, leaving his son Piero in charge. His last years were spent at his villa at Careggi, having his uricemia and his bad joints treated, gardening and philosophizing with his neo-Platonic friends from Marcilius Ficino's circle; his intellectual pursuits enabled him to remain serene and good-humoured in spite of his 70 years and more. His was, of course, a gilded old age, a humanist old age, but also a Christian one. The preachers' sermons had not been forgotten. Cosimo spent hours meditating on death and when his wife showed surprise, he answered: 'When we plan to go to our villa, you make your preparations a fortnight beforehand. Surely you understand that I, who must quit this existence for the life to come, have much thinking to do about it.'[81] He passed away peacefully at the age of 75, in 1464.

At the end of the fourteenth century, another Florentine, Gregorio Dati, did not wait so long before preparing for death, devoting himself to prayer at the age of 42 in order to earn salvation.[82] Bartolomeo Colleone, the famous condottiere lived his last few years rather less devoutly, though his retirement was just as gilded. He fought his last battle at the age of 67, against Federigo de Urbino, and then spent his last eight years in his castle at Malpaga, hunting and setting up an irrigation system until his last day. Again, this was a case of voluntary retirement, since he had no shortage of job offers, in spite of his advanced age. His reputation as a war leader was such that his age was of no account to rulers. In 1468, Pope Paul II asked this 68-year-old to conduct the war against the Turks; at the age of 72, Colleone received a further offer from Charles le Téméraire (Charles the Rash) who was looking for a good general. But he was sensible enought to turn down these propositions. He received Christian, King of Denmark, at the age of 74, and there is a fresco at Malpaga showing them hunting together.[83] He died the following year, in 1475.

Two other famous retired people died in Italy just a century earlier – Petrarch and Boccaccio. Their last few years were spent piously and peacefully in their country villas, the former at Arguà and the latter at Certaldo. Boccaccio retired first at the age of 49, meditating on the problems he might encounter in the great beyond arising from his licentious tales in the *Decameron*. He died aged 62. Petrarch, who only retired at the age of 66, died several months before him, aged 70.

THE PERSONALIZATION OF OLD AGE

A final indication of the growing number of old people during the fourteenth and fifteenth centuries is provided by their appearance in paintings and sculptures. These appearances were no longer symbolic but personal representations: old people were portrayed for themselves and as themselves, not just as stereotyped allegorical representations of Dame Old Age. This evolution was primarily the fruit of the artistic development towards an increasingly accentuated realism at the end of the Middle Ages. The portraits were not all of old people, but painters were perhaps able to make best use of these to display their original creativity, given the extent to which the physical signs of old age had been stereotyped. The change occurred gradually and one of its first stages produced the bronze effigy of Edward III in Westminster Abbey. The king died in 1377 at the age of 65, and the effigy head was cast from his death mask; his forehead is wrinkled, his cheeks hollow, and his expression weary, but his long beard and hair are in keeping with tradition.

The first real portrait did not appear until the birth of the fifteenth century and the emergence of wealthy patrons, the Maecenes. When someone commissioned a painting, he would have himself included in it in a recognizable fashion as part of the religious scene which, once finished, he would then present to a church; or else he might simply order a portrait of himself. The works of Jan Van Eyck illustrate both ways. *The Virgin of Canon Van der Paele* offers a realistic picture of the elderly, dignified and timid divine, with his lined face, his protruding veins and his flabby skin, clutching his spectacles, whereas the portrait of Cardinal Albergati shows an old man with a wise, calm and kindly face and a touch of bitterness, confirming our previous knowledge of the sitter, who was ambassador to the Holy See and known for his love of peace.

In Italy, Filippo Lippi painted his very sober *Portrait of an Old Man*, in which the subject's head is covered with a large bonnet and his forehead simply criss-crossed with a few lines. Here, too, the expression is everything: his slight smile is that of someone witnessing a scene which will soon end; the old man is meditating but his portrait records his fundamental kindliness. The symbolic old man had not entirely disappeared. In pictures of the Adoration of the Magi, one of the three often represents old age: the sculptures in the choir of Notre-Dame de Paris from the second half of the fourteenth century show him as the one offering gifts, with his bald head, long hair and a white beard. In the *Très Riches Heures du Duc de Berry* Melchior also sports a white beard and hair, whereas Balthazar has a brown beard and Caspar is clean-shaven: they represent the three ages of life. From then on, however, old age was depicted less and less and old people more and more, portrayed in a personalized and realistic manner. These old men still retain their dignity; a balance has been struck. For the moment, old people had been granted their place in society and were portrayed respectfully. It was during the sixteenth century, however, when youth and beauty were exalted, that the cruel caricatures of old men and women were painted.

In spite of their undeniably strong position during the fourteenth and fifteenth centuries, the situation of the old was still precarious and ambiguous. Their social importance was fleeting, due to transitory and particular conditions – the devastation of the young by the Black Death. The demographic recovery which started in 1480 provided for an influx of young and demanding people, who were to push the elderly people aside and make fun of them. In a sense, the relative acceleration of history, the challenging of certain traditions and the appearance of new techniques turned to the disadvantage of old age. As parish registers became more systematized and printing was more widespread, the old were gradually stripped of their role as the community's memory.

9

The Sixteenth Century:

Humanists and Courtiers versus Old Age

Then heed me, sweet, while life is yours
And still untainted, still endures.
While youth is fresh and still to friend.
Gather your youth while yet you may.
Gather it, gather it! Age one day
Your beauty too will swiftly end.[1]

All the poets of the sixteenth century, whether Ronsard's precursors or his imitators, intoned this refrain. Romance poets, essayists, artists, litterati, all types of thinkers and every talent was to chorus it: its echoes were to reach every sphere of life in the four corners of Renaissance Europe. The Renaissance, like every time of renewal and rebirth, celebrated youth, the fullness of life, beauty and novelty. It abhorred everything that presaged decline, decrepitude and death: 'I feel Winter coming, whose cold breath / Makes my skin shudder in trembling horror' Du Bellay was to moan. By re-establishing its links with ancient Greece, the Renaissance instinctively rediscovered the Hellenes' horror of old age. Far from seeking to conceal, camouflage or ignore it, however, the Renaissance displayed and exposed it, showing all its repugnant aspects. At the same time, knowing how useless such efforts were, the Renaissance railed against old age, blackening, demeaning and damning it.

The unprecedented violence of attacks against old age in the sixteenth century was derived from the impotent rage of a generation which worshipped youth and beauty. This optimistic and creative age measured the vanity of its efforts to exorcize ageing, and its cruelty towards the old reveals the depths of its hidden despair. For this formed the great obstacle to the deification of man, rendering it impossible: this world would always lack eternity. Was it not a cause of despair for humanists to know that ageing and death were to render all their intellectual achievements vain? Ageing was their supreme adversary: its absolute invincibility made it both detestable and fascinating.

LITERATURE AND ART: A CULT OF YOUTH DAMNING OLD AGE

The Renaissance conducted a bitter struggle against old age, employing every available means to prolong youth and life: medicine, magic, witchcraft, fountains of youth and utopia, all in vain. Old age and death constituted the greatest of scandals, for the two went together: one announced the other; old people's faces were henceforth to be viewed above all as death masks. At the age of 60 Ronsard experienced this sensation with regard to his whole body:

> All that's left of me is bones. I resemble a skeleton,
> Unfleshed, unstrung, unmuscled and unpadded,
> Unmercifully struck down by the delineaments of death.
> I daren't view my arms for fear lest they tremble.

Hans Baldung Grien depicted this fatal alliance most horribly in his *Ages of Woman and of Death*, now in the Prado. Against a background of fighting, of glowing fires, under the wan light of the moon, three women stand: the young one is naked, lovely, her body firm and pale, but her face already hard and anxious; beside her is an old woman with a dark body, pendulous breasts and angular features; arm in arm with her is a terrible female skeleton, covered in only a few tatters of skin and some hair: worms gyrate in her stomach and she holds an hourglass. Old age and death are sisters.

Faced with this destiny, sixteenth-century man was to oscillate between lamentations and invective. Lamentations before the ineluctable passage of youth and beauty; exhortations to make the best of these years, which, like the rose, were to fade away. Ronsard led the field in this genre of poetry, whether addressing his mistress:

> When you are old, one night while candles flare,
> Spinning before the fire, you'll sit and say
> 'Once Ronsard praised me . . .'
> Huddled about the hearthstone you will stay,
> Feeling remorse at heart for your cruel scorn.
> Live, live, my love: tomorrow's never born:
> Gather the roses of life; begin today.

or bemoaning his own decline:

> Gone is my youth that was so sweet.
> My prime of life has met defeat,
> Black teeth I have and hair of snow.
> My muscles limp, a body chilled.
> And all my veins so poorly filled
> Red water runs where blood should flow . . .[2]

In a text printed at Lyons in 1538, an old woman laments, leaning on her staff and flanked by a pair of skeletons:

> In pain I've lived so long
> That I no longer wish to live
> But indeed I know full well
> That death is preferable to life.[3]

In England, George Peele (1556–96) was also deploring the inanity of man's efforts against ageing:

> His golden locks time hath to silver turned;
> O time too swift, o swiftness never ceasing!
> His youth against time and age hath ever spurned,
> But spurned in vain; youth waneth by increasing.[4]

The knight that he was is now reduced to spending his time praying, and he begs the queen to give him a chaplaincy. One of his contemporaries, Edmund Spenser (1552–99), adopted the rose theme:

> Gather therefore the Rose, whilest yet is prime.
> For soone comes age, that will her pride deflowre.[5]

Samuel Daniel (1562–1601) developed the same idea in his sonnets to Delia:

> Short is the glory of the blushing rose
> The hue which thou so carefully dost nourish,
> Yet which at length thou must be forced to lose.
> When thou, surcharged with burden of thy years,
> Shalt bend thy wrinkles homeward to the earth,
> And that, in beauty's lease expired, appears
> The date of age, the Kalends of our death
> But ah, no more, this must not be foretold,
> For women grieve to think they must be old.[6]

Thomas Wyatt (1503–42) wished old age on his fair lady out of revenge for her coldness:

> Perchance thee lie withered and old,
> The winter nights that are so cold
> Plaining in vain unto the moon: –
> Thy wishes then dare not be told.[7]

The same tune recurs, whether in France, England or Spain. In 'The Rogue or the Life of Guzman of Alfarach', a romance from the end of the sixteenth century, the hero, on returning home after a long absence, finds that his mother has grown old:

> I found her toothless, thin and wrinkled, quite different from her former self. I saw in her how time undermines and devours all things. I bent my gaze on my wife and said to myself: In a few days the same will happen to her. And even if a woman escapes the ugliness caused by old age, she will inevitably have to succumb to the ugliness of death.[8]

The same language was employed in Italy, where the *commedia dell'arte* rediscovered the comic vein of Plautus and Terence by exploiting the ridiculous and odious aspects of old age in three principal forms; the old lover, the old pedant and the rich old exploiter. The first type, who had so graced Roman comedy, was resurrected in the character of Pantalone. This retired merchant, with his gout, his catarrh, his avarice and lechery, was arrayed in a costume which emphasized his erect phallus and spent his time trying to corrupt young girls with his gold, in spite of being regularly tricked, deceived and beaten. In 'The Second Rustic Dialogue', Ruzante (1502–42) staged an old man who has won a young woman. She expresses her disgust as follows:

> He is half sick. He coughs like a rotten sheep all night long. He never sleeps; he tries to embrace me all the time, he covers me with kisses . . . Sure his breath stinks more than a dungheap. He smells of death a hundred miles away and his arse is so covered in filth it must come out the other end.

In 1525, Machiavelli himself did not disdain writing a comedy on the same theme for the Florence carnaval. '*Clizia*' is an uneven work, but one which testifies to the popularity of its subject, once again copied from the plays of antiquity. Nicomaco is a ridiculous old man of 70, who loves young Clizia. He swallows an aphrodisiac in order to revitalize his failing virility: 'Good God!' he says, 'What a lot of worries this damned old age brings us. Still, I'm not so old yet that I cannot break a lance with Clizia'. The old man is ridiculed by his entourage: 'An old soldier is a hideous thing; an old lover is even more hideous': 'Love is as gracious in a young heart as it is revolting in a man who has seen the flowers of age fade away'. When they are not trying to corrupt women, old men relapse into bigotry: 'If you meet an old man, he goes off and sticks his nose into every church that stands along his way, and there he is mumbling a Paternoster at every altar'. Of course, Nicomaco is cheated; his plan to sleep with Clizia is foiled and he finds himself in bed with one of his menservants.

This theme travelled around Europe at that time. It can be found in a Breton comedy, written in a savoury populist language, and printed in 1647 as *Les Amourettes du Vieillard* (The Old Man's Love Affairs).[9] The eroticism of old men was illustrated just as vividly by the works of Matteo Bandello, Bishop of Agen, who published three books of 'Tragic Stories' at the age of 70 in 1554; they are full of rapes and lascivious adventures. Lucas Cranach was to illustrate the subject in an acerbic painting, the *Genre Scene* in the Vice-Queen's palace at Barcelona. It depicts a rich old man, sumptuously dressed, embracing a young woman. His face expresses both concupiscence and ugliness, with his toothless mouth and angular features contrasting with the smooth curves of the young woman's face. She enters into the game smiling pleasantly, dipping with light fingers into the old man's purse the while; he is duped by his own lubricity.

Italian comedy employed the character of the doctor to make equal fun of the exasperating old pedant: in *L'Aconitana*, Ruzante attacked old men who use their wealth to exploit the poor. In *La Piovana*, he established a cruel parallel between youth and old age:

> Youth is like a lovely flowery bush where all the birds flock to sing; whereas old age is like a skinny dog pursued by swarms of flies who devour his ears . . . Everything touching old age is far more exposed to misery . . . Old age is in truth a swamp where every sort of unhealthy water gathers and which has no outlet other than death. Do you want to wish someone evil? Just say to him:—May you grow old.[10]

The painters of the Renaissance frequently revived the theme of violent contrast between youth and old age. An allegorical painting by Bernardino Luini (1480–1532), *Roman Charity*, provides a curious illustration in the form of a young woman suckling her father. Their flesh is thereby brought into brutal and ambiguous confrontation, with the bald, white-bearded father drawing life avidly from his daughter's breast. Albrecht Altdorfer went further still when he illustrated the theme of incest between father and daughters in *Lot and his Daughters*, painted in 1525 and now in Vienna. Here the wrinkled old man reclines alongside a young woman whose white flesh contrasts with his dark skin. Raphael was not so daring but in his *Holy Family*, now in the Prado, by placing Mary and Elizabeth side by side, he confronts the former's freshness and slight smile with the latter's tanned and lined skin and meditative expression.

INVECTIVE AGAINST OLD WOMEN

The rage felt by Renaissance man against old age was given particular vent in paintings of old women, because ageing appears to have an even more devastating effect on women than on men. As the image of beauty, love and worldy pleasure, the young woman was relegated by age to the other extreme; ugliness, hatred and suffering. Woman was destined to experience extremes; from being the symbol of beauty, she could only become the symbol of ugliness; having been fairy-like, she became a witch. In the eyes of the Church, however, whether seductive or horrible, she was still the agent of the devil. So she could expect no pity; spurned by her former and revolted lovers, condemned by her constant detractors, she was rejected by all.

While the Italians preferred to avert their eyes, Flemish and German painters rivalled one another in their invective against, and horror of, old women. This has given us the *Ugly Duchess* by Quentin Metsys in the National Gallery, a hag dressed in lace, whose décolleté allows her flabby and wrinkled flesh to overflow; *The Ugly Sorceress* by Niklaus Manuel Deutsch (now in the Berlin Kupferstichkabinett), shamelessly exposing her naked old body, her long white pubic hair and her sagging breasts. Quentin Metsys re-offends in his *Temptation of St Anthony*, now in the Prado; behind the three pretty young women attempting to seduce the saint appears a toothless, wrinkled and hideous witch, her paps exposed to reveal her flabby flesh.

The men of letters threw themselves wholeheartedly into the game, and their enthusiasm appears all the more excessive in that they also acted as the minstrels of love. Du Bellay's *Antiérotique* is characteristic in this respect:

> Observe (oh old and hideous
> Old woman, this world's dishonour)
> She who (if I remember right)
> Barely touches her fifteenth year.

In his 'Rustic Games' he speaks of courtesans who have necessarily grown old and repentant. The old woman possessed evil powers:

> You can bloody the moon.
> On dark night you can summon

Shadows from their sepulchres
And flout nature's laws.

In the same way, Ronsard's 'Catin' an 'ungilded picture' with her teeth 'rotted and black', her hair white, her 'eye weepy' and her 'dripping nose', wanders

Sad, pensive and solitary
Between the cemetery crosses.

Maynard reproaches an old woman on account of her 'toothless mouth' which emits 'a putrid smell which makes the cats sneeze', and Sigogne compares her with a 'black carrion crow':

a breathing mummy
Whose anatomy can be perceived
Through its transparent skin.
Whose dry and bony body
Would, in some shop, make
An ignorant barber wise . . .
Living portrait of death, dead portrait of life,
Colourless carrion, tomb's plunder,
Disinterred carcase, crow's prey.

The theatre, in the shape of plays by Jodelle, Odet de Turnèbe and Larivey, also made fun of old women. *La Célestine*, by Rojas, is an old prostitute full of vices, who ends up being punished. The picaresque tales also swarm with old beggarwomen, half magicians and half nurses. In 'The Adventurer's Life', by Francisco de Quevedo, one of the characters has an aunt, aged 70, who becomes governess to the hero and his friends:

God knows what evils we suffered with this old woman. She was so deaf we always had to yell ourselves hoarse, and she couldn't see a thing. She was such a great teller of her paternoster beads that one day her rosary slipped into the pot, and that day we were served the most devout soup you ever ate.[11]

The most savage detractor of old women was also the prince of humanists: Erasmus' *Praise of Folly* is quite merciless:

Yet it's even more fun to see the old women who can scarcely carry their weight of years and look like corpses that seem to have risen from the dead. They still go around saying 'life is good', still on heat, 'longing for a mate', as the Greeks say, and seducing some young Phaon they've hired for large sums of money. They're forever smearing their faces with make-up and taking tweezers to their pubic hairs, exposing their sagging, withered breasts and trying to rouse failing desire with their quavery whining voices, while they drink, dance among the girls and scribble their little love-letters. All this raises a general laugh for what it is — absolute foolishness.[12]

Literature was joined by practice in condemning old women; unfavourable prejudice turned them into witches much more frequently than young women. The average age of the 164 witches and witch-masters judged by the Paris Parlement between 1565 and 1640 was over 50.[13] As the most useless of all, old women were the first to be expelled from towns under siege: on 25 January 1555, 400 old women were driven from Sienne during the long blockade imposed by the imperial army.[14] One voice alone was raised in defence of old women in the sixteenth century, that of Brantôme, who felt it normal that they should still seek love; some, he states, are still beautiful and loved at 70. Diane de Poitiers was one of these exceptions; when Henry II died in 1559, she was still extraordinarily lovely at the age of 60.

HUMANISTS AND COURTIERS VERSUS OLD AGE

The sixteenth century had two models; the courtier and the humanist. At the dawn of the century, in 1515, Balthazar Castiglione established the norms of the former, and Erasmus provided a manifesto for the latter. Both joined in condemning old age. That same year, a young king aged 21 initiated his reign following his victory at Marignan. His future rivals, Charles Quint and Henri VIII, were 15 and 24 years old respectively. The century was opening under the sign of youth. Both *The Book of The Courtier* and the *Praise of Folly* became the new age's mentors. The ideals they presented were to establish the human model of the Renaissance; as it was, both the courtier and the humanist rejected old people.

This is easy to believe of the former. Young, handsome, courteous, witty, brave and decisive, the courtier was in every way the opposite of the greybeard. The speakers in *The Book of the Courtier* easily agreed in this. The work is presented in the form of a fictional conversation between real individuals, and supposed to take place in 1507 at Urbino. The participants were in the prime of life, mostly aged between 30 and 40. They included Alfonso Ariosto, aged 32, Pietro Bembo, aged 37, Lodovico Canossa, aged 31, Bernardo Dovizi, aged 37, Ottaviano Fregoso, aged 37, Cesare Gonzaga, aged 32, Elizabeth Gonzaga, aged 36 and Guidobaldo da Montefeltro, aged 35. The slightly older ones were Bernardo Accolti, aged 49, Calmeta, aged 47, Giovan Cristoforo

Romano, aged 42, Fra Mariano, aged 47, whereas the youngest were Michael de Silva, Francesco Maria della Rovere, aged 17, Gasparo Pallavicino, aged 21, and Giuliano de Medici, aged 28. All these beautiful people were agreed; the old are hateful. They regret the past, do not cease denigrating the present, finding that everything is going wrong and that everything went better in their time. Nor is this an exceptional fault; all old people are the same:

> Not without marvel manie a time and often have I considered with my selfe, how one errour should arise, the which because it is generallye seene in olde men, a man may beleve it is proper and naturall unto them; and that is, how (in a manner) al of them commend the times past, and blame the times present; dispraysinge our doings and maners, and whatsoever they did not in their youth:
>
> Affirming moreover every good custome and good trade of living, every vertue, finally each thinge to decline alwaies from evil to worse . . . And yet doe we see not onely in our dayes, but also in times past that this hath alwaies beene the peculiar vice of that age.

The cause of this plaintive state of mind was both physical and psychological:

> The cause therfore of this false opinion in olde men, I beleve (in mine opinion) is, for that, yeares wearing away, carry also with them many commodities, and among other take away from the bloud a great part of the lively spirites that altereth the complexion, and the instruments waxe feeble, whereby the soule worketh her effects.
>
> Therefore the sweete flowers of delyte fade away in that season out of our harts, as the leaves fall from the trees after harvest, and in steade of open and cleare thoughts, there entreth cloudie and troublous heavinesse accompanied with a thousand heart griefes; so that not onely the bloud, but the minde is also feeble; neither of the former pleasures receiveth it any thing els but a fast memorie, and the print of the beloved time of tender age, which when wee have upon us, the heaven, the earth, and each thing to our seeming rejoyceth and laugheth alwaies about our eyes, and in thought (as in a savorie and pleasant Garden) flourisheth the sweete spring time of mirth, so that peradventure it were not unprofitable, when now in the cold season, the Sunne of our life (taking away from us our delites) beginneth to draw towarde the West, to lose in like case therewithall the mindfulnes of them, and to finde out (as Themistocles saith) an arte to teach us to forget; for the senses of

our bodies are so deceivable, that they beguile many times also the judgement of the minde . . .

Because therefore the minde of old age is without order subject to many pleasures, it can not taste them; and even as to them that bee sicke of a Fever, when by corrupt vapours they have lost their taste, all wines appeare most bitter, though they be precious and delicate in deede; so unto olde men for their unaptnesse, (wherein notwithstanding desire faileth them not) pleasures seeme without taste and cold, much differing from those that remember they have proved in foretime, although the pleasures in themselves be the selfe same.

Therefore when they feele them selves voide of them, it is a griefe, and they blame the time present for ill, not perceiving that this chaunce proceedeth of them selves, and not of the time.

And contrariwise, when they call to minde the pleasures past, they remember therewithall the time they had them in, and therefore commend it for good, because to their weening it carrieth with it a savour of it, which they felt in them when it was present.[15]

These old courtiers harp on about how in their time the court was more refined, how the men in it were superior to the ones there today, how there were neither assassinations, nor quarrels, nor plots, nor treachery and how loyalty and goodwill reigned everywhere. The good times were those of Filippo Maria Visconti, Duke of Milan (1391–1447) and of Borso d'Este, Duke of Ferrara (1413–71). In those days, courtiers behaved like monks and an insincere word was never heard. Now, however, they lead dissolute lives, the women are debauched and the fashions indecent. Castiglione made fun of these weakminded old chatterboxes as follows:

Therefore may it be lawfull for us also to follow the custome of our times, without controlement of these olde men, which going about to prayse themselves, say:

When I was twentie yeares olde I lay with my mother and sisters, nor a great while after wist I what women ment; and now children are not so soone crept out of the shell, but they know more naughtinesse, than they that were come to mans state did in those dayes.

Neither be they aware in so saying, that they confirme our children to have more wit than their old men.

Let them leave therefore speaking against our times, as full of vices; for in taking away them, they take also away the vertues. And let them remember that among the good men of auntient time, when as the glorious wits florished in the world, which in very deede were of most perfection in every vertue, and more than manly, there were also many most mischievous, which if they had still lived, shoulde have excelled our ill men so much in ill, as those good men in goodness: and of this doe all Histories make full mention.[16]

The generation gap was thus wider than ever before, and the courtier circle demonstrated their profound disdain for old age. Castiglione reproached them not only with dotage, but also with debauchery and drunkenness; 'What can be saide to bee more wider from the continencie of an old man, than dronkennese?' Luckily, since old men are all halfway impotent, 'the thing which olde men covete more than the battailes of Venus' is wine.[17] This accusation is as ancient as literature, and occurs regularly from ancient Greece onwards.

Erasmus knew his classics and employed it in his turn in the *Praise of Folly*: 'There are some men, especially old men, who are more given to wine than women, and find their greatest pleasure in drinking parties.'[18] Was this a fact or a literary device? If one believes the saying that there can be no smoke without fire, one might be tempted to think that old people did indeed abuse the gift of wine. Antonio de Guevara, Bishop of Cadiz, reproached them in his turn and even told how the ancient Goths were accustomed to drinking as many glasses of wine as they had years.[19] The medical theories of the age encouraged the consumption of wine as a remedy against loss of heat and moisture which, according to the ideas of the time, characterized old age.[20] Given, too, the fact that old peoples' resistance to intoxication is reduced and that the spectacle of a drunken old man, who is supposed to embody wisdom, is incongruous, to say the least, the popularity of this theme becomes self-explanatory.

It is easy to suppose that the old man was banished from the circle of courtiers, whose ideal was superman, a handsome, intelligent and strong swashbuckler. It is more surprising that he was condemned by the humanists' circle. Wisdom and erudition were in fact qualities commonly felt to belong to the old, and ones which humanism placed in the foreground. However old age did not find grace in the eyes of the greatest thinkers of the sixteenth century. Erasmus was merciless in this respect, and the old man held an eminent place in his gallery of fools. From a certain age onwards, old people relapse into infancy:

I know they're called silly and foolish, as indeed they are, but that is exactly what it means to become a child again . . . There really is no difference between them except the old man's wrinkles and the number of birthdays he has. Otherwise they are exactly alike; white hair, toothless mouth, short stature, liking for milk, babbling, chattering, absurdity, forgetfulness, thoughtlessness,

everything in fact. The nearer people approach old age the closer
they return to a semblance of childhood, until the time comes for
them to depart this life, again like children, neither tired of living
nor aware of death. It is lucky that this is the case, says Folly,
since who could carry on doing business or having dealings with
an old man if his vast experience of affairs was still matched by a
vigorous mind and keen judgement? So I see to it that the old
man is witless, and this sets him free meanwhile from all those
wretched anxieties which torment the man in his senses.[21]

This indeed is the secret of eternal youth, revealed in derisory fashion;
thanks to Folly, childhood is prolonged into extreme old age;
philosophers and ernest folk age sooner than others on account of their
worries and the serious questions bothering them. Folly is the true
remedy for old age, as illustrated by Erasmus's compatriots:

And there's good reason for what is generally said about the
natives of Brabant, that increasing age brings other men wisdom,
but they grow more and more foolish the nearer they approach
old age. At the same time there's no people so cheerful in company
or so little affected by the misery of growing old. Close to them
as neighbours and also in their way of life are my Hollanders –
for why shouldn't I call them mine? They're my devoted followers,
so much so that they've earned a popular epithet of which they're
not at all ashamed, indeed they make a special boast of it.[22]

This was a reference to the Dutch proverb: 'the older a Dutchman the
stupider.'
    Old age is a painful burden; 'old age, with its troubles, unwelcome
not only to others but just as much to oneself'; 'Nothing is better than
youth, nothing so hateful as old age'; 'Old age is a burden and death
a harsh necessity.' [23] In spite of this, the old are so foolish that they
do not want to leave this life.

The less reason they have for staying alive, the more they enjoy
living – so far are they from feeling at all weary of life. Thanks
to me you can see old men everywhere who have reached Nestor's
age and scarcely still look human, mumbling, senile, toothless,
white-haired or bald, or rather, in the words of Aristophanes,
'dirty, bent, wretched, wrinkled, hairless, toothless, sexless'. Yet
they're still so pleased with life and eager to be young that one
dyes his white hair, another covers up his baldness with a wig,
another wears borrowed teeth taken from a pig perhaps, while
another is crazy about a girl and outdoes any young man in his
amorous silliness. For any real old drybones with a foot in the

grave can take some tender young girl for a wife today – even if she has no dowry and is ready for others to enjoy her.[24]

Money is the sole reason why people still associate with old men and women.

We have come a long way from the traditional image of the wise old man in his study, which the humanist type so often evokes. In fact, behind Erasmus's merciless criticism of old age lie the Greek and Roman models; his images and ideas are often borrowed from Plautus, Horace, Ovid and Aristophanes; the second childhood theme is derived directly from Lucian. Erasmus's personal and profound opinion was certainly more subtle than his caricatures in the *Praise of Folly* would suggest. Nevertheless, some passages do reveal a certain bitterness and harsh irony directed by the author against himself. He wrote these words at the age of 45, the onset of his own maturity, when he realized that his youth had been entirely dedicated to study, which had made a wise man of him, but an ageing wise man who had never enjoyed life:

> Imagine some paragon of wisdom to be set up against him, a man who has frittered away all his boyhood and youth in acquiring learning, has lost the happiest part of his life in endless wakeful nights, toil and care, and never tastes a drop of pleasure even in what's left to him. He's always thrifty, impoverished, miserable, grumpy, harsh and unjust to himself, disagreeable and unpopular with his fellows, pale and thin, worn-out and dying before his time. Though what difference does it make when a man like that does die? He's never been alive. There you have a splendid picture of a wise man.[25]

THE RELATIVITY OF PEOPLE'S OPINION OF OLD AGE

Such irony is bitter; a profound malaise may be glimpsed behind the optimistic mask of the humanist age. Was it not also an age of 'regrets' and 'sadness', of nostalgia? How could it have been otherwise? Every age which rediscovers the charms of life here below must feel the passage of time even more cruelly. Man shook off his shackles, improved his environment, constructed machines and dreamt of the triumph of reason – and this pleasanter world built by him seemed but to elude him all the faster. History seemed to speed up; printing, Turks, America, Reformation, Copernicus, inflation, so many revolutions in his intellectual world, so many subjects for meditation. History was no longer moving in a circle, but in a specific direction, and ever faster.

Fashions changed ever more rapidly, styles followed one on another, and people on this revolving planet felt they were growing old faster than on their old static world at the centre of the universe. People felt they were being overtaken sooner than formerly. Erasmus felt he was ageing prematurely when he was 45. At the same age, Montaigne reckoned he was lucky to have lived so long:[26] at the age of 53, he considered himself old and behaved accordingly:

> I am now in another state. The conditions of age do but overmuch admonish, instruct, and preach unto me. From the excesse of jollity, I am falne into the extreame of severity; more peevish and more untoward . . . My yeares read me daily a lesson of coldnesse and temperance. My body shunneth disorder, and feares it; it hath his turne to direct the minde toward reformation; his turne also to rule and sway; and that more rudely and imperiously. Be I awake or a sleepe, it doth not permit me one houre but to ruminate on instruction, on death, on patience, and on repentance.[27]

Such mental states belonged, however, to intellectuals, people with the time to watch themselves grow old, and who dedicated themselves to introspection. We should not draw conclusions from such men about the real longevity of sixteenth-century men nor about their precocious ageing. Men of action felt quite differently about age. Blaise de Monluc, when 53, was a competent soldier who dedicated very little time to meditation; he considered himself a young captain and was still courting the ladies during the Piedmont campaign. When he was 58, he announced that one should never stop, because nothing is ever won; one must go on fighting in order to preserve one's reputation: 'Don't be like those who, as soon as they make theirs, are satisfied and think that whatever they do they will always be reckoned valliant.' He set an example by going to fight in Lorraine with François de Guise. He was still fighting in Aquitaine at the age of 62, sometimes travelling over 100 kilometres in under two days, and repeating 'that he wasn't the man to put things off'. Two years later, he was undertaking great improvements to his castle of Estillac, and that same year married a young woman, Isabeau-Paule de Beauville, who was to bear him three children. On 20 September 1569, when he was 69 years old, he led the attack against Mont-de-Marsan, at the head of his troops. Although badly wounded in the face at 70 by an arquebus shot, he led the seige of La Rochelle three years later and even took part in an assault. At the age of 74, he became Marshall of France, besieged and took Gensac when 75, and then gradually retired to die at the age of 77.

The previous year, Jean Bodin had published his 'On the Republic'. In it he took pains to show by means of numerous historical examples that the age at which most men die is a multiple of seven. This constituted an extension of the artificial and symbolic notion of age. Old age begins at 56, and ends for most people seven years later: 'The number of 63, which is the multiple of seven by nine, ordinarily entails the end for old men.' Those who lived beyond this term went on till they were 70, 'which removes nearly all old men', or till the age of 77: 'There is a tiny number which is observed to die at this age.'[28] Monluc would have agreed with him.

Another man of action, Benvenuto Cellini, has left us a precious record in the shape of his memoirs. He presents us with the image of a man who cared not a whit about his age. He was as hot-blooded as a young man at the age of 52, when he challenged a captain to a duel. The following year, he engaged in gross practical jokes worthy of a lad – and he went on begetting children; at 62, at 66, at 69 . . . He admitted, nevertheless, to having suffered from attacks of gout since he was 58 or 59, with a further very severe attack at the age of 66. When he was 69 years old, he described himself as ill and lame.

WHAT ROLE FOR THE OLD? MONTAIGNE'S OPINION

The literature of the sixteenth century was much exercised with the question of what role old people ought to play in society. Opinions were divided on this point, and depended to a great extent on prejudices inherited from the humanists' eduction, which were frequently unfavourable. Montaigne often returns to this problem, surveying it with subtle pessimism. In his chapter 'Of the affection of fathers to their children', he thinks that an old man should try above all to win his family's love, and not play the domestic tyrant, for if he is weak, he is very easily made fun of and cheated:

> There are so many sorts of defects in age, and so much impuissance. It is so subject to contempt, that the best purchase it can make, is the good will, love and affection of others. Commandement and feare are no longer her weapons. I have knowen one whose youth had beene very imperious and rough, but when he came into mans age, although hee live in as good plight and health as may be, yet he chafeth, he scoldeth, he brawleth, he fighteth, he sweareth, and biteth, as the most boistrous and tempestuous master of France, he frets and consumes himself with carke and care and vigilancy (al which is but and jugling and ground for his family to play upon, and cozen him the more) as for his goods, his garness, his cellars, his coffers, yea his purse, whilst himself keepes the keyes of them close in his bosome, and under his boulster, as charily as he doth his eyes, other enjoy and command the better part of them; whilst he pleaseth and flattereth himselfe, with the niggardly sparing of his table, all goth to wracke, and is lavishly wasted in divers corners of his house, in play, in riotous spending, and in

soothingly entertaining the accomts or tales of his vaine chafing, foresight, and providing. Every man watcheth and keepeth sentinell against him, if any silly or heedlesse servant doe by fortune apply himselfe unto it, he is presently made to suspect him: A quality on which age doth immediately bite of it selfe.[29]

The time of commandment is over, for 'the steps of age are so slow, the senses so troubled' that he is no longer able to make himself feared.

What occupations did an old man have? Certainly not bigotry. Montaigne was totally opposed to this notion, which was so widespread at the end of the Middle Ages and according to which the only viable task for an old man was to prepare himself for death. Humanists were Christians, but they were above all children of this world, and they meant to enjoy it to the end. An old man should take every opportunity to have fun:

> It is meere simplicity, as most men do, to prolong and anticipate humane incommodities. I had rather be lesse while olde, than old before my time. I take hold even of the least occasions of delight I can meet withall.[30]

Unfortunately, such occasions are very few:

> I was heretofore wont to note sullen and gloomy daies, as extraordinary; now they are my ordinary ones; the extraordinary are my faire and cleere days. I am ready to leape for joy, as at the receaving of some unexpected favour, when nothing grieveth me. Let me tickle myself, I can now hardly wrest a bare smile from this wretched body of mine. I am not pleased but in conceit and dreaming, by sleight to turne aside the way-ward cares of age; but sure there is need of other remedies, then dreaming. A weake condition of arte against nature.[31]

So an old man must try to wrest a few pleasures from life yet: 'Yeares entrain me if they please; but backward!' He must seek entertainment by watching the games and exercises of the young, and by remembering his own exploits. Since his body is now too weak, his mind must seek for amusement. Alas! even the mind is paralysed by physical ills, like ivy on a dead tree. 'This wretched condition, where to my age forceth me' is miserable indeed, and philosophy can do nothing to alleviate the ills of old age.

> Well may my judgement hinder me from spurning and repining at the inconveniences which nature allots me to indure; from feeling them it cannot. I could finde in my heart to runne from

one ende of the world to another, to searche and purchase one yeare of pleasing and absolute tranquility; I who have no other scope, then to live and be mery.[32]

Like Erasmus, Montaigne thought that old age, 'this calamity of age', makes us return to childhood.

He was violently opposed to the hypocrisy of those who claimed that old age was a good thing because it brings wisdom. It is an imposture to owe one's virtue to one's inability to enjoy life and one's decrepitude: 'O miserable kind of remedie, to bee beholden unto sickeness for our health.' There is no merit in not being able to indulge in debauchery when one has become impotent: 'Our appetites are rare in old age; the blowe overpassed, a deepe society seazeth upon us: Therein, see no conscience. Fretting care and weakenesse, imprint in us an effeminate and drowzie vertue.'[33]

If one must make a virtue of one's decrepitude, it is still preferable to lead an enjoyable life. How dishonest to pretend to be happier and more virtuous in old age, and to repudiate and reject our best years! The virtue of the old is but impotence; it stinks of sour grapes and mustiness:

> But mee thinkes our soules in age are subject unto more importunate diseases and imperfections, then they are in youth. I said so being young, when my beardlesse chinne was upbraided me; and I say so againe, now that my gray beard gives me authority. We entitle wisdome, the frowardnesse of our humours, and the distaste of present things; but in truth wee abandon not vices, so much as we change them; and in mine opinion for the worse. Besides a sillie and ruinous pride, combersome tattle, wayward and unsotiable humours, superstition and ridiculous carking for wealth, when the use of it is well-nigh lost, I finde the more envie, injustice and leaudnesse in it. It sets more wrinckles in our mindes, then on our foreheads; nor are there any spirits, or very rare ones, which in growing old taste not sowrely and mustily.[34]

What was to be done about old age then? Or, rather, what was not to be done? For everything is negative at that age. The height of the ridiculous consisted in throwing oneself into long-drawn-out enterprises, when approaching death. Montaigne here reveals his lack of respect for classical models: Cato was an idiot for starting to learn Greek in his extreme old age:

> It is properly that which we cal doting or to become a child againe. All things have their season, yea the good and all . . . Eudemouindas, seeing Xenocrates very old, laboriously apply

himself in his Schoole-lectures, said, when wil this man know something, since he is yet learning? And Philopoemen, to those who highly extolled king Ptolomey, because he daily hardned his body to the exercise of arms: It is not (said he) a matter commendable in a king of his age, in them to exercise himselfe, he should now really and substancially imploy them. Wise men say, that young-men should make their preparations, and old-men enjoy them. And the greatest vice they note in us, is, that our desires do uncessantly grow yonger and yonger. We are ever beginning new to live. Our studies and our desire should sometimes have a feeling of age. We have a foote in the grave, and our appetites and pursuits are but new-borne.[35]

Had he known of them, Montaigne would have considered follies our universities of the third age. Once he was 50, he no longer undertook any project lasting over a year: 'The longest of my desseignes doth not extend to a whole yeare; now I only apply my selfe to make an end: I shake off all my new hopes and enterprises: I bid my last farewell to all the places I leave, and daily dispossesse my selfe of what I have.' He goes on to poke fun at elderly students: 'This man learneth to speake, when he should rather learne to hold his peace for ever. A man may alwaies continue his studie, but not schooling. O fond-foolish for an old man to be ever an Abcedarian.'[36]

On the other hand, he recommends tourism and even long-distance journeys:

Of which age, few that travell farre journies returne home againe. What care I for that? I undertake it not, either to returne or to perfect the same. I onely undertake it to be in motion: So long as the motion pleaseth me, and I walke that I may walke. Those runne not, that runne after a Benefice or after a Hare: But they runne, that runne at barriers and to exercise their running. My desseigne is every where divisible, it is not grounded on great hopes; each day makes an end of it. Even so is my lifes voiage directed. Yet have I seene divers farre countries, where I would have beene glad to have been staied. Why not? If Chrysippus, Diogenes, Cleanthes, Antipater and Zeno, with so many other wise men of that roughly-severe, and severely-strict Sect, foresooke their Countries (without just cause to be offended with them) onely to enjoy another aire? Truly the greatest griefe of my peregrinations, is, that I cannot have a firm resolution, to establish my abiding where I would. And that I must ever resolve with my selfe to return, for to accommodate my selfe unto common humours. If I should feare to die in any other place, then where I was borne; if I thought I should die lesse at my ease, farre from mine owne people: I would hardly goe out of France, nay I should scarcely goe out of mine owne parish, withot feeling some dismay. I feele death ever pinching me by the throat, or pulling me by the backe: But I am of another mould; to me it is ever one, and at all times the same. Nevertheles if I were to chuse, I thinke it should rather be on horsebacke, than in a bed; from my home, and farre from my friends. There is more harts-sorrow, than comfort, in taking ones last farewell of his friends.[37]

Old people are moaners, who exaggerate their ills in order to win sympathy:

by our griefs and pains we ever desire to moove our friends to compassion and sorrow for us, and with a kinde of sympathy to condole our miseries and passions. We endeare our inconveniences beyond measure, to exact teares from them: And the constancy we so much commend in all others, undauntedly to endure all evill fortune, we accuse and upbraid to our neerest allies, when they molest us; we are not contented they should have a sensible feeling of our calamities, if they doe not also afflict themselves for them.[38]

This is indeed a gloomy picture; Montaigne did not consider the old much good for anything. Relying on his historical knowledge and his own case, he proclaimed an opinion which was to be taken up and amplified in our age by Harvey C. Lehman:[39] every great thing has been achieved by young people aged under 30. Once over this age, all our faculties, physical as much as intellectual, diminish:

Of all humane honourable and glorious actions, that ever came unto my knowledge, of what nature soever they be. I am perswaded, I should have a harder taske, to number those, which both in ancient times, and in ours, have beene produced and atchieved before the age of thirtie yeares, than such as were performed after; yea, often in the life of the same men. May not I boldly speak it of those of Hanniball, and Scipio his great adversarie? They lived the better part of their life with the glorie which they had gotten in their youth: And though afterward they were great men, in respect of all others, yet were they but meane in regard of themselves. As for my particular, I am verily perswaded, that since that age, both my spirit and my body, have more decreased than encreased, more recoyled than advanced. It may be, that knowledge and experience shall encrease in them, together with life, that bestow their time well; but vivacitie, promptitude, constancie, and other parts much more our owne, more important and more essentiall, they droope, they languish, and they faint . . .

It is the body, which sometimes yeeldeth first unto age; and other times the mind; and I have seene many, that have had their braines weakned before their stomacke and legges. And forasmuch, as it is a disease, little or nothing sensible unto him that endureth it, and maketh no great shew, it is so much the more dangerous.[40]

So it is a mistake to set a man's entry into active life or into official duties at 25 or 30 years of age; the effect of this is to deprive oneself of the most efficient years of one's life, which is anyway so brief.

POLITICAL THEORISTS AND HOSTILITY TO OLD AGE

On this point, Montaigne was in agreement with most of the political theorists of his age, who put their trust in youth and were wary of the old. This was especially true of Italy at the beginning of the century. In his treatise on Livy, Machiavelli praised the Romans of the first republican period, who appointed magistrates without taking their age into account, since if a young man possesses great qualities 'it would be a great pity were the State obliged to deny itself their use and wait for old age to chill his courage.'[41] He went even further in *The Arte of Warre* in 1523, when he accused the wise old men of his city of responsibility for the humiliations suffered by Florence, because of their resigned and pacifist attitudes:

> for that I beleve, that youthfulness, wil make you lovers of warlike thinges, and more easie to beleve the same, that of me shal be saied . . . These other, be reason of having nowe their hedde white, and for havyng upon their backes their bloude congealed, parte of theim are wonte to bee ennemies of warre, parte uncorrrectable, as those, whom beleve, that tymes, and not the naughtie maners, constraine men to live thus.[42]

At this time too, Lodovico Alamanni, a member of the Medici faction, was writing a practical manual about the government of Florence, in which he stigmatized the errors of their elders, who were responsible for having introduced mercenaries into the militia: 'We owe our forefathers very little. Subverting Italy's good order, they reduced it to the governance of priests and merchants.' As the partisans of traditional republican government, the old men's ideas were out-of-date and, being too timorous, they were no longer dangerous, because they had been overtaken by events: 'The republican fantasies of the old can never be eliminated. But the *vecchi* are wise, and the wise do not have to be feared, because they never do anything.'[43]

Francis Bacon, Chancellor of England, also reproached the old with being too timorous and consequently bad rulers. As a philosopher, a scientist and a politician of the first rank, his interest in old age encompassed all three points of view. In his essay *Of Youth and Age*, he considered the principal fault of aged politicians to be indecision:

> The errors of young men are the ruin of business; but the errors of aged men amount to this, that more might have been done, or sooner . . .
> Men of age object too much, consult too soon and seldom drive business home to the full period, but content themselves with a mediocrity of success.[44]

Around the year 1525 Donato Giannotti, another Florentine, was attacking the old men in power:

> These *vecchi* who made and make such professions of civic wisdom . . . Living of their own free will under the tyranny they have made . . . They say the *giovanni* should not discuss public affairs, but pursue their sexual needs . . . Saying that a giovane of twenty-five years is still a *fanciullo* . . . I want to stop talking about the perversity of the *vecchi*, because every time I think about their evil ways, I get very sick to the stomach.[45]

His contemporary, Pierfilippo Pandolfino took the same line:

> It might not appear reasonable to you that the giovani, who have no position at all, come before the oldest, constituted by the popolo in the supreme honour, and commend to them the public welfare . . . But . . . in each person, even if young and inexperienced, one can find something of use to the public good.[46]

Jean Bodin provided the only discordant note in this concert of opposing voices, and even he did not wholeheartedly support elderly politicians. In his great treatise 'On the Republic', he recapitulated all the examples from antiquity favourable to the old: 'It is not only the Greeks and Latins who have given old men the prerogative of advising the Republic; the Egyptians, Persians and Hebrews have also taught other peoples how to govern their states well and wisely.' Moses had composed a council of 70 old men; Lycurgus and Solon had given power to the old. According to him, then, antiquity had trusted in gerontocracy, and he was ready to do likewise. However, he attributed old men with consultative rather than decisive powers, and on condition they were still fully in command of their faculties:

> Not without cause have the laws bestowed the prerogative of honour, privilege and dignity on old men, given the presumption that they are wiser, better listened to and more worthy of giving advice than young men. I do not mean that the quality of old age is in itself enough to bestow entry into the Senate of a Republic, and similarly, if old age is advanced and already decrepid, weakening the natural forces, and if the softened brain can no longer do its duty.[47]

Generally speaking, then, the political theorists of the sixteenth century favoured youth, in accordance with preferences of the courtiers and the populace. Although the texts quoted above do not agree with practice, as we will see, they nevertheless agreed with general opinion. Old leaders were often ill-received, especially by armies, whose soldiers preferred young and bold commanders. In 1555, when Henri II appointed Paul de La Barthe, lord of Termes and aged 73, his lieutenant-general in the Piedmont, the officers all came out in revolt; Termes was nonetheless made *maréchal* of France at the age of 76 and died at his post at the age of 80. Even the favour enjoyed by Monluc faded away in his last years, when the old soldier was seen as an old fogey who had lived too long. In another sphere of life, Benevuto Cellini, although only 60, was cheated in a financial transaction by unscrupulous characters who, according to him, reckoned him an old man who would not live out the year.[48]

RESEARCH INTO THE CAUSES AND TREATMENT OF OLD AGE

Humanist doctors and philosophers were especially concerned with the problem of their enemy old age. Albeit an old problem, and one which Aristotle claimed Galen had definitively solved, it was taken up again by the thinkers of the sixteenth century, who were driven by their insatiable curiosity. Flagrant proof of the interest taken in the subject at that time is the unprecedented number of works on the origin and treatment of old age produced in the 1500s, not repeated until our period. Every path, albeit passably muddled and confused, was explored; medicine, philosophy and religion combined in their efforts to resolve the enigma and put an end to the scandal of old age.

Their aim was in reality a practical one, that of discovering the causes of old age in order to eliminate it or at least distance it. Every work on the subject involves these two aspects simultaneously. Their ambition was immense; their means of investigation puerile and muddled, confusing serious aspects with the most extravagant fantasies. Consequently, they achieved but meagre practical results: overall, only a little dietary and hygienic advice conducive to better health in old age. Such results were disappointing indeed, given the humanists' extravagant hopes. Their research into eternal youth ended up investigating cold prevention after the age of 60. Longevity was not extended by a single day, and, in the end, they added nothing to Galen's theories. From our point of view, however, it is not the results but the efforts involved which are interesting, the passion with which so many thinkers searched for a remedy for that incurable sickness, old age. Nothing is more illustrative of the horror inspired by great old age and its ills in the sixteenth century.

Luigi Cornaro's *A Treatise of Health and Long Life with the Sure Means of Attaining It* recommended moderation in all things, in food and drink as in the emotions, and his own longevity was the best guarantee of the efficacy of his method, since he lived 96 years (1470–1566).[49] His compatriot Jerome Cardan also dealt with old age in his medical works, but his notions were confused and muddled by references to astrology. He lived long enough to learn to detest old age (1501–76): 'Old age, when it comes, must make every man regret that he did not die in infancy.'[50]

Paracelsus was a Swiss with an original and outstanding mind, who invented a complete theory of old age in his treatise *Liber de Longa vita*.[51] His work is obscure, prolix, full of contradictions and references to astrology, but it provides a global vision of the life process, its decline and the means of prolonging it. Paracelsus refuted the Greek notion of pathology and substituted another, personal one, which insisted on the independent nature of different illnesses. He thought that life was a 'spirit' derived from the air and endowed with 'power and virtue'. Every material thing had a 'spirit', whether animal, vegetable or mineral, animate or inanimate, celestial or earthly. Each different part of the body had a 'spirit' which carried function and individual specificity. Man has an innate and natural tendency to corruption, the separation of the elements which go to make him up. This gives rise to illness and also to ageing and final decomposition. Paracelsus compared ageing to rust on metal, leading to decomposition. This process may be slowed down, thanks to a balanced diet, to living in a pleasant climate and especially to taking a magic elixir which he claimed to have perfected, which can repair ageing tissue and regenerate the individual. However, he refused to use this potion, which he call *quinta essentia*, or *prima substantia*, or *lignum vitae*, or *lignum anima*, or *arcanum* of gold or mercury, because it was against nature and unChristian. Life has a natural and predetermined end, and no one has the right to extend it artificially. This was not the least of the paradoxes presented by this strange doctor.

The French had their version of old age as well. In 1599, Andŕe Du Laurens (Laurentius, 1558–1609), chancellor of the University of Montpellier and court doctor, published a *Discourse of the Preservation of the Sight; of Melancholike diseases; of Rheumes, and of Old Age.* His notion of the ageing process was based on the traditional theories of Hippocrates, Galen, Avicenna and Celsus; the contrariety of the four elements in the body and the accumulation of excrements derived from nutrition. The lack of originality in Laurentius' conclusions contrasts with the modern methods he employed. As an adept in the experimental method, he engaged in a series of dissections on human bodies which allowed him to dismiss an ancient belief, that the heart of old men grew smaller with age and ended by disappearing, thus causing death:

> The men of Egypt and Alexandria did beleeve that the naturall cause of olde age did come of the diminishing of the heart: they said that the heart did growe till fiftie yeeres the weight of two drams every yeere, and that after fiftie yeeres it waxed lesser and lesser, till in the end it was growne to nothing: but these are nothing but vaine imaginations and meere fooleries. We have caused many old men to be opened, whose hearts have been found as great and heavie as those of the younger sort.[52]

To start off with, the scientific method did not furnish more probing results than the traditional speculative method had done. This may also be observed of the works of an Italian, Santorio Santorio (Sanctorius, 1561–1636). He was professor of theoretical medicine at Padua until 1629, and dedicated the last years of his life to his private experiments. His last great work, *Ars de Statica Medicina*, dates from 1614 and went to several editions.[53] His theory rested on the notion of 'insensible perspiration' which Sanctorius was determined to measure. This striving for quantification provided the principal original element in his works, but its bearing was limited by the fact that he remained a prisoner of the Greek doctrine of humoral pathology. Sanctorius believed that the human body contained spirits which enabled it to carry out its functions. Ageing was the effect of the progressive decay of these spirits, whose residues encumber and harden the tissues, thus hindering insensible perspiration. The body, which can no longer rid itself of its superfluous substances, hardens, and old men die 'because their fibres are grown hard, and such as possibly cannot be renewed: whence proceeds death'.[54] Old age is a 'universal hardness of the fibres'.[55] This notion, which seems so bizarre to us nowadays, was nevertheless to be taken up again by serious doctors such as Rowbotham in the nineteenth century.[56]

At the end of the sixteenth and beginning of the seventeenth century, two English philosophers and men of politics were attentively studying the phenomenon of ageing from the theoretical point of view: they were

Henry Cuffe and Francis Bacon. The former (1563–1601) was professor of Greek at Oxford and known for his attempts at reconciling Greek philosophy with Christianity; he was involved in the Duke of Essex's plot and was beheaded. His work on old age, *The Differences of the Ages of Man's Life*,[57] was printed posthumously in 1607. In it, the Greek humours are strangely mingled with the Christian soul. Originally, man's body and soul had been in perfect harmony, and their separation, meaning death, unknown:

> But after that man's pride set abroch by the divels suggestion, ventured to taste of the forbidden fruite for desire of knowledge; the light of reason being the life of the soule, overcast by unavoidable cloudes of ignorance, there grew a disagreement and quarrell among the subject interior parts of the soule, from whence followed the warre of the elements in the bodie, never to bee ended till the field were lost by blood.[58]

Cuffe then tries to explain the ageing process. His very prolixity, however, distracts the reader, who has great difficulty in following his tortuous arguments.

In fact, Cuffe presents three possible explanations. The first explanation is derived directly from the Greeks; ageing is the result of the body's diminished internal heat and moisture. Cuffe, however, was aware of another theory to account for ageing and death, which he set down in another part of his book. It is reminiscent of Bacon's mechanistic attitude:

> For in the violent notion of things naturall, we see it comes to passe, that the virtue or power of moving, imprinted by the unnatural mover, by little and little decaying, at length by continuance of moving, or rather by the resistance of the bodies about it, is cleane extinguished: So in the naturall proceeding toward the enemie and end of nature, death, the preserving meanes of life (either by the toilsomenesse of their never-ceasing operation, or by the corruption and mixture of impure moisture, infeebled and disabled to the sufficient performance of their functions, more and more every day) at length of force yeelds to the oppressing violence of their resisting adversaries, not able any longer to maintaine their conquering action . . .[59]

The third theory is that ageing proceeds from the ever-warring four elements. Fire, Aire, Water, Earth, and their four first qualities, Heat, Cold, Drinesse and Moisture, within the body. Indeed, such beings as do not have these four elements warring within them last eternally; angels, for instance.

Francis Bacon (1561–1621) enjoyed a reputation far superior to that of his friend Henry Cuffe. His political success, which brought him the post of Chancellor of England in 1618, and his brilliant scientific theories, which were expounded in his *Novum Organum* in 1620, revealed him as one of the precursors of the experimental and inductive method and fully justified his renown. His notions about ageing were nevertheless no more modern than those of his contemporaries, although he had dedicated an important part of his oeuvre to the subject in *The Historie of Life and Death, with Observations Naturall and Experimentall for the Prolonging of Life*, in a treatise *The cure of old age, and Preservation of Youth*, and again in *De augmentis scientiarum*, where a whole section is devoted to the means of prolonging a man's life.[60] For him, this was the crux of the matter: might it not be possible to extend human longevity? With this practical aim in mind, he undertook to study the ageing process in order to slow it down, if possible. He felt that this constituted the most noble aspect of medicine. While he was not searching for eternal youth, since we do but pass through life in this world, he was well aware of the advantages of our bodies and minds not wearing away. Consequently, Bacon was astonished to find that no one had as yet written seriously on the subject, apart from Aristotle's short treatise. Doctors themselves were totally ignorant in this field, although 'prolongation of life is a work of labour and difficulty and consisting of a great number of remedies, and those aptly connected one with another.'[61]

Bacon attacked the traditional theory of the humours, which queered all serious study and obfuscated research:

> For when I hear men on the one side speak of comforting Natural heat, and the Radical moisture, and of Meats which breed good blood, such as may neither be burnt nor phlegmatick, and of the cheering and recreating of the spirits, I suppose them to be no bad men which speke these things: but none of these worketh effectually towards the end.[62]

In spite of this promising statement, Bacon himself succumbed to another traditional and theoretical theory that 'there is in every Tangible body a Spirit, or body Pneumatical, enclosed and covered with the Tangible parts',[63] which is supposed to enable the parts of the body to function: the blood, flesh, fat, muscles, arteries, veins, bones, cartilege, intestines and so on, all have their own spirits. This view was inherited from neo-Platonic realism, according to which these spirits, notably the spirit in the blood, are the ultimate source of bodily energy.

Having, in spite of his initial announcements, thus rejected the experimental method, our author oscillates between alchemy and popular potions in his search for remedies prolonging life. From the start, he was convinced that the secrets of nature could be discovered and the course of nature thus changed, suggesting that the spirit of youth, once inoculated into an old body, could reverse the course of nature. Such a notion simply presented a new version of the elixir of long life. Since the body's collapse is derived from the collapse of the spirits ruling the body, renewing these spirits ought to restore youth. In the meantime, it is important to spare them, in order not to age prematurely: do not commit excesses, do not get excited, avoid the sun's rays, live in the open, take baths, eat sweetened but not acid things, follow a strict diet, do not abuse cosmetics, take physical exercise but without overdoing it or seeking to excel, 'for the Olympic Games are over long since; and besides in such things mediocrity is enough for use, excellency in them serving for the most part only for mercenary ostentation.'[64] No professional or competitive sports, then, no excessive laughter (this being tiring) and no excessive sorrow.

On the other hand, he recommends the occasional petty worries: 'Grief and sadness, if it be void of fear, and afflict not too much, doth rather prolong life, for it contracteth the spirits and is a kind of condensation.'[65] In the same way, the occasional little bout of anger can only fortify the heart. The contemplation of a lovely painting, which satisfies the spirits, may also prolong them. Longevity, however, does not depend on living conditions, it is due just as much to the parents' state of health and to the moment of conception, preferably in the morning, after sleep. Some physical signs do not deceive: 'hairiness of the lower parts, as of the thighes and legs, is a sign of long life.'[66] Small heads and thighs live longer than big ones.

None of this constitutes much of an advance on the scientific level. However, it is clear that the Renaissance was passionately involved in the fight against old age, in listing its symptoms and the prescriptions for prolonging longevity and improving the health of old people. At this point, the 'Tree of Life' by Edward Madeira Arrais (1530–1600), doctor to John IV of Portugal, and the *Methusala Vivax* by Dornavus, in which the author seeks the causes of the patriarchs' extraordinary longevity before the Flood, should be mentioned.

Which was more to be feared, old age or death? The ideal would be to remove the latter indefinitely while preserving youthful health. Imagination provided two means of achieving this end: the elixir of long life and the fountain of youth. Several versions of the former exist. Gabriele Zerbi suggested a mixture of viper's flesh, distilled human blood and liquid gold. Erasmus himself did not entirely reject the notion of a 'quintessence'. The fountain of youth, for its part, inspired Juan Ponce de Léon in his exploration of Florida as well as Cranach the Younger in his splendid painting of 1546 which shows infirm and ugly old women recovering their youth and beauty. People also dreamt of the Happy Isles, the memory of which was transmitted via Hesiod, Homer, Pindar,

Pliny and Horace, to turn up again in Erasmus; isles where work, old age and illness are unknown.

As in all times of crisis and accelerating history, the Renaissance saw the emergence of a profusion of Utopias, which revealed the reformers' aspirations. By its very nature Utopia assumes that men are unalterable and incorruptible, know not ageing and reject time, which undoes all things, and so is destined to do away with old age. Gilles Lapouge, who has studied this type of literature, remarks very aptly that

> The current model of Utopian . . . functions like a terrifying disinfectant machine, a science-fiction autoclave. The pox, senility, death and sin have no existence in his home. Illness, like sadness, are forbidden entry, by decree, and old age is done away with. If sin does manage to slip in, it is bombarded and knocked out, running the risk of crushing a few heads with the same bludgeon. Mercenaries and guard dogs are unleashed to purge the city for ever, although this may mean carrying out a few legal assassinations.[67]

The Utopia of the sixteenth century matches this description in every respect. Firstly, in doing away with old age. Aware that they could not eliminate this cancer, since Utopia claimed not to be a fairy-tale, the utopians simply avoided all mention of it. Few indeed are the allusions to it in Campanella's 'City of the Sun', or Bacon's *New Atlantis*, or Stiblin's 'Country of Macaria', or in Rabelais' Abbey of Thélème. In the latter, one of the few aged individuals is 'an old French Poet, named Raminagrobis', whose only function was to predict the future:

> It has been likewise told me frequently, That old decrepit Men upon the Brinks of Charon's Banks, do usher their Disease with a Disclosure, all at ease (to those that are desirous of such Informations) of the determinate and assured truth of future Accidents and Contingencies. I remember also, that Aristophanes, in a certain comedy of his, calleth Folks Sibyls . . .[68]

Utopia was visibly the land of rational perfection, which has nothing to do with old people. What role could be given them in these worker-bee societies? Nor indeed were they to be seen in the earthly paradises which the pastoral romances and shepherd-tales had made fashionable. They would undoubtedly have spoiled the pretty world, inhabited by young people, of the Arcadian romances, Tasso's *Arminta*, Cervantes'

Galatea, Honoŕe ďUrfé's *Astrée*, Guarani's *Pastor fido* and Montemayor's *Diane*. As soon as people escaped from reality, they tried to forget the nightmare of old age. But they were well aware of its constant presence, marking its prey from behind the scenes. Consequently some utopians did not shrink from suggesting instituting the legal assassinations mentioned by Gilles Lapouges in their abominable barracks-cities. In Utopia, the priests were to advise excessively feeble old people to commit suicide by taking poison. Antonio de Guevara, Bishop of Cadiz, took an even more radical stance. In his *Diall of Princes* he suggests the straightforward elimination of old age: everyone over 50 should commit suicide in order to avoid decrepitude. 'What stroke of fortune; what whippe for the fleshe!' the bishop enthuses, taking care not to appear to advocate suicide by setting this custom among the inhabitants of a distant land in the time of Pompey, and putting his words in the mouth of Marcus Aurelius.[68]

The only Utopia to take precise account of the old is also the most famous one: Thomas More's *Utopia*. Henry VIII's chancellor took an honest interest in the problem and revealed the extent of its gravity. His actions testify to his sincerity, since Erasmus tells us that he rented a house in Chelsea which took in infirm old men. In the first part of *Utopia*, he delineates the problem lucidly, showing how in his time, the old were profoundly despised and rejected. In a conversation between a cardinal and a fool, we learn that common opinion classes all old people among the more or less parasitical poor, whose existence society must underwrite. They belong within the same category as vagabonds, the sick and even robbers. The fool gives brutal expression to the general feeling about them:

> For I had rather than any good that this kind of people were driven somewhere out of my sight, they have so sore troubled me many times and oft, when they have with their lamentable tears begged money of me; and yet they could never to my mind so tune their song that thereby they ever got of me one farthing.[70]

He suggests shutting them up in monasteries. Old people were surplus to a world enamoured of youth and beauty; they cast an irritating shadow over its official optimism.

Thomas More undertook to rehabilitate them within society, and to this end eliminated all notions of retirement from his ideal city. Professions and offices were to be exercised for life, at a rate of six hours' work a day. Deference and respect were due to the elders, who were to be served by the young, a feature reminiscent of Plato's *Republic* and in contrast with the practice and feelings of other utopians. A century and half later on, Cyrano de Bergerac was to write: 'Old men should render every kind of respect and deference to the young . . . for youth alone is fit for action.'[71] In *Utopia* the family is 'governed by the eldest and ancientest father, unless he dote for age; for then the next to him in age is placed in his room.'[72] If anyone wants to travel, he had to secure the consent of his wife and father. Old women, far from being despised, may be admitted to the priesthood. The specific role of the old in society would be to moderate the ardour of the young, to temper their petulance by imparting the lessons of their experience to them. This is the wise old man's traditional position, and Thomas More provides practical dispositions to enchance it. During the meals, which are of course taken communally, 'two of the ancientest and eldest' are seated at the table of honour, in company with the governor and his wife:

> On both sides of them sit young men, and next unto them again old men. And thus throughout all the house equal of age be set together, and yet be mixed and matched with unequal ages. This, they say, was ordained, to the intent that the sage gravity and reverence of the elders should keep the youngers from wanton licence of words and behaviour . . . The dishes be not set down in order from the first place, but all the old men (whose places be marked with some special token to be known) be first served of their meat, and then the residue equally. The old men divide their dainties as they think best to the younger on each side of them. Thus the elders be not defrauded of their due honour, and nevertheless equal commodity cometh to every one . . .
>
> The elders take occasion of honest communication, but neither sad nor unpleasant. Howbeit they do not spend all the whole dinner-time themselves with long and tedious talks, but they gladly hear also the young men.[73]

Finally, when the old man grows too old, becomes decrepit and absolutely useless, he had best commit suicide. This constitutes More's recognition of the final failure; in every society which places the common good above that of individuals, a powerless old man is entitled only to death. Every legislator who reckons in terms of the commmunity, of communism, of the masses, of the generality, of the people, the greatest number, is led to sacrifice the non-productive elements, if he is logical with himself. 'If there is a Paradise, let the foolish not imagine that they will return to the restful pleasures of Eden, where it is enough to put out one's hand to cull the fruits of a delicious garden! Happiness must pass through exhaustion, total sacrifice, the abnegation of the individual in the interest of Public Safety and the greater well-being of the collective'; Jacques Minois has thus fairly described the Utopian world.[74]

Thomas More did at least try to attribute healthy old people with an honourable role, which Antonio de Guevara did not even attempt at. He told the old what he thought of them without mincing his words:

> I let you know, if you do not knowe it, that you are poore aged folkes, your eyes are sonke into your heades, the nosetrelles are shutte, the heares are white, the hearinge is loste, the tongue faltreth, the tethe fall, the face is wrinckled, the fete swolne, and the stomake cold. Finally I saye, that if the grave could speake unto his subiectes, by iustyce he might commaund you to inhabite his house.[75]

He felt that the classical writers had made a great fuss of old people: Aulus Gellius, in his 'Attic Nights' tells us that the Romans honoured the old, that old age took precedence over everything, even the greatest men, and that old people were worshipped like gods; in Sparta, Lycurgus had ordered that the old be respected; in Greece, the bandits used to disguise themselves as old men in order to elude justice; a philosopher is supposed to have told Pyrrhus one day that the best city in the world was Molerda, in Achaia, because all its rulers were white-haired. But, Guevara continues, the 'Ancients' were also aware of the miseries of old age. He recalls how Cato, on meeting a weeping old man, asked him the reason why. It was because of the miseries of old age, the other replied, since he, being 77 years old, had already buried his father, his mother, his grandfather, two aunts, five uncles, nine sisters, 11 brothers, two wives, five bondwomen, 14 children, seven married daughters, 37 nephews, 15 nieces and two friends:

> The man whiche is laden with yeares, turmented with dyseases, pursued with enemies, forgotten of his frendes, visyted with mishappes, and with evyll wyl and poverty: I know not why he demandeth long life.[76]

Thus, suicide at the age of 50 is the best solution for everyone.

Was Antonio de Guevara serious when he set forth this proposition, given that he was 49 when he published the *Diall of Princes* in 1529? In any case, far from attributing the old with a positive role in his ideal society, he limited himself to imposing a code of conduct on them which was intended to make them as discreet as possible and to have them pass unnoticed. If they cannot be killed, let them at least be forgotten. Let them stop claiming the best places and always wanting to be the first to speak, when they often behave like madmen; let them cease their gossiping, nonsense, dressing like youngsters and pursuing pleasures unsuited to their age:

It is a confusion to tell it, but it is greater shame to do it, that is to mete, that maye olde men of our time take no small felicity to put caules on their heades, everye man fayre, to weare jewels on their neckes, to lave their cappes with agglettes of golde, to leke out divers inventions of metalles, to loade their fingers with riche ringes, to go perfumed with odiferous favoures, to wear new fashioned apparyle, and finally I saye, that though their face be full of wrincles, they can not suffer one wrincle to be in their gowne.[77]

All that is asked of them is that they be virtuous and keep silence. At their age, no one has the right to commit the slightest indiscretion:

For oftentymes if the yonge do offende, it is for that he wanteth experyence; but if the olde man offende, it is for the aboundance of malyce.[78]

The utopians, who assessed everything in a normative manner, were consequently merciless towards old age. Starting from a preconceived and ideal image of the old man, they expected wisdom and virtue from him; in him, the slightest fault was intolerable. Rendered useless by his physical decrepitude, he was no longer really a man, but an example, and if he did not conform to this role, he had to disappear. This extreme notion can be found in varying degrees among all the intellectuals of the period. As far as these humanists were concerned, an old man had to be a Nestor – or not exist. At the level of daily life in a family of good bourgeois standing, Machiavelli drew a picture of how the existence of an old head of family ought to be. It will be noted that he uses the terms resolved, reserved, honourable, grave, honest, serious, regular and exemplary to describe the stereotyped picture of the ideal old man:

He was then a serious man, resolved and reserved. He spent his time honourably, and rose early in the morning, heard Mass, and ordered the food for the day; after which he went out on business in the piazza, in the market place, or in the law-courts, and did it; when he had none, he would engage in honourable conversation with some citizen, or else would retire home into his study, where he would collate his writings and bring his accounts up to date; after which he would chat cheerfully with his family over lunch, and having lunched, he would chat with his son, advising him to learn more about men, and teaching him how to live by means of a few examples from antiquity and modern life; he would then go outside, and spend the rest of the day either doing business or in grave and honest recreation; once evening had come, he was always back home for the Hail Mary; if it was winter, he would stay a while with us by the fire; then, he would return to his study to look over his business again; at the third hour he would dine merrily. His regular life was an example for everyone else in the house, and everyone would have been ashamed not to imitate him. Thus everything ran along in a regular and smooth fashion.[78]

OLD AGE IN THE SHAKESPEARIAN UNIVERSE

To move from the normative to the descriptive; the greatest social and psychological fresco of the sixteenth century is offered by the 'human comedy' of the Renaissance, or William Shakespeare's great corpus of plays. It presents, in its incomparable diversity, a living picture of how the Stratford master viewed the old. Shakespeare reflected the opinions of his age at the same time as subjecting them to penetrating analysis, and he was able to give expression to the ambiguous position of old age, not only in a period when the Middle Ages and modern times met, but in its timeless and universal dimension.

Although old age constitutes life's ending, it also seems to be a return to the beginning. It is the last role to be played out on the stage of life, and one strangely similar to the first. Shakespeare took up the theme of the ages of life, associated with his favourite image of the theatre, and made the drama of human destiny unfold in seven acts:

> All the world's a stage,
> And all the men and women merely players;
> They have their exits and their entrances:
> And one man in his time plays many parts.
> His acts being seven ages. At first the infant,
> Mewling and puking in the nurse's arms.
> And the whining school-boy, with his satchel
> And shining morning face, creeping like a snail
> Unwillingly to school. And then the lover,
> Sighing like furnace, with a woeful ballad
> Made to his mistress' eyebrow. Then a soldier.
> Full of strange oaths and bearded like the pard,
> Jealous in honour, sudden and quick in quarrel,
> Seeking the bubble reputation
> Even in the cannon's mouth. And then the justice,
> In fair round belly with good capon lined,
> With eyes severe and beard of formal cut,
> Full of wise saws and modern instances:
> And so he plays his part. The sixth age shifts
> Into the lean and slipper'd pantaloon,
> With spectacles on nose and pouch on side,

> His youthful hose, well saved, a world too wide
> For his shrunk shank; and his big manly voice,
> Turning again toward childish treble, pipes
> And whistles in his sound. Last scene of all,
> That ends this strange eventful history,
> Is second childishness and mere oblivion,
> Sans teeth, sans eyes, sans taste, sans everything.[80]

The final scene is thus nothing to rejoice over. The old man is ugly and weak; his beauty fades from his fortieth year onwards:

> When forty winters shall besiege thy brow,
> And dig deep trenches in thy beauty's field,
> Then youth's proud livery, so gazed on now,
> Will be a tatter's week, of small worth held . . .[81]

No physical advantage can resist old age: 'A good leg will fall; a straight back will stoop; a black beard will turn white; a curled pate will grow bald; a fair face will wither; a full eye will wax hollow . . .'[82] And so the old man is an object of scorn on the part of the young: 'But old folks, many feign as they were dead; / Unwieldy, slow, heavy and pale as lead', says Juliet ironically. [83] Young people 'may jest / Till their own scorn return to them unnoted / Ere they can hide their levity in honour . . .' declares the old king in *All's Well That Ends Well*; but at the same time he laments that 'On us both did haggish age steal on / And wore us out of act . . .'[84] In *Henry IV, Part 2*, the Lord Chief Justice classed Falstaff among the category of the old simply by looking at his ugly face: 'Do you set down your name in the scroll of youth, that are written down old with all the characters of age? Have you not a moist eye? a dry hand? a yellow cheek? a white beard? a decreasing leg? an increasing belly? is not your voice broken? your wind short? your chin double? your wit single? and every part about you blasted with antiquity? and will you yet call yourself young? Fie, fie, fie, Sir John!'[85] Old people, who judge everything in the bitterness of their bile are liars and dotards because, as with beer, 'when the age is in, the wit is out',[86] and 'as with age his body uglier grows, / So his mind cankers . . .'[87] In *The Passionate Pilgrim* Shakespeare takes up the classical theme of the conflict between youth and age, to the exclusive advantage of the former:

> Crabbed age and youth cannot live together:
> Youth is full of pleasance, age is full of care;
> Youth like summer morn, age like winter weather;
> Youth like summer brave, age like winter bare.
> Youth is full of sport, age's breath is short;

Youth is nimble, age is lame;
Youth is hot and bold, age is weak and cold;
Youth is wild, and age is tame;
Age, I do abhor thee; youth I do adore thee;
O, my love, my love is young!
Age, I do defy thee: O, sweet shepherd, hie thee
For methinks thou stay'st too long.[88]

The night of the abysses of age is ruled by suffering, weakness and infirmity. Old Aegeon, a merchant of Syracuse, laments the effects of time on his old body:

O time's extremity,
Hast thou so cracked and splitted my poor tongue
In seven short years, that here my only son
Knows not my feeble key of untuned cares?
Though now this grained face of mine be hid
In sap-consuming winter's drizzled snow,
And all the conduits of my blood froze up,
Yet hath my night of life some memory . . .[89]

In his lucid madness, Hamlet declares that

old men have grey beards, that their faces are wrinkled, their eyes purging thick amber and plum-tree gum and that they have a plentiful lack of wit, together with most weak hams.[90]

Achilles and Hector make similar fun of old Nestor, aping his infirmities:

And then, forsooth, the faint defects of age
Must be the scene of mirth: to cough and spit
And, with a palsy-fumbling on his gorget,
Shake in and out the rivet: and at this sport
Sir Valor dies: O, enough, Patroclus![91]

In *The Winter's Tale*, Polixenes asks his son Florizel, who does not recognize him, how his aged father does:

Is not your father grown incapable
Of reasonable affairs? is he not stupid
With age and altering rheums? can he speak? hear?
Know not man from man? dispute his own estate?
Lies he not bed-rid? and again does nothing
But what he did being childish . . .[92]

This idea of a return to childhood occurs several times in Shakespeare, as we have seen in *As You Like It*. In *King Lear*, Goneril mocks her father:

> Idle old man,
> That still would manage those authorities,
> That he hath given away! Now, by my life,
> Old fools are babes again, and must be used
> With checks as flatteries,— when they are seen abused.[93]

The body and soul decay together. Timon of Athens recalls the theory of the humours in his invective castigating the coldness of old people:

> These old fellows
> Have their ingratitude in them hereditary:
> Their blood is caked, 'tis cold, it seldom flows;
> 'Tis lack of kindly warmth they are not kind;
> And nature, as it grows again toward earth,
> Is fashion'd for the journey, dull and heavy.[94]

One character sums up all the distress and ambiguity of old age: King Lear. He is a victim indeed, but no innocent victim. His old man's vanity makes him prefer Goneril and Regan's flatteries to Cordelia's apparent coldness and, in an act of characteristic injustice, he disinherits her. This is his first fault. His second is to cede power, to seek for a comfortable retirement:

> 'tis our fast intent
> To shake all cares and business from our age;
> Conferring them on younger strengths, while we
> Unburthen'd crawl toward death . . .[95]

Vanity and weakness are thus at the root of his misfortunes, and the scorn with which his daughters treat him is not entirely unjustified:

Goneril: You see how full of changes his age is; the observation we have made of it hath not been little: he always loved our sister most; and with what poor judgement he hath now cast her off appears too grossly.
Regan: Tis the infirmity of his age; yet he hath ever but slenderly known himself.
Goneril: The best and soundest of his time hath been but rash; then must we look to receive from his age, not alone the imperfections of long-engraffed condition, but therewithal the unruly waywardness that infirm and choleric years bring with them.[96]

'A poor, infirm, weak and despised old man', Lear was also, by his own admission,

> a very foolish fond old man,
> Fourscore and upward, not an hour more nor less;
> And, to deal plainly,
> I fear I am not in my perfect mind.[97]

The main reproach made him is that of lacking wisdom, which is the principal duty of the old, and in his moment of lucidity, he acknowledges the truth of this. 'As you are old and reverend, you should be wise',[98] his daughter Goneril tells him. Even his Fool grumbles: 'Thou should'st not have been old till thou hadst been wise.'[99] So it is not old age which stands condemned here, but one old man, the victim of his personal faults. His tragedy is nonetheless the result of the situation in which the old find themselves, placed as they are in a hostile environment which allows them no shortcomings. The slightest weakness is fatal to them; faults which are forgiven the young are not forgiven them; mistakes which the young recover from are for them definitive. For they must be wise; everyone expects this attribute of them. Society, which maintains the old, demands wisdom of them, and its judgement is merciless.

King Lear is not the only old man in the play. The honest Duke of Gloucester is also very old, and he too will be a victim. He presents another aspect of the distress old people suffer, the conflict between the generations, the impatience of the young who drive their elders towards oblivion: 'The younger rises when the old doth fall.'[100] Edmund, Gloucester's bastard son, gets rid of his father in order to inherit the title. He rejects the social and family order and expresses the claims of youth in the face of their parents' authority, a conflict which was illustrated many times in the political life of the sixteenth century:

> This policy and reverence of age makes the world bitter to the best of your times; keeps our fortunes from us till our oldness cannot relish them. I begin to find an idle and fond bondage in the oppression of aged tyranny; who sways, not as it hath power, but as it is suffered.[101]

While old age was granted certain prerogatives, this was but condescension towards its frailty. This is why Leonato defends his desire to take advantage of them:

> I speak not like a dotard or a fool,
> As under privilege of age to brag

What I have done being young, or what would do
Were I not old.[102]

Respect and wisdom were among the attributes of the stereotyped image
of old age rather than that of current practice: 'Respect and reason, wait
on wrinkled age!';[103] 'And that which should accompany old age, / As
honour, love, obedience, troops of friends, / I must not look to
have'.[104] 'Priam, why art thou old and yet not wise?' Lucrece asks.[105]
Indeed, if the old do possess a common attribute, it does not appear to
be wisdom. 'If to be old and merry be a sin, then many an old host
that I know is damned',[106] declares Falstaff, 'the very model of well-
being. As for Adam, his merit derives from his ability to retain his
physical strength:

> Though I look old, yet I am strong and lusty;
> For in my youth I never did apply
> Hot and rebellious liquors in my blood,
> Nor did not with unbashful forehead woo
> The means of weakness and debility;
> Therefore my age is as a lusty winter,
> Frosty, but kindly: let me go with you;
> I'll do the service of a younger man
> In all your business and necessities.[107]

Such sprightly old men occur more frequently than the wise variety,
and none of the them conform to the traditional type. Whatever the
outcome, old age is a sad business, the miserable end to a life which
itself is but an illusion. In *Measure for Measure*, the Duke reasons thus
with life:

> Thou hast nor youth nor age,
> But, as it were, an after-dinner's sleep,
> Dreaming on both; for all thy blessed youth
> Becomes as aged, and doth beg the alms
> Of palsied eld; and when thou art old and rich,
> Thou hast neither heat, affection, limb, nor beauty,
> To make thy riches pleasant. What's yet in this
> That bears the name of life? Yet in this life
> Lie hid moe thousand deaths: yet death we fear,
> That makes the odds all even.[108]

The literary assessment of old age in the sixteenth century was thus
entirely negative. The humanists thought of great age as the skeleton at
the feast, which comes with its ugliness, infirmities and dotage to ruin
the charms of existence and to provide a ridiculous and unhappy death

for every life. Why should everything end tragically? One poet alone appears to have appreciated old age; he was Agrippa d'Aubigny, for whom 'an autumn rose more exquisite than another is'. He retained his vigour until his death at the age of 78, and enjoyed his comfortable retreat as a country gentleman in the Château of Crest to the full. He married Reñee Burlamachi as his second wife when he was around 70 andd she 20 years younger, and recorded his appreciation of the charms of 'happy old age' in poetic form:

> Here is less pleasure but also less sorrow;
> The nightingale falls silent as do the mermaids.
> We no longer pluck the fruits or the flowers.
> Hope has left me who so often betrayed me
> And winter reigns everywhere; happy old age,
> The worn-out season when no one need work.[109]

D'Aubigny is the exception and, dying as he did in 1630, he belonged to another period, that of a powerful religious revival, which would alter people's perspectives yet again. For Renaissance man, both the humanist and the courtier, old age remained the sign of the ultimate failure of their attempts to create superman. For old age makes us lose all the virtues of ideal man: beauty, strength, the capacity for decision and intellectual growth. It robs us of love and the worldly pleasures. It brings suffering and frailty. It was indeed that century's bugbear, which the utopians dreamt of abolishing.

10

The Sixteenth Century:

The Real Weight of Old People

Not least of the paradoxes of the sixteenth century was the flagrant contradiction between what was said about old age and the role actually played by old people in society, economy, politics and art. The Renaissance proclaimed its execration of the old through its humanists, while simultaneously giving them even greater responsibility and conferring the highest honours on them. The century began under the aegis of youth with the glittering trio François I, Henry VIII and Charles V, but it ended under the aegis of gerontocracy and the equally famous triumvirate of Queen Elizabeth, Philip II and Suleiman, all of whom were over 70 when they died.

Though vilified, old people made up a cohort of sovereigns, ministers, warriors, diplomats, merchants, churchmen, thus illustrating the total indifference of practice in the face of current opinion . . . that is, if opinion is not just a reaction against practice. At a time when modern propaganda was as yet unknown, this was the opinion generally held by independent people, the thinkers, writers and artists, whose personal feelings were inspired by the context of their age, by tradition and intellectual trends. There were no newspapers, radio or television to provide society with models. Very few men during the sixteenth century ever saw their rulers, whether lay or ecclesiastical, who remained abstractions and whose existence was demonstrated only by their decisions, their taxes, their wars and their justice. Power and opinion evolved independently, taking no account of each other. It is hardly surprising, therefore, that under such conditions the old were held in low esteem on the one hand, whereas they were being given more responsibility than ever before by their governments.

OLD PEOPLE IN POPULATION STATISTICS: TENTATIVE RESULTS

This state of affairs is by no means due to any increase in longevity or of the proportion of elderly people in the population. The figures, which multiply steadily and grow more accurate with the passage of time, demonstrate this. People began knowing their age with greater precision, although not everyone had access to such minute information as Benvenuto Cellini, who knew that he 'was born during the night after All Saints' Day, at exactly half past four, in the year 1500.'[1]

In his study of Breton demography during the sixteenth and seventeenth centuries, Alain Croix has observed that old people in hospital usually gave their ages with a fair degree of accuracy: less than ten per cent of them were wildly out. One old man, who said that he was 'over 80', was found to be actually 81 years 6 months old.[2] The means of checking such information already existed:

> in fact, registration became generalised, from the Reformation onwards, in Catholic as much as in Protestant lands; all the more so in the latter given that the Lutheran, Anglican and Calvinist Churches were trying to prevent the proliferation of religious sects. The lay authorities often intervened, aware of the interest registration held, from the point of view both of public order and the state of the people and its property . . .[3]

In Catholic lands, registers of baptisms, marriages and burials were already multiplying prior to the Reformation: in regions as diverse as Avignon (1509), Seville (1512), Angers (1504), Vezprem (1515) and Lisieux (1505), parish priests were obliged to record the names, Christian names and dates of birth of those baptized, and the ages of deceased persons.

At the same time, population censuses were multiplying; at Dresden (1430), Ypres (1431), Nuremberg (1449), Basle (1454) and Strasbourg (1470), etc. On a state level, censuses were taken in the kingdom of Valencia (1527), in Sicily (1548), in Savoy (1561) and in Saxony (1571), added to which were Philip II's inquisitions.[4] There was usually a fiscal or religious reason for these investigations (checking on baptism and degrees of consanguinity). A further practice, however, encouraged the compilation of statistics regarding longevity, and ended by drawing up mortality tables. This involved life annuities and life assurance. Life annuities have existed since antiquity, when Ulpian's Table was compiled to evaluate their worth in terms of inheritance credits and debits during the third century. During the Middle Ages, some of the Flemish municipalities issued loans repayable through life annuities, which suggests that calculations of average life expectancy may have already

Table 10.1 Scarcity of old people in medieval Italy

Age at death	Pozzuoli (in 1489)		Sorrento (in 1561)	
	Of 1394 men	Of 1133 women	Of 1483 men	Of 1435 women
60–4	30	32	51	54
65–9	4	5	25	38
70–4	15	21	11	6
75–9	0	2	9	11
80–9	3	9	7	5
90–9	1	3	0	3
100+	0	2	2	0

Source: J.C. Russell, 'Late ancient and medieval population', *Transactions of the American Philosophical Society*, vol. 48, part 3 (1958).

existed. The system really took off during the seventeenth century with the advent of the tontines.[5] Life assurance took off rather more slowly because of opposition from the Church, which considered speculation on the life and death of men heinous. Although prohibited in the Spanish Netherlands (1570), in Genoa (1588) and in Holland (1598), it was undoubtedly practised more or less clandestinely in England, since Thomas Wilson referred to it in his 'Dissertion on Usury' of 1569.[6]

The results of these various enquiries, whether political or economic, have mostly been lost. Modern demographic research has, however, to some extent reconstructed the demographic situation in the sixteenth century with regard to the position and life span of old people. Two conclusions emerge from this: that the retreat of the epidemics, which had chiefly affected the young, meant that the global proportion of old people within the population as a whole decreased; and that longevity remained at a level similar to that during the Middle Ages. Let us give some examples. In Italy, J.C. Russell has studied the age at death of 2,527 people in Pozzuoli in 1489 and of 2,918 people in Sorrento in 1561.[7] The results are shown in table 10.1.

These figures are surprising because of the relative lack of old people and the larger proportion of women: in Pozzuoli 3.9 per cent of the men and 6.5 per cent of the women were over 60 when they died; in Sorrento the figures were 7 per cent and 8 per cent respectively. Was this a sign of a reduction in female mortality due to childbearing? Further studies would be required to confirm this.

The situation was very different in Brittany, where the number of elderly people appeared far greater, as demonstrated by Alain Croix's figures, which do however overlap largely into the seventeenth century (table 10.2).[8]

Table 10.2 Age at death of adults in some Breton parishes (sixteenth to seventeenth centuries)

	60–9 yrs (%)	*70+ yrs (%)*
Couffé	22.2	15.2
Notre-Dame-de-Guimgamp	20.7	18
Notre-Dame-d'Hennebont	17.8	11.4
Loudéac	17.3	9.8
Menéac	17	?
St Jacques-de-Nantes	18.4	13
Névez	25.2	16.4
Ossé	16.4	19.3
Piriac	15	?
Plozevet	20.4	14.2
Le Theil	26.6	12.4

Source: Alain Croix, *La Bretagne aux XVIe et XVIIe siècles*, Paris 1981.

The parish registers of Saint-Malo for 1601–25 do not give the age at death, just the degree of age. Thus, 'old man' or 'old woman' is given for 32 of the 97 deaths registered, that is, in 32.9 per cent of cases.[9]

OLD PEOPLE IN THE ARISTOCRACY: A SHARP INCREASE,
PARTICULARLY WOMEN

In England, detailed studies of the aristocracy were drawn up during the sixteenth century.[10] Although limited to a numerically restricted social class, the conclusions confirm the general tendency of the time, since the figures can be compared with those of previous periods. In general, life expectancy had barely increased since the time of the Romans and if one refers to Ulpian's Table, an English nobleman of 50 could expect to live 2.5 years longer than a third century Roman, and if he were 70 years old, he would have lived only another year on average. The life expectancy of the nobility was helped by one factor, however, and this was the significant decrease in the number of violent deaths, due above all to the cessation of the civil wars. Whereas between 1330 and 1479 46 per cent of the aristocracy aged over 15 had died in battle, the percentage had fallen to 19 per cent between 1480 and 1679. Consequently many more men attained the age of 60, whereas the proportion of women remained unchanged: of 100 male births, only eight survived to the age of 60 between 1330 and 1479, whereas the number was 15 between 1480 and 1679. This fact is significant, given that this stratum of society furnished almost all the political leaders: the

Tudors had more than twice the number of elderly servants than did the Yorks or the Lancasters. The great slaughters of the Wars of the Roses having cut short many political careers, noblemen in the sixteenth century had the opportunity to prolong their activities into advanced age; we shall see that this really was the case. To a lesser extent the same can be said of Europe as a whole where, in spite of the Habsburg and Valois wars and the wars of religion, the nobility suffered less than in previous times.

On the other hand this same English research also confirms the reversal of the trend observed for Italy: more women were attaining old age and they generally lived longer than the men; of 100 female births, 19 were still alive at 60 between 1330 and 1479, and 17 between 1480 and 1679. Life expectancy at the age of 60 was ten years for men and 8.2 years for women between 1330 and 1479, and improved to 9.2 and 10.3 years respectively between 1480 and 1679. In this respect, the sixteenth century was a turning point. Of 100 people born between 1500 and 1599, there remained:

    aged 70: 6.9 men and 9   women
    aged 80: 0.6 men and 2   women
    aged 85: 0.1 men and 0.6 women
    aged 90: 0   men and 0.1 women

In other terms: a man of 70 born between 1500 and 1599 could expect, on average, to live a further 4.9 years and a woman 6.8 years.

If the figures provided in an article by T.H. Hollingsworth [11] are to be believed, the difference became more marked during the last quarter of the sixteenth century (table 10.3).

It does, therefore, seem to be an established fact (and one which has not changed even now) that, although women died earlier than men from antiquity until the fifteenth century, and old men were far more numerous than old women, the situation was reversed during the sixteenth century, at least in aristocratic circles, where childbirth occurred under more hygienic conditions. Given the scarcity of figures it is impossible to apply this result to the popular classes. It is, however, vital to note that the relative proliferation of old women in aristocratic circles was one of the novelties of the sixteenth century.

Surely this was one of the reasons for the hatred which the men of letters expressed towards old women, and the success of the fading rose motif? 'When you are old, one night while candles flare . . .' Such a prediction would have been out of place before the sixteenth century, since any beauty would have very likely died before the age of 50. If Ronsard was able to write such a gracious poem, it was undoubtedly due to the demographic changes in his time, when numerous women really did start living to an old age in the chateaux and manor houses.

Table 10.3 Longevity in men and women in England 1550–1600

Age at death (yrs)	Born 1550–1574		Born 1575–1600	
	Men(%)	Women(%)	Men(%)	Women(%)
50–4 yrs	12.8	10.2	6.6	10.6
55–9	6.3	13.2	7	10.3
60–4	6.3	5.8	7.1	7.6
65–9	2.5	4.4	5	5.4
70–4	5.1	4.4	3	2.9
75–9	2.5	4.4	3.8	2.4
80–4	1.3	0	1.9	0.7
85+	1.3	0	0.9	17.2 (?)
Total 50 and more	38.1	42.4	35.3	57.1

Source: T. H. Hollingsworth, 'Mortality in the British peerage families since 1600', *Population Review*, September 1977.

It was a phenomenon which unconsciously marked their contemporaries among the wealthy classes, whence the poets and humanists were recruited. Coming across 'ugly duchesses' more often than before, they were impressed to a greater extent by the effect of time's ravages on female beauty and were filled with apprehension about the future of their loved ones. Having discovered the old woman, they pitted themselves against the scandal of hideous feminity.

CONTEMPT FOR OLD AGE AND ADMIRATION FOR OLD PEOPLE

Very old people could now be observed at all levels of society, generating a certain degree of pride, in contrast with the literary criticisms reported above: 'A few years since there was in the County of Hereford a May-game or Morrice dance, consisting of eight men whose age computed together made up eight hundred years, insomuch that what some of them wanted of an hundred, others exceeded as much.'[12] The tomb of a certain Mary Ellis can be seen in a tiny cemetery in Essex. Her exceptionally long life overlapped three centuries: born in 1490, she died on 3 June 1609, aged 119.[13] Benvenuto Cellini refers proudly to his grandfather, Andrea, who lived over a hundred years, and whenever he can he informs us with sympathy about the age of the old people he came across: thus one of his workmen had a good old man aged over 70 for his uncle, who was both doctor and surgeon, and even practised a bit of alchemy. Elsewhere he remarks on the painter Giuliano

Burgiardini's 79 years. Francis Bacon appreciated the fact that, in his opinion, of all living creatures, it is man who lives the longest even though, three centuries after the flood, his life expectancy has been reduced by three-quarters. He was also of the opinion that longevity was progressing and that his contemporaries were living longer than their ancestors of antiquity. On the one hand, 'the ages of the nymphs, the fauns and the satyrs, once revered almost superstitiously, are nothing but dreams and fables, contrary to philosophy and to religion', and on the other the historical characters from the Near East of antiquity certainly did not live as long as is claimed. Ramses II's hundred years were part of his legend, and the pharaohs couldn't have lived longer than 40 or 45 years. The term of human life has been around 80 years since Moses, but this varies according to climate and occupation and Bacon saw some extremely ancient madmen at Bedlam Hospital in the London suburbs.

Pride in their advanced years and admiration for very old men were sentiments which represented the other face of people's attitude towards old age in the sixteenth century. Reaching the age of 80 was akin to a sporting triumph. This period, with its cult of hero worship, could hardly remain indifferent to such an achievement. In any case, had not Plato, their idol and demi-God, lived 81 years and produced his greatest works late in life? His influence certainly removed a great deal of weight from the prevailing gerontophobic sentiments. Had not Raphael included several old men in his *School of Athens*? Although quick to denigrate their elderly contemporaries, people liked to depict the ancient philosophers as old men; although the faults of living old people were hard to tolerate, once dead, they were idolized; age, which does present-day man no service, actually gave him prestige in the past. Once again, ambiguity and contradiction were human nature's lot.

And what a difference there was between the portraits of imaginary old men and those of men who really lived! The former, as symbols bearing the miseries of old age, as scapegoats loaded with the hatred felt for the faults and weaknesses of old age, are ugly, whereas the latter are dignified, expressing as they do the wisdom and experience of frequently remarkable individuals. Naturally, no portrait painter could allow himself to turn his client's face into an image of ugliness; he had to be recognizable and his picture a work of art and a pleasure to look at. But there was no reason why Dürer, who was capable of painting repulsive imaginary people, should endow the living old people whose portraits he painted with quite so many qualities. He rendered the face of his master, Michael Wolgenut, sharp and bony, but invested it with an expression of extraordinary purity, emanating intense life and energy.[14] He painted Jerome Holtzschuher, a Nuremberg senator, giving him a white beard and hair which do little to detract from his energetic, not to say hard, expression,[15] and Saint Jerome,[16] who is really Rodrigo d'Almada, John III's ambassador, meditating on a skull, and, finally, he painted his mother at the age of 63 with a great deal of realism and vivacity in her expression.[17]

Neither Raphael nor Titian were obliged to make the Renaissance popes appear pleasant, lessening Julius II's haughty refinement and tyrannical energy with a touch of bitterness, and detracting from the deformities of the 80-year-old Paul III's little shrunken body by painting a face glowing with intense malice.[18] And what grandeur in the wholly puritanical austerity of those Tudor faces in the National Portrait Gallery! The grandeur of those men in black: William Warham, Archbishop of Canterbury, aged 82; Hugh Latimer, aged 70; William Paulet, Marquis of Winchester, aged 87; William Cecil, Elizabeth I's Treasurer, aged 78; Nicholas Heath, Bishop of Rochester and Worcester, aged 77 and William Whitgift, aged 74. In all these works, as in Pedro Berruguete's *Saint Jerome*,[19] Jacob of Amsterdam's *Jan Gerritsz*,[20] Bäcker's *Old Woman*,[21] and later in Gossaert's *Elderly Couple*,[22] the artist is close to his subject, which enables him to capture their qualities. In it he contrasts antipathy towards old age in the abstract with sympathy for actual old people, thus turning the old quarrel between realists and nominalists on its head: old age was detestable, but every old person was worthy of respect.

OLD AGE AND POLITICAL POWER

It was precisely because of their personal qualities that many old people played important political or military roles. There is no shortage of examples.

Among the military leaders were Blaise de Monluc (who died aged 75), Andrea Doria (94) and his adversary Barbarossa (over 80), Villiers de l'Isle Adam (70) and Anne de Montmorency (74).

Among the heads of state, were Queen Elizabeth (died aged 70), Suleiman (72), Bajazid II (65), King Henry of Portugal (68), Emperor Frederick III (78), Frederick I of Denmark (62), Frederick II, Elector Palatine (74), his successor Frederick III (61), his namesake Frederick III of Saxony (62), Sigismund I of Poland (81), Sigismund III (66), Ivan III (65), Cosimo de'Medici (75), Philippe le Bon (71) and the successive doges of Venice, among them Tommaso Mocenigo (80), Francesco Foscari (84), Pietro Mocenigo (70), Giovani Mocenigo (77), Agostino Barbarigo (82), Andrea Gritti (83), Alviso Mocenigo (70).

Among the popes were Martin V (63), Calixtus II (80), Eugenius IV (64), Sextus IV (70), Alexander VI (72), Pius III (64), Julius II (70), Adrian VI (64), Paul III (81), Julius III (68), Paul IV (83), Pius IV (66), Pius V (68), Gregory XIII (83), Sixtus Quintus (70), Urban VII (69), Innocent IX (72), Clement VIII (69) and Leo XI (70).

Among the royal advisers were Cardinal Gattinara (65), Nicolas de Granvelle (64), Hurtado de Mendoza (72), Antoine Duprat (72), Michel de L'Hospital (68), Cheverny (71), Olivier de Serres (80), President Jeannin (82), Brûlart de Silléry (80), Achille du Harlay (83), Claude de L'Aubespine (67), Chancellor Pomponne de Belliévre (78), Duplessis Mornay (74), Sully (81), Treasurer William Cecil (78), Thomas Howard (81), and his son of the same name (81), Chancellor John Gage (77) and Chamberlain William Paulet (87).

The list is far from exhaustive. Of course, these people had not always been old and we should examine that period of their lives when they were performing their duties. Although most of them remained active right up to the end, some retired from political life and spent their last few years in retirement. Sully, for example, was dismissed as early as 1611, at the age of 51. On the other hand, sovereigns, popes and doges, who were normally nominated for life, almost always remained in power to the end. Thus, whenever possible, a statistical approach is more satisfactory. One circle is particularly suited to this; that of the royal councillors, especially in England, where the monarchical institutions, being well defined, allow lists of the various post-holders to be drawn up. By studying these people's careers, thanks to the inestimable Dictionary of National Biography, the following question may be answered: from which age group did the Tudors choose their advisers? Table 10.4 gives the average age of entry into service, of retirement and of death for 100 holders of the highest administrative posts in England between 1485 and 1558.

The Tudor administration was therefore in the hands of experienced people, the more important the job the older they were. The most important positions were only reached after the age of 50, but they were rarely held for life. The post of Treasurer was the highest in the land, and was often retained over and beyond the age of 70; Thomas Howard held it for 21 years, from the age of 58 to 79, and died three years after his resignation, in 1524. The changing reigns, further complicated by religious changes, did not cause any upheavals. The new sovereigns retained their predecessors' advisers because their experience of administration rendered them indispensible. Henry VIII's irascible temper alone brought about an interruption in some careers, notably that of Chancellor Thomas More, who was executed in 1535 at the age of 57.

William Paulet, first Marquis of Winchester, provides the best example of this continuity. His career spanned the reigns of Henry VIII, Edward VI, Mary Queen of Scots and Elizabeth without hiccup, his knowledge and experience respected by all. Born in 1485, he became sheriff of Hampshire at the age of 27, a member of the Privy Council at the age of 40, in 1525, Comptroller of the King's Household in 1532 (at 47), then ambassador to France and charged with various missions, Treasurer

Table 10.4 Longevity of 100 Tudor administrators

Posts	No. of holders	Average age at		
		Entry	Retirement	Death
Chamberlain	6	58 yrs	64 yrs 9 mths	68 yrs 9 mths
Chancellor	12	54 yrs 1 mth	60 yrs 2 mths	67 yrs
Treasurer	4	53 yrs 3 mths	71 yrs	74 yrs
Marshall	6	53 yrs 1 mth	62 yrs 1 mth	63 yrs 4 mths
Treasurer of King's Household	4	51 yrs 6 mths	61 yrs 3 mths	71 yrs 3 mths
Keeper of Privy Seal	10	51 yrs 4 mths	59 yrs 2 mths	64 yrs 5 mths
Comptroller of Royal Household	11	49 yrs 3 mths	54 yrs 4 mths	65 yrs 8 mths
Admiral	9	47 yrs 4 mths	51 yrs 5 mths	60 yrs 6 mths
Steward to Royal Household	8	46 yrs 6 mths	55 yrs	62 yrs
Master of Rolls	14	42 yrs 8 mths	48 yrs	56 yrs 9 mths
Secretary to the King	16	40 yrs 5 mths	48 yrs 4 mths	63 yrs 5 mths

of the King's Household from 1537 to 1539 (at 52–4), Chamberlain in 1543 (at 58) and Master of the King's Household between 1545 and 1550 (from 60 to 65). Held in great regard by all on account of his great restraint, he was appointed to the Regent's Council in Henry VIII's will. He became Treasurer in 1550, which he remained for 22 years, until his death at the age of 87. Mary Tudor confirmed him in all his appointments and entrusted him with the Privy Seal in 1556, although he declared himself against the Spanish marriage. Under Elizabeth, furthermore, he became Speaker of the House of Lords, from 1559 to 1566. His splendid portrait in the National Portrait Gallery shows a dignified old man of 85, of whom Queen Elizabeth said: 'Were my treasurer a young man, I should marry him above any other man in England.' A compliment indeed from a young queen of 27. When he died, William Paulet had 103 children and grandchildren.

Although the oldest of all the Tudor monarchy's servants, William Paulet was by no means an isolated example. Thomas Howard's career was less glittering, but no less remarkable: Treasurer from the ages of 58 to 79, Earl Marshall from 67 to 81 and Lord Admiral from 70 to 81; his son and namesake (1473–1554) was Lord Marshall from 60 to 64 and Treasurer from 49 to 74; John Gage (1479–1557) was Comptroller of the King's Household from 61 to 68 and Chamberlain from 74 to

77; William Warham (1450–1532) died whilst Archbishop of Canterbury at the age of 82; he was also Chancellor from 54 to 65. His portrait, which also hangs in the National Portrait Gallery, shows him at the age of 77, and Lord Burghley's may be found a little further ɔn (1520–98). He was Elizabeth's Treasurer for 26 years from the ages of 52 to 78. His portrait was painted by Marcus Gheeraerts the Younger, when Cecil was 70, and is a splendid witness to the de facto power exercised by old men in England during the sixteenth century. More than any other monarchy, the Tudors trusted in age and experience, confiding the most senior posts to elderly men still in full possession of their faculties.

With the Valois, however, the elderly were more exceptional amongst the senior servants of state. Antoine Duprat was undoubtedly the most remarkable among them. He was the first president of the Paris Parlement in 1508 at the age of 45, Chancellor for 20 years, from 52 to 72 years (1515–35), he was also cardinal from 1527 onwards. One of his successors, Michel de L'Hospital held the post of Chancellor between the ages of 55 and 68 (1560–73). It was Henri IV, the first of the Bourbons, who gave most power to the elderly. In 1590 he took back into service the old chancellor Hurault de Cheverny, who had been dismissed by Henri III; in 1599 he called on Olivier de Serres (1539–1619), an elderly Calvinist gentleman from Vivarais, for his advice in agricultural matters; that same year he replaced his defunct 69-year-old chancellor with another of 70, Pomponne de Belliévre, who held his post until 1607, when he was 78. His successor, Brûlart de Silléry (1544–1624) was 63 and died at the age of 80. The Secretary of State Nicolas de Neufville de Villeroy remained in power for 22 years, from the age of 54 to 76 (1594–1616). President Jeannin was one of the most important members of the Council of State (1540–1622) and one of the men held in highest regard by the King was Achille de Harlay, Count of Beaumont, who died at the age of 83 in 1619.

Did a 'policy of greybeards' wiser and less adventurous than that of younger men really exist? Were the elderly members of the government bent on moderation? There is nothing to confirm this. Certainly Michel de L'Hospital played a 'political' hand, but there were equal numbers of young and old among the ranks of extremists and moderates; Anne de Montmorency and Blaise de Monluc, who died at 74 and 75 years respectively, were opposed to any form of compromise right up to the end. In 1609–10, a 'young' 50-year-old Sully persuaded the king to intervene actively in Europe, whereas Villeroy (aged 68) counselled caution, but, apart from the fact that his advice was ignored, his example does not suffice to demonstrate that old age guided policy towards moderation.

The Mediterranean world also offered numerous examples. In Venice, the doges employed elderly diplomats for their more delicate missions.

Table 10.5 The sixteenth-century popes

Age group	No. of popes elected	No. of popes deceased
30–9 yrs	1	0
40–9 yrs	1	1
50–9 yrs	3	3
60–9 yrs	9	7
70–9 yrs	4	9
80–9 yrs	—	3

In 1540, Tomaso Contarini, aged 88, was sent to Sultan Suleiman the Magnificent; the Serenissima, as we have seen, retained her elderly condottieri, such as Colleone, who fought his last battle for her at the age of 67, her 90-year-old painter, Titian and her 80-year-old merchants, such as Francesco Balbi. At sea, the 70-year-old Andrea Doria from Genoa competed with the octagenarian Barbarossa; on land, the formidable Turkish army started its campaign east of Hungary under the command of the 71-year-old Suleiman in 1565 and its general in chief, Mustapha Pasha, was 70 years old. In the depths of the Escorial, Philip II brooded on his revenge against the Infidel and listened to the advice of Hurtado de Mendoza (1503–75), a septuagenarian, and Antoine de Granvelle (1517–86), while Marineo Siculo, the royal historiographer, ran from one Spanish battlefield to another at the age of 70, and died aged 89, still writing. In Rome, finally, the popes were not getting any younger. Their average age had never, in fact, been higher. Of the 18 pontiffs elected between 1503 and 1605, 13 were over 60 when they acceeded to office and four were aged over 70 (table 10.5).

Their average age at election was 61 years and 8 months; at death, 67 years and 2 months. The oldest popes were even the most active, though the nature of their activities varied: Julius II (1503–13), pope from the age of 60 to 70; Paul III (1534–49), who convoked the Council of Trent, reformed the Inquisition, tried to promote a new crusade and died aged 81; Paul IV (1555–9), who fought against ecclesiastical abuses, was elected at the age of 79 and died at the age of 83. The statues of these last two pontiffs by Guglielmo Della Porta (in the Vatican) and Giacomo da Cassignola (Santa Maria in Araceli) render them as two tall old men with long beards, the former dignified and pensive, the latter with an ascetic face. Gregory XIII (1572–85), whose pontificate ran from the ages of 70 to 83, began applying the decrees of the Council of Trent, and his successor Sixtus V (1585–90), pope from the age of 65 to 70, worked extensively on the legislation.

Conflicts between the generations: illusion or reality?

The advanced age of Peter's successors has led some historians to consider the question of the Reformation in terms of a generation struggle. While there is no question of reducing the Protestant schism to a relatively secondary level, once one starts looking at the age of the first protagonists of the crisis, one may legitimately enquire into the part played by youth in the daring ideas which resulted in the separation from Rome, and into the part played by the elderly in the Catholic refusal to consider fundamental changes. The generation problem also contributed to hardening and accelerating the course of events. 'The young were for Luther, the old for tradition', wrote Hermann Tüchle.[23]

It is indeed startling to note the homogeneity of the ages of the first great Reformation leaders. When Luther pinned his 95 propositions to the church door at Wittemberg in 1517, he was 34, and he secured the loyalty of men of his own generation: Karlstadt, his university contemporary, was aged 37, Franz von Sickingen, who was put in command of the German cavalry, was aged 36, Oecolampade, a man of compromise, was aged 35, and Zwingli, who was to start up his own movement in Berne, was 33 years old. Luther was also followed by some young and brilliant minds: Ulrich von Hutten, a humanist aged 29, Thomas Müntzer, who led a peasants' revolt, aged 28, Martin Bucer, a Dominican from Selestat, aged 26, Philip Melanchton, master at Tübingen University, aged 20, and Johannes Brenz, the future reformer of the Duchy of Wurttemberg, who was 18 years old. At the beginning, the Reformation seemed to be a movement led by fervent young people, the oldest of whom was 37. In contrast, their adversaries were mostly over 50, and from the start they took the part of tradition: the Dominicans Prieras and Hochstraten, a Franciscan called Thomas Murner, and the Duke of Saxony's chaplains, Jerome Emser and Cochläus.

It would, however, be difficult to generalize from these few examples. As we have already seen, new ideas, which in any case are never wholly new, have often been expounded by older men. In the same way, it must not be forgotten that Johann Eck, the papacy's most dedicated theologian and greatest defender, was three years younger than Luther, and that Leo X, who was pope in 1517, was the youngest the Church had known for two and a half centuries: he was then 42 years old. It is not hard to find people of very dissimilar ages on both sides: how many youthful bishops did Rome have on her side? And on the Reformation side, Calvin appealed to the elderly to join the Genevan consistory he was creating to supervise religious life.

Although age does not appear to have had a decisive influence on the allocation of religious and philosophical positions, it still played an important part in the political conflicts which were perpetually rocking the small Italian states, Florence in particular. Pamphlets and treatises for and against the old continued to flourish there, as we have seen. And events within the republic were always marked by discord between the generations. Between 1512 and 1527, the Medicis were again in power, together with a band of friends and partisans made up of young people: Lorenzo, the grandson of Il Magnifico, was in control of the city from the age of 21 to 27 (1513–19), as was his son Alessandro from the age of 13 to 17 years (1523–7), together with his young uncle Ippolito. The opposition was led by the old, the Albizzi, Vettori, Valori and Rucellai families, the latter busily plotting a conspiracy in 1522. Its failure inspired young Niccolo Martelli to send a memorandum to the Medicis, demonstrating once again that the fundamental gulf in society lay between the young and the old, and listing the categories of old people who needed to be watched.

The events of 1527–30 served to aggravate the conflict. The Medicis lost power in 1527, when the republicans took over and elected Niccolo Capponi, a staunch opponent of the young, as gonfalonier; this was the revenge of the old. The following year, they were nevertheless forced to accept the lowering of the minimum age for entry into the Grand Council to 24, and Donato Giannotti, a member of the government, favoured the idea of entrusting certain responsibilities to the young. He maintained that there was no direct opposition between the young and the old and that the psychological barrier was not insurmountable; the existing social order should be changed to allow the young to take part in politics and so become more experienced. A new order should be instituted in which 'the young would have to try to be old before being young.'[24] In 1528, partly under Gianotti's influence, the government agreed to the formation of a militia of young men, which was to cover itself with glory during the 1529–30 siege, when the old men were prepared to compromise and surrender.[25]

During the sixteenth century, there was, therefore, a marked gap between the way people talked about old age, with contempt, bitterness and rancour, even hatred, and the attitude they actually adopted towards old people. As in Florentine politics, instances of opposition were rare and were confined to small republican-type states, where the monarchies made greatest use of the experience of elderly advisers. Active old men fulfilled many important roles in all spheres. Gerontocracy did not occur during the sixteenth century any more than it had during preceding eras. But old men were often regarded as trustworthy, and if a dislike for old women existed, it was mainly a literary device. The theoretical attitude of the humanists and courtiers towards old age was no more than a front, striking because of its exponents' talent, but concealing their real attitude towards the old, which was one of sympathy rather than sarcasm.

Affective ties between grandparents and grandchildren grew ever stronger during the Renaissance. Although the passage of time can affect a great gulf between parents and children, it can, paradoxically, bring remoter generations closer together: 'The time of grandparents is ruled by a different thread; it evokes the haziness of ancient pictures in fairy tales, a maternal time, a time of grandmothers, of women so old in years that they may well have eluded the hours, whereas the father is time's workman.'[26] Again, it is Benvenuto Cellini who tells us how much his grandfather loved his grandchildren and how he played with them. At the age of three, little Benvenuto got hold of a scorpion while playing, at which his grandfather almost dropped dead from shock and anxiety. Again, it was the formidable Blaise de Monluc who, at the age of 70, began to regret not having shown more affection towards his children, having been rough towards them and worn an 'empty mask'.[27] There was more genuine feeling between the generations during the sixteenth centuries than its literature would lead us to suppose. But this affection was not open; it was not until the early romantic period that tenderness towards the venerable old became the norm.

Conclusion

'It is the tendency of every society to live and to go on living: it extols the strength and the fecundity that are so closely linked with youth and it dreads the worn-out sterility, the decrepitude of age.'[1] Simone de Beauvoir's statement is particularly well confirmed by the ancient societies we have studied. Over and above their minor variations, the general impression is one of pessimism and hostility towards all-conquering age. In spite of the various pleas in defence which we have met, it is clear that youth has always and everywhere been preferred to old age. Since the dawn of history, old people have regretted their youth and young people have feared the onset of old age. According to western thought, old age is an evil, an infirmity and a dreary time of preparation for death. Even the latter is often envisaged with more sympathy than is decrepitude, because death means deliverance. Christian thought has always tried to reconcile and familiarize its adherents with death, the door to eternal life. Pagan and neo-Platonic thought preferred suicide to decrepitude. This is an incontrovertible fact, which cannot be concealed behind a few rare instances of peaceful and happy old age. Such people may appear happy, but their lives were bitter indeed. The fountain of youth has always constituted western man's most irrational hope.

The situation of old people expresses the ambiguity of the human condition more fully than do the other ages of life. Living in this world, they are already felt no longer to belong to it. The activities, attitudes and distractions of the young are forbidden them. The only role allowed them is an inhuman one: unfailing wisdom, without error or frailty. To be accepted, an old man must be a saint. Condemned to veneration or detestation, he no longer has the right to commit the slightest mistake, he who enjoys so much experience, he can no longer surrender to the slightest urge of the flesh, he who is so worn and shrivelled, he must be perfect, or he will become revolting and doting.

If old people show the same desires, the same feelings and the same requirements as the young, the world looks upon them with disgust: in them love and jealousy seem revolting or absurd, sexuality repulsive and violence ludicrous. They are required to be a standing example of all the virtues. Above all, they are called on to display serenity; the world asserts that they possess it, and this assertion allows the world to ignore their unhappiness. The purified image of themselves that society offers the aged is that of the white-haired and venerable sage, rich in experience, planing high above the common state of mankind; if they vary from this then they fall below it; the counterpart of the first image is that of the old fool in his dotage, a laughing-stock for his children. In any case, either by their virtue or by their degradation, they stand outside humanity.[2]

This is undoubtedly the main conclusion. From antiquity to the Renaissance, however societies evolved, they remained fundamentally based on physical strength and bodily vigour; the conditions were unfavourable to old age from the start. However, variations of detail appear within this framework, which contribute towards the local and temporary amelioration or deterioration of the situation of old people. Any search for a regular evolution from ancient Egypt to the Renaissance would indeed be vain, given the great difference between the countries and civilizations involved. Even though the societies examined successively by us were to a certain extent one another's heirs, in no case was there absolute continuity between them. The course of history traces neither a hyperbola nor a parabola, but a capricious arabesque which eludes every attempt at equation by the human brain. The condition of the old was determined by several components which did not necessarily evolve in the same way, and an improvement in one sector might well be accompanied by a deterioration in another. At no time did all the favourable conditions combine.

What were these different factors which came into play to define the social status of the old? The first was undoubtedly their physical frailty. Consequently, the condition of the old was worst in those societies which were most anarchical and least policed, relying on the law of the strongest, as in the Merovingian world and in the Middle Ages as a whole. Conversely, in more structured societies, where the state and the law had more authority and could enforce order, the weaker elements were more protected against physical aggression by the strong. This was the case in Rome and under the absolute monarchies of the sixteenth century.

The second factor making up old age was the knowledge and experience due to long life. Thus civilizations which relied on oral tradition and custom were kinder towards the old. In such societies, they acted as links between the generations and as the collective memory. They were called on during the long evenings and at legal proceedings, as was the case in Greece and especially in the Middle Ages. On the other hand, the advance of the written word, of archives and laws recorded in writing, were unfavourable to them. Their knowledge of custom was rendered useless. The printed book was for a while the old man's enemy. In this sense, Rome and the Renaissance boded ill for him. These legalist civilizations had less need of their old people's customary experience. Added to which the relative acceleration of history during the Renaissance contributed to relegating them to the category of antiquated and useless things.

Harvey C. Lehman assessed the positive and negative qualities of old age as regards cultural evolution as follows:

> Whatever the causes of growth and decline, it remains clear that the genius does not function equally well throughout the years of adulthood. Superior creativity rises relatively rapidly to a maximum which occurs usually in the thirties and then falls off slowly. Almost as soon as he becomes fully mature, man is confronted with a gerontic paradox that may be expressed in terms of positive and negative transfer. Old people probably have more transfer, both positive and negative, than do young ones. As a result of positive transfer the old usually possess greater wisdom and erudition. These are invaluable assets. But when a situation requires a new way of looking at things, the acquisition of new techniques or even new vocabularies, the old seem stereotyped and rigid. To learn the new they often have to unlearn the old and that is twice as hard as learning without unlearning. But when a situation requires a store of past knowledge then the old find their advantage over the young.[3]

The third factor is their altered features. Societies which indulged in a cult of physical beauty tended to depreciate old age. This was particularly obvious in Greece and during the Renaissance. Societies which entertained a more abstract and symbolic aesthetic ideal were, conversely, less revolted by wrinkled faces because they were aiming at a spiritual beauty above and beyond the visible; this was the case in the Middle Ages especially.

Age also serves to increase the number of one's relations, as new generations appear and matrimonial alliances are contracted. Civilizations which experienced the extended and patriarchal family, which supported those members who were incapable of work, did help the old more. This was generally the case in the remotest ages, at the beginning of a new civilization, for instance, or during periods of crisis; in archaic Greece, at the beginning of the Roman republic, or during the early

Middle Ages. Periods of relative equilibrium, on the other hand, generally witnessed the disintegration of the group in favour of the conjugal family—as in classical Greece, imperial Rome, the 'classical' Middle Ages and the Renaissance, which all tended to neglect their old.

Old age can also be a time when worldly goods accumulate, ensuring the material security and prestige of old persons in the ruling classes. Societies where movable wealth, which is essentially personal, played a great role, allowed many old people to achieve a superior status, as in the merchant and banking circles in Rome, at the end of the Middle Ages and the Renaissance. However, the corollary to this concentration of wealth within the hands of old people was that the young were impatient and sometimes murderously jealous of them. Where landed property predominated, belonging to the family group, the inverse situation arose and was less favourable towards the elder members.

Generally speaking, the periods known as transitional were less unfavourable towards the old than the stable periods known as classical. The times of upheaval, when the prejudices and rigid structures characteristic of settled times were lost, were more open to a variety of talents, more friendly towards difference and less encumbered by aesthetic, moral or social taboos. While these periods were undoubtedly difficult for everyone, old people were less rejected; every age suffered the common lot of a precarious existence. The Hellenistic world, the time of the Germanic invasions and the early Middle Ages were less hard on the old than were classical Greece and Rome, or the Renaissance.

Added to which, the general attitude towards the old of every society tends to assume a particular colour within each social category. It has always been better to be old and rich than old and poor. Charity is all that can be hoped for in the latter event, where the elderly are totally dependent on others. In short, there has never been a golden age for the old, but a chaotic evolution at the whim of the desynchronized values of civilizations.

The concept of retirement did not exist in any of these ancient periods, with the exception of a few privileged cases. Such distinctions as existed were between two categories of old people: the active old, who, in spite of their age, continued to exercise a profession and who merged into the mass of adult people so far as their contemporaries were concerned; and the inactive old, who were forced by their decrepitude to rest, and were classed by the sources among the infirm and the sick. There was thus no limit and old age disappeared. This constituted their main difficulty, resulting in the weakness and misery of the old in the past. In societies which were still very closed, where a person's status and membership of a group were the sole guarantors of his social acceptance, where an isolated individual could not survive, an old person was not recognized as such. So he had no rights and was entirely at the mercy of those around him. This was the social circle which, in the final analysis, created the image of old people, starting from the norms and human ideals of their age.

Each civilization has its model old person, and judges all its old accordingly. The more this model is idealized, the more demanding and cruel the society is, and so long as this trend is not reversed, old people will not be truly integrated within the group. Every description encountered above has in fact been a judgement; there have always been good or bad old people, who conform to a greater or lesser degree to the established ideal. When these societies begin with reality and experience as they know them instead of starting off with an abstract model, they take a great step forward. For this, we must wait for the advent of the social sciences, of psychology and geriatric medicine. The old should be studied and society adapted to meet their needs, rather than the reverse. It should be recognized that old people have their needs, including physical ones, and that they should be allowed to satisfy these needs, instead of decreeing that the old man is wise and trying to force him so to become.

Notes

INTRODUCTION

1 Ladislas Robert, 'Biologie du vieillissement', *Communications* no. 37. 1983, p. 17.

2 Edgar Morin, 'Vieillissement des théories et théorie du vieillissement'. *Communications* no. 37, 1983, p. 203.

3 G. Calot and J.C. Chesnais, *La Situation démographique de la France: diagnostic et perspectives*, Rapport au Conseil Central de Planification, March 1979, Paris, Cahiers de l'INED, 1980.

4 Simone de Beauvoir, *Old Age*, trans. Patrick O'Brian, Harmondsworth 1977, p. 100.

5 *Communications* no. 37, 1983, entitled 'Le continent gris', is a compilation of studies from every discipline on old age. Each article is followed by a bibliography.

6 Michel Philibert, 'Le status de la personne agée dans les sociétés antiques et préindustrielles', *Sociologie et sociétés* 16(2), October 1984.

7 Paul-Laurent Assoun, 'Le vieillissement saisi par la psychanalyse', *Communications* no. 37, 1983, p. 167.

8 Edgar Morin, 'Vieillissement', p. 211.

9 Simone de Beauvoir, *Old Age*, p. 100.

10 Philippe Ariès, 'Une histoire de la vieillesse', *Communications* no. 37, 1983, p. 54.

11 Jean-Pierre Bois, *Les Anciens Soldats dans la société française au XVIIIe siecle*, PhD thesis submitted to the Sorbonne on 21 June 1986. J.P. Bois has also written numerous articles on the subject.

12 Simone de Beauvoir, *Old Age*, p. 99.

13 Konrad Lorenz, 'La place des anciens ches les animaux sociaux', *Communications* no. 37, 1983, p. 7.

14 Georges Condominas, 'Ainés anciens et ancêtres en Asie du Sud-Est', *Communications* no. 37, 1983, p. 63.

15 Louis-Vincent Thomas, 'La vieillesse en Afrique Noire', *Communications* no. 37, 1983, p. 85.
16 Ibid.

CHAPTER 1 THE MIDDLE EAST OF ANTIQUITY: THE EXPERIENCE OF OLD AGE BETWEEN MYTH AND HISTORY

1 *La Vieillesse, problème d'aujourd' hui*, Groupe lyonnais d'études medicales, SPES, Paris 1961.
2 Louis-Vincent Thomas, *Anthropologie de la mort*, Payot, 1975, p. 362.
3 Leo Simmons, *The Role of the Aged in the Primitive Society*, Yale, 1945, p. 140. See too Michel Philibert, 'Le statut de la personne agée dans les sociefes antiques et preindustrielles', in *Sociologie et sociétés*, 16(2) October 1984, pp. 15–27.
4 J. Roumeguere-Eberhardt, *Pensée et société africaines*, Mouton, Paris-la-Haye 1963, p. 73.
5 Louis-Vincent Thomas, *Anthropologie*, pp. 361–2.
6 Herodotus, *The Histories*, trans. Aubrey de Selincourt, Harmondsworth 1954, book I.CCXVI, p. 101.
7 Ibid., book III.XCIC, p. 217.
8 Simone de Beauvoir, *Old Age*, trans. Patrick O'Brian, Harmondsworth 1977, pp. 96–8.
9 D.B. Bromley, *The Psychology of Human Ageing*, Harmondsworth 1974.
10 Inca Garcilaso de La Vega, *Commentaires royaux sur le Pérou des Incas*, Maspero, 1982, vol. 1, p. 220.
11 Ibid., vol. 2, p. 9.
12 Ibid., vol. 2, p. 19
13 Ibid., vol. 2, p. 67.
14 Ibid., vol. 2, p. 95.
15 Ibid., vol. 2, p. 102.
16 J.B. Pritchard, ed., *Ancient Near Eastern Texts relating to the Old Testament*, Princeton 1955, p. 412.
17 Ibid., p. 483.
18 *Papyrus Insinger*, trans. F. Lexa, Paris 1926, XVII.11.14.
19 J.B. Pritchard, ed., *Ancient Near Eastern Texts*, p. 439.
20 Herodotus, *The Histories*, book III. CXXXIV, p. 230.
21 *The Papyrus Ebers*, trans. B. Ebbell, London 1937, p.117.
22 *Huang Ti Nei Ching Su We, The Yellow Emperor's Classic of Internal Medicine*, trans. I. Veith. Berkeley 1966, p. 183.
23 *Kaviraj Kunja Lal Bhishagratna, An English Translation of the Sushruta Samhita*, Calcutta 1907–16, vol. 2, p. 530.
24 J.H. Breasted, *The Edwin Smith Surgical Papyrus*, Chicago 1930, vol. l, p. 498.
25 D.B. Bromley, *Psychology*, p. 37.
26 I. Veith, *The History of Philosophy of Knowledge of the Brain and its Functions*, New York 1958, p. 35.
27 J.B. Pritchard, ed., *Ancient Near Eastern Texts*, p. 265.
28 Samuel Noah Kramer, *History begins at Sumer*, London 1958, p. 197.

29 Ibid., pp. 243–4.
30 J.B. Pritchard, ed., *Ancient Near Eastern Texts*, p. 101.
31 Herodotus, *The Histories*, book III.XXII and XXIII, p. 183.
32 Ibid., book I.CXXXXIII, p. 69.
33 D.B. Bromley. *Psychology*, pp. 36–7.
34 *Papyrus Insinger*, XVIII.4.
35 Paul Faure, *La Vie quotidienne en Crète au temps de Minos*, Hachette, 1973.
36 Herodotus, *The Histories*, book II.LXXVII.
37 Jacques and Michel Dupaquier, *Histoire de la démographie*, Perrin, 1985, pp. 28–32.
38 J.B. Pritchard, ed., *Ancient Near Eastern Texts*, p. 505.
39 *Cambridge Ancient History*, II, part 2A, Cambridge 1975, p. 390.
40 J.B. Pritchard, ed., *Ancient Near Eastern Texts*, p. 350.
41 James Hastings, ed., *Encyclopaedia of Religion and Ethics*, Edinburgh 1917, article on 'old age'.
42 Paul Garelli, *Le Proche-Orient asiatique. Des origines aux invasions des peuples de la mer*, Nouvelle Clio, 1969, p. 56.
43 Ibid., p. 92.
44 Ibid., p. 119.
45 Ibid., p. 267.
46 *Cambridge Ancient History*, p. 264.
47 Herodotus, *The Histories*, book III.XXXI, p. 187.
48 Xenophon, *Cyropaedia*, trans. W.H. Bulgarcie, London 1897, I.2.4.
49 *Cambridge Ancient History*, pp. 154–5.
50 Ibid, p. 159.
51 J.B. Pritchard, ed., *Ancient Near Eastern Texts*, p. 422.
52 Ibid., p. 420.
53 Ibid., p. 415.
54 Ibid., p. 414.
55 Herodotus, *The Histories*, book II.LXXX, p. 132.
56 Ibid., book II.XXXV, p. 116.
57 Ibid., book I.CXXXVII. p. 70.
58 *Cambridge Ancient History*, pp. 39–40.

Chapter 2   The Hebraic World: From Patriarch to Old Man

1   Most of the quotations in this chapter have been taken from:

The Holy Bible containing the Old and New Testaments (King James Bible).
The Apocrypha translated out of the Greek and Latin tongues in the 1611 version.
The Babylonian Talmud, trans. Rabbi Dr I. Epstein, London 1948.

The following works have also been used with reference to Jewish society:

André Chouraqui, *La Vie quotidienne des hommes de la Bible*, Hachette, 1978.
Charles F. Jean, *Le Milieu biblique avant Jésus-Christ*, Paris 1963.

F. Vigouroux, *Dictionnaire de la Bible*, Paris 1912.
R. de Vaux, *Les Institutions de l'Ancien Testament*, Cerf 1960.
Andre Baruq, *Écclésiaste Qohélet*, Paris 1968.
Joseph Bonsirven, *Textes rabbiniques des deux premiers siècles chrétiens*, Rome 1955.
James Hastings, ed., *Encyclopaedia of Religion and Ethics*, Edinburgh 1917.

2   *The Babylonian Talmud*, trans. I. Epstein, p. 128.
3   Ibid., vol. l, p. 49.
4   Ibid., p. 55.
5   'Discernment' ch. 4. 20, *The Book of Knowledge from the Mishnah Torah of Maimonides*, Edinburgh 1981, p. 39.
6   *The Babylonian Talmud*, p. 76.

Chapter 3   The Greek World: Sad Old Age

1   For these interpretations, see 'Early cosmogonical and theogonical myths', in *Cambridge Ancient History*, II, part 2B, Cambridge 1975, pp. 887–93;
2   'The Homeric poems as history', in ibid., ch. XXXIX, pp. 820–50.
3   Homer, *The Iliad*, trans. Martin Hammond, Harmondsworth 1987, I.245, p. 56.
4   Ibid., I.260, p. 56.
5   Ibid., IX.50, p. 167.
6   Ibid., X.76, p. 183.
7   Homer, *The Odyssey*, trans. E.V. Rieu, Harmondsworth 1964, II.16, p. 37.
8   Ibid., II.150, p. 41.
9   Ibid., VII.155, p. 116.
10 Ibid., II.225, p. 43.
11 Ibid., II.179, p. 42.
12 Ibid., XXIV.240, p. 357.
13 Simone de Beauvoir, *Old Age*, trans. Patrick O'Brian. Harmondsworth 1977, p. 99.
14 See Henri-Irenee Marrou, *Histoire de l'éducation dans l'Antiquité, I, Le Monde grec*, Seuil, 1948, ch. 1.
15 The translations of the extracts from *Oedipus at Colonos* are from Sophocles *Three Theban Plays*, trans. T.H. Banks, Oxford 1956.
16 Euripides, *Medea and Other Plays*, trans. P. Vellacott, Harmondsworth 1963, p. 173.
17 *Euripides V: Electra, The Phoenician Women, The Bacchae*, trans. E. Wykoff, Chicago 1959, p. 129.
18 *The Complete Poems of Aeschylus*, trans. G. Murray, London 1952, p. 38.
19 Aristophanes, *The Eleven Comedies*, New York 1943, p. 119.
20 Ibid., p. 249.
21 Ibid., p. 305.
22 Aristophanes, *Lysistrata*, trans. Alan H. Sommerstein, Harmondsworth 1973, p. 205.
23 Diogenes Laertius, *Lives of Eminent Philosophers*, trans R.H. Hicks, London 1925, I.111.

24 See especially the book by Bessie Ellen Richardson, *Old Age among the Ancient Greeks*, Baltimore 1933.

25 Diogenes Laertius, *Lives*, II.132.

26 Ibid., VI.34.

27 Ibid., X.122.

28 Ibid., V.171.

29 Ibid., IV.48.

30 Ibid., I.60.

31 Ibid., VIII.35.

32 Ibid., I.56.

33 Ibid., VI.33.

34 Plato, *The Republic*, trans. D. Lee, Harmondsworth 1975, I.328, p. 62.

35 Ibid., I.328–30, pp. 62–4.

36 Plato, *Phaedrus*, trans. R. Hackford, Cambridge 1952, p. 45.

37 Plato, *The Republic*, III.412, p. 178.

38 Plato, *The Laws*, trans. A.E. Taylor, London 1960, III.690.

39 Ibid., II.666.

40 Ibid., XI.929.

41 Aristotle, *The Politics*, trans. T.A. Sinclair, Harmondsworth 1976, p. 88.

42 Aristotle, *The Ethics*, trans. J.A.K. Thomson, Harmondswoth 1959, IV.I; VIII.3; VIII.4; VIII.5; VIII.6.

43 Aristotle, *Rhetoric*, trans. Lane Cooper, New York 1932, II.13, pp. 134–6.

44 Quoted in Simone de Beauvoir, *Old Age*, p. 124.

45 Plato, *The Laws*, XI.928.

46 Jacques Ellul, *Histoire des institutions de l'Antiquité*, PUF, 1961, p. 44.

47 James Hastings, ed., *Encyclopaedia of Religion and Ethics*, Edinburgh 1917, article on 'old age', p. 471. See too M.S. Haynes, 'The supposedly golden age for the aged in Ancient Greece (a study of literary concepts of old age)', *The Gerontologist* III, 1963.

48 Diogenes Laertius, *Lives*, I.55.

49 Robin Lane Fox, *Alexander the Great*, London 1975.

50 Xenophon, *Anabasis and Memorabilia*, trans. J.S. Watson, London 1894, ch.VIII.1, pp. 504–5.

51 B.E. Richardson, *Old Age among the Ancient Greeks*, Baltimore 1933, p. 225.

52 Aristophanes, *The Acharnians*, II.673–8, trans. A.H. Sommerstein, Harmondsworth 1973, p. 74.

53 Vitruvius, *De Architectura*, trans. Fabio Calvo Ravennate, Rome 1975, book III.111.

54 The details about Alexander's expedition have been taken from Robin Lane Fox, *Alexander the Great*.

55 Aristotle, *Constitution of Athens*.

56 J. and M. Dupaquier, *Histoire de la démographie*, Perrin, 1985, p. 34.

57 B.E. Richardson, *Old Age among the Ancient Greeks*.

58 Hippocrates, *The Genuine Works of Hippocrates*, trans. F. Adams, New York 1929, p. 197.

59 Hippocrates, *Aphorisms*, ed. W.H.S. Jones, London 1931, III.31.

60 Richard L. Grant, 'Concept of Ageing: an Historical Review', in *Perspectives in Biology and Medicine*, 1963, p. 450.

61 Aristotle, *On Youth and Old Age, on Life and Death and on Respiration*, trans. W. Ogle, London 1897.

62 D.B. Bromley, *The Psychology of Ageing*, p. 41.

63 Plutarch, 'Nine Books of Table Talk', trans. P.A. Clement and H.B. Hoffleit et al., included in his *Moralia* VIII and IX, Cambridge, Mass. 1969, 1961.

64 Ibid., VIII 'Table Talk' III.3, 650, p. 227.

65 Ibid., VIII 'Table Talk' I.8, 625, p. 81.

66 Ibid., VIII 'Table Talk' I.8, 626, pp. 83–4.

67 Plutarch, 'Whether an old man should engage in public affairs?, *Moralia*, X, 'Old men in public affairs' 784, p. 81.

68 Ibid., 786, p. 91.

69 Ibid., 786, p. 97.

70 Ibid., 788, p. 103.

71 Ibid., 793, p. 129.

72 Ibid., 797, p. 151–3.

73 Plutarch, 'Table talk' III.3, 650 p. 229, *Moralia* VIII.

74 Plutarch, 'Consolation to his wife', *Moralia*, VII.611, p. 603.

75 Plutarch, 'On praising oneself inoffensively', *Moralia*, VII.546, p. 161.

76 Plutarch, 'On moral virtue', *Moralia*, VI.450, pp. 75–7.

CHAPTER 4   THE ROMAN WORLD: THE OLD MAN'S GRANDEUR AND DECADENCE

1 Jacques Heurgon, *La Vie quotidienne chez les Etrusques*, Hachette, 1961.

2 Patrick Galliou, *L'Armorique romaine*, Le Bibliophiles de Bretagne, 1984, p. 224.

3 K. Hopkins, 'On the probable age structure of the Roman population', *Population Studies* XX.2, November 1966.

4 Trebellius Pollio, 'Divius Claudius II', *Historiae Augustae Scriptores*.

5 Quoted in J. and M. Dupaquier, *Histoire de la démographie*, Perrin, 1985, pp. 38–9.

6 Ibid., pp. 39–40.

7 Jacques Heurgon, *La Vie quotidienne*.

8 J.C. Russell, 'Late ancient and medieval population' *Transactions of the American Philosophical Society*, vol. 48, part 3, (1958).

9 These figures for the period from the third century BC to the seventh century AD are according to Hombert, M. and C. Preaux, 'Note sur la durée de la vie dans l'Égypte gréco-romaine', *Chronique d'Égypte* 20, 1945.

10 Livy, *The Early History of Rome*, trans. Aubrey de Selincourt, Harmondsworth 1986, I.9, p. 43.

11 Plutarch, *Lives*, trans. J. and W. Langhorne, London 1829, X, p. 130.

12 Ibid., X, p. 140.

13 Ibid., XVIII, pp. 253–4.

14 Ibid., XXII, p. 307.

15 Juvenal, Satire X, *Sixteen Satires upon the Ancient Harlot*, trans. Stephen Robinson, Manchester 1983.

16 Suetonius Tranquillus, *The Twelve Caesars*, trans. Robert Graves, Harmondsworth 1980, p. 85.
17 Ibid., p. 95.
18 Eugen Cizek, *Néron*, Fayard, 1982, pp. 214–15.
19 Tacitus, *Annals*, VI.20.
20 Ibid., VI.23.
21 Eugen Cizek, *Néron*, p. 185. ᛫
22 Suetonius, *The Twelve Caesars*, p. 198.
23 Eugen Cizek, *Néron*, p. 206.
24 P. Galliou, *L'Armorique romaine*.
25 Jacques Heurgon, *La Vie quotidienne*.
26 Juvenal, Satire X.118–288, *Sixteen Satires*, p. 147.
27 Seneca, *Letters to Lucilius*, trans. E.P. Barker, vols I and II, Oxford 1932, Letter LVIII, I, pp. 190–1.
28 Pliny, *The Letters of the Younger Pliny*, trans. Betty Radice, Harmondsworth 1963. III.1, pp. 83–4.
29 Juvenal, Satire XIV, *Sixteen Satires*.
30 Eugen Cizek, *Néron*, p. 125.
31 Jean Gaudemet, *L'Église dans l'Empire romain*, Paris 1958, p. 698.
32 Plautus, 'The Merchant', v. 985–8, in *The Comedies*, trans. Paul Nixon, vol. 3, p. 113.
33 Ibid., v.1015–20, p. 117.
34 Plautus, *Three Comedies*, trans. Erich Segal, New York 1969: 'The Brothers Menaechmus, v.756–70. p. 189; 'The Braggart Soldier', pp. 642–54, p. 59.
35 Terence, *The Plays*, trans. William Ritchie, London 1927, v. 879–81 and v.833–5.
36 Cato, *Moral Distichs, a literal English translation*, Edinburgh 1737, liber III.10, p. 66; liber I.16, p. 40; liber IV.18, p. 79.
37 M.S. Haynes, 'The supposedly golden age for the aged in Ancient Greece (a study of literary concept of old age)', *The Gerontologist* III, 1963, p. 28.
38 Ibid., p. 34.
39 Tibullus, *Elegies*, trans. Guy Lee, Cambridge 1975, I.4, v.31.
40 Ibid., I.4, v.79–80.
41 Ibid., I.8, v.41–2.
42 Ibid., I.8, v.44–8.
43 Ibid., I.10, v.33 and 39–44;
44 Ovid, *Tristia*, trans. W.S., London 1681, IV.8.
45 Ibid.
46 Ovid, *Metamorphoses*, trans. A.P. Melville, Oxford 1986, VII, v.287–94.
47 Horace, Epode VIII, *The Odes and Epodes*, trans. C.E. Bennett, London 1978, p. 387.
48 Ode XXV, in ibid., p. 71.
49 Horace, 'The Art of Poetry', v.169–76, *Satires, Epistles, Ars Poetica*, trans. H. Rushton Fairlough, London 1876, p. 465.
50 Horace, Satire II.5, v.9–26, v.70–83, *Satires and Epistles*, trans. Niall Rudd, Harmondsworth 1986, pp. 110–12.
51 Pliny, *The Letters*, IV.2, p. 110.
52 Celsius, *De medicina*, II.1.
53 Charles C. Thomas, *A Translation of Galen's Hygiene*, Oxford 1952, p. 7.

54   Ibid., p. 15.
55   Ibid., pp. 217–18.
56   Ibid., pp. 15–17.
57   Cicero, 'De senectute II, in *Two Essays on Old Age and Friendship*, trans.
     E.S. Schuckburg, London 1900, p. 28.
58   Ibid., III, pp. 32 and 33–4.
59   Ibid., V, p. 40.
60   Ibid., VI, pp. 40–2.
61   Ibid., VIII, pp. 49–50.
62   Ibid., IX, pp. 52–3.
63   Ibid., XI, pp. 58–9.
64   Ibid., XI, pp. 61–2, XII, pp. 62–4.
65   Ibid., XVI, p. 82.
66   ibid., XVIII, pp. 89–90 and pp. 86–7.
67   *Letters and Treatises of Cicero and Pliny*, New York 1909, p. 261.

CHAPTER 5   THE EARLY MIDDLE AGES: THE OLD MAN AS A SYMBOL IN
CHRISTIAN LITERATURE

1   Maurice Bouvier Ajam, *Dagobert*, Tallandier, 1980, p. 95.
2   Philippe Ariès, *Centuries of Childhood*, Harmondsworth 1973, translated
    from *L'Enfant et la vie familiale sous l'Ancien Régime*, Seuil, 1973.
3   St Augustine, 'De la Genèse contre les manichéens', ch. 23, *Oeuvres
    complètes de saint Augustin*, Paris 1873, 32 vols, vol. III. Translated for
    this volume from the French, and below.
4   St Augustine, 'Les 83 questions diverses', *Oeuvres complètes*, vol. XXI, p.
    41.
5   Philippe Ariès, *Centuries*, p. 17.
6   *On the Properties of Things, John Trevisa's translation of Bartholomaeus
    Anglicus, De Proprietatibus Rerum*, ed. M.C. Seymour, 2 vols, Oxford
    1975.
7   St Gregory the Great, *Les Morales sur le livre de Job*, Paris, 3 vols, 1969
    edn, vol. III, book 34, p. 814.
8   St Eucherius, *Lettre à Valerien sur le mepris du monde*.
9   Philo, *The Migration of Abraham*, 10 vols, trans. F.H. Colson and Rev.
    G.H. Whitaker, London 1932, vol. IV, p. 249. l. 199.
10 St Jerome, Letter 10, *Letters*, trans. C.C. Mierow, 2 vols, London 1962,
    vol. I, p. 50.
11 Dhuda, *Manuel pour mon fils*, trans. B. de Vregille and C. Mondesert. Le
    Cerf, coll. 'Sources chrétiennes', 1975, VI.4.
12 St John Chrysostom, 'Apologie de la vie monastique' *Oeuvres complètes*,
    11 vols, trans. M. Jeannin, Paris 1865, vol. II, pp. 22–3. Translated for
    this volume from the French, and below.
13 Lactantius, *Works*, trans. W. Fletcher, 2 vols, Edinburgh 1871, vol. II, ch.
    IV, p. 57.
14 St Augustine, 'Livre des enseignements salutaires', *Oeuvres complètes*,
    XXIII, p. 40.
15 Gregory the Great, Prologue, in *Dialogues*, trans. P.W. (Philip Woodward),
    London 1911, book II, p. 51.

16 Hilary of Arles, '*Discourse on the life of St Honoratus, Bishop of Arles*', in *The Western Fathers*, trans. F.R. Hoare, London 1954, vol. II, ch. 11, p. 256.

17 Ibid., vol. II, ch. 10, p. 255.

18 Defensor, *Liber Scintillarum*, ed. E.W. Rhodes, London 1889.

19 Origen, Sermon XVI, *Homelie sur Josué*, Le Cerf, coll. 'Sources chrétiennes', no. 71, trans. A. Jaubert, 1960, p. 359.

20 St Ambrose, *Traité sur l'Évangile de saint Luc*, le Cerf, coll. 'Sources chrétiennes', no. 52, 1958, VIII.7.

21 St John Chrysostom, *Oeuvres complètes*, vol. X, p. 260.

22 St Augustine, *Oeuvres complètes*, vol. X, p. 457, vol. XIV, p. 464.

23 'Discours sur le psaume 91', in ibid., vol. XIV, p. 13.

24 St John Chrysostom, *Oeuvres complètes*, vol. X, p. 457; vol. XIV. p. 464.

25 'Des douze sortes d'abus', in ibid., vol. XXIII, p. 63.

26 'Traité XXIII sur l'Évangile de saint Jean', in ibid., vol. XI, p. 605.

27 'Troisième Discours sur le psaume 26', in ibid., vol. XII, p. 199.

28 Sermon 81, in ibid., vol. XVI, p. 582.

29 St Jerome, Letter 10, *Letters*, vol. II, p. 255.

30 Salvian of Marseille, Letter IV.15, in *Oeuvres*, 2 vols, trans. G. Lagarrigue, Le Cerf, coll. 'Sources chrétiennes, 1971 and 1975.

31 Ephraim of Nisbe, Hymn XI, 1, *Hymnes sur le paradis*, trans. R. Lavenant, Le Cerf, coll. 'Sources chrétiennes', 1968.

32 Hymn VII, 10, in ibid.

33 *Vie des pères du Jura*, Le Cerf, coll. 'Sources chrétiennes', 1968.

34 Theodoretus of Cyr, 'Vie de saint Jacques', vol. 1 (IV) of *Histoire des Moines de Syrie*, trans. P. Canivet and A. Leroy-Moliglen, 2 vols, Le Cerf, coll. 'Sources chrétiennes', 1977.

35 See chapter 4, note 27.

36 St Jerome, Letter 10, *Letters*, p. 50–1.

37 St Augustine, Sermon 161, in *Oeuvres complètes*, vol. XVII, p. 509.

38 Salvian of Marseille, 'Du gouvernement de Dieu', in *Oeuvres*, VI.73. Translated for this volume.

39 Ibid., VII.2.

40 St Ambrose (Ambroise de Milan), *La Pénitence*, trans. R. Gryson, Le Cerf, coll. 'Sources chrétiennes', 1971, book II, ch.8.

41 St John Chrysostom, 'Commentaire sur l'Épitre de saint Paul aux Hebreux', homélie VIII, *Oeuvres complètes*, vol. XI, p. 485.

42 'Homélies sur la Genèse', homélie XXXVII, in ibid., vol. V, p. 254.

43 '4e homélie sur Anne', in ibid., vol. V, p. 509.

44 Ibid.

45 'Commentaire sur l'Épitre de saint Paul à Tite', in ibid., vol. XI, pp. 420–1.

46 Ibid.

47 St John Chrysostom, *Oeuvres complètes*, vol. V, p. 509.

48 'Commentaire sur Isaïe', ch. 3, in ibid., vol. VI, p. 364.

49 St Augustine, *Oeuvres complètes*, vol. XXII, p. 258.

50 Sermon 138, in ibid., vol. XVII, p. 279.

51 Justin, I, Apol., XV.6.

52 Tertullian, *La Toilette des femmes*, trans. M. Turcan, Le Cerf, coll. 'Sources chrétiennes', 1971, VI.6.

53 Cyril of Alexandria, *Dialogues sur la trinité*, trans. G.M. de Durand, Le Cerf, coll. 'Sources chrétiennes', 1978, III.33, 4–5.

54 Gregory the Great, *Dialogues*, book III, ch.33, p. 160.

55 Lactantius, *Works*, ch.X, p. 71.

56 John Moschus, *Le Pré spirituel*, Le Cerf, coll. 'Sources chrétiennes', p. 113.

57 St Patrick, *His Writings and Muirchu's Life*, trans. A.B.E. Hood, London 1978, p. 43.

58 Sermon IV, *XIV homelies du IXe siècle*, Le Cerf, coll. 'Sources chrétiennes', 1970.

59 St Augustine, Letter 166, *Oeuvres complètes*, vol. V, p. 451.

60 Gregory the Great, *Dialogues*, book I, ch. 10, p. 41; ch. 4, p. 23; ch. 10, p. 43.

61 Ibid., book IV, ch. 47, p. 243.

62 Ibid., book I, ch.9,15; book III, ch. 12, 2; book III, ch. 21,1.

63 Origen, Homélie 6, *Homélies sur les Nombres*, p. 124.

64 Hilary of Arles, in *The Western Fathers*, vol. II, ch.12, p. 257.

65 Ibid., vol. I, ch.8, p. 254; ch.6, p. 252; ch.7, p. 252.

66 St Jerome, *Letters*, p. 60–1, Letter XIV.

67 Dhuoda, *Manuel*, III.1.

68 *The Rule of St Benedict*, trans. David Parry O.S.B., London 1984, ch. XXXVII, p. 63.

69 Ibid, ch. XXI.4, p. 43.

70 'Vie de saint Oyend', 171.3; 'Vie de saint Romain', 21.5; 28.2; 'Vie de saint Lupicin', 68.7; in *Vie des pères du Jura*.

71 *La Règle du maitre*, Le Cerf, coll. 'Sources chrétiennes', 1964, ch. 94.

72 Guigue I, *Coutume de Chartreuse*, Le Cerf, coll. 'Sources chrétiennes', 1984, 78.2.

73 Salvian of Marseille, 'Les Livres de Timothée a l'Église', *Oeuvres*, IV.4.

74 St Jerome, Letter 10 (Letter to Paul, an old man of Concordia), *Letters*, p. 10.

CHAPTER 6   THE EARLY MIDDLE AGES: INDIFFERENCE TO AGE

1 Edwin Morgan, *Beowulf, a verse translation into modern English*, London 1952.

2 Tacitus, *Germania*, London 1970, pp. 149–55.

3 Procopius, *De Bello Gothico*, II.4.

4 H.M. Chadwich, *The Cult of Othin*, London 1899, p. 99.

5 James Hastings, ed., *Encyclopaedia of Religion and Ethics*, Edinburgh 1917, article on 'old age'.

6 Ammianus Marcellinus, *The Later Roman Empire*, trans. Walter Hamilton, Harmondsworth 1986, book 31, ch.2, p. 414.

7 Bede, *Ecclesiastical History of the English People*, ed. Bertram Colgrave, Oxford 1969, IV.13.

8 Pierre Riché, *Daily Life in the World of Charlemagne*, trans. Jo Ann McNamara, Liverpool 1978, pp. 269–79.

9 Of especial interet are the *Études sur l'histoire de la pauvreté (Moyen*

Age – XVI siècle), publications de la Sorbonne. 1974.

10 A.D. Kapferer, 'Des images de la pauvreté dans le haut Moyen Age anglo-saxon', *Cahiers de la pauvreté* no. 9. 1972–4.

11 C. Mirabel, 'Les pauvres et la pauvreté en Italie du Nord d'après Rathier de Verone', *Cahiers de la pauvreté* no. 6, 1967–8.

12 M. Rouce, *Le matricule des pauvres*, Études sur l'histoire de la pauvreté, publications de la Sorbonne, 1974.

13 Pierre Biché, *Daily Life*, p. 249.

14 Salvian of Marseille, 'Livres de Timothée à l'Église' II.62, *Oeuvres*, Le Cerf. coll. 'Sources chrétiennes', 2 vols, 1971 and 1985.

15 Sermon VII, *XIV Homélies du IX siècle*. Le Cerf, coll. 'Sources chrétiennes', 1970.

16 Caesar, *De Bello Gallico* VI.19; Gaius, *Institutionum comment.* I.51,52,55.

17 Henri Hubert, *Les Celtes et la civilisation celtique*, Albin Michel, 1974, p. 224.

18 J. Ellul, *Histoire des institutions de l'Antiquité*, PUF 1961, p. 631.

19 Ibid., pp. 682–683.

20 Lex, Bavar, II.9, *Monumenta Germaniae Historica*, Leges V.2.

21 P. Laslett, *Household and Family in Past Time*, Cambridge 1972; the article by Laurent Theis, 'Saints sans famille? Quelques remarques sur la famille dans le monde franc à travers les sources hagiographiques', *Revue historique* no. 517. January-March 1976, pp. 3–20.

22 *Récits et poèmes celtiques. Domaine Britonique (VIe – XVe siècles)*: Stock, 1981, pp. 54–5; translated for this volume. See, too, *Early Welsh Gnomic Poetry*, edited by K. Jackson, Cardiff 1961, pp. 50, 51, 54–55.

23 *L'Épopée Irlandaise*, Presses d'aujourd'hui, 1980, p. 43.

24 Anatole Le Braz, *La Légende de la Mort chez les Bretons armoricains*, Marseille 1974, vol. I, p. 439; vol. II, pp. 149, 164, 244; vol. I, p. 391.

25 B. Merdrignac, *Les Saints témoins de Dieu ou témoins des hommes? L'hagiographie et son public d'après les Vitae bretonnes armoricaines des origines au XVe siècle*, PhD thesis, 3e cycle, Rennes 1982.

26 Nennius, *'Kentish Chronicle'* and *'Welsh Annals'*, in *History from the Sources. Arthurian Period Sources*, vol. VIII. London 1980.

27 M. Bouvier-Ajam. *Dagobert*, Tallandier, 1980, pp. 44–5.

28 Caesar, *The Commentaries*, trans. W. Duncan, 2 vols. London 1819, vol.I.XXI. p. 249.

29 Pierre Riché, 'Problèmes de démographie historique du haut Moyen Age, Ve–VIIIe siècles'. *Annales de démographie historique*, 1966, pp. 37–55.

30 Gregory of Tours, *Historia Francorum*, VI.15.20; IX.26.

31 M. Bouvier-Ajam, *Dagobert*.

32 This account follows that of Monroe Stearns, *Charlemagne, Monarch of the Middle Ages*, London–New York 1971.

33 John Morris, *The Age of Arthur*, London 1973.

34 D. Whitelock, ed., *English Historical Documents 500–1042*, Oxford, 1979, vol I.

35 B. Guérard. *Cartulaire de l'abbaye Saint-Victor de Marseille*, Paris 1857.

36 R. Étienne, 'La démographie de la famille d'Ausone', *Études et chronique de démographie historique*, 1964, pp. 15–24.

37 R. Étienne. 'A propos de la démographie de Bordeaux aux trois premiers

siècles de notre ère', *Revue historique de Bordeaux.* vol. 42, 1955; and G. Fabre, *Esclaves et affranchis impériaux: essai de démographie différenciée*, thèse de 3e cycle, Bordeaux 1970.

38 St. Anathasius. 'Vie et conduite de notre saint père Antoine', in *Vie des pères du desert, Lettres chrétiennes*, no. 4. Grasset, 1961.

39 St. Augustine. *Oeuvres Complètes*, vol. VI, pp. 125, 15,50.

40 Simone de Beauvoir, *Old Age*, p. 143.

41 *Nouvelle Histoire de l'Église*, vol. 1, Seuil, 1963, p. 281.

42 Ibid., p. 249.

43 Gregory of Nazianzus, *Poem About My Life*, v. 1680ff.

44 Nennius, 'Kentish Chronicle', pp. 28 and 32.

45 M. Bouvier-Ajam, *Dagobert*, p. 129.

46 Ibid.

CHAPTER 7   THE ELEVENTH TO THE THIRTEENTH CENTURY: THE SOCIAL AND CULTURAL DIVERSIFICATION OF OLD PEOPLE

1   Poème des milieux goliards, quoted in J. Le Goff. *La Civilisation de l'Occident médiéval*, Flammarion, 1982, p. 142.

2   *On the Properties of Things, John Trevisa's translation of Bartholomaeus Anglicus' De Proprietatibus Rerum*, ed. M.C. Seymour. 2 vols, Oxford 1975, vol. I, pp. 291–3.

3   'Grant kalendrier et compost des bergiers', publ. 1500, in J. Morawski, *Les douze mois figurés. Archivum romanicum*, 1926, pp. 351–63. Translated for this volume.

4   Ibid.

5   Arnold of Villanova, ed., *Regimen sanitatis, schola salernitania*.

6   Didron, 'La vie humaine', *Annales archéologiques* XV, p. 413.

7   Didron. *Annales archéologiques* XVII, pp. 69 and 193. See, too, Philippe Aries, *Centuries of Childhood*, p. 22.

8   Philippe Ariès, *Centuries of Childhood*, p. 21.

9   Philippe De Novare, *Des quatre tenz d'aage d'ome*, ch. 36.

10 C.V. Langlois, *La Vie en France au Moyen Age d'après quelques moralistes du temps*, Paris 1908, p. 27.

11 'Aucassin et Nicolette', in *Poètes et romanciers du Moyen Age*. Bibliothèque de la Pléiade, p. 453.

12 Ibid., p. 461.

13 Chaucer's *Romaunt of the Rose and Le Roman de la Rose*, ed Ronald Sutherland, Oxford 1967, pp. 8–9. Il. 349–412.

14 Hélinant de Froidmont, *Les Vers de la mort*.

15 J. Le Goff. 'Temps de l'Église et temps des marchands', in *Annales ESC*, 1960, pp 417–33. See, too, G. Poulet, *Études sur le temps humain*, 1949; H.I. Marrou, *L'Ambivalence du temps de l'histoire chez saint Augustin*, 1950.

16 J. Le Goff, *La Civilisation de l'Occident médiéval*, p. 149.

17 Gilles Lapouge, *Utopie et civilisations*, Champs, 1978, p. 62.

18 Ibid., p. 77.

19 Isaac de L'Etoile, Sermon 6, *Sermons*, trans. G. Salet, Le Cerf, coll. 'Sources chrétiennes' no. 130, 1967.

20 Philo, *De opificio mundi*, 105, 107; St Gregory, *Moralia*, XXV.17 and 18; Isidore of Sevile, *Liber numerorum*, VIII. 34–7; Rabanus Maurus, *De laudibus s. Crucis*, I.107 and 225: John Salisbury, *De septem septenariis*.

21 Hélène Étienne, *Marbode, évêque de Rennes, 1096–1120*. DES, Rennes 1967.

22 Thomas Aquinas, 'Sin' Q.85. Art.5; 'The origins of man', Q.97. Art.1; in *Summa Theologica*.

23 St Bernard, *Oeuvres complètes*, trans. Abbé Dion, 8 vols, Paris 1867. vol. IV, *Traité du réglement de la vie et de la discipline des moeurs*, pp. 59–83. Translated from the French for this volume.

24 St Bernard, *Life and Works*, ed. Dom. J. Mabillon. 4 vols, trans. S.J. Eales, London 1889. vol. II. p. 253.

25 Ibid., vol. I, p. 275.

26 Ibid., vol. II, p. 534.

27 St Bernard, *Oeuvres complètes*, vol. VI, pp. 59–83.

28 Ibid., vol.II *Traité sur les moeurs et devoirs d'un évêque*, ch. VI, p. 207.

29 St Bernard. Letter CCLIV, in *Life and Works*, vol. II, p. 747.

30 St Bernard, *Vie et gestes de saint Bernard, premier abbé de Clairvaux, en sept livres, par Guillaume qui, apres avoir été abbé de saint Thierry, près de Reims, devint simple religieux de Ligny, ou il ecrivit*, vol. I of *Oeuvres Complètes*, p. 5.

31 St Bernard, *Life and Works*, vol. II, pp. 744–5; p. 747.

32 St Bernard, *Oeuvres completes*, vol. VII, p. 257.

33 Georges Duby, *Le Temps des cathédrales, L'art et la société, 980–1420*. Gallimard, 1976, p. 182.

34 Joinville and Villehardoin, *Chronicles of the Crusades*, trans. Margaret Stuart, Harmondsworth 1970, pp. 33, 44.

35 Christopher Brooke, *Europe in the Central Middle Ages, 962–1154*, London 1964, p. 92.

36 *Monuments originaux de l'histoire de saint Yves*, Saint-Brieuc 1887.

37 T.H. Hollingsworth, *Historical Demography*, London 1969, pp. 220–2.

38 Orderic Vitalis, *Historia Ecclesiastica*, ed. and trans. Marjorie Chibnall, Oxford 1978, vol. VI, book XII, ch.45, p. 551.

39 Harry Rothwell, ed., *English Historical Documents 1189–1327*, vol. III, London 1975, p. 826, no. 195.

40 J.G. Frazer, *The Golden Bough*, London 1980, Harmondsworth 1980, p. 402.

41 D.B. Bromley, *The Psychology of Human Ageing*, Harmondsworth 1981, p. 44.

42 Avicenna, *The Canon of Medicine of Avicenna*, trans. O. Cameron Gruner, London 1930, p. 74.

43 Arnold of Villanova, *The Defence of Age, and Recovery of Youth*, London 1540, p.A.II.

44 Roger Bacon, *The Cure of Old Age and Preservation of Youth*, trans. Richard Browne, London 1683, p. 15.

45 Roger Bacon, *Of the Wonderful Power of Art and Nature*, quoted in R.L. Grant, 'Concepts of aging; an historical review', *Perspectives in Biology*

and Medicine VI, 1963, p. 456.

46   Roger Bacon, *The Cure of Old Age*, p. 1.
47   T.H. Hollingsworth, *Historical Demography*, p. 378.
48   Roger Bacon, *The Cure of Old Age*, p. 22.
49   Ibid., pp. 23, 31, 139.
50   Ibid., p. 148.
51   J.C. Russell, 'Population in Europe, 500–1500', in Carlo M. Cipolla, ed., *The Fontana Economic History of Europe, The Middle Ages*, Harmondsworth 1978, p. 46.
52   Éric Fugedi, 'Pour une analyse démographique de la Hongrie médievale', *Annales ESC*. 1969, pp. 1299–1312.
53   J.C. Russell,'*Population in Europe*', p. 46.
54   J.C. Russell, *British Medieval Population*, Albuquerque 1958, p. 181.
55   J.C. Russell, '*Population in Europe*', p. 44.
56   Robert Fossier, *La Terre et les hommes en Picardie jusqu'à la fin du XIII siècle*, Paris-Louvain 1968.
57   Ibid.
58   Thomas Walsingham, *Gesta abbatum monasterii Sancti Albani*, ed. H.T. Riley, vol. I, London 1867, pp. 24–8.
59   St Bernard, *Oeuvres complètes*, vol. I, p. 352.
60   St Bernard of Clairvaux, *The Story of his Life*, trans. Geoffry Webb and Adrian Walker, London 1960, p. 10.
61   Ibid., p. 217.
62   St Bernard, Letter XLI, in *Life and Works*, vol. I, p. 217.
63   Malcolm Barker, *The Trial of the Templars*, Cambridge 1978, p. 59.
64   Joinville and Villehardouin, *Chronicles of the Crusades*, trans. Margaret Stuart, pp. 352–3.
65   Pierre Mandonnet, *Saint Dominique*, Paris 1937, vol. I, p. 72.
66   Christopher Brooke, *Europe in the Central Middle Ages*, p. 93.
67   A.L. Poole, *From Domesday Book to Magna Carta*, Oxford 1970, p. 445.
68   Leon Lallemand, *Histoire de la charite*, 4 vols, Paris 1902–12, vol.III, p. 133.
69   J. Le Goff, *La Civilisation de l'Occident médiéval*, p. 286.
70   'La chanson de Roland', in *Poètes et romanciers du Moyen age*, Bibliothèque de la Pléiade, 1967, p. 124. Translated for this volume.
71   *The Laxdale Saga*, trans. Muriel Press, London 1964, p. 12.
72   Ibid., p. 82.
73   *Njal's Saga*, trans. Magnus Magnusson and Hermann Palsson, Harmondsworth 1960, ch. 159, p. 354.
74   *Egil's Saga*, trans. Gwyn Jones, Syracuse 1960, p. 237.
75   Ibid., p. 256.
76   *Hrafnkel's Saga and other Icelandic Stories*, trans. Hermann Palsson, Harmondsworth 1971, p. 20.
77   *Three Northern Love Stories and Other Tales*, trans. Magnus Magnusson and William Morris, London 1910, pp. 251, 258, 261.
78   *Four Icelandic Sagas*, trans. Gwyn Jones, Princeton–New York 1935, p. 57.
79   Georges Duby, *Guillaume le Maréchal ou le meilleur chevalier du monde*, Fayard, 1984.
80   Joinville and Villehardouin, *Chronicles*, pp. 43–4.

81 Ibid., p. 71.
82 Pierre Aubé, *Godefroy de Bouillon*, Fayard, 1985.
83 Joinville and Villehardouin, *Chronicles*, p. 316.
84 O. Forst de Battaglia, *Traité de généalogie*, Lausanne 1949.
85 Brunetto Latini, *Il tesoretto*. Translated here from the French, 'Le Livre du trésor', in *Jeux et sapience du Moyen age*, Bibliothèque de la Pléiade, p. 826; publ. in English as *The Little Treasure*, trans. J. Bolton Holloway, New York–London 1981.
86 E. Le Roy Ladurie, *Montaillou, village occitan, de 1294à1324*, Gallimard, 1975. Publ. in English as *Montaillou*, trans. B. Bray, Harmondsworth 1980.
87 Ibid., p. 65.
88 Ibid., p. 64.
89 'La Housse partie', in *Romans et contes du Moyen Age*, Bibliothèque de la Pléiade.
90 Robert Fossier, *La Terre et les hommes en Picardie*..
91 Monique Bourin, Robert Durand, *Vivre au village au Moyen Age. Les solidarités paysannes du XI au XIII siècle, Messidor*, Temps actuels, 1984, p. 42.
92 Jacques Poumarède, 'Puissance paternelle et ésprit communautaire dans les coutumes du sud-ouest de la France au Moyen Age', in *Recueil de memoires et travaux publié par la société d'histoire du droit et des institutions des anciens pays de droit écrit*, Melanges Roger Aubenas, Universife de Montpellier I, pp. 651–63.
93 E. Le Roy Ladurie, *Montaillou*, p. 317, note 2.
94 A. Briod, *L'Assistance des pauvres au Moyen Age dans le pays de Vaud*, Lausanne 1976.
95 St Bernard, *Oeuvres complètes*, vol. I, pp. 131, 135, 138, 170, 175, 196, 197.
96 C.H. Hefele, *Histoire des conciles*, Paris 1914.
97 Léon Lallemand, *Histoire de la charité*.
98 D.B. Bromley, *The Psychology of Human Ageing*, p. 54.
99 E. Le Roy Ladurie, *Montaillou*, p. 363.
100 Ibid., p. 365.
101 *Histoire de la France urbaine*, sous la direction de Georges Duby, Seuil, 1980, vol.II, *La ville médiévale*, p. 163.
102 J. Le Goff, *La Civilisation de l'Occident médiéval*, p. 286, translated for this volume. The book has recently been published in English as *Medieval Civilization 400–1500*, trans. Julia Ballow, Basil Blackwell 1988.
103 Brunetto Latini, *Le Livre du trésor*, p. 735.

CHAPTER 8 THE FOURTEENTH AND FIFTEENTH CENTURIES: OLD PEOPLE ASSERT THEMSELVES

1 Quoted in Richard C. Trexler, *Public Life in Renaissance Florence*, New York–London 1980, p. 362.
2 *The Fontana Economic History of Europe*, vol. I, The Middle Ages, ed. C.M. Cipolla, New York 1976, pp. 56–7.

3   Ibid.
4   Monique Zerner, 'Une crise de mortalité au XVe siècle d'après les testaments et les roles d'imposition', *Annales ESC*, 1979, no. 3.
5   H. Dubois, 'L'histoire démographique de Chalon-sur-Sâone à la fin du XIVe siècle d'après les crèches de feux', in *Annales de la faculté des lettres de Nice* no. 17, 1972, pp. 89–102.
6   Maurice Berthe, *Famines et épidémies dans les campagnes navarraises à la fin du Moyen Age*, 2 vols, SFIED, 1984.
7   Ibid., p. 417.
8   Ibid., p. 552.
9   Ibid., p. 152.
10 Ibid., p. 155.
11 Much later, during the 1603 Plague in London, it was also observed that far more children died than old people; cf. M.F. and J.M. Hollingsworth, 'Plague mortality rate by age and sex in the parish of St Botolph's without Bishopsgate, London 1603', *Population Studies*, vol. XXV.1, March 1971.
12 *Two Memoirs of Renaissance Florence, The Diaries of Buonaccorso Pitti and Gregorio Dati*, ed. G. Brucker, New York 1967.
13 *The Fontana Economic History of Europe*, p. 47.
14 J.J. Rosenthal, 'Medieval longevity: the secular peerage. 1350–1500', *Population Studies*, vol. 27, July 1973.
15 Christiane Klapish, 'Fiscalité et démographic en Toscane, 1427–1430', *Annales ESC*, 1969, pp. 1313–37; C. Klapisch and D. Herlihy, *Les Toscans et leur famille: une étude du catasto florentin de 1427*, Paris, École des Hautes Études et Fondation nationale des Sciences Politiques, 1978.
16 This case is cited by J. and M. Dupaquier, *Histoire de la demographie*, Perrin, 1985, p. 45.
17 J. Heers, *Le Clan familial au Moyen Age*, PUF, 1974.
18 P. Desportes, *La Population de Reims au XVe siecle d'après un denombrement de 1422*, Le Moyen Age, 1966, pp. 463–509.
19 *Histoire de la France urbaine*, Seuil, 1980, p. 485.
20 Arlette Higounet-Nadal, *Périgueux aux XIVe et Xe siècles. Étude de démographie historique*, 2 vols, Paris 1977, on pp. 805–15.
21 Jacques Rossiaud, 'Crises et consolidations, 1330–1530', in *Histoire de la France urbaine*, p. 487.
22 Ibid.
23 Georges Minois, *L'Évéché de Tréguier au XVe siècle*, Thèse de 3e cycle, typescript, Rennes 1975, p. 189.
24 Jean-Pierre Poussou, 'Pour une histoire de la vieillesse et des vieillards dans les sociétés européennes', *VII colloque national de démographie*, Strasbourg 1982, *Les Ages de la vie*, Actes du colloque, vol. II, PUF, 1983, pp. 149–60.
25 Georges Minois, *L'Evéché de Tréguier*, pp. 174–6.
26 Ibid., p. 194.
27 M. Le Mené, *Les Campagnes angevines a la fin du Moyen Age*, Nantes 1982.
28 C. Klapisch, 'Fiscalité et démographie en Toscane', *Annales ESC*, p. 1336.
29 J. Heers, *Le Clan familial au Moyen Age*, PUF, 1974, p. 253.
30 Maurice Berthe, *Famines et épidémies*, p. 143.

31   Anne Le Duc, 'Familles et lignages d'artisans', in *Artistes, artisans et production artistique en Bretagne au Moyen Age*, Rennes 1983, pp. 39–40.
32   These quotations are from Christine de Pisan, *The Treasure of the City of Ladies or the Book of the Three Virtues*, trans. Sarah Lawson, Harmondsworth, 1985, pp. 162–7.
33   G.M. Trevelyan, *English Social History*, London 1946, p. 65.
34   D. Herlihy, 'Vieillir à Florence au Quattrocento', *Annales ESC*, 1969, pp. 1338–52.
35   Christine de Pisan *The Treasure*, p. 160.
36   Gilles Bellemère, Les Quinze Joies de mariage', in *Pòetes et romanciers du Moyen Age.*, éd. de la Pléiade, 1967, p. 611. Translated for this volume.
37   Ibid., p. 662.
38   Ibid., p. 643.
39   Ibid., p. 645.
40   Ibid., p. 661–2.
41   Ibid., p. 662–3.
42   Chaucer, *The Canterbury Tales*, trans. Nevill Coghill, Harmondsworth 1951, p. 112.
43   Ibid., pp. 287–8.
44   Ibid., p. 289.
45   Ibid., pp. 396–7.
46   Ibid., pp. 129–30.
47   Ibid., pp. 385–6.
48   Ibid., pp. 311–12.
49   Francois Villon, *Poems*, trans. Norman Cameron, London 1952.
50   Olivier de La Marche, *Le Parement et triomphe des dames*. Translated for this volume.
51   ´Emile Male, *L'Art religieux de la fin du Moyen Age en France*, Paris 1922.
52   Chaucer, *The Canterbury Tales*, p. 314.
53   Arlette Higounet-Nadal, *Perigueux*, p. 829.
54   *Histoire de la France urbaine*, p. 510.
55   B. Pullan, *Rich and Poor in Renaissance Venice*, Oxford 1971.
56   Richard C. Trexler, *Public Life*, p. 362.
57   Ivan Cloulas, *Laurent le Magnifique*, Fayard 1982, p. 277.
58   Richard C. Trexler, *Public Life*, p. 518.
59   Piero Parenti, quoted by Richard C. Trexler, ibid., p. 515.
60   C. Puelli-Maestrelli, 'Savonarole, la politique et la jeunesse à Florence', in *Théorie et pratique politiques à la Renaissance*, XXIIe colloque international de Tours, Paris 1977, pp. 1–14.
61   Robert Henryson, *The Poems*, ed. Denton Fox, Oxford 1987, p. 166.
62   E. MacLeod, *Charles of Orleans, Prince and Poet*, London 1969.
63   Charles d'Orléans, Ballade XXII. Translated for this volume.
64   François Villon, *Poems*, p. 57.
65   J. Huizinga, *The Waning of the Middle Ages*, London 1924, p. 26 and note.
66   Jehan Regnier, in *Poètes et romanciers du Moyen Age*, éd. de la Pléiade, pp. 1131–2. Translated for this volume.
67   Chaucer, *The Canterbury Tales*, p. 41.
68   Ibid., pp. 275–6.

69 Ibid., pp. 314–15.
70 Émile Male, *L'Art religieux.*
71 *Histoire de la France urbaine*, pp. 528–9.
72 Marcilio Ficino, *De vita libri tres.*
73 Alviso Cornaro, *Discorsi intorno alla vita sobria*, ed. Pietro Pancrazi, Florence 1946, p. 80.
74 Quoted by J.R. Hale, 'Renaissance Europe, 1480–1520', *Fontana Economic History of Europe*, London 1971, p. 18.
75 Hélène Millet, *Les Chanoines du chapitre cathédral de Laon 1272–1412*, École française de Rome, 1982.
76 Quoted by Simone de Beauvoir, *Old Age*, pp. 334–5.
77 Ibid., p. 333–4.
78 Jean Deviosse, *Jean le Bon*, Fayard, 1985, p. 225.
79 *Histoire de la France urbaine*, p. 536.
80 Leon Lallemand, *Histoire de la Charité*, vol. III.
81 Yvan Cloulas, *Laurent le Magnifique*, p. 84.
82 *Two Memoirs of Renaissance Florence. The Diaries of Buonaccorso Pitti and Gregorio Dati.*
83 Geoffrey Trease, *The Condottieri, Soldiers of Fortune*, London 1970.

CHAPTER 9   THE SIXTEENTH CENTURY: HUMANISTS AND COURTIERS
VERSUS OLD AGE

1 *Lyrics of Pierre de Ronsard*, trans. Charles Graves, Edinburgh and London 1967, p. 59.
2 Ibid.
3 Quoted by Jean Delumeau, *La Civilisation de la Renaissance*, Arthaud, 1967, p. 391.
4 George Peele, *Plays and Poems*, Glasgow and New York 1887, p. 285.
5 Edmund Spenser, *Fairie Queene*, ed. J.C. Smith, 2 vols, Oxford 1961, II. xii, 74–5.
6 Samuel Daniel, *Delia*, Sonnet XLVIII, in *Daniel's Delia and Drayton's Idea*, ed. Arundel Esdaile, London 1908.
7 *Elizabethan Lyrics, a critical anthology*, ed. Edwin Muir, London 1952, p. 44.
8 Mateo Aleman. 'Le gueux ou la vie de Guxman d'Alfarache', in *Romans picaresques espagnols*, éd. de la Pléiade, 1968, p. 704. Translated for this volume.
9 Gwennolé Le Men, 'La Littérature en moyen breton de 1350 à 1650', *Actes du 107e congrès national des Sociétés savantes*, Brest 1982, p. 95.
10 Ruzante, *Teatro*, Turin 1967.
11 *Romans picaresques espagnols*, p. 774.
12 Erasmus of Rotterdam, *Praise of Folly*, trans. Betty Radice, London 1974, cap.31.
13 A. Soman, *Annales ESC*, 1977, p. 799.
14 Jean-Charles Sournia, *Blaise de Monluc*, Fayard, 1981, p. 138.
15 Baldassare Castiglione, *The Book of the Courtier*, trans. Sir Thomas Hoby, lst edn 1561, London and New York 1974, book II, pp. 86–8.

16 Ibid., p. 91.
17 Ibid., p. 227.
18 Erasmus, *Praise of Folly*, cap. 18.
19 Antonio de Guevara, *The Diall of Princes*, English trans., London 1557, reprinted Amsterdam 1968, fol. 190 v.
20 Francis Bacon, 'De augmentis scientiarum', in *Francis Bacon Philosophical works*, ed. John M. Robertson, London 1905.
21 Erasmus, *Praise of Folly*, cap. 13.
22 Ibid.
23 Ibid., caps 13, 14 and 31.
24 Ibid., cap. 31.
25 Ibid., cap. 37.
26 Montaigne, *The Essayes of Michael, Lord of Montaigne*, trans. John Florio, 6 vols, London 1897.
27 Ibid., book III.6, pp. 86–7.
28 Jean Bodin, *De la République*, IV.2.
29 Montaigne, *The Essayes*, book II.8, pp. 107–8.
30 Ibid., book III.5, p. 89.
31 Ibid., book III.5, pp. 88–9.
32 Ibid., book III, ch.5, p. 91.
33 Ibid., book III.2, p. 44.
34 Ibid., book III.2, p. 47.
35 Ibid., book II.28, p. 244.
36 Ibid., book II.28, pp. 244–5
37 Ibid., book III.9, pp. 62–3, 65.
38 Ibid., book III, ch.9, p. 65.
39 Harvey C. Lehman, *Age and Achievement*, Princeton 1953.
40 Montaigne, *The Essayes*, book I.57, p. 270.
41 Niccolo Machiavelli, 'On the first Decade of Titus Livy', ch.60.
42 Niccolo Machiavelli, *The arte of Warre*, English trans., London 1560, reprinted Amsterdam–New York 1969, firste booke, fol. vii.
43 Quoted in Richard C. Trexler, *Public Life in Renaissance Florence*, New York–London, 1980, pp. 519, 520.
44 Francis Bacon, 'Of Youth and age', *Philosophical Works*, ed. John Robertson, London 1905, pp. 787.
45 Richard C. Trexler, *Public Life*, p. 321.
46 Ibid., p. 525.
47 Jean Bodin, 'Du senat et de sa puissance', *De la République*, book III, ch.1. Translated for this volume.
48 Benvenuto Cellini, *Autobiography*, trans. G. Bull, Harmondsworth 1974.
49 Luigi Cornaro, *A Treatise of Health and Long Life with the Sure Means of Attaining it*, English trans., ed. T. Smith, London 1743.
50 Quoted in D.B. Bromley, *The Psychology of Human Ageing*, Harmondsworth 1981, p. 47.
51 Paracelsus *Sämtliche Werke*, ed. K. Sudhoff, Munich and Berlin 1930, vol. III.
52 See Richard L. Grant, 'Concepts of ageing: an historical review', *Perspectives in Biology and Medicine*, 1963, p. 462.
53 Cf. S. Santorio, *Medicina Statica, being the aphorisms of Sanctorius*, trans. John Quincy, London 1728.

54 Ibid., Section I, Aph.LXXX, p. 45.

55 Ibid., Section V, Aph.XXXV, p. 235.

56 S. Rowbotham, *An Inquiry into the Cause of Natural Death, or Death from Old Age*, Manchester 1842.

57 H. Cuffe, *The Differences in the Ages of Man's Life: together with the Original Causes, Progresse, and End thereof*, London 1607.

58 Ibid., p. 73.

59 Ibid., pp. 4–5.

60 Francis Bacon, *The Historie of Life and Death, with Observations Naturall and Experimentall for the Prolonging of Life*, London 1648; *The Cure of old age and preservation of youth*, London 1683; 'De augmentis scientiarum', in *Francis Bacon, Philosophical Works*, ed. John M. Robertson, London 1905.

61 Francis Bacon, 'De augmentis scientiarum', ibid., p. 490.

62 Francis Bacon, *The Historie of Life and Death*, p. 26.

63 Ibid., p. 3.

64 Francis Bacon, 'De augmentis scientiarum', p. 491.

65 Francis Bacon, *The Historie of Life and Death*, p. 33.

66 Ibid., p. 23.

67 Gilles Lapouge, *Utopie et civilisations*, pp. 67–8.

68 François Rabelais, *The Works of Mr. Francis Rabelais*, lst edn 1653. 2 vols, London 1921, p. 405.

69 Antonio de Guevara, *The Diall of Princes*, fol. 190v.

70 Sir Thomas More, *The Utopia*, trans. Ralph Robinson, London 1958, book I, p. 39.

71 Cyrano de Bergerac, *L'Autre Monde*, éd. sociales, p. 113.

72 Thomas More, *The Utopia*, book II, ch.V, p. 80.

73 Ibid., book II, ch.V, pp. 84–5.

74 Jacques Minois, *L'Idéalité du réel comme réalité de l'idéal*, p. 193.

75 Antonio de Guevara, *The Diall of Princes*, fol. 191r.

76 Ibid., fol. 182v.

77 Ibid., fol. 130r.v.

78 Ibid., fol. 183v.

79 Niccolo Machiavelli, *Theatro Andria, Mandragola, Clizia*, Turin 1979, pp. 160–1. Translated from the Italian for this volume.

80 William Shakespeare, *As You Like It*, II.7.138–66, in *The Complete Works*, ed. W.G. Clarke and W. Aldis Wright, New York 1853 (used also in the following extracts).

81 Sonnet no. 2.

82 *Henry V*, V2.165–70.

83 *Romeo and Juliet*, II.5,16–17.

84 *All's Well That Ends Well*, I.2.28–9.

85 *Henry IV, Part 2*, I.3.201–10.

86 *Much Ado About Nothing*, III.V.37.

87 *The Tempest*, IV.1.191–2.

88 *The Passionate Pilgrim*, XII.

89 *Comedy of Errors*, V.1.6–13.

90 *Hamlet*, II.2.197–202.

91 *Troylus and Cressida*, I.3.172–6.

92 *The Winter's Tale*, IV4.407–13.

93 *King Lear*, I.3.15–20.
94 *Timon of Athens*, II.2.224–9.
95 *King Lear*, I.1.39–42.
96 Ibid., 291–302.
97 Ibid., III.1.20: IV.7. 60–3.
98 Ibid., I.4.261.
99 Ibid., I.5.49.
100 Ibid., III.3.26.
101 Ibid., I.2.50–9.
102 *Much Ado About Nothing*, V.I.59–62.
103 *The Rape of Lucrece*, v.275.
104 *Macbeth*, V.3.275.
105 *The Rape of Lucrece*, v.1550.
106 *Henry VI, Part 1*, II.4.518–19.
107 *As You Like It*, II.3.47–56.
108 *Measure for Measure*, II.1.32–41.
109 Translated for this volume from Minois's citation.

Chapter 10 The Sixteenth Century: The Real Weight of Old People

1 Benvenuto Cellini, *Autobiography*, trans. G. Bull, Harmondsworth 1974, p. 19.
2 Alain Croix, *La Bretagne aux XVIe et XVIIe siècles*, 2 vols, Paris 1981.
3 Jacques et Michel Dupaquier, *Histoire de la démographie*, Perrin, 1985, p. 52.
4 Ibid., pp. 79–80.
5 Ibid.
6 F. Hendricks, *Contributions to the History of Insurance and of the Theory of Life Contingencies*, London 1851.
7 J.C. Russell, 'Late ancient and medieval population', *Transactions of the American Philosophical Society*, vol. 48, part 3 (1958).
8 Alain Croix, *La Bretagne*.
9 Nicole Lucas, *Saint-Malo, étude démographique, 1601–1625*, mémoire de maîtrise, Rennes 1969.
10 S. Peller, 'Birth and death among Europe's ruling families since 1500'; T.H. Hollingsworth, 'A demographic study of the British ducal families'; in D.V. Glass and D.E.C. Eversley, ed.,*Population in History: Essays in Historical Demography*, London 1965.
11 T.H. Hollingsworth, 'Mortality in the British peerage families since 1600', *Population Review*, September 1977.
12 Francis Bacon, *The Historie of Life and Death*, p. 20.
13 Leigh on Sea cemetery.
14 Germanisches Nationalmuseum, Nuremberg.
15 Staatliches Museum, Berlin.
16 National Museum, Lisbon.
17 Staatliches Museum, Berlin.

18 Raphael, *Portrait of Julius II*, in the Uffizi Gallery, Florence; Titian, *Paul III with his great-nephews*, in the Capodimonte Gallery, Naples.
19 Retable of Santo Thomaso d'Avila.
20 The Louvre, Paris.
21 Wallace Collection, London.
22 National Gallery, London.
23 'Reforme et Contre-Reforme', *Nouvelle Histoire de L'Eglise*, Seuil, vol. III, 1968, p. 67.
24 R. Starn, ed., *Donato Gianotti and his epistolae*, Geneva 1968.
25 The argument is taken from Richard C. Trexler, *Public Life in Renaissance Florence*, New York–London 1980.
26 Gilles Lapouges, *Utopie et civilisations*, pp. 126–7.
27 Cf. J.C. Sournia, *Blaise de Montluc*, p. 307.

CONCLUSION

1 Simone de Beauvoir, *Old Age*, p. 46.
2 Ibid., p. 10.
3 Harvey C. Lehman, *Age and Achievement*, Princeton 1953, p. 330.

Bibliography

Given that the history of old age has never been broached for the early period up to the Renaissance, it is very difficult to provide a bibliography. Useful snippets are generally dispersed among a multitude of chronicles, articles and social, demographic, economic, institutional and political histories, not forgetting the history of mentalities. Only a few English and American works have begun to approach the question, and they are often hard to obtain. The following titles are merely the most useful, and further references may be found in the notes to each chapter.

Ariès, P., *L'Homme devant la mort*, Seuil, 1977.
——*Centuries of Childhood*, Peregrine, 1979.
Bailbe, J., 'Le thème de la vieille femme dans la poésie satirique du XVIe siècle et du début du XVIIe', *Bibliotheque d'humanisme et Renaissance*, XXVI, 1964.
Beauvoir, S. de., *Old Age*, trans. P. O'Brian, Harmondsworth 1977.
Berelson, L., *Old Age in Ancient Rome*, University of Virginia, 1934.
Birren, J.E., 'A brief history of the psychology of aging', *The Gerontologist*, vol. I, 1967.
Bois, J.P., *Less Anciens soldats dans la sociéte française au XVIIIe siècle*, thesis, typescript, Paris 1986.
Bromley, D.B. *The Psychology of Human Ageing*, Harmondsworth 1974.
Cassedy, J.H., *Mortality in Preindustrial Times. The Contemporary Verdict*, Farnborough 1973.
Chamoux, F., *La Civilisation hellenistique*, Arthaud, 1981.
Cipolla, C.-M., *Economic History of World Population*, Harmondsworth 1962.
Coffman, G.R., 'Old age from Horace to Chaucer', *Speculum* IX, 1934.
Creighton, B., 'When did Renaissance man grow old?', *Studies in the Renaissance*, XIV, 1967.
Delumeau, J., *La Civilisation de la Renaissance*, Arthaud, 1967.
Duby, G. and Le Goff, J., *Famille et Parenté dans l'Occident médiéval*, Rome 1977.
Dupaquier, J. and M., *Histoire de la démographie*, Perrin, 1985.
Eversley, D.E.C., Laslett, P., Wrigley, E.A., *An Introduction to English*

Historical Demography from the Sixteenth to the Nineteenth Century, London 1966.

Gaudemet, J., *Les Communautés familiales*, Paris 1963.

Glass, D.V. and Eversley, D.E.C., *Population in History*, London 1965.

Grant, R.L., 'Concepts of aging: an historical review', *Perspectives in Biology and Medicine*, vol. VI, 1963.

Grimal, P., *La Civilisation romaine*, Arthaud, 1960.

Gruman, G.J., 'History of ideas about the prolongation of life', *Transactions of the American Philosophical Society*, vol. 56, 1966.

Haynes, M.S., 'The supposedly golden age for the aged in Ancient Greece', *The Gerontologist* II, 1962.

——'The supposedly golden age for the aged in Ancient Rome', *The Gerontologist* III, 1963.

—— *Literary Concept of Old Age in the Late Middle Ages, with Special Reference to Chaucer*, University of California, 1956.

Heers, J., *Le Clan familial au Moyen Age*, Paris 1974.

Herlihy, D., 'Vieillir à Florence au quattrocento', *Annales ESC*, XXIV, 1969.

Hopkins, K., 'On the probable age structure of the Roman population', *Population Studies* XX.2, 1966.

Laslett, P., 'Famille et ménage', *Annales ESC*, 1972.

—— *The History of Ageing and the Aged*, Cambridge 1977.

—— *Household and Family in Past Time*, Cambridge 1972.

Le Goff, J., *La Civilisation Médiévale*, Arthaud, 1964.

—— *Medieval Civilization 400–1500*, trans. Julia Barrow, Oxford 1988.

Lehman, H.C., *Age and Achievement*, Princeton 1953.

McKenzie, 'Antonio Pucci on old age', *Speculum* XV, 1940.

Poussou, J.P., 'Pour une histoire de la vieillesse et des vieillards dans les sociétés européennes', *Actes du VII colloque national de démographie*, P.U.F., 1983.

Reinhard, M., Armengaud, A., Dupaquier, J., *Histoire générale de la population mondiale*, Paris 1968.

Richardson, B.E., *Old Age among the Ancient Greeks*, Baltimore 1933.

Russell, J.C., *British Medieval Population*, Albuquerque 1948.

—— *Late Ancient and Medieval Population*, Philadelphia 1958.

Salmon, P., *Population et dépopulation dans l'Empire romain*, Brussels 1974.

Smith, S.R., 'Growing old in early Stuart England', *Albion* VIII, 1976.

Thomas, Keith, *Age and Authority in Early Modern England*, London 1976.

Willcox, W.F., 'The length of life in the early Roman empire', *Congrès international de la population*, Paris 1927.

Zeman, F.D., a series of articles in the *Journal of Mount Sinai Hospital*, New York:

'Old age in ancient Egypt', vol. 8, 1942.
'The Gerontocomia of Gabriele Zerbi', vol. 10, 1944.
'Life's later years, studies in the medical history of old age', vol. 11, 1944.
'The ancient Hebrews', 1944.
'The contribution of Greek thought', 1944.
'Roman attitudes and opinions', 1945.
'The medicine of Islam', 1945.
'The medieval period', 1945.
'The revival of learning', 1945.

Index

Index by Barbara Hird